AF477675

The Uncertain Foundation

The Uncertain Foundation

France at the Liberation, 1944–47

Edited by

Andrew Knapp
Professor of French Politics and Contemporary History
University of Reading

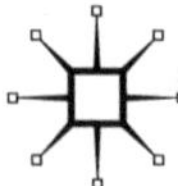

First published 2007 by
PALGRAVE MACMILLAN
Houndmills, Basingstoke, Hampshire RG21 6XS and
175 Fifth Avenue, New York, N.Y. 10010
Companies and representatives throughout the world

PALGRAVE MACMILLAN is the global academic imprint of the Palgrave
Macmillan division of St. Martin's Press, LLC and of Palgrave Macmillan Ltd.
Macmillan® is a registered trademark in the United States, United Kingdom
and other countries. Palgrave is a registered trademark in the European Union
and other countries.

ISBN-13: 978–0–230–52121–6   hardback
ISBN-10: 0–230–52121–5   hardback

This book is printed on paper suitable for recycling and made from fully
managed and sustained forest sources.

A catalogue record for this book is available from the British Library.

Library of Congress Cataloging-in-Publication Data

The uncertain foundation : France at the Liberation, 1944–1947 / edited by
Andrew Knapp.
       p. cm.
   Includes bibliographical references and index.
   ISBN-13: 978-0-230-52121-6 (cloth)
   ISBN-10: 0-230-52121-5 (cloth)
     1. France—History—German occupation, 1940–1945. 2. France—Politics
and government—1945–1958. I. Knapp, Andrew.

DC397.U63 2007
940.53'44—dc22

                                                                  2007060086

10   9   8   7   6   5   4   3   2   1
16   15   14   13   12   11   10   09   08   07

Printed and bound in Great Britain by
Antony Rowe Ltd, Chippenham and Eastbourne

Aux artisans de la liberté

Contents

Preface

Vichy, the Occupation, even the Resistance inform France's dark subconscious; if the Liberation era, too, has its dark secrets, it also, more importantly, shaped France's public post-war destiny. This is most clearly true of an economic and social transformation which, though anticipated before 1939, represented a step change against the pre-war system and a model to which the French remained deeply attached after six decades. It is true of the great political forces to emerge from the period, Gaullism and Communism, or of France's ambiguous relationships with the newly-ascendant superpowers. Post-war France was shaped, too, by the frustrations and false starts of the period – by the partial integration of women into politics, by a new constitutional order that so closely resembled the old, by the failure to define a satisfactory relationship with an increasingly restless empire.

So the Liberation era always repays closer inspection. My first encounter with it, as I prepared an undergraduate dissertation in 1975, left a lasting impression – of the fierceness of ideological conflict (and the universal belief that it *mattered*), of the continuing harshness of material conditions, of the resilient capacity of the French to enjoy themselves anyway (I became an early addict of Django Reinhardt). Added to that was Georgette Elgey's talent, still unsurpassed, for bringing the élite politics of the period to life.

An invitation to the Fondation Charles de Gaulle's conference on the Rassemblement du Peuple Français brought me back to the Liberation in 1997. Its attraction was undiminished, and the gap in the historiography – a deluge of work on the war, a trickle on the years that ensued – even more marked. Could I, as a Fifth Republic specialist, seriously hope to narrow it? It seemed more prudent to recruit a team.

They assembled in Reading for two intensive days in September 2005. That they were able to do so, in the conference which gave birth to this book, was due to financial help from the British Academy (Conference Grant no. BCG40204), the Institut Français du Royaume-Uni, the Society for French Studies, and the Centre for the Advanced Study of French History at the University of Reading.

Money aside, I am extremely grateful to each of the contributors, for their care in producing papers in time for our meeting, and for their patience in transforming them into the chapters that follow. The project has benefited from the advice of Philippe Buton and David Goldey – contributors themselves – and from the comments, during the conference, of able discussants, including Joël Félix, Robert Gildea, Julian Jackson, and Frank Tallett, and after it of anonymous readers. My own contributions were read, with his usual discernment, by Wilfrid Knapp.

But an even greater debt is owed to all those, French and Allies, who paid the price without which the 'dark years' would have been indefinitely prolonged, and the Liberation would have remained the stuff of dreams. It is to them, in all humility, that this volume is dedicated.

Andrew Knapp
Reading, November 2006

Notes on the Contributors

Nicholas Atkin is Professor of Modern European History at the University of Reading. His many publications include *Church and Schools in Vichy France, 1940–1944* (1991); *Pétain* (1997); *The French at War* (2001); *The Forgotten French. Exiles in the British Isles, 1940–1944* (2003), and (with Frank Tallett) *Priests, Prelates and People. A History of European Catholicism since 1750* (2003). He has also edited (with Frank Tallett), *Religion, Society and Politics in France since 1789* (1991); *Catholicism in Britain and France since 1750* (1996), and *The Right in France from the Revolution to Le Pen* (2nd edition, 2003).

Philippe Buton is Professor of Contemporary History at the University of Reims. His publications include *La Joie douloureuse: la Libération de la France* (2004); *Communisme: une utopie en sursis* (2001); *Les lendemains qui déchantent: le Parti communiste français à la Libération*, as well as (edited, with Jean-Marie Guillon and François Bédarida), *Les Pouvoirs en France à la Libération* (1994).

Emmanuel Cartier is Lecturer in Public Law at the Université de Bourgogne, Dijon. His doctoral thesis in law, *La transition constitutionnelle en France (1940–1945): la reconstruction révolutionnaire d'un ordre juridique républicain*, won the Prix de thèse de l'Assemblée Nationale in 2004, and was published by the Librairie Générale de Droit et de Jurisprudence in 2005.

Herrick Chapman is Associate Professor of History at New York University. He is the author of *State Capitalism and Working-Class Radicalism in the French Aircraft Industry* (1991), and has edited several works including (with Mark Kesselman and Martin A. Schain) *A Century of Organized Labor in France: a Union Movement for the Twenty-First Century?* (3rd edition, 1998).

Charles Cogan is a Senior Associate Fellow at the Kennedy School of Government, Harvard University. He is author of *Oldest Allies, Guarded Friends: the United States and France since 1940* (1994); *Charles de Gaulle: a Brief Biography with Documents* (1996); *The Third Option: the Emancipation of European Defense, 1989–2000* (2001); and *French Negotiating Behavior: Dealing with La Grande Nation* (2003).

Hilary Footitt is Senior Research Fellow in French at the University of Reading. She is the author of *War and Liberation in France: Living with the Liberators* (2004), and of *Women, Europe and the New Languages of Politics* (2002) and co-author, with John Simmonds, of *France, 1943–1945* (1988).

David Goldey is Emeritus Fellow in Politics at Lincoln College, University of Oxford. He has written numerous articles on French parties and elections over nearly half a century of visits to the grass roots, and is the co-author, with Philip Williams, of *French Politicians and Elections, 1951–1969* (1971).

Andrew Knapp is Professor of French Politics and Contemporary History at the University of Reading. He is the author of *Le gaullisme après de Gaulle* (1996), and *Parties and the Party System in France* (2004), and co-author (with Yves Mény) of *Government and Politics in Western Europe* (3rd edition, 1998) and (with Vincent Wright) of *The Government and Politics of France* (5th edition, 2006). His published articles include work on international views of the first Gaullist party, the RPF (1947–53), as well as on party politics and local government under the Fifth Republic.

Natalia Naoumova is Senior Lecturer in European History at Lomonossov University, Moscow. Her publications include (in Russian) *The Rassemblement du Peuple Français in the Politics of the Fourth Republic* (1991), and as joint author, *Class Struggle and Party Strife in Fourth-Republic France* (1988) and *Liberalism in France* (2001).

Martin Shipway is Lecturer in French Contemporary History and Politics at Birkbeck College, University of London. He is the author of *The Road to War: France and Vietnam, 1944–1947* (1996) and of *Decolonization and its Impact. A Comparative Approach to the End of Colonial Rule* (2007).

Paul Smith is Associate Professor in French and Francophone Studies at the University of Nottingham. He is author of *Feminism and the Third Republic: Women's Political and Civil Rights in France 1918–1945* (1996) and editor of 'Irreconcilable differences? Centre, periphery and the space between in French history' (*Nottingham French Studies*, 44.1, Spring 2005). His most recent publication is *A History of the French Senate* (2 vols.: 2005–6). A shorter study of the same subject will shortly be published by PalgraveMacmillan.

Olivier Wieviorka is Professor of Contemporary History at the École Normale Supérieure, Cachan. He is author of *Les Orphelins de la République. Destinée des députés et sénateurs français. 1940–1945* (2001); *Une certaine idée de la Résistance: Défense de la France* (1997); *Nous entrerons dans la carrière. De la Résistance à l'exercice du pouvoir* (1994), and, as co-author (with Jean-Pierre Azéma), of *Vichy 1940–1944* (1997), and *Les Libérations de la France* (1993).

List of Abbreviations

ACA	Assembly of Cardinals and Archbishops
ACJF	Association Catholique de la Jeunesse Française
AFL	American Federation of Labor
ALP	Action Libérale Populaire
AMGOT	Allied Military Government of Occupied Territories
CDL	Comité de Libération
CFDT	Confédération Française Démocratique du Travail
CFLN	Comité Français de Libération Nationale
CFTC	Confédération Française des Travailleurs Chrétiens
CFU	Council of the French Union
CGC	Confédération Générale des Cadres
CGT	Confédération Générale du Travail
CIA	Central Intelligence Agency
CNIP	Centre National des Indépendants et des Paysans
CNPF	Conseil National du Patronat Français
CNR	Conseil National de la Résistance
CPL	Comité Parisien de Libération
DRAC	Ligue des Droits des Religieux Anciens Combattants
ECSC	European Coal and Steel Community
EDF-GDF	Électricité de France-Gaz de France
FFI	Forces Françaises de l'Intérieur
FNC	Fédération Nationale Catholique
FNOSS	Fédération Nationale des Organismes de la Sécurité Sociale
FO	Force Ouvrière
GPRF	Gouvernement Provisoire de la République Française
GRECE	Groupement d'Études et de Recherches sur la Civilisation Européenne
IBRD	International Bank for Reconstruction and Development
INED	Institut National des Études Démographiques
INSEE	Institut National pour la Statistique et des Études Économiques
JAC	Jeunesse Agricole Chrétienne
JEC	Jeunesse Étudiante Chrétienne
JOC	Jeunesse Ouvrière Chrétienne
JR	Jeune République
LOC	Ligue Ouvrière Chrétienne
MLN	Mouvement de Libération Nationale
MLP	Mouvement de Libération du Peuple
MPF	Mouvement Populaire des Familles
MRP	Mouvement Républicain Populaire

OCM	Organisation Civile et Militaire
OSS	Office of Strategic Services
PCF	Parti Communiste Français
PDP	Parti Démocrate Populaire
PPF	Parti Populaire Français
PRL	Parti Républicain de la Liberté
RATP	Régie Autonome des Transports Parisiens
RPF	Rassemblement du Peuple Français
SFIO	Section Française de l'Internationale Ouvrière
SNCF	Société Nationale des Chemins de Fer Français
STO	Service du Travail Obligatoire
UCP	Union des Chrétiens Progressistes
UDSR	Union Démocratique et Socialiste de la Résistance

France in 1945

1
Introduction: France's 'Long' Liberation, 1944–47

Andrew Knapp

France was liberated by force of arms: those of the French Resistance, but also, on an altogether larger scale, by those of the Allies. On 6 June 1944, 156,000 British and American troops landed on five beaches in Normandy. For seven weeks they were largely confined to a narrow coastal belt. But after the 1st US Army broke through at Avranches late in July, German defences in Normandy collapsed in less than three weeks. On 18 August, the internal Resistance, grouped as the Forces Françaises de l'Intérieur (FFI), which had harassed German forces across France since June, felt strong enough to launch an insurrection in Paris. Six days later General Leclerc's French Second Armoured Division, which had landed in Normandy on 1 August, led the Allies into the capital. De Gaulle would walk triumphantly down the Champs-Élysées on 26 August. Meanwhile French and American armies landed in southern France on 15 August, secured Marseilles and Grenoble within eight days, and joined northern Allied forces in Dijon on 11 September. Fierce battles remained to be fought in the Vosges, Alsace, and the Ardennes, and a few coastal garrisons held out against the Allies till 9 May 1945; these aside, the end of September saw France's territory freed. Between D-day and late August, over 238,000 Allied soldiers and airmen, as well as several thousand FFI combatants and over 30,000 French civilians, had been killed or wounded or gone missing.[1]

The focus of this book is political and social rather than military. But the course of the fighting left its mark in other domains. One was the contrast between experiences of liberation in what Buton has called 'two Frances'.[2] One France was fought over: Allied armies removed German armies, and death often visited the French in the form of crossfire, or British and American bombs.[3] Elsewhere, chiefly in the south and east but also Paris, the FFI and the (often Communist-led) Comités de Libération had the impression of having freed their own territory, sometimes after fierce fighting before the occupiers were withdrawn to the main battlefronts. The fact of large swathes of French territory falling directly under the control of local Resistance groups proved one of the main short-term issues in the re-establishment of a French state.

For as well as a victorious military operation the Liberation was a process of régime change and restoration. It was also a social and economic transformation, and a repositioning of France in the world. To get the full measure of these changes, this book covers the 'long' Liberation period as it defined the post-war settlement up to late 1947.[4] It also examines the varied interpretations given to the Liberation over the six decades that separate us from it.

Régime change

The Third Republic's Parliament signed its own death warrant on 10 July 1940, in the wake of France's catastrophic defeat by Nazi Germany, when it gathered at Vichy to vest full constituent powers in Marshal Pétain, by 569 votes to 80. For followers of General Charles de Gaulle, whose broadcast from London on 18 June had launched the Free French movement, committed to continuing the struggle against Germany from beyond France's frontiers, the Vichy régime was illegal from the start. The question of the regime, therefore, was posed by the clash of these two competing legitimacies.

Endorsed by the British and backed in a sprinkling of French colonies, the Free French mutated from a group of diehards and adventurers into a provisional government in exile. In spring 1943, installed on French territory (liberated by the Allies from Vichy six months earlier) in Algiers, de Gaulle's Comité National Français received the allegiance of France's internal Resistance organisations, represented in the Conseil National de la Résistance (CNR), and transformed itself into the Comité Français de la Libération Nationale (CFLN). By November, a Consultative Assembly, drawn from the major pre-war parties and from the internal Resistance, gave the CFLN some trappings of representativeness; on 4 April 1944 de Gaulle brought two Communist leaders into the CFLN; and on 3 June 1944, the CFLN took the title of Gouvernement Provisoire de la République Française (GPRF). Yet over the summer of 1944 the contours of the political transition, and of the ensuing regime, were far from clear.

The short term was dominated by three issues. These were the relationship between the GPRF and the Allies (who recognised the GPRF formally only on 23 October 1944); the scope and severity of the purge of collaborators and Vichy officials (the purge, though more wide-ranging than many knew, satisfied almost no one at the time); and the GPRF's ability to impose its authority across France over the FFI and Comités de Libération (the GPRF, with the co-operation of the Communist leadership, disbanded the FFI and other 'people's militias' and held municipal elections in April–May 1945 to re-establish a system of elected local government).

The longer-term issue concerned the Constitution. This was only opened to the people after the end of hostilities and the return of prisoners and deportees, and only resolved 27 months after the liberation of Paris. The process opened on 21 October 1945, when the French were invited both to vote at a double referendum and to elect an Assembly. At the double referendum nearly three-quarters of the electorate, and 96.4 per cent of those voting, laid the Third Republic to rest by giving the new Assembly the power to draft a new constitution. Half the electorate, and two-thirds of those voting, also agreed to limit the Assembly's powers: its mandate would end after seven months, and the final decision on whether to adopt the constitution it drafted would rest with the people, via a new referendum.

On the same day, the people chose their Deputies, and confirmed a swing to the Left already seen at that spring's municipal elections. The Parti Communiste Français (PCF) added ten points to its pre-war score and topped the poll with 26.2 per cent of the vote, overtaking its Socialist ally and rival, the Section Française de l'Internationale Ouvrière (SFIO), which won 23.4 per cent. With 305 seats between them, these two parties held an overall majority in the new Assembly. At the same time much of the Catholic vote (and nearly 24 per cent of the overall popular vote) went to the Mouvement Républicain Populaire (MRP), the new Christian Democratic party, which boasted a Resistance pedigree for many of its leaders and a willingness to embrace both the Republic and social measures. The chief losers of the process were the main governing parties of the Third Republic, the conservative groups and the Radicals, with under a quarter of the vote, and just 96 Deputies, between them.

Throughout this process de Gaulle, still at the head of the GPRF, had remained aloof from party politics, and had not organised his considerable, but dispersed, following. Although the new Assembly unanimously confirmed him as head of the GPRF on 13 November 1945, he had no single bloc of loyalists under his control, found it increasingly difficult to work with political parties newly legitimised by the voters, and resigned on 20 January 1946. His expectation of a quick return to power, on his own terms, was frustrated. Instead, de Gaulle was succeeded by the Socialist Félix Gouin, supported by a 'tripartite' coalition of Communists, Socialists, and MRP. But these three parties failed to agree on the first task before them: the first draft Constitution, which vested political power in France in a single-chamber Assembly, was supported by Communists and Socialists only. That made the referendum of 5 May 1946 the cleanest Left–Right confrontation that France would see in three decades.[5] But the lack of checks and balances in the Left's first draft, alarming to anyone who feared the PCF, helped ensure its rejection by 53 per cent of the voters; the narrow Communist-Socialist parliamentary majority was not confirmed in the country. At the ensuing elections, to a second constituent Assembly, the MRP emerged briefly as the leading party with 28.2 per cent of the vote to the Communists' 25.9 per cent.

The MRP had presented itself as the party of 'fidelity' to de Gaulle, to the ideals of the Resistance, and to a certain Catholic-inspired vision of social and economic reform. But it was also the refuge for a conservative electorate that had rallied to Pétain and was much less reform-minded than the party leadership. De Gaulle, in any case, had no wish to tie himself to the MRP or any single party. The constitutional issue caused a final separation between them.

At Bayeux on 16 June 1946, de Gaulle had called for strong executive leadership and set out the bases of the future constitution of 1958. The MRP leaders, attached to French republican traditions of parliamentary supremacy and reluctant to break with their coalition partners, rejected de Gaulle's arguments. The second draft constitution was chiefly the MRP's. It included a second chamber but not a strong executive and therefore resembled the constitutional laws of the Third Republic. What the voters had consigned to the history books in October 1945, however, they were prepared to endorse, wearily and in a modified form, at the referendum of 13 October 1946. The second draft was approved by 53.5 per cent of those voting – or just 36.2 per cent of the electorate, against 31.3 per cent who voted No and 32.6 per cent who abstained or spoilt their ballots. This was enough to secure adoption, if not adherence. The first National Assembly of the new Fourth Republic was duly elected on 10 November 1946 (Socialist support declined below 18 per cent of the vote, the Communists reached their all-time peak level of support with 28.2 per cent, and the MRP fell back to 25.9 per cent); elections to the upper house followed in December; and the final piece of the new regime fell into place when the Socialist Vincent Auriol was elected President of the Republic on 16 January 1947.

Tripartisme survived the elections by less than six months. Colonial policy (with the start of insurrections in Madagascar and Inchochina) and incomes policy (with growing working-class resistance to wage restraint) both set the PCF against its coalition partners. Early in May, the Socialist Prime Minister Paul Ramadier manœuvred the Communists into voting against the government on a confidence motion, and then dismissed the PCF ministers from his cabinet (their Belgian and Italian counterparts were removed from government that same spring). Philip Williams refers to 5 May 1947 as 'the most important date in the history of the Fourth Republic' because it ensured – despite the PCF's efforts to destabilise the country through strikes later in the year – that France would not go the way of Czechoslovakia.[6] France's Communists remained out of office for 34 years. With their departure, the constitutional transition closed and the Fourth Republic settled down to its characteristic routine: a succession of more or less short-lived governments drawn from what became known as the 'Third Force' – from the ranks of Socialists, MRP, Radicals and conservatives (whose support in parliament was now needed to replace that of the Communists), prey to their own divisions and to the slings and arrows of far Left and far Right.

Regime change and constitutional law

Four chapters cover different aspects of the process of regime change. That the outcome was so similar to the Third Republic was, as Emmanuel Cartier shows, partly the result of the constraints within which the constitutional debate had been carried on since the 1930s. The French political tradition associated strong executives – the most direct remedy to the Third Republic's instability – with the Empires that had buried the first two Republics. Vichy had only confirmed this association with authoritarianism. De Gaulle's Bayeux constitution therefore stood little chance of winning the support either of a big party or a majority in the country.

Yet there were innovative aspects to the transition process too. Some arose from the complex legal arguments that the GPRF developed to uphold its own legitimacy, to establish Vichy's illegality, and, crucially, to preclude a simple return to the *status quo ante* of the Third Republic. For de Gaulle, it was essential to give voters the final say on the constitution via a referendum. As the tool used by the two Napoleons to legitimate their rule, the referendum was opposed by the consultative assembly, the parties, and the press – but imposed by de Gaulle and the GPRF in August 1944, and finally accepted by the electorate as compatible with the Republic. This reflected a wider post-war aspiration to establish a reformed republican regime, more stable and reflecting the 'economic and social democracy' evoked in the charter of the Conseil National de la Résistance. Despite its limitations, it was the Fourth Republic constitution which first incorporated a 'bill of rights' including the 1789 Declaration of the Rights of Man and the Citizen; which established a form, albeit very constrained, of judicial review; which gave the *Président du Conseil* a clear leading role within the government; and which established that motions of censure against the government could only be passed by an absolute majority of all Deputies. Although the caution of the constitution-makers and the constraints of the party system prevented any real exploitation of these features under the Fourth Republic, they set out important markers for its successor.

The upper house

The constitution of the Fourth Republic differed from the rejected first draft chiefly by its inclusion of an upper legislative house. The Left's unicameral model of 1946 had been inspired by an ideal, inherited from 1789, of government by a popularly-elected Assembly; by the Senate's record of obstruction of left-wing governments before 1940; and probably, in the case of the PCF, by its promise of a quick route to power. The Centre and Right opposed it because they were attached to a 'chamber of second thoughts' rooted in the good sense of France's mayors and local councillors, and fearful of an all-powerful Communist-dominated single chamber. But as Paul Smith observes, the defeat of the unicameral model at the May 1946 referendum, after the rejection of the Third Republic at that of October 1945, raised difficult questions about the powers and electoral base of any future upper house, and about its relationship to France's colonies, whose aspiration for representation in post-war France had been recognised, in the first draft, in the form of a Council of the French Union.

It fell to the prime minister from June 1946, the MRP's leader Georges Bidault, to try to steer a middle line. Out of respect for the majority vote at the May referendum (and his own party's conservative voters) there would be an upper house. But to satisfy his Communist and Socialist coalition partners, it would be denied the title of Senate (in favour of the more neutral Council of the Republic), as well as all but the most basic powers, and any French Union role. At this point, as Smith notes, the French Union stepped in. Its spokesman, Gaston Monnerville, the Constituent Assembly member for French Guiana, forced Bidault to concede the inclusion of its representatives in a stronger upper house. Once elected president of the Council of the Republic in 1947, Monnerville carved as much power as he could for it from the unpromising material of the new constitution. A neglected constitution-maker of the Liberation era, Monnerville presided over the upper house long enough to see a decade of confrontation with de Gaulle after 1958.

Regime change and party system change

Like the process of regime change, the renewal of the party system was, as David Goldey observes, less dramatic than expected. The major novelties of the immediate post-war elections were the reinforcement of the PCF, the arrival of the MRP, and the weakening of the Radicals and the Right. To these would be added, in April 1947, the launch by de Gaulle of the Rassemblement du Peuple Français, and its spectacular success in winning 40 per cent of the vote in France's cities – and control over many of them – at that October's municipal elections. That result aroused expectations of the General's imminent return and another change of constitution. But the Fourth Republic survived another decade against permanent challenges from far Left and far Right. The average longevity of its governments – about six months – resembled the pre-war pattern. So did some of the governments. In September 1948 a pre-war Radical Agriculture Minister, Henri Queuille, formed what proved to be the Fourth Republic's second-longest ministry.

Continuity also marked the way in which grass-roots politics was carried on. Third-Republic politics had been centred on local notables focused on the narrow interests of their *arrondissements*, or single-member constituencies. At the Liberation, however, a consensus emerged against the *arrondissement* as an electoral district, and in favour of proportional representation. This, it was hoped, would distance politics from the parish pump and promote truly national political debate between structured and disciplined parties. It would also limit the risk of a majority system amplifying a big swing to one party (for example, the Communists). And indeed, the parties of *tripartisme* were, or tried to be, different in kind from the loose collections of notables who had run the Third Republic. They boasted a mass membership: 355,000 in 1946 for the SFIO, over 800,000 for the PCF, and 80,000 even for the MRP, against a mere 20,000 for the Radicals and fewer for the Right (until the arrival of the RPF, whose members probably numbered 400,000). But all of these figures would drop after 1947. Moreover, the hundred or so multi-member constituencies designed under the new electoral system (most of them corresponding to a *département*) remained small enough to be close to local interests. France's economic and social regression under the Occupation, which briefly produced a nation *more* rural than in 1940, was also reflected in a pattern of rural over-representation that failed to keep pace with rapid post-war urbanisation. Parish pump politics continued to thrive, and every party but the PCF was factionalised. It was the notables who destroyed de Gaulle's RPF by flouting the discipline it sought to impose: in May 1953 the General disowned his creation and withdrew from politics, keeping most of his political credit intact for his return to power five years later.

Regime change, purges, and the political élite

Continuity in political processes did not entail continuity of politicians. As Olivier Wieviorka shows, the Liberation saw a wide-ranging replacement of the French political élite. The first step in this was a very untidy purge of collaborators and others linked to Vichy. The summary executions of summer 1944, numbering about 5,000 (in addition to some 2,500 before this period) gave way to more careful judicial proceedings as the state was re-established.[7] The process still varied greatly between regions, satisfied few, and was widely believed to have punished the small fry but spared the powerful. This reproach was less than justified. Some 350,000 people were investigated for collaboration. Retribution ranged from the death penalty (carried out in 1,502 cases) to 'national indignity' and loss of civil rights, or sacking for civil servants. Within the political élite, the turnover caused by this *épuration* was compounded both by an extensive weeding-out by political parties of Right and Left and by the leftward shift of France's post-war political representation. The political agenda, too, underwent a sea-change, away from Third-Republic disputes long out of season and towards social and economic issues.

Yet the scope of the political *renewal* was limited. The much hoped-for 'party of the Resistance', the Union Démocratique et Socialiste de la Résistance (UDSR) turned out to be a tiny, though strategically placed, group of notables. The MRP, though a new party able that mobilised Catholic former *résistants*, was led by élites of the pre-war Christian Democratic Parti Démocrate Populaire and, as we have noted, attracted disoriented right-wing voters (Communists took to calling it the *Machine à Ramasser les Pétainistes*). Among Socialists and Communists, established pre-war activists won promotion more readily than the 'new men' of the Resistance. Even the Left's electoral 'landslides' could be seen as optical illusions, depending on where the MRP – of ambiguous leanings, as we have seen – is placed. And despite the *épuration*, men who had served under Vichy were by no means disqualified by the voters.

Gendering regime change?

Long neglected in the historiography, the role of women in the Occupation and Liberation periods has been much researched in recent years. By 1932, women's suffrage existed in nineteen democracies, but not in France. The Chamber of Deputies passed four votes in its favour between the wars, only to be frustrated by the Senate, on the pretext (especially dear to the Radicals) that women were too susceptible to clerical influence. Ironically, it was Vichy that opened the door a chink by allowing women onto municipal councils.[8] The (considerable) activities of French women in the Resistance were, to say the least, under-appreciated: just six women, against 1,030 men, were made *Compagnons de la Libération*. By contrast, women accused of 'horizontal collaboration' with Germans were held up to the scorn of their communities, with as many as 20,000 having their heads shaven at the Liberation.[9] At least the Resistance record of women, and above all the Radicals' relative marginalisation within the CFLN, led to a consensus between the parties and de Gaulle in favour of female suffrage.[10] This was granted, with the Consultative Assembly's support, by the CFLN on 21 April 1944, and first exercised in 1945 at the municipal elections of April–May, and at the parliamentary elections and double referendum of October.

This was a modest foothold in French politics that has left feminist historians understandably underwhelmed. Even the small proportion of women in the National Assembly of November 1946 – 6.48 per cent – was not equalled for another four decades. Women as politicians were largely confined to education and the family; women as citizens were denied full civil rights until the 1960s. Yet as Hilary Footitt argues, it would be misleading to limit analyses of French women at the Liberation to this 'discourse of failure'. Her case studies of three French women Deputies, one from each of the three parties of *tripartisme*, show the variety of women's political engagement in the Assembly, from the pursuit of a liberal equality agenda, through to addressing women's rights at work, and mainstreaming so-called 'women's' issues like food and children. In the long liberation of women, this post war period tells us a great deal about how we might represent the relationship of women with political power in France, directing our attention to the political hinterland from which women politicians came, the diversity of their political commitments, and the breadth of the political spaces they occupied.

The results of regime change occupied much of political France for over two years, but disappointed many. The Fourth Republic resembled the Third, and its defects were clear within months. But the provisional regime was important in itself. For over a year, until November 1945, the GPRF governed France by decree, unimpeded by serious checks from the Consultative Assembly; for another year it had only the single-chamber Constituent Assemblies to worry about. This freedom was used to effect wide-ranging social and economic reforms.

A society transformed?

If the human cost to France of the Second World War was less than that of the First – some 400,000 deaths against 1,300,000 – the material damage was greater.[11] Most of the French, especially in the cities, were ill-housed and hungry in the Libération years, and cold, thanks to fuel shortages, in winter. In towns, food was even lower than in Britain: in August 1947, the daily bread ration was cut to 200 grammes, below its level under the Occupation. One home in twenty had been destroyed, one in five seriously damaged; France's housing crisis, perceptible from the pre-war years, would last a generation. Less of everything was being produced: in 1945, food production was at 61 per cent of pre-war levels, industrial production at 50 per cent.[12] What was produced could not readily be transported; only one railway locomotive in six, two-fifths of French rolling-stock, and less than half of the rail network were working; most of France's ports and merchant fleet were destroyed. Without the tough currency reform suggested by Economics Minister Pierre Mendès France but refused by de Gaulle, the franc lost two-thirds of its purchasing power between 1944 and 1947. By 1948, three successive devaluations had cut its rate against the dollar by 80 per cent compared to ten years earlier.[13] In a still rural country, rationing failed to ensure 'fair shares for all', and the black market thrived. A worker's purchasing power in 1944 was some 60 per cent of its (hardly princely) pre-war level; it rose to perhaps 85 per cent a year later, but had returned to 60 per cent by May 1947.[14] Milward cites France and Belgium as the only two West European countries where real wages were clearly falling in the course of 1947.[15] Meanwhile, in a ravaged Europe, few wanted either to buy the luxury items that France had traditionally sold abroad, or to visit France as tourists. Exports in 1945 had fallen by 90 per cent against 1938. That meant that over the Liberation period, France could only pay for between one-third and two-thirds of even a much reduced volume of imports. The resulting balance of payments deficit could only be covered by American loans.

Enter the state – and the workers

Yet it was in these unpromising conditions that French couples embarked on a thirty-year baby-boom (the first signs of which can be dated to 1943) while French governments – crucial players in a capital-starved country – undertook vast reforms. In a little more than three years, nationalisations covered the energy sector (coal, electricity, and gas), air, sea and rail transport plus the Paris metro and buses, the aircraft industry, France's biggest car maker, the five biggest banks and most of the insurance sector. At the same time de Gaulle's provisional government, through its *ordonnance* of 4 October 1945, laid the foundations of a modern social security system, and three months later, on 3 January 1946, created Jean Monnet's Planning Commissariat. As Herrick Chapman argues, this panoply of measures did not represent a 'year zero'. Each had been imagined by reformers and revolutionaries in the inter-war years; state intervention in the economy had already been extended in the First World War, in the 1930s, and under Vichy. Yet the contrast remains striking between the timidity of the political record and the scope of the social and economic reforms. They were facilitated by a consensus extending through the three parties of *tripartisme* to the left wing of the Radicals, and (crucially) de Gaulle.

But the consensus, Chapman notes, was always an ambiguous one. Disagreements – new in the Liberation years, familiar over the next four decades – soon surfaced over the extent of nationalisations; over their purpose (punishment of collaborators, economic modernisation, or 'economic and social democracy'); and, especially, over the respective roles in running nationalised firms of their managers, the workforce, parliament, and the supervising ministries. The answers as they developed in practice were, as Chapman shows, varied and untidy. Meanwhile a newly confident breed of senior civil servants, who would graduate, from 1946, from the new École Nationale d'Administration, prepared to give nationalisations a modernising thrust: the practice of *pantouflage*, of switching between senior positions in the Industry or Finance ministries to top posts in nationalised firms, was rapidly established.

Worries about Communism, which as we have seen played a role in the constitutional debate, were seldom far from negotiations over industrial democracy. Senior PCF members such as Benoît Frachon had come to dominate the main trade union confederation, the Confédération Générale du Travail (CGT), which claimed some 3.8 million members – about three times as many as all other unions combined – in 1945. Under the benevolent eye of Communist ministers, the CGT made strongholds out of the new *comités d'entreprise* in industries such as EDF, aviation, or Renault, securing monopoly positions and opportunities to place and pay full-time union officials. From the point of view of industrial recovery, this could be a positive development as long as the PCF was in government, calling for industrial peace to win the 'battle of production', even at the cost of wage restraint, in order to show its responsibility and indispensability within the governing coalition. But the PCF could only back austerity among its core working-class supporters for so long. It was the outbreak of a strike at Renault in April 1947, against all attempts by the CGT to rein it in, that finally broke the dam, forced the Communist leadership into tardy backing of the workers, and offered the opportunity for Ramadier to remove them from government. Within six months the PCF would be backing a series of quasi-insurrectionary strikes in public-sector firms across France, which themselves would lead to the split of the CGT. The removal of the Communists from government was followed by what Chapman compares to the post-revolutionary Thermidor period after 1794: months and years of reaction in which gains of the Liberation years, notably in the area of industrial democracy, were rolled back.

Yet the transformations wrought in the French economy were too great to be simply reversed. The resulting 'settlement' was more unstable in some respects than those reached at the same period in Britain or West Germany. The continuing existence of a nationalised sector, whose boundaries remained roughly the same till the 1980s, was accepted. So were other forms of state intervention in the economy such as the Plan or price controls. So, even after 1947, were the CGT's strongholds, which helped it remain France's strongest union over half a century. On the other hand the whole area of industrial relations, workplace control and industrial democracy remained unsettled, unpredictable and confrontational, and re-emerged to drive the legendary strike wave of May 1968.

The Church turns Left

A remarkable feature of the Liberation, which it had in common with May 1968, was the manner in which hitherto deeply conservative institutions could take on a leftish hue, albeit temporarily. This could be said of France's Catholic Church, whose hierarchy, with a handful of honourable exceptions, emerged from the Occupation with little credit. Too many bishops had not merely worked with Vichy out of obligation but identified with its values; too few protested, and too quietly, at the regime's violence, especially towards Jews. But neither the hierarchy nor the Vatican undertook more than the most token *épuration*; (though the cardinal-archbishop of Paris, most closely identified with Vichy, resigned under pressure from de Gaulle). No apology for the Church's 'silence' over the persecution of Jews came until 1997. If the Catholics' wartime record had been limited to this, it might have done lasting damage to the Church.

In fact, as Nicholas Atkin points out, the Liberation period was one of effervescence within the Church, thanks in no small measure to the decent behaviour of many grass-roots Catholics under the Occupation. Lay Catholics had been active in most of the Resistance networks; trade unionists of the Confédération Française des Travailleurs Chrétiens (CFTC) had taken part in the big strikes of the Nord, and their leaders joined the CGT on the Conseil National de la Résistance; monks, nuns, priests, and lay Catholics had all protected Jews. As France's bishops lost confidence and authority at the Liberation, many of the same grass-roots Church members reached out to touch French society in all its diversity, often building on pre-war Catholic Action movements for students, workers, and farmers. But the Catholics of the Liberation went further. The MRP, formed without consulting either the hierarchy or the Vatican, chose the Marxist parties for allies. A strong Catholic press reinforced the confidence of the laity. Open Catholic belief was no longer *mal vu* for a senior civil servant. Among the clergy, the most adventurous became worker-priests. Above all, Catholics demonstrated an unaccustomed acceptance, born of the Resistance, of a pluralistic society.

The Church's Liberation years came to a more or less abrupt end in 1947. With the PCF once more designated as a public enemy in France as in Italy, reaching out to left-wing constituencies could appear naïve or positively dangerous. The hierarchy and the Vatican steadily reasserted their control over laity and priests alike. The worker-priests' movement was banned altogether. By the early 1950s the Church was again looking more inwards, to its own institutional concerns, than outwards to the society around it. But the 'liberal moment' would find its echo after the Second Vatican Council in 1962.

While the process of regime change came to a natural close in 1946–47, as the French voted unenthusiastically for the new constitution, the economic and social changes associated with the Liberation met their 'Thermidor', as Chapman calls it, in part for external reasons. These were linked to events beyond France's borders.

Beyond the *métropole*: France in the world

The politics of France's Liberation era were played out in a rapidly-changing international context, within which France's position was both unprecedented and ambiguous. It was unprecedented in that France, like Britain, suddenly had to learn to live in the second rank in a world dominated by the new superpowers. It was ambiguous because France's decline was masked by trappings appropriate to a great and victorious nation – a permanent seat on the United Nations Security Council, an occupation zone in Germany, and a more or less intact empire.

Imperial ambiguities

Intact, but badly shaken. For French colonial administrators, hostilities between Vichy and de Gaulle had entailed an obvious conflict of loyalties. For nationalists, meanwhile, the débâcle of 1940 broke the myth of the colonists' invincibility. But the French were even less inclined than the British to liquidate their empire, as vital now for continued great-power status as it had seemed indispensable during Germany's wartime occupation of mainland France.

Martin Shipway's chapter outlines France's postwar hopes for empire as they took shape at the Brazzaville conference early in 1944. Brazzaville went down as a landmark of liberal colonialism. De Gaulle's opening speech called for 'structural reforms' within the empire, and insisted that colonial 'progress' should enable the colonised peoples 'to take part in running their own affairs'.[16] But they would do so within the 'French community'; even Commonwealth-style self-government was ruled out by the conference. This was, after all, a meeting of colonial administrators, not colonised peoples. Within the Corps Colonial, liberals coexisted with former Vichyites (few of whom were purged), while Gaullism did not necessarily equate with reformism. Moreover, the colonial administration proper did not include Algeria, a part of 'France' run from the Interior Ministry, or Morocco and Tunisia, technically protectorates and dependent on the Foreign Ministry; Indochina, meanwhile remained loyal to Vichy and was unrepresented at Brazzaville. Perhaps it was unsurprising, then, that deliberations there tended to the abstract and the general.

Within months of the liberation of metropolitan France, the generalities of Brazzaville were confronted with alarming realities on almost every watch of the Empire. In Algeria, riots in Sétif on 8 May 1945, and above all the police and settler repression that followed, left between 8,000 and 20,000 Moslem dead. In the Levant, the League of Nations-mandated territories of Syria and Lebanon insisted on the independence promised to them. In Tunisia, the departure for Cairo of the nationalist leader Habib Bourguiba, after being virtually outlawed by the colonial authorities, deprived the French of an impeccably moderate and pro-Western interlocutor. In Indochina, after a complex interlude which saw the presence of Japanese, Chinese and British as well as French troops within one year, a full-scale rebellion against French rule broke out in Tonkin on 20 December 1946. The spring of 1947 was marked by a major insurrection in Madagascar, brutally repressed, as well as by public statements from the Sultan of Morocco that clearly placed him in the nationalist camp. In September of that year, the National Assembly voted a *statut* for Algeria that included a 120-member Algerian Assembly, with limited powers and members, elected in equal numbers by two colleges (sixty members for a million Europeans, sixty members for eight million Algerian Moslems). Even properly applied, these arrangements might well have been insufficient to assuage nationalist sentiment in Algeria. As it was, the elections to the Assembly in 1948 were rigged, leaving the French with yes-men, but no moderate and credible partners in the Moslem population. It was not a reassuring record.

The bulk of Shipway's chapter evaluates colonial policy in Liberation France in three very contrasting cases. In Indochina, an apparently promising agreement signed in March 1946 between the French and the Vietnamese nationalists led by Ho Chi Minh soon unravelled. When French troops left eight years later they had been defeated in a full-scale colonial war. Sub-Saharan Africa, by contrast, began to send elected representatives to Paris, where they sat in the two Constituent Assemblies and the parliaments of the Fourth Republic – a rare direct consequence of Brazzaville. The representative system was grossly biased towards white minorities and disregarded boundaries between colonies. But the presence of African and colonial Deputies in the French Parliament made differences that were both practical (the abolition of forced labour) and symbolic (provisions for a citizenship and for an Assembly of the French Union). After May 1947, moreover, the narrowness of many Third Force majorities gave such Deputies significant leverage in the Assembly – an element that contributed to Defferre's relatively liberal legislation of 1956 and the fairly peaceful transition of French sub-Saharan Africa to independence. This was far from true in Shipway's last case, Madagascar – 'sub-Saharan' but quite distinct from continental Africa – where the clash between the apparently liberal colonial policy of the post-war period and the reality of French imperial mastery provoked one of France's bloodiest colonial uprisings of the twentieth century. The colonial record of the Liberation period was thus a messy combination of liberal rhetoric, partial citizenship rights, limited concessions to colonial aspirations, and administrative and military rigidity, all varying between territories, which set the pattern for the troubled history of French decolonisation over the next fifteen years.

France and the Allies: the Soviet Union

France's diplomatic demotion was most obviously symbolised by the absence of any Frenchman alongside the 'Big Three' at the big conferences of Tehran, Yalta, and Potsdam. Weakened as a major power, France nevertheless remained of consequence to each of the Big Three in Europe's rapid and complex transition from Grand Alliance to Cold War.

None shaped France's internal politics more directly than the Soviet Union. After all, France's biggest post-war party, the PCF, took its orders from the Kremlin – as is clear from Naoumova's chapter. As the European war drew to a close Stalin aimed, firstly, to avoid the nightmare of a separate Anglo-American peace with Germany, and, secondly, to secure recognition for the establishment of Soviet satellite states in Central and Eastern Europe. In that context, Stalin's pathological mistrustfulness, well documented in the cases of Roosevelt and Churchill ('he will pick your pocket for a kopek if you don't watch him', he told Milovan Djilas of the latter) actually encouraged co-operation with the West.[17] Advisers such as Litvinov, Maisky and Gromyko, and even Foreign Minister Molotov, all envisaged such co-operation lasting at least until the Soviet Union's full recovery from the conflict.[18] So France's suggestion of an alliance won a favourable response. Signed during de Gaulle's visit to Moscow in December 1944, the Franco-Soviet treaty was of largely symbolic importance: for the French, a diplomatic fillip, for the Soviets, a gesture to reinforce a provisional government independent from Washington and London, and willing to govern with the PCF. But the policy of co-operation with the West also meant restraining the revolutionary ardours of Western Communists, at a time when former FFI fighters with access to arms competed for power on the ground with the representatives of the GPRF. In November 1944 Stalin instructed the PCF leader Maurice Thorez, who had spent his war as a guest of the Soviet Union, to work solely within 'bourgeois' democratic institutions and to eschew any attempt at a violent takeover. Thorez's careful implementation of Stalin's orders on his return to Paris was crucial first in establishing that the GPRF, not the *Comités de Libération* or the people's militias, had the right to rule France, second in buttressing the reform governments of 1944–47, and third in holding back workers' demands, especially on pay.

Yet from the Allies' victory in Europe, Stalin turned slowly away from co-operation with the West. Abroad, the Western Allies had proved reluctant to endorse the dictatorships he was setting up in Eastern Europe, especially Poland; the Americans temporarily acquired a monopoly in atomic weapons, and sent at times contradictory signals about their own commitment to co-operation. At home, a political clamp-down, seen as necessary after a victory which had brought Soviet troops into contact with the West for the first time, would be facilitated by an atmosphere of international tension. By February 1946, Stalin, Malenkov and Beria had all publicly evoked a renewed threat from the 'imperialist powers', while the most serious East–West confrontation since the war took place over Iran.[19] The transition to Cold War was gradual rather than sudden, however, and for a further 18 months the PCF was still invited to follow Stalin's line of participation within France's 'bourgeois' political system.

No Western Communist leader was more loyal to Moscow than Thorez, but the line was hard to follow in France. The dissolution of the FFI dampened the expectations of many serious activists, without wholly allaying the suspicions of the PCF's allies in the *tripartite* coalition, for whom both history (the Nazi-Soviet pact of 1939) and current events (the establishment of Soviet-style regimes in Eastern Europe) suggested prudence. Among the electorate, it was clear in 1946, as in the 1960s, that millions of French men and women voted Communist but did not 'yet' want a Communist-led government.[20] That the party did not, under these conditions, press its claim to the premiership for Thorez too hard, was logical but disappointing to its committed supporters. And the PCF's willingness, as a responsible party of government, to condone austerity policies and condemn strikes as 'fomented by the trusts', inevitably tried the patience of its working-class supporters. That was the background to the Renault strike which broke out in April 1947, and thence to the Communists' removal from government.

Throughout that summer they behaved as if their return to government in tandem with the Socialists was both imminent and necessary. The turning-point only came in September. Then, at a meeting of European Communist parties at Sklarska-Poreba, in Poland, the French and Italian delegates received a memorable dressing-down for following the moderate strategy of the post-war years – although they had done so on Stalin's instructions. The new order for the world's Communists was confrontation with the 'imperialist' camp led by the United States, in which category all other forces, including the Socialists, were considered to fall. The global Cold War was reproduced within the French political system, with France's Communists out of government till 1981.

The Liberation years are important for what they reveal about the position of a Soviet-style Communist party in a Western democratic system. The PCF's Moscow links, as Stalin knew, aroused suspicion. To win voters' trust and stake a claim to lead government, the Communists therefore sought to establish credentials as responsible and moderate members of a ruling coalition. But they thereby risked breaking faith with the promises of radical change and better tomorrows that had attracted their core electorate to them in the first place. To remain out of government and press for change on Communist terms, on the other hand, would be to court voter mistrust and political isolation. The PCF's dilemma remained intact even forty years later; by then, the assets that had kept it relatively strong even after 1947 – a robust organisation and the continued prestige of the Resistance and even of the Soviet role in winning the war – had gone, and the party faced precipitate decline.

France and the Allies: the United States

Relations with the United States present something close to a mirror image of the Franco-Soviet record. They got off to a memorably bad start, as Charles

Cogan notes. For Roosevelt, France was finished as a great power and de Gaulle was practically a fascist. France's empire, and French ideas about Europe's future, had little place in the Rooseveltian vision of the post-war world, where peace and security would be assured on a multilateral basis through the new United Nations Organisation, differences with the USSR settled through negotiation, and American forces stationed in Europe only for as long as it took to denazify Germany. It was Roosevelt's obstruction that delayed the Allies' recognition of the GPRF till 23 October 1944. Yet even for the United States, France mattered. Half a million French soldiers and sixteen French air squadrons had been equipped by the Americans by the summer of 1944 (though as Cogan points out, Roosevelt was reluctant to do much more). As long as the European war persisted, France was *the* indispensable supply-line, its stability vital to the swift defeat of Germany. After the war, France's economic and political stability, as well as Western Europe's integration into a future multilateral trading system, were considered important enough for the Americans to prop up the faltering French economy with a succession of loans and grants, culminating with the European Recovery Programme (Marshall Aid) in 1948.

Economic aid to France became all the more important as the Rooseveltian vision gave way, during the 2–3 years after the Yalta conference of February 1945, to the mindset of the Cold War. That the change began, more or less, with the succession to the presidency of Harry Truman at Roosevelt's death on 12 April 1945, was largely coincidental. Its landmarks include the unease of Truman and the American delegation with Soviet behaviour, especially in relation to Poland and other East European countries, at the Potsdam conference of July–August 1945; George Kennan's 'long telegram' of 22 February 1946 from the Moscow Embassy about the direction of Soviet policy worldwide and the impossibility of finding an amicable *modus vivendi* with the Soviet Union; Churchill's 'Iron Curtain' speech given just twelve days later on Truman's home territory of Missouri; the crisis of March 1946 over the continued presence of Soviet troops in Iran, which was only ended after Iranian and American complaints to the Security Council of the United Nations; the report on US–Soviet relations submitted to the President by his adviser Clark Clifford that September; the enunciation of the 'Truman doctrine' on 12 March 1947, in which the President used a request for congressional funds to assist the Greek and Turkish governments against Communist threats to make a forceful declaration of America's role as world power, stating that 'I believe that it must be the policy of the United States to support free peoples who are resisting attempted subjugation by armed minorities or by outside pressures'; and the offer from Secretary of State George Marshall, on 5 June 1947, of large-scale aid for European recovery, on terms that only the Western countries were likely to accept.

The process was, of course, vastly more complex than such a bald chronology would suggest. Political leaders in the executive branch and in Congress, officials, and public opinion moved at different speeds from seeking to work with the Soviets, to 'getting tough' with Moscow and requiring a *quid pro quo* for every American concession, to a readiness to oppose perceived Soviet expansionism not only with diplomacy but with tax dollars and ultimately military force. The fact that the Democrat Truman had to build a bipartisan foreign policy with his Republican congress complicated the process further. But the evolution inevitably engaged America's European partners, especially France and Italy, with their big Communist parties.

The record of Franco-American relations up to the start of 1947 remained a source of frustration to both sides. Americans saw France as obstructive on the German question (the French clung to the idea of a punitive peace for over two years longer than the 'Anglo-Saxons'), reluctant to commit to the West in the emerging world conflict, economically unstable despite American loans, and politically a mess with Communists still in office and de Gaulle about to attempt a return to power. For the French, American credits were insufficient (especially compared to the largesse awarded to the British), and the Americans and British insensitive both to France's need both for coal and for security from Germany. By the end of 1947, however, the accelerating pace of the Cold War had transformed the situation. The Communists were removed from office – a step encouraged and welcomed, but did not dictated, by the Americans; and the Third Force governments had resisted both the Communist-led strikes and de Gaulle's peremptory demands for a change of regime. France had co-operated with Britain in the organisation of Marshall Aid, and would receive the highest share of any country except the United Kingdom. Acceptance of Marshall Aid had anchored France to the West, and French demands over Germany had been moderated, with preparations under way for a merger of France's occupation zone with the Anglo-American 'bizonia'. French relations with the United States did not suddenly become simple, but they were closer in the ensuing decade than at any other time in post-war history.

France and the Allies: Britain

France was more important for the British in 1945 than for either of the emerging superpowers. In a Europe expected to be free of American troops by 1947, Britain needed a major continental ally, and France was the only one available. The resulting wish to build up France, particularly well-established within the Foreign Office, hardly varied whether the principal threat was seen as coming from a resurgent Germany (as it was in 1945) or a newly unfriendly Soviet Union (as it was beginning to be in 1947). It was chiefly through Britain's efforts that France obtained an occupation zone in Germany and positions alongside the Big Three in the international institutions of the post-war era. Moreover, de Gaulle was acknowledged by most British policy-makers, far earlier than by the Americans, as France's natural leader at the Liberation. To avoid repetition of the errors of the inter-war period, the British were ready, at almost any point in the two-and-a-half years after the Liberation, to conclude a formal alliance with France; powerful French voices sought the same.

But no Anglo-French Treaty was concluded till March 1947. It was hindered by personalities – notably Churchill's stormy relations with de Gaulle – but also by more fundamental issues: the distribution of Ruhr coal, which fell within the British occupation zone, and wider Anglo-French differences over the future of Germany; a French hesitation, until 1947, to give the impression of having 'chosen' the Anglo-Saxons; and a deeply-held British reluctance, among both the military and the economic ministries, to make a lasting commitment to the European continent. Dunkirk became one of history's forgotten treaties, quickly overtaken by the Brussels Treaty of a year later and above all by the North Atlantic Treaty of April 1949. It forged no special Anglo-French relationship; economic co-operation would advance (slightly) within the framework of the Marshall Plan, military co-operation within that of NATO – both, therefore, under the American aegis. And France's key European partner would turn out to be, not Britain, but Germany.

Remembering the Liberation: the uncertain foundation

Vincent Wright has remarked that 'The dates which figured (and continue to figure) most prominently in the French historical consciousness – 1789, 1793, 1830, 1848, 1871, 1936, 1940 and 1944 – all recall periods when French people were at their most bitterly divided. When a British politician invokes history it is normally to buttress an unconvincing appeal to national unity; a French politician will cite historical examples to illustrate the perfidy of his adversaries.'[21] Certainly memories of the Liberation include moments of consensus, whether symbolic – the liberation of Paris on 25 August 1944 and de Gaulle's walk down the Champs-Élysées the following day – or practical – the decrees of October 1945 that founded France's Social Security system. Buton's closing chapter, however, stresses the extreme diversity of French views of the period – a diversity that was affected from the start by varied political positions, but which has also been shaped by the passage of time and by generational effects. To make sense of this kaleidoscope, Buton divided the six decades since the Liberation into three periods: that of the 'resistentialist myth' lasting until 1968, that of confrontation between radically opposed views from 1968 till the mid-1990s, and a calmer, more consensual decade since then. Within each period, a variety of memories have coexisted, more or less peacefully.

Over the immediate post-war generation, French memories of the Liberation were dominated by the myth of *la France résistante* sustained, in different ways, by the two great political forces to have emerged from the war, Gaullism and Communism. The positive gloss of 'resistentialism', argues Buton, contributed both to the re-establishment of 'Republican legality' in 1944–45 and to France's subsequent recovery. But there were longer-term costs. The concealment of France's role in the Holocaust damaged the power of the Republic to assimilate citizens of all races; the denial of the defeat of 1940 encouraged the illusion that France could hang on to her colonies; the refusal to acknowledge Vichy's daily 'accommodations' with Nazis led to blindness over what French officials were capable of – with dramatic consequences as French politicians and civil servants condoned torture under the Fourth Republic. And the truth, when it came out, smelt all the worse for having been shut away for two decades and more. Hence the generation of debunking that opened in the late 1960s. The balance was certainly redressed, despite an official view that clung to the old myth; few, by 1995, could seriously believe that Vichy was a tiny band of criminals, or that more than a small minority of the French had engaged in active resistance. But this period too had its costs. In particular, it created an environment in which the far Right, and especially the Front National, could attempt seriously to relegitimise Vichy and to deny or minimise the reality of the Holocaust.

The relative calm of the third and most recent period owes much to a change in generations and in official attitudes. Both a neo-Gaullist president, Jacques Chirac, and a Socialist prime minister, Lionel Jospin, admitted that *France*, and not merely a band of right-wing adventurers, had behaved dishonourably. Meanwhile, historians showed that support for Pétain especially early in the war, did not exclude, especially after 1942, the rejection of Vichy by many of the French, who gave assistance to those whom it excluded. If France did not emerged unblemished from the dark years, it would be wrong to claim that the French had behaved worse than other peoples under occupation.

What traces did the 'long' Liberation, as distinct from the Occupation and its close, leave on the face of France? De Gaulle had written in June 1942 that the French people were 'uniting for victory and gathering for a revolution'.[22] What happened was less than a revolution, but still, in some respects, a founding moment. This is most obviously true of the social and economic settlement. Whatever their antecedents in pre-war debates and measures, and whatever their ambiguities, the characteristic features of France's post-war social and economic structures – the big public sector, the place of planning, the social security system – were forged in the Liberation era. It is also true of one aspect of the political system – the tardy recognition of basic democratic rights for the whole adult population, and not just half of it. France's alignment with the West, sealed by the end of 1947, also falls into this category – even if the French would continue, before as well as after de Gaulle's return to power, to try and retain the greatest available freedom of action vis-à-vis their new American ally.

Other aspects of the record show less of a dramatic break than a moment of acceleration, speeding up processes already under way which would continue in ensuing years and decades. The position of French women, though transformed much less radically than many had hoped by the tardy extension of political rights, was nevertheless advanced in important ways. The renewal of France's political élite may also be placed in this category: many politicians, especially of the Right, simply disappeared (or were removed) from the scene at the Liberation, though their replacement by wholly new arrivals was rarer than the sudden advancement of men already active at junior levels in the pre-war years.

Yet the Liberation also had its false starts, turning-points of history where, finally, nothing turned. The 'liberal moment' of the Catholic Church came and went – not without leaving traces, but nothing corresponding to the expectations of 1945. The brief promise of a new deal for the colonies, even in the limited form of Brazzaville, was largely betrayed: although a return to the *status quo ante* was widely agreed to be impossible, there was little consensus about what constituted desirable or possible change, and even such change as was agreed went wrong. The Franco-Soviet treaty fell an early victim of the Cold War. The Treaty of Dunkirk, signed nearly two years after the end of hostilities in Europe, of March 1947, was a minimal alliance that failed to set Franco-British relations on a new course.

But it is in the domestic political settlement that the sense of false starts and frustrated hopes is strongest. The Communists, of course, did not get their revolution, thanks in part to Stalin. The party system, which had appeared transformed by the first post-war elections, though not unchanged, saw a speedy return, especially after May 1947, of 'delights and poisons' of before 1940. The Third Republic, though decisively rejected by the electorate in October 1945, returned a year later as the Fourth, altered in significant details but instantly familiar in its basic architecture, after parties and people had turned down the Left's option of an all-powerful single chamber and de Gaulle's of a strengthened executive. The most striking contrast of the Liberation years, indeed, was between economic and social renewal, unnoticed for too long by outside observers, and an all too recognisable political continuity. The opposite would be true of 1958, when France's economy continued on its course as the political system was transformed and the empire finally dismantled. Only then would the lopsided character of France's post-war foundation be corrected.

Notes

1. L.F. Ellis, *Victory in the West*, Vol. I (London: HMSO, 1962), pp. 488, 493. The figures, which include 36,976 army dead, cover the period from 6 June to the end of August 1944, plus Allied air operations preparatory to D-day.
2. P. Buton, *La Joie douloureuse: la Libération de la France* (Brussels: Complexe, 2004), pp. 230–1.
3. Buton, in *La Joie douloureuse* (pp. 43, 245), puts current estimates of French deaths from Allied bombing at between 48,000 and 60,000, a figure comparable to that for British victims of German bombing. Many of them, though far from all, died in the campaigns of 1944–45.
4. Karen Adler uses the term 'long' liberation, stressing its elasticity, in her *Jews and Gender in Liberation France* (Cambridge: Cambridge University Press, 2003). On a long view, she observes (p. 5), for those who immediately rejected the defeat, 'Liberation started the day the armistice was signed' in 1940. And because the victory

against Germany still left important groups – most obviously colonised peoples and women – rather less than fully liberated, the Liberation era could could be said to have closed at any point up to 1995. This book's time frame, with necessary spillover at either end, is the period between the D-Day landings and the end of 1947, when the political, economic, imperial, and diplomatic settlements of post-war France were, for better or worse, broadly complete: compared to Adler's, then, a 'short long Liberation.'

5. F. Goguel, *Chroniques électorales*, Vol. III (Paris: Presses de la Fondation Nationale des Sciences Politiques, 1983), p. 44.
6. P.M. Williams, *Crisis and Compromise: Politics in the Fourth Republic* (London: Longman, 1964), p. 24.
7. Buton, *La Joie douloureuse*, p. 106.
8. F. Muel-Dreyfus, *Vichy et l'éternel féminin* (Paris: Le Seuil, 1996), pp. 213–14.
9. F. Virgili, *La France 'virile': des femmes tondues à la Libération* (Paris: Payot-Rivages, 2000), p. 223.
10. J. Jenson, 'The Liberation and new rights for French women' in M.R. Higonnet and J. Jenson (eds), *Behind the Lines. Gender and the Two World Wars* (New Haven: Yale University Press,1987), pp. 272–84: p. 279.
11. Buton, *La Joie douloureuse*, p. 209.
12. Buton, *La Joie douloureuse*, pp. 162–3.
13. F.M.B. Lynch, *France and the International Economy: From Vichy to the Treaty of Rome* (London: Routledge, 1997), p. 89.
14. Buton, *La Joie douloureuse*, p. 164.
15. A. Milward, *The Reconstruction of Western Europe, 1945–51* (London: Routledge, 1992 (original edition 1984)), p. 15.
16. C. de Gaulle, *Discours et messages*, Vol. I, 1940–1946 (Paris: Plon, 1970), p. 373.
17. M. Djilas, *Conversations with Stalin* (New York: Harcourt Brace, 1962), p. 73.
18. V. Zubok and C. Pleshakov, *Inside the Kremlin's Cold War: from Stalin to Khrushchev* (Cambridge, Mass.: Harvard University Press, 1996), pp. 28–32; C. Cogan, *Forced to Choose: France, the Atlantic Alliance, and NATO – Then and Now* (London: Praeger, 1997), p. 6.
19. P. de Senarclens, *From Yalta to the Iron Curtain: the Great Powers and the Origins of the Cold War* (Oxford: Berg, 1995), p. 123.
20. G. Lavau, 'Le Parti communiste dans le système politique français', in Fondation Nationale des Sciences Politiques, *Le communisme en France* (Paris: Armand Colin, 1969), pp. 7–81: pp. 27–35.
21. V. Wright, *The Government and Politics of France*, 3rd edn (London: Unwin Hyman, 1989), p. 170.
22. de Gaulle, *Discours et messages*, Vol. I, p. 205.

Bibliography

Adler, K., *Jews and Gender in Liberation France* (Cambridge: Cambridge University Press, 2003).
Buton, P., *La Joie douloureuse: la Libération de la France* (Brussels: Complexe, 2004).
Cogan, C., *Forced to Choose: France, the Atlantic Alliance, and NATO – Then and Now* (London: Praeger, 1997).
de Gaulle, C., *Discours et messages*, Vol. I, 1940–1946 (Paris: Plon, 1970).

de Senarclens, P., *From Yalta to the Iron Curtain: the Great Powers and the Origins of the Cold War* (Oxford: Berg, 1995).

Djilas, M., *Conversations with Stalin* (New York: Harcourt, Brace, 1962).

Ellis, L.F., *Victory in the West*, Vol. I (London: HMSO, 1962).

Goguel, F., *Chroniques électorales*, Vol. III (Paris: Presses de la Fondation Nationale des Sciences Politiques, 1983).

Jenson, J., 'The Liberation and new rights for French women' in M.R. Higonnet and J. Jenson (eds), *Behind the Lines. Gender and the Two World Wars* (New Haven: Yale University Press, 1987), pp. 272–84.

Lavau, G., 'Le Parti communiste dans le système politique français', in Fondation Nationale des Sciences Politiques, *Le communisme en France* (Paris: Armand Colin, 1969), pp. 7–81.

Lynch, F.M.B., *France and the International Economy: From Vichy to the Treaty of Rome* (London: Routledge, 1997).

Milward, A., *The Reconstruction of Western Europe, 1945–51* (London: Routledge, 1992 (original edition 1984)).

Muel-Dreyfus, F., *Vichy et l'éternel féminin* (Paris: Le Seuil, 1996).

Virgili, F., *La France 'virile': des femmes tondues à la Libération* (Paris: Payot-Rivages, 2000).

Williams, P., *Crisis and Compromise: Politics in the Fourth Republic* (London: Longman, 1964).

Wright, V., *The Government and Politics of France*, 3rd edn (London: Unwin Hyman, 1989).

Zubok, V., and Pleshakov, C., *Inside the Kremlin's Cold War: from Stalin to Khrushchev* (Cambridge, Mass.: Harvard University Press, 1996).

2
The Liberation and the Institutional Question in France

Emmanuel Cartier[1]

The question of France's institutions may at first sight seem secondary compared to other pressing issues confronting the Gouvernement Provisoire de la République Française (GPRF) on its move to Paris at the end of August 1944. Yet it had absorbed the attention of the Resistance movement and of political parties, both established and new, as early as 1941. It was therefore soon aired in the legislative or quasi-legislative organs of the Resistance and Liberation authorities. The first of these was the Provisional Consultative Assembly, set up in Algiers in September 1943 to enhance the democratic legitimacy of the Comité Français de la Libération Nationale (CFLN), the predecessor to the GPRF, by representing the main political parties, and reconstituted a year later in Paris. It was replaced in October 1945 by the first of the two National Constituent Assemblies. This, like its successor elected in June 1946 (and unlike the Consultative Assembly), was a legislature legitimated by universal suffrage, in which the parties wielded deliberative power via their Deputies.

The 'reform of the State' had been debated in France (and elsewhere) in the 1930s. Constitutional issues reappeared in the work of the various committees created by the Free French from 1941;[2] in Algiers a Commission for the Reform of the State was created within the Provisional Consultative Assembly and an interdepartmental working committee also considered constitutional reforms.[3] Traditionally interested in such issues, the French had a new forum within which to debate them in the early days of the Liberation, thanks notably to legislation protecting the independence and diversity of the press. Institutional questions therefore moved to the centre of political debate, with an underlying awareness that the future liberty, dignity, and daily lives of human beings, all severely tried during the Occupation, were linked to them. Two unifying factors appeared in these debates. First, the internal Resistance reflected the widespread desire for renewal, notably through the many constitutional drafts addressed to the French National Committee in London, and to its successor the CFLN, by movements in occupied France.[4] Second, however, 'the Republic' had become a unifying symbol of the fight against fascism. As in former struggles against the Monarchy, and then the Empire, it acquired the status of an ideal, with which the words democracy, liberty, and welfare came to merge. The desire for renewal meant that no project suggested a return to the Third Republic and what were viewed as its failed institutions; the ideal of the Republic meant that none advocated a regime that was not republican.

But as the Liberation turned from a mystical goal into a real political event, the institutional question became more, not less, intractable. Its task over, the Resistance lost its (always transitory) unity and the *résistants'* revolutionary faith faded.[5] De Gaulle's hopes for a republic with strong executive leadership were dashed, as were the Left's dreams of a 'purer', unicameral constitution. In the end, the French accepted a compromise, but without enthusiasm, adopting the second draft for the Constitution of a Fourth Republic in which many of them had placed excessive hopes for renewal and for democratic and social progress.

The laborious construction of the new Republic had two phases. The first laid the groundwork for transition, ensuring *both* that the new regime would leave past institutions – Vichy, but also the Third Republic – behind it *and* that a founding myth – the continuity of the Republic – would take root. The second phase defined the new regime itself, within the framework of two aspirations not easily reconciled – to renew the bases and modes of expression of French democracy, and to establish a form of rationalised parliamentarianism. The important debate over the upper house, however, is left to Chapter 3.

The preliminaries of transition: a consensus over essentials

The leaders of Free France needed to agree an official doctrine on two issues relating to the constitutional transition: the status of France's institutional past and the legal and democratic basis of the transitional regime.

The selective liquidation of the past

To break with the institutional past of Vichy was easy and consensual. To break with the Third Republic – the parliamentary regime born in 1875 and in force until 10 July 1940 – was harder and more controversial, for with the Liberation once achieved, voices were raised in favour of a return to it. The consensus eventually reached had a twofold base: the legal void of Vichy and the myth of the continuity of 'the' Republic.

The Free French in London had denied Vichy's legal existence from 1940. They viewed it as illegitimate for having compromised with the enemy (in the Franco-German armistice of 22 June 1940), and as unconstitutional (from the vote of constituent powers to Marshal Pétain on 10 July). In principle, then, the Third Republic remained in force, and could be 'restored' at the moment of liberation. In the meantime, however, a state of emergency existed which prevented the normal application of the constitutional laws of 1875 (the basic laws of the Third Republic). The Free French authorities founded their right to pass acts in the name of France on this state of emergency. But they soon felt the need to underpin this with a legal system with all the makings of a constitution. The Brazzaville manifesto of 27 October 1940, complemented by the organic declaration of 16 November, gave form for the first time to the official doctrine of Free France. It would figure in the *ordonnances* (decrees) of 27 October 1940, 24 September 1941 and 3 June 1943;[6] and these in turn would be the authority on which rested the early texts of 1942 restoring republican legality in the colonies. The consensus of the Provisional Consultative Assembly and the GPRF was given formal existence by the *ordonnance* of 9 August 1944 re-establishing republican legality on the French mainland and declaring as 'null and void' the whole body of acts passed by the Vichy government since 16 June 1940, while restricting the whole effect of this nullity only to the acts directly concerned by the *ordonnance* and its decrees of application – chiefly institutional dispositions and anti-Semitic measures.[7] This *ordonnance* thus safeguarded political appearances for the GPRF, reasserting the absence of legitimacy of Vichy and, *a contrario*, the legitimacy of Free France, regarded as early as 16 June 1940 as the only legal authority in charge of the interests of the Republic, which 'legally' had never ceased to exist.

If the legal non-existence of Vichy required the careful construction of a legal and constitutional edifice to justify it, this was even more true of the notion of the continuity of the Republic. Indeed, in practical terms, precise continuity with the pre-war regime was *not* what the GPRF sought. In the early days of Free France, General de Gaulle used the words 'France', in the name of which he claimed to be speaking, or 'democracy', so as to foster the political union of the Free French in their fight alongside the Allies, but 'Republic' with far greater caution. For an effective riposte to Vichy's accusation of 'dissidence' required a high degree of unity among the Free French, and this was not likely to be achieved by referring to a regime – the Third Republic – which had been guilty of institutional and moral weakness. Gradually, however, the word Republic became synonymous with fighting for Free France, in particular because the internal Resistance was so deeply attached to it. Thus an enquiry conducted by the Free French General Committee of Studies, showed that members of the internal Resistance associated the word *République* with the ideas of '*liberté*', '*justice*', '*patrie*', '*égalité*', even '*justice sociale*'.[8] For the internal and external Resistance alike, no other type of regime was conceivable. On this basis, therefore, there would legally be merely a transition between a provisional republic embodied in a *de facto* government since 16 June 1940, and a legal and permanent Republic.

This would therefore have implied – when the exceptional circumstances necessitating a state of emergency came to an end – a straightforward return both to the constitutional laws of 1875 and to France's institutions as they had existed on 16 June 1940. That choice might be viewed as a natural solution. Even though, as Olivier Wieviorka observes elsewhere in this book, 173 Deputies or Senators of the Third Republic had died during the Occupation, and 321 more would be banned from election by virtue of their wartime activities, the legal provisions existed for exceptional circumstances of this sort. The so-called Tréveneuc law of 15 February 1872 stated that if the National Assembly was illegally dissolved or prevented from meeting, the *conseil général* in each of the French *départements* should immediately designate two representatives. These representatives would form an Assembly, which would assure order and provisionally carry out administrative measures, aimed primarily at the recovery of the National Assembly's full powers. That achieved, the *ad hoc* Assembly would be dissolved and new elections held.[9]

But the CFLN ruled out this course as early as April 1944. Instead, it sought a transition marking a clear break with the Third Republic. The legal bases for this choice go back to an exchange of letters between de Gaulle and Jules Jeanneney, president of the Senate since 1932. Answering de Gaulle's request for confidential legal advice on the transition, Jeanneney argued, firstly, that the National Assembly (the designation under the Third Republic for the two Houses, Chamber of Deputies and Senate, meeting together) had acted illegally in delegating constituent powers to Pétain in its session of 10 July 1940 (which, ironically, Jeanneney had presided). Under the law of February 25, 1875, one of the Third Republic's founding texts, amendments could only be passed by an absolute majority of the whole National Assembly itself.[10] Moreover, Pétain had used his illegally-delegated powers without delay, issuing, on 11 July, Constitutional Law No. 3 prohibiting Parliament from meeting unless convoked by him. For Jeanneney, therefore,

> The power thus wrongly delegated was, in explicit terms as well as in the minds of the principals, with a view towards a republican Constitution. However, use was made of it against the institutions of the Republic and even its very designation. Since this power has been abused it should be revoked.[11]

Jeanneney concluded that national sovereignty could not legally be exercised by a National Assembly which, though still existing, was non-functioning, and which had defaulted on its responsibilities. Consequently it was up to the 'Nation' to assume them through a free vote concerning the institutions and the leadership of France. But such a free vote could not be arranged until order had been restored, prisoners of war returned and voting lists established. In the meantime there was no alternative but to 'cross the Rubicon' and set up a provisional government until a new National Assembly could be created – and the earlier constitutional laws for setting up a government (24 and 25 February and 16 July 1875) would be suspended.[12]

Jeanneney's advice was, broadly, followed. A first step in the break was marked by the *ordonnance* of 21 April 1944 relating to the provisional post-Liberation authorities, issued with support from the Consultative Assembly. This provided for the election of a single constituent assembly within a year of the complete liberation of French territory.[13] More generally, the *ordonnance* provided for a gradual return to representative institutions working on democratic principles – though these were, in practice, overtaken both by the speed of military operations and by the massive return of prisoners and deportees from May 1945.

In a second *ordonnance*, dated 17 August 1945, the GPRF decided on a national vote combining a referendum with the election of a constituent assembly. This *ordonnance* was adopted *against* the opinion of the Consultative Assembly, for reasons to be discussed more fully below. The provision for a referendum meant that the responsibility for the break with former institutions, *formally* attributable to a *de facto* government, the GPRF, would be *politically* attributable only to the French people. And the constitutional power given to the text appended to the questions put to voters on 21 October 1945 enabled the provisional to be formalised and the Republic to be given a new foundation, resting on a new democratic pact.

Formalising the present

The legal texts issued by the provisional authorities before the Liberation formed the basis for a provisional regime, officially justified by the state of emergency, which ruled until the constitutional law of 2 November 1945 came into force.[14] This latter date marks what Maurice Duverger calls 'the end of the era of autocratic provisional governments'.[15] Although the GPRF retained the title of provisional government it had taken in 3 June 1944, and would continue to do so until the inauguration of the Fourth Republic in January 1947, what had been the *de facto* government of the Republic now became a *de jure* authority, constituted in conformity both with the democratic principles upheld by the internal and external Resistance and with the requirements of the Allies in the West.

The first formally constitutional law of the 'provisional' Republic, dated 2 November 1945, re-established, in eight concise articles, the republican principles of the separation of powers and representative and accountable government. The National Constituent Assembly and the GPRF would share the right to table bills. The Assembly alone could vote the budget and pass laws. Adopted against the Consultative Assembly's adverse opinion of 29 July 1945, the law of 2 November 1945 was nevertheless something of a compromise between the Assembly's views and those of the GPRF. It attempted to rationalise relations between executive and legislature, reconciling the stable government aimed at both by the GPRF and by the Consultative Assembly with the requirement that the executive be accountable to the future Assembly.[16] Thus Article 1 stated, firstly, that the president of the GPRF was elected directly by the Assembly, which was to approve both its composition and its programme; and, secondly, that the absolute majority of the Assembly required to pass a no-confidence motion should mean a majority of its total membership and not merely of those voting. This provision, which would reappear in the

Constitutions of the Fourth and Fifth Republics, sought to reinforce government stability by setting a limit to the scope of no-confidence motions. The same paragraph, which gave rise to the political crisis of December 1945 between de Gaulle and the parties of the Left, stated that the rejection of a finance bill should not automatically result in the resignation of the government.

But the most striking and controversial innovation, as France took the first step towards a return of representative government, lay in the restrictions placed on the powers of the newly-elected Assembly. The constituent assemblies convened by the provisional governments of 1848 and 1870 had enjoyed complete freedom both to draft and vote on the future Constitution and to define the provisional organisation of the public authorities. By contrast, the National Constituent Assembly elected on 21 October 1945 was limited, both in its competences and in its term of office, by a constitutional law adopted by the French electorate in the double referendum of the same day. This law clearly established the new Assembly's subordination to the will of the people. Under its Article 3, the constitutional draft was to be ratified by referendum. Under Articles 6 and 7, moreover, the mandate of the Assembly's Deputies would end immediately if the voters rejected their constitutional draft; as soon as the new constitution came into force, if the draft was accepted; and in any case, within a maximum of seven months. These limitations corresponded to the same logic of restraining the so-called 'sovereignty' of the constituent assemblies, to which republican doctrine had been attached ever since 1789 and which members of the Provisional Consultative Assembly had vainly tried to defend. Unlike its predecessors of 1848 and 1870, the National Constituent Assembly was not empowered to change the constitution; this power was legally vested in the citizens of France. Moreover, the Constituent Assembly had no right to modify the *provisional* constitution (the law of 2 November 1945), for example by changing the competence and the status of the GPRF.[17] This was confirmed by an opinion of the Conseil d'État on 17 April 1946.[18]

André Philip referred to the work of the Committee on the reform of the Constitution as one of *'clearing up'* the basic institutional questions before the discussion of the new regime could begin.[19] The Committee's answers commanded a broad consensus on one issue: the referendum of 21 October 1945 buried the Third Republic, as nearly three-quarters of the electorate, and 96.4 per cent of those voting, chose to give the new Assembly the task of drafting a new constitution. Only the Radicals, badly weakened by their record since 1940, had supported a return to the old regime, and barely a third of their voters had followed them. A very clear majority, but a less overwhelming one – half the electorate, and two-thirds of those voting – also agreed to limit the Assembly's powers. Here, the Radicals, faithful to the principle of parliamentary rights, were joined by the Communists, who saw a strong and unchecked Assembly as the surest legal route to power. These divisions foreshadowed the more fundamental political quarrels that appeared as discussion of the new constitution got seriously under way and the unity of the Resistance disintegrated. Meanwhile, the general public increasingly focused on the everyday problems of food, housing, and jobs, and lost interest in institutional debates.[20]

The constitutional outcome: a compromise on fundamentals

Partially tackled by the Resistance during the war, the question of France's future institutions was fully debated by the two Constituent Assemblies elected successively on 21 October 1945 and (after the No result at the constitutional referendum of May 1946) on 2 June 1946. The first Assembly's Standing Orders, voted on 22 November 1945, set up a Constitutional Committee responsible for producing a draft Constitution. It was chaired by two Socialists, first André Philip and then (from January 1946) Guy Mollet. Throughout all the debates over all the issues dealt with by the Committee one can notice a desire both for a renewed democracy and for the rationalisation of French parliamentarianism.

Renewing democracy

The desire for democratic renewal, clear since before the Liberation, found three main expressions. First, the suffrage was (finally) extended to women. Second, there were steps, however cautious and limited in the final version of the Constitution, towards widening democratic expression to include referendums. Third, ways were sought to give constitutional status to social and economic democracy, a particular concern of the dominant parties at the Liberation.

On 18 March 1944, a few days before the Provisional Consultative Assembly in Algiers was due to discuss the draft *ordonnance* on the provisional organisation of public authorities in post-Liberation France, General de Gaulle made it clear that the future 'Fourth Republic' desired by the French people should embody a 'renewed democracy' and 'include a representation elected by all the men and women of our country, which would discipline itself to follow political and legislative procedures quite different from those which had ended up by paralysing the parliament of the Third Republic'.[21] By the *ordonnance* of 21 April 1944, the GPRF extended the vote to women and, later on in 1945, to the military and to the peoples of France's overseas territories, even if the latter, as Martin Shipway notes elsewhere in this book, was a long-awaited but still very incomplete measure.[22] With wider bases of national representation went a reinforcement of the voters' right of deliberation thanks to the new procedure established by the *ordonnance* of 17 August 1945: the constituent decisional referendum. The institution of the constituent decisional referendum epitomised Free France's attitude, thanks to a bold and original combination of two theories of sovereignty, national and popular. Criticised as resembling the authoritarian style of plebiscite typical of the two Napoleonic eras, but in fact quite distinct from them, the referendum gave the French people the right of direct expression, and thereby aimed to confirm and to ensure national unity on the fundamental principles of Free France. The double referendum of 1945 allowed the Republic to be founded on a renewed contractual basis, based on the spirit of the previous regime – the tradition of liberties, the principle of national sovereignty, and parliamentarianism – rather than its letter.

This innovative process did not go smoothly. Indeed, in its debates of January and March 1944, the Provisional Consultative Assembly established a cross-party agreement to *reject* the use of the referendum, which it viewed as comparable to a plebiscite, characteristic of 'personal power', and thus opposed to the Republican spirit supposed to guide everybody's deliberations. De Gaulle himself had avoided mention of the referendum in his speeches, preferring references to the 'Nation' or to the 'French People', and making it clear on repeated occasions that he thereby meant its 'representatives' and not the nation as a whole political body vested with a decision-making competence. It was, moreover, to a fully constituent National Assembly that Article 1 in the *ordonnance* of April 21 1944 referred. Hence the political parties' shocked reaction to the General's allusion, in his press conference of 2 June 1945, to the referendum as a third way between a return to the Third Republic and the election of a fully sovereign constituent assembly. Contemporary press articles again assimilated the referendum to a plebiscite: for the press, the true Republic meant the rejection of all forms of 'personal power'.[23] Among politicians, only a minority – such as André Hauriou, Robert Lecourt or Robert Salmon – favoured the referendum, while the Radicals and the Communists levelled the most scathing criticisms of the GPRF's project.[24]

The Provisional Consultative Assembly's Committee for the Reform of the State and Legislation, to which the project of the GPRF was referred, declared on 20 July 1945 against the referendum, which it deemed contrary to the 'French constitutional tradition'. Following the Committee's lead, the members of the Provisional Consultative Assembly first rejected the draft *ordonnance* on 29 July, by 210 votes to 19, and then, by 179 votes to 37, declared for a *sovereign* constituent assembly. After consulting the Conseil d'État, the GPRF nevertheless adopted the *ordonnance* of 17 August 1945 providing for the referendum and stating the moment when the powers of the Provisional Consultative Assembly would lapse.[25] Again, the *ordonnance* received harsh criticism from the press and the parties. The referendum was termed 'dangerous', 'antidemocratic', 'plebiscitary and Bonapartist . . . smacking of His Majesty's pleasure'.[26] Alone among the parties in August, the SFIO found the GPRF's decisions 'acceptable'. Léon Blum went so far as to recognise the referendum's democratic character, conceded that it did not, in this instance, amount to a plebiscite, and remarked that the historic Socialist leader Jaurès had favoured direct consultation of the people.[27]

Given this hostility to the referendum embedded in the French republican tradition, and its vigorous articulation by parties and press in summer 1945, why did the French electorate, in its vote of 21 October, choose to limit the Constituent Assembly's powers in favour of direct democratic consultation?

Three answers can be suggested. First, by deciding to use the constituent referendum, the provisional government was resuscitating another strand of France's revolutionary tradition which had fallen into oblivion after being diverted from its aim: that of the social contract. The concept of a semi-representative or 'mixed' democracy, as Carré de Malberg termed it,[28] had been developed in the constitutional debates of the 1930s: André Tardieu coined the term 'captive sovereign' to denote a people whose democratic rights were circumscribed by the fiction of national representation so precious to the Revolutionary theorist Sieyès.[29] The referendum made it possible for the people to pass from this 'fictitious sovereignty', to its own 'real sovereignty'.[30] The second answer is altogether more pragmatic. With the Communists widely expected to dominate the new Assembly, any check on its powers would appear welcome to the millions of voters who mistrusted the PCF and feared a Communist takeover of France: by polling day, both the MRP and the conservative groups had joined the SFIO in supporting limits on the Assembly's powers, leaving only the Communists and Radicals campaigning for a No to this question. The third and final answer is linked to Gaullism and to the founding myths of the Liberation, analysed more fully in this book by Philippe Buton. For Gaullists, it was the French people who had cast off the yoke of the enemy and of a 'usurping' power unaided.[31] The notion of Resistance lay at the heart both of the Gaullist myth of the Liberation and of the process of democratic transition which permeated the legal domain as well as French society as a whole after 1944. From this two consequences flowed. On the one hand, France was a mature nation, fit to decide by itself what its future Constitution should be. On the other, as the Gaullist legal expert René Capitant pointed out, while Vichy founded its legitimacy on a parliamentary vote, the Resistance was 'the expression of the people's spontaneous revolt against that regime'.[32] To break away from the logic of parliamentary sovereignty, which had resulted in Vichy, therefore appeared quite logical.[33] The break with the Third Republic therefore becomes conceivable only in conjunction with the break with Vichy. It is worth noting, finally, that the referendum of October 1945 – in effect de Gaulle's entry onto France's national electoral stage – was marked by one of the General's typical political ploys: an appeal to the voters over the heads of established opinion-makers in parties and press. A measure of his success is that the draft constitution of April 1946, supported by Communists and Socialists, formalised a 'mixed' conception of democracy: its Declaration of Rights, contrary to the 1789 Declaration, stated that 'The principle of any Sovereignty lies primarily in the people', and again its article 43 stated that 'Sovereignty belongs to the people'. Article 123, moreover, required any revision to the constitution to be approved by referendum – an interesting switch in favour of the referendum on the part of parties, particularly the Communists, hitherto hostile to it.

The first Chapter of the Constitution of October 1946 gave the people and semi-direct democracy their rightful place in its formulations on sovereignty.

Thus Article 2 stated that the principle on which the Republic rests is 'government of the People for the People and by the People.' Article 3, defining sovereignty as 'national', stated that it 'belongs to the French People' and not only to the 'Nation' which, during the Third Republic, had found its exclusive representation in the Chambers. Although the referendum was not adopted as a technique for ordinary legislation, it appears in Chapter XI as the guiding *principle* for constitutional amendments. However, unlike in the April draft, the referendum was compulsory only if the proposed amendment had not either been adopted by a two-thirds majority of the National Assembly in a second reading, or voted by a three-fifths majority of each of the two houses of parliament. This effectively turned the rule into the exception.

The referendum aside, the other components of the future Fourth Republic can be considered as part and parcel of the long-term heritage of 1875 – with one exception. The economic and social references, underpinned by the doctrines of Free France as well as of most of the internal resistance, were new.[34] The Third Republic's political liberalism had been widely supported in a general sense, even at the Liberation; its economically liberal character much less so. The various constitutional drafts produced by the internal Resistance testify to a vigorous demand for social measures within most of the Left, and especially the PCF.[35] Fully aware that France, when the time for reconstruction came, would be in great need of new structures able to ensure social unity and cohesion, de Gaulle's French National Committee in London declared, as early as June 1942, for the restoration of a social and democratic Republic.[36] General de Gaulle reasserted that stance in his address to the Provisional Consultative Assembly on 18 March 1944:

> French democracy will have to be a social democracy, that is one organically ensuring for everybody the right to and the liberty of their work, guaranteeing the dignity and the safety of all citizens, in an economic system aimed at the development of national resources and not at the satisfaction of private interests, one in which the main sources of common wealth will be the nation's property and in which the direction and the control by the State will be carried out with the regular participation of those who work and show a spirit of enterprise.[37]

A number of post-war democracies found inspiration in comparable political philosophies, driven by Christian democratic or social democratic ideals, and viewing the individual as the basis of an economic and social structure which, when built into political institutions, would create the conditions for true political democracy.

Thus for left-wing parties, social rights, linked both to people's daily lives and to the laws of the Third Republic, were considered deserving of a higher place in the category of fundamental rights, in order to facilitate the reconstruction of European nations. The formalisation of those rights in post-war constitutions is evidence of this concern. So the first Constituent Assembly drafted a new declaration adding social and economic rights to the political rights, of liberal inspiration, of 1789. Its successor simply decided to complement the 1789 Declaration of Rights by mentioning in a Preamble, separate from the main body of the Constitution, new rights and principles related to the economic and social dimension of the republic, such as gender equality, a ban on different types of discrimination, and the protection of workers. It also defined principles for the regulation of the nation's economy that offset the liberal dimension in the legacy of 1789, such as nationalisations and a role for employees in the management of firms. The first chapter both of the April draft and of the approved 1946 Constitution therefore characterised France as an 'indivisible, democratic and social' Republic, to which the 1946 Constitution added (a guarantee from the MRP to the left-wing parties with which it shared power) – the word 'secular'. The attempts of Liberation governments to realise these social and economic aspirations on the ground are analysed in Herrick Chapman's contribution to this volume.

Rationalised parliamentarianism à la française: *change and its limits*

The necessary complement of widening democratic expression and rights, for the constitution-makers, lay in greater provisions to stabilise and thereby safeguard democracy itself. The interwar years in Europe had seen a representative democracy succumb in country after country to autocratic regimes of Right and Left. The textbook case was that of Germany, where, it was argued, democracy had been both undermined by governmental instability and left unprotected by any serious constitutional safeguards. Within the established democracies, this crisis gave birth to institutional reformist movements. Interwar theorists, in France and elsewhere, sought to give a better definition to concepts at the basis of democracy, such as that of national sovereignty, in order to give them clearer and more accurate meaning.[38]

In the opinion of the Resistance as of many other French people, the Third Republic, whatever its liberal aspirations, embodied an outmoded regime, incapable of reforming itself, which had made the 'coup' of 10 July 1940 possible through the excesses of parliament and the impotence of the executive. Thus the majority in the Algiers Provisional Constituent Assembly approved the *ordonnance* of 21 April 1944, which excluded a simple restoration of the 1875 Republic. The debates over the constitutional law of 2 November 1945, as well as those bearing on the adoption of the future Constitution, reasserted this standpoint. Everybody cried out for parliamentary government to be renewed, or 'rationalised', as Boris Mirkine-Guetzévich put it.[39] In particular, they sought, first, to safeguard the executive from the instability seen as one of the Third Republic's major weaknesses, and, secondly, to go a little way towards limiting, through judicial review, the absolute rights of the legislature to pass whatever laws it saw fit. Neither attempt yielded many short-term results; both, however, represented important breaks with French republican tradition.

Stabilising the executive by strengthening its power and rationalising the procedures of accountability to the legislature were among the recurrent concerns of interwar reformers, echoed in the draft constitutions prepared by the internal Resistance as well as in the *ordonnances* of 21 April 1944 and 17 August 1945. So too, the Provisional Consultative Assembly's resolution of 29 July 1945 against the constitutional bill 'for the provisional organisation of the public authorities' reasserted the need to ensure the stability of the executive by limiting the conditions under which the legislature could force the government to resign. The constitutional law of 2 November 1945 took this concern into account. Similarly, the members of both Constituent Assemblies accepted the two procedures of a vote of confidence initiated by the government and a no-confidence motion initiated only by the lower house (the National Assembly), to which they added the government's right of dissolution.

For the Deputies of the Constituent Assembly, the no-confidence motion as provided under the constitutional law of 2 November 1945 appeared an accepted institution: the first constitutional committee therefore merely gave it form and expression. The rejection of the April draft did not call into question the procedure, which appears in article 50 of the October 1946 constitution. But it was a technical solution that did not work. Although, as Philip Williams has observed, 'in eleven years of the Fourth Republic fewer than twenty censure motions were proposed, only five were discussed, and none passed',[40] this was no guarantee of government stability; indeed, the best-known statistic about the Fourth Republic is that it went through twenty-five governments in its short existence. The constitution-makers of 1958, though they retained the same procedures, transformed them by integrating them into a new balance of power giving functional and organic primacy to the executive. The 1946 Constitution, however, had not achieved this result. At the most, it instituted a real head of government in the shape of the *Président du Conseil*, in whom (as in the Italian Constitution of 1947 or the German Constitution of 1949), the executive power came to be vested. The function of the President of the Republic was thereby weakened – until 1958.

At the same time, aware of the need to rationalise the usual means for governments to influence the legislature, namely the right of dissolution of the Assembly and the vote of confidence, the makers of the Fourth Republic paradoxically strengthened the role of the National Assembly. Clear evidence of this is the first constitutional committee's decision to deprive the government of any right of dissolution and thus of an important instrument of pressure on the legislature. Under the influence of the MRP, the Constituent Assembly went back on this, in part. It allowed governments to initiate a dissolution but maintained the restrictive conditions stipulated in the previous drafts – namely the occurrence of two cabinet crises during one annual parliamentary session. The second constitutional committee, despite the Communists' token opposition, did not fundamentally go back on the draft but prescribed a compulsory period of eighteen months before this measure could be invoked in a new legislature. On the committee's proposal, the Constituent Assembly restricted the process even more by excluding cabinet crises occurring within a fortnight of the government's appointment. This process, which was far removed from the classical parliamentary tradition according to which dissolution is 'a right unconditionally granted to the executive',[41] was used only once, in December 1955: it failed to secure the emergence of a stable majority from the resulting parliamentary elections.

The vote of confidence, a classical feature of rationalised parliamentarianism which enabled governments to secure the legislature's confidence by staking its responsibility on its general policy or on a bill, was the object of stormy debates. While the procedure was of unquestionable value, its prodigal abuse by the governments of the Third Republic led some parties and politicians in the first committee, especially the Socialists, to advocate its abolition. De Gaulle's successful use of the technique on 31 December 1945 made them all the keener to avoid a long-term precedent being created. The General had viewed the Socialist Deputies' demand for a 20 per cent reduction in the defence budget as an act of defiance against his programme as president of the GPRF: in the name of 'the principles of the parliamentary regime', he had therefore put his government's responsibility at stake before the Assembly – and won.

However, the committee did not think it necessary to prevent governments from calling votes of confidence. It merely limited the right of initiative to the *président du conseil*, and specified that confidence could be refused only by an absolute majority of the members of the Assembly. The final text, decided on 28 March 1946, was passed with practically no discussion by the Constituent Assembly. The second Constituent Assembly left the initial text virtually unchanged; its conditions of application were met only five times in the course of the Fourth Republic. The precautions taken by the constitution-makers to secure the stability of the executive did not hinder 'deviant' practices. Governments still resigned after losing a vote of confidence by a simple majority, or under pressure from volleys of aggressive parliamentary questions. The reality of politics thus thwarted legal techniques which, it must be admitted, proceeded from compromises unfit to define a coherent political system. This coherence would only be achieved by the Constitution of 1958, built around the presidential 'keystone'.

The second aspect of the constitution-makers' attempts to rationalise French parliamentarianism lay in their provision, however limited, for judicial review. As we have seen, the limitations placed on the powers of the Constituent Assembly by the law of 2 November 1945 opened a breach in the traditional Jacobin conception of absolute representative democracy. The well-meaning members of the two Constituent Assemblies also set limits to this doctrine. But they failed to develop to the full the logic of the law-based state (the *État de droit*), in which the law, backed by the judicial authorities, sets clear boundaries on what the other two branches of government can do.

A case in point was the issue of delegated legislative power. Forbidden by Article 13 of the 1946 Constitution – a reaction against the abusive use of decree-laws during the 1930s – decree-laws nevertheless reappeared within a few months of the Fourth Republic coming into force.[42] This was possible because the constitution-makers had baulked at the only really decisive step they might have taken in the direction of the *État de droit*, the provision for judicial review of laws on grounds of their constitutionality. Judicial review, so vigorously supported by interwar theorists like Maurice Hauriou and Raymond Carré de Malberg, was adopted by the first constitutional committee at the suggestion of its president André Philip, but eventually rejected by the first Constituent Assembly after violent opposition from the Communists, with whom the Socialists had joined forces. The second Constituent Assembly reconsidered very slightly, accepting an embryo of judicial review in the form of a Constitutional Committee provided for under Articles 91–93, dealing with revision of the constitution. These provisions rested in part on the major institutional addition of the second Constituent Assembly, the revival of an upper house, albeit a weakened one, in the Conseil de la République, and with it the return of a major office of the Republic in the person of its president (provisions discussed more fully in this book by Paul Smith). Thus the October 1946 constitution stated that laws passed by the National Assembly might be referred to the Constitutional Committee jointly by the President of the Republic and the President of the Conseil de la République, but only after an absolute majority vote of the upper house. It would then be the Committee's task to determine whether the law in question entailed a revision of the Constitution. To be promulgated in the event of a negative decision by the Constitutional Committee, the law would have to be confirmed by a new vote in the Assembly, and the Constitution would have to be revised. But review by the Committee also remained limited to articles 1 to 10 of the Constitution – excluding the Preamble, which constitutes, in the Constitution of the Fourth Republic as of the Fifth, a sort of Bill of Rights. Under the Fourth Republic, the Constitutional Committee therefore had a purely symbolic role. However, it did pave the way for a real judicial review of constitutionality under the Constitution of 1958.

Conclusion

Every constitution is a creature of circumstance, defined in part by the context of its drafting. By definition, that context is one of regime change. It is therefore often a context of crisis, in which constitution-makers seek to make a clean break with past errors associated with unintended, even catastrophic, outcomes. Yet one of the many paradoxes of the Liberation era is that despite the near-unanimous desire, expressed in the vote of 21 October 1945, to draw the curtain on *both* old regimes – the Third Republic as well as Vichy – the regime that France got, a year later, resembled the Third Republic so much, and embodied the same mistakes. These, and especially the pride of place given in France's institutions to the National Assembly, led to paralysis over the Algerian crisis, and to the Fourth Republic's failure. Some of the reasons for the failure to change much were wholly political. For example, it is tempting to wonder if the April 1946 draft, which in its plan to abolish the second chamber certainly represented a radical break, would not have won the voters' acceptance if the PCF had not seemed so strong and so frightening. But other reasons for the Fourth Republic's resemblance to its predecessor lie more in the realm of the constitutional debate as it was shaped by the context. If a break with Vichy did not mean a return to the Third Republic, it did mean the restoration of what were seen as the constitutive elements of the French Republic – a certain tradition, dating from the Revolution, of representative government and of parliamentary freedom. Every attempt at innovation – whether to strengthen the executive, to bring political issues directly to the people, or to verify the constitutionality of laws – was viewed in some quarters (chiefly but not exclusively on the Left) as an affront to these traditions, and resisted accordingly.

The traditions usually won, but not entirely. The constitution of the Fourth Republic included attempts, which broke with the Third, to address the issues identified by the inter-war reformers: the Preamble setting out basic human rights, the partial rehabilitation of the referendum, the provisions to safeguard the stability of the executive, and the embryo of a constitutional court. The importance of each of these was largely formal, for the moment. But their reappearance and amplification in the Fifth Republic suggest that the Fourth should be viewed as an intermediate point in a republican continuity stretching from 1875 to 1958.

Notes

1. My special thanks to Françoise and Rolland Bourié for their help with the translation of this chapter.
2. At the end of August 1941, Britain's Royal Institute of International Affairs encouraged both the Free French and the governments-in-exile in London each to create groups to study post-war problems. 'Political and institutional reconstruction' was among the most important of these issues. By a decree of 2 December 1941, de Gaulle created four committees for the study of post-war problems, of which one, entitled *Problèmes intérieurs et internationaux d'ordre juridique et intellectuel*, rapidly generated a whole edifice of sections and sub-committees which occupied some of the leading figures of Free France, including René Cassin and Félix Gouin. Cf. Décret no. 53 du 2 décembre 1941, *Journal Officiel de la France Libre*, no. 1, 20 January 1942, p. 2.
3. Chaired by Paul Giacobbi and then, from April 1944, by René Cassin, the Commission for the Reform of the State had the task of preparing discussions of planned *ordonnances* to be passed to the Consultative Assembly, and to draw up proposals itself. The interdepartmental working committee was created on 31 January 1944 (*Journal Officiel de la République Française*, 17 February 1944, p. 147).
4. Cf. J.-E. Callon (ed.), *Les projets constitutionnels de la Résistance* (Paris: La Documentation française, 1998).
5. A. Dansette, *La libération de Paris* (Paris: Fayard, 1946), p. 12.

6. Cf. *Journal Officiel de la France Libre*, no. 1, 20 January 1941, p. 3; no. 11, 14 October 1941, pp. 1–2; *Journal Officiel de la République Française* (hereafter *JO*), no. 1, 10 June 1943, p. 1.
7. Ordonnance du 9 août 1944, *JO*, no. 65, 10 August 1944, pp. 688–94, rectificatif p. 830.
8. *Les Cahiers politiques*, no. 2, juillet 1943, Londres, 'Pourquoi je suis républicain', reproduced in Henri Michel and Mirkine-Guetzevitch (eds), *Les idées politiques et sociales de la Résistance*, pp. 88–104. In a mere five numbers – all that appeared – *Les Cahiers politiques* attracted high-level contributions from the leading political and legal thinkers of the Resistance, including François de Menthon, Pierre-Henri Teitgen, René Lacoste, Alexandre Parodi, Michel Debré, Georges Bidault, Paul Bastid, Marc Bloch and others. Cf. D. de Bellescize, *Les neuf sages de la résistance: le Comité général d'études dans la clandestinité* (Paris: Plon (collection Espoir), 1979), p. 81.
9. Cf. *JO*, 23 February 1872, p. 1281.
10. L. Duguit, H. Monnier and R. Bonnard, *Les Constitutions et les principales lois politiques de la France depuis 1789* (Paris: LGDJ, 1952), p. 292.
11. J. Jeanneney, *Journal Politique: septembre 1939–juillet 1942*, ed. J.-N. Jeanneney (Paris: Armand Colin, 1972), p. 315.
12. Jeanneney, *Journal Politique*, pp. 315, 317.
13. Ordonnance du 21 avril 1944, *JO*, no. 34 du 22 April 1944, p. 325.
14. Loi du 2 novembre 1945 portant organisation des pouvoirs publics, *JO*, no. 258, 2–3 November 1945, p. 7159.
15. M. Duverger, *Manuel de droit constitutionnel et de science politique*, 5th edn (Paris: PUF, 1948), p. 298.
16. For example, Marcel Plaisant, *rapporteur* of the Commission for the reform of the State and for legislation, stressed the need to 'introduce palliatives to the extreme movements of the parliamentary pendulum': *JO*, *Débats de l'Assemblée Consultative Provisoire*, no. 64, 28 July 1945, pp. 1550–3.
17. By contrast, in the period before the 1875 constitutional laws were passed, the National Assembly made significant changes to the powers of the Thiers government in the laws of 31 August 1871 and 13 March 1873.
18. The Conseil d'État's opinion (no. 238–373), marked '*très confidentiel*', is in Assemblée Nationale, fonds personnel René Cassin, 382 AP 75, Dossier 4. It is partly reproduced in *Etudes et Documents du Conseil d'État* 1947, p. 45. The Conseil d'État specified that the Constituent Assembly could only change the law of 2 November 1945 by the same method used for its adoption – the referendum.
19. *JO*, *Débats de l'Assemblée Consultative Provisoire*, no. 20, 4 March 1944, p. 3.
20. O. Wieviorka, 'Le poids du quotidien de la Libération au départ du général de Gaulle', *Historiens et géographes* 357(April–May 1997), pp. 205–13.
21. 'Communication du gouvernement sur la politique générale présenté par le général de Gaulle à l'ACP lors de la séance du 18 mars 1944', *JO*, *Débats de l'Assemblée Consultative Provisoire*, no. 25, 25 March 1944, p. 9.
22. Women first voted at the municipal elections of 29 April and 13 May 1945, at a time when prisoners and deportees were beginning to return from Germany. Cantonal elections followed on 23 and 30 September. The *ordonnances* of 7 March 1944 and 22 August 1945 (*JO*, no. 24, 18 March 1944, pp. 217–18, and no. 197, 23 August 1945, p. 5266) created, in Algeria and in other major colonies, two electoral colleges, one for French citizens and one for natives. The latter, though not citizens, therefore still had the right to vote – a dissociation unprecedented in French constitutional history between citizenship and voting rights. This political freedom was, however, limited by gross inequalities in representation (cf. Chapter 9, pp. 151–2).

23. F. Ferry, *Le Problème constitutionnel et l'opinion publique en France de 1940 à 1946*, unpublished thesis, Faculté de droit de Paris, 1947 (2 vols.): vol. I, p. 160.

24. *JO, Débats de l'Assemblée Consultative Provisoire*, no. 64, 28 July 1945, pp. 1554 ff., 1561 ff., 1566 ff., 1579 ff., and 1596 ff.

25. Ordonnance no. 45-1836 du 17 août 1944, *JO* no. 194, 19 August 1945, pp. 5154–5.

26. August 1945 also saw the congresses of the SFIO and the Radical Party, which determined their strategy for the referendum campaign. Cf. *L'année politique, 1944–1945* (Paris: éd. du Grand Siècle, 1946), pp. 274–79.

27. Léon Blum in *Le Populaire*, 30 August 1945. In January 1914, Jaurès had supported the proposal of a 'republican bonapartist' Deputy to use a referendum to fix France's electoral system. The proposal was rejected as unconstitutional. Cf. *JO, débats, Chambre des députés*, 30 janvier 1914, p. 379, and M. Mopin, *Les grands débats parlementaires de 1875 à nos jours* (Paris: La Documentation française, 1988), p.184.

28. Cf. R. Carré de Malberg, 'Considérations théoriques sur la combinaison du référendum avec le parlementarisme', *Revue de droit public* 2 (1931), pp. 256–84.

29. A. Tardieu, *La Révolution à refaire: Vol. I: Le souverain captif* (Paris: Flammarion, 1936). This expression was used by de Gaulle himself on 18 mars 1944 before the Consultative Assembly in Algiers, (*JO, Débats de l'Assemblée Consultative Provisoire*, no. 25, 25 March 1944, p. 9).

30. R. Capitant, *Écrits constitutionnels* (Paris: Éditions du CNRS, 1982), p. 267.

31. De Gaulle, speech of 2 March 1945 to the Provisional Consultative Assembly, in C. de Gaulle, *Discours et Messages*, Vol. I (Paris, Plon, 1970), pp. 521 ff.

32. Ibid., p. 276.

33. Ibid., p. 276.

34. On the social character of the Republic and its acceptance in French law, cf. B. Mathieu, 'La République sociale' in B. Mathieu and M. Verpeaux (eds) *La République en droit français* (Paris: Économica, 1996), pp. 77–88.

35. Cf. Callon (ed.), *Les projets*.

36. Déclaration aux mouvements de résistance du 23 juin 1942, published in clandestine papers in France, in C. de Gaulle, *Discours et Messages*, Vol. I (Paris, Plon, 1970), pp. 205–7.

37. Communication du gouvernement sur la politique générale présenté par le général de Gaulle, président du CFLN. à l'ACP lors de la séance du 18 mars 1944, *JO, Débats de l'Assemblée Consultative Provisoire*, no. 25, 25 March 1944, p. 9. For reflections on the choice of a form of democracy in the immediate post-war period, cf. also G. Vedel, 'Existe-t-il deux conceptions de la démocratie?', *Études* CCXLVIII-2 (January 1946) reproduced in A. de Laubadère, A. Mathiot, J. Rivero, and G. Vedel (eds), *Pages de doctrine* (Paris: LGDJ, 1980), pp. 191–212: p. 191.

38. Cf. J. Barthelémy, 'La crise de la démocratie', *Annuaire de l'Institut international de droit public* 1 (1930), pp. 43–165: pp. 45ff.; H. Kelsen, *La démocratie, sa nature, sa valeur* (Paris: Economica, 1931, (new edition 1988)), p. 15; L. Duguit, *Traité de droit constitutionnel*, 3rd edn, Vol. I (Paris: de Boccard, 1927), p. 585; M. Vauthier, 'La crise de la démocratie parmlementaire', *Annuaire de l'Institut international de droit public* 1 (1930), pp. 185–214: p. 186; A. Lawrence Lowell, 'La crise des gouvernements représentatifs et parlementaires dans les démocraties modernes', *Revue du Droit Public* (2) 1928, pp. 166–84.

39. B. Mirkine-Guetzévich, *Les Constitutions de l'Europe nouvelle*, 2nd edn (Paris: Librairie Delagrave, 1929), p. 565.

40. P.M. Williams, *Crisis and Compromise: Politics in the Fourth Republic* (London: Longman, 1964), p. 240.

41. G. Vedel, 'Questions de confiance et dissolution', *Études juridiques*, 3–4 (1954), pp. 26–9: p. 28.
42. J. Soubeyrol, *Les décrets-lois sous la IVe République* (Bordeaux: Imprimerie Samie, 1955).

Bibliography

Barthelémy, J., 'La crise de la démocratie', *Annuaire de l'Institut international de droit public* 1 (1930), pp. 43–165.

Callon, J.-E. (ed.), *Les projets constitutionnels de la Résistance* (Paris: La Documentation française, 1998).

Capitant, R., *Écrits constitutionnels* (Paris: Éditions du CNRS, 1982).

Carré de Malberg, R., 'Considérations théoriques sur la combinaison du référendum avec le parlementarisme', *Revue de droit public* 2 (1931), pp. 256–84.

Dansette, A., *La libération de Paris* (Paris: Fayard, 1946).

de Bellescize, D., *Les neuf sages de la résistance: le Comité général d'études dans la clandestinité* (Paris: Plon (collection Espoir), 1979).

de Gaulle, C., *Discours et Messages,* Vol. I (Paris, Plon, 1970).

Duguit, L., *Traité de droit constitutionnel*, 3rd edn, Vol. I (Paris: de Boccard, 1927).

Duguit, L., Monnier, H., and Bonnard, R., *Les Constitutions et les principales lois politiques de la France depuis 1789* (Paris: LGDJ, 1952).

Duverger, M., *Manuel de droit constitutionnel et de science politique*, 5th edn (Paris: PUF, 1948).

Ferry, F., *Le Problème constitutionnel et l'opinion publique en France de 1940 à 1946*, unpublished thesis, Faculté de droit de Paris, 1947 (2 vols.): vol. I, p. 160.

Jeanneney, J., *Journal Politique: septembre 1939–juillet 1942*, ed. J.-N. Jeanneney (Paris: Armand Colin, 1972).

Kelsen, H., *La démocratie, sa nature, sa valeur* (Paris: Economica, 1931, (new edition 1988)).

Lawrence Lowell, A., 'La crise des gouvernements représentatifs et parlementaires dans les démocraties modernes', *Revue du Droit Public* 2 (1928), pp. 166–84.

Mathieu, B., 'La République sociale' in B. Mathieu and M. Verpeaux (eds) *La République en droit français* (Paris: Économica, 1996), pp. 77–88.

Mirkine-Guetzévich, B., *Les Constitutions de l'Europe nouvelle*, 2nd edn (Paris: Librairie Delagrave, 1929).

Mopin, M., *Les grands débats parlementaires de 1875 à nos jours* (Paris: La Documentation française, 1988).

Soubeyrol, J., *Les décrets-lois sous la IVe République* (Bordeaux: Imprimerie Samie, 1955).

Tardieu, A., *La Révolution à refaire: vol. I: Le souverain captif* (Paris: Flammarion, 1936).

Vauthier, M., 'La crise de la démocratie parmlementaire', *Annuaire de l'Institut international de droit public* 1 (1930), pp. 185–214.

Vedel, G., 'Existe-t-il deux conceptions de la démocratie?', *Études* CCXLVIII-2 (January 1946), reproduced in A. de Laubadère, A. Mathiot, J. Rivero, and G. Vedel (eds), *Pages de doctrine* (Paris: LGDJ, 1980), pp. 191–212.

Vedel, G., 'Questions de confiance et dissolution', *Études juridiques*, 3–4 (1954), pp. 26–9.

Wieviorka, O., 'Le poids du quotidien de la Libération au départ du général de Gaulle', *Historiens et géographes* 357 (April–May 1997), pp. 205–13.

Williams, P.M., *Crisis and Compromise: Politics in the Fourth Republic* (London: Longman, 1964).

3
Sénat ou pas Sénat? The 'First' Council of the Republic

Paul Smith

On 21 October 1945, French men and women were invited to elect a new Assembly and to respond to a two-part referendum. The first asked if the Assembly should be constituent. Ninety-six per cent of the voters (73 per cent of the electorate) voted yes and thereby dissolved the Third Republic. They also approved a series of 'pre-constitutional' conditions within which the assembly would operate, including a time limit of six months to produce a constitution: the parties were not happy with the restriction, but no-one wanted a drawn-out period of provisional government. In the event, twelve months, fresh general elections and two more referenda would come and go before the Republic had a new constitution. There were many obstacles to overcome and while the question of the second chamber may not have been the most prominent in the minds of contemporaries, it was one which drew together a number of the issues discussed elsewhere in this collection beyond the apparently straight-forward question of whether such a chamber should exist at all. Where would it fit in relation to the other institutions (president, government, lower house), what or who it would represent (*métropole* and/or empire and in what measure) and how would the parties prevent it from re-emerging as a Senate?

The shadow of the past

Each of France's constitutional moments has experienced the tension between the urge to adapt existing institutions and the impulse to invent new ones, but the popular rejection of the old regime appeared to give the upper hand to those who wanted to start with a *tabula rasa*, expressed on the Left through a profound 'sénatophobie'.[1] '[O]n the 21 October 1945', said the Communist Jacques Duclos, 'the country condemned the regime of 1875, which means the Senate'.[2] Socialists were no less adamant: 'No Senate', insisted Georges Depreux, 'either open or hidden. No second Assembly with the least share of popular sovereignty.'[3] Clearly, as far as the left-wing parties were concerned, the Senate was *persona non grata*, the very word signifying not simply an upper house, but an insurmountable obstacle to 'la véritable démocratie'. Neither party had the remotest ideological attachment to bicameralism, much less any practical reason for wanting to resurrect it: in 1939 the SFIO had 15 senators, the PCF two.

The other parties all wanted a second chamber, but not the Senate. Between the wars, some of the ideological forerunners of the Mouvement Républicain Populaire (MRP) had argued for a corporatist second chamber and although the Vichy experience had undermined corporatism, many rank-and-file members favoured an assembly representing local councils, professional and social organisations and family associations. Moderate Independents and the Parti Républicain de la Liberté (PRL) were small parties of local notables and bicameral through an instinct of self-preservation, though open to experimentation. Some, such as the Catholic Georges Pernot (PRL), warmed to a corporatist assembly, but one did not have to be a Catholic to believe corporatism had a future. Jules Jeanneney, a Radical and the last president of the old Senate, and René Capitant of the Union Démocratique et Socialiste de la Résistance (UDSR) also advocated a corporatist chamber; both men had some influence on de Gaulle. Other Moderates were less convinced. Jacques Bardoux simply wanted to revive the Senate, stripped of its veto. For once in his career, Bardoux found himself in agreement with the Radicals, the notable party par excellence, who had dominated the old Senate and who, barring a handful of *progressistes* on their left wing, had wanted a second chamber included as one of the pre-constitutional conditions in the October referendum, though even they accepted that its powers must be reduced.[4] All had prosaic reasons for favouring a second chamber. Unicameralism threatened to give all the spoils to the victor, and a Communist victory at a future general election could not be ruled out. To the MRP, Radicals and Moderates, a single assembly presented an incalculable and unacceptable risk – as it had to their bicameralist predecessors of 1789, 1795 and 1875.

The problem for the bicameralists was that they were too few in the first Constituent Assembly. The commission appointed to draft the constitution swung towards a single chamber thanks to Pierre Cot, a Radical *progressiste* who before the war had opposed the Senate's right (exercised in 1937 against the left-wing Popular Front coalition) to bring down a government. In April 1946 Cot became *rapporteur* to the commission and he and the Socialist Guy Mollet, who had replaced André Philip in the chair in January 1946, were mainly responsible for the resulting draft. It featured a weak head of state and a prime minister answerable to a single, sovereign National Assembly, flanked by two consultative, non-parliamentary bodies, an Economic Council and a Council of the French Union. The Economic Council was a more robust version of the National Economic Council created in 1925, conceived as a forum where the social partners would discuss legislation and offer an opinion to the National Assembly. Its brief was restricted, however, to whatever Deputies – not the government – deemed 'social' legislation. The Council of the French Union (CFU), by contrast, was an innovation: two-thirds were to be elected by the general councils of *départements* in the *métropole* and one-third by the various assemblies of the overseas *départements* and territories. If the CFU looks today like the vestige of doomed colonialism, it demonstrated that in the wake of the Brazzaville conference, the constituents were grappling with the question of how best to federate *métropole* and *outremer*.[5]

The Cot–Mollet constitution split the tripartite PCF–SFIO–MRP coalition that had governed France since de Gaulle's resignation in January. The MRP tried to insert an amendment giving the CFU parliamentary status and though all parties except the SFIO and the PCF rallied to them, the motion was defeated by 28 votes. Even so, right up until the final vote on the whole constitution, MRP leaders continued to press the SFIO to raise the status of the Council.[6] Mollet and Vincent Auriol, president of the Assembly, made half-hearted representations to the Communists, but the reply was unequivocal. The constitution of the 'new Convention' was approved in the Assembly on 19 April 1946 by 309 votes to 249.

There was, of course, more to the first constitution than just the number of parliamentary chambers, but the subsequent referendum campaign divided the parties in exactly the same way. The Left pushed the constitution as the most authentic possible expression of the sovereign national will and a bulwark against the threat of personal dictatorship (meaning de Gaulle). The opposition focused on the danger of one assembly becoming the basis of a single-party dictatorship (meaning the Communists). André Siegfried, the veteran centre-right political scientist, described the campaign as a struggle between the defenders of the *régime parlementaire* ('let us not fear the word') and pluralist republicanism, against the threat of a *régime d'assemblée*, the new Convention and, by extension, the Terror, which in the context of the Liberation implied a rather more terrifying process of *épuration* than had hitherto been the case.[7] The 'no' campaign promised to interpret a successful outcome as a vote for a meaningful upper house and a reinforced presidency, though in the event it achieved neither to its complete satisfaction.

The opposition was vindicated on 5 May, when the constitution was rejected by ten million votes to nine, but fresh general elections on 2 June were a disappointment. The Communists and Socialists lost seats and the MRP became the largest single party in the new Constituent Assembly. The Radicals and the UDSR (campaigning together as the Rassemblement de la Gauche Républicaine – RGR), the PRL and the Independents all failed to perform as well as the referendum had led them to hope. The challenge facing the new Assembly was to reconcile the votes of 21 October and 5 May. The Left argued that only modest revisions of the April draft were needed. A government crisis also influenced the outcome. After the elections, Socialist premier Félix Gouin resigned, but nearly a month passed before the MRP's Georges Bidault was confirmed as his replacement. Faced with the threat to his party by the looming presence of de Gaulle, whom he detested, Bidault was determined to rebuild tripartism and would not jeopardise the coalition for the sake of some bicameral chimera. Thus, while the MRP rank and file might well favour a corporatist upper house with teeth, the leadership was prepared to make considerable concessions. Bidault's willingness to compromise with his coalition partners was reinforced by de Gaulle's first direct intervention in the constitutional debate.

De Gaulle used a speech at Bayeux on 16 June to break the political silence he had diligently observed since leaving government five months earlier. His principal theme was the need to restore the authority of the state through strong political institutions, in particular the presidency, but he also gave considerable prominence to a second *chambre de réflexion*. He sketched the outline of a composite, tripartite upper house, representing the communes and *départements*, professional and social groups and the empire, in what he called, in a very deliberate echo of Léon Gambetta, the Grand Council of the French Union. De Gaulle's second chamber was by no means original, but for ideologues of Gaullism like René Capitant, a corporatist upper chamber became part of the 'pure' vision of the *République gaullienne*; when he returned to power in 1958, de Gaulle first spoke of a Senate *à la Bayeux*.[8] There was also of course a calculation behind the speech. Gaullism was not simply a call to form a new party but an attempt to rally and/or undermine others. The immediate effect, however, was to push MRP leaders towards their coalition partners, not into the arms of Capitant's hastily organised Union Gaulliste. The paradox of Bayeux was that it weakened the short-term possibility of achieving balanced bicameralism, though that was hardly de Gaulle's concern.

Bimonocameralism

Meanwhile, the Assembly had elected a new commission. André Philip, a more conciliatory figure than Mollet, returned to the chair, with the MRP's Paul Coste-Floret as *rapporteur*. The commission was bombarded with proposals for a second chamber, but only two really mattered. The Communists refused to take responsibility for a second chamber and delegated the SFIO to negotiate. Mollet suggested simply linking the National Assembly to a marginally more substantial Council of the French Union, parliamentary in the sense that members would participate in electing the President, but in reality largely consultative: its president and the *rapporteur* of the appropriate commission would be heard by the National Assembly during the second reading of any bill.[9] Above all, Mollet was determined to prevent the resurrection of a *navette* (shuttle) between chambers, the process by which the old Senate had slowed down or killed off legislation.

The MRP left the two consultative assemblies untouched and instead inserted a new body, a Council of the Republic, elected only by local councillors from the *métropole*. All legislation would receive a first reading in the National Assembly, and then pass to the Council, which had three months to examine it, unless Deputies passed the bill under emergency procedures. Deputies could accept amendments by simple majority, reject them by absolute majority, or ask the upper house to consider a new text, thereby resurrecting the *navette* in all but name. The Council was explicitly forbidden from overturning governments. The MRP leadership removed all corporatist references from its earlier plans, settling instead for a consultative Social and Economic Council. But in contrast to the Socialists, the MRP made no attempt to integrate the empire in the Council of the Republic, instead corralling overseas representation into a consultative Assembly of the French Union, a sure sign of the way that men like Bidault conceived the future of the empire.

If the May referendum revived bicameralists' hopes, it had dealt a blow to the Union. In sub-Saharan Africa the April constitution, which abolished forced labour in the *territoires*, extended political and civil rights to native populations and established the Union as a free association of peoples, opening the door to federation or even (in principle) secession, had been endorsed by 85 per cent of voters.[10] The 'no' vote in the *métropole* gave the colonial lobby time to regroup and apply pressure on the Constituent Assembly to drop the concessions, infamously described by Edouard Herriot as liable to turn France into 'the colony of its colonies'.[11] A cross-party *intergroupe* of overseas representatives, led by Gaston Monnerville, Radical deputy for Guyane, and including Ferhat Abbas of Algeria, Léopold Senghor of Senegal and Aimé Césaire of Martinique, responded by threatening to resign their seats. The commission panicked and invited the government to intervene. Bidault had never had any sympathy for creating a federal partnership out of the empire, but Marius Moutet, Socialist minister for the colonies, and Monnerville, who had served under Moutet as a junior minister during the Popular Front, struck a compromise that provided for overseas representation in both houses of parliament as well as retaining the Assembly of the French Union. The SFIO's Council of the French Union thus provided *la forme* of the second chamber, if not its *fond*.

Parliament would comprise the National Assembly and a Council of the Republic, elected by indirect suffrage by the *collectivités territoriales*, a neologism that happily covered all levels of local representation in both *métropole* and *outremer*. The Council had parliamentary status insofar as its members participated in electing the head of state and examined and voted on all legislation, though only after a first reading in the National Assembly. The second chamber had the right of amendment, which could be rejected out of hand by deputies, though the MRP insisted that amendments that passed the Council by absolute majority could only be rejected by an absolute majority in the lower house. There was, however, no scope for a *navette*, at least on paper. The constitution fixed the number of councillors at between 250 and 320, between two-fifths and one-half the size of the National Assembly, a mechanism intended to ensure the majority in the upper house could not join with the minority in the lower when electing the President of the Republic. The Left also insisted that up to fifty seats would be nominated by the National Assembly. To confirm that it was the junior partner, only four members of the upper house – the president *ex officio* and three other nominees – sat on the new Constitutional Committee, compared to eight Deputies.

Coste-Floret suggested that opponents of a second chamber should see the arrangement as 'tempered unicameralism', while its advocates should regard it as 'incomplete bicameralism'.[12] Paul Ramadier explained the Socialist position: 'We interpreted the decision [of 5 May 1946] as obliging us to give this Council of the Republic not greater power, but greater moral authority.'[13] But in the Communist daily *L'Humanité*, Pierre Hervé was more critical. 'Sénat ou pas Sénat?' – Is this a Senate or not?'[14] Hervé denounced the 'Socialist–MRP compact' as a frame on which organic and special laws as well as judiciously drafted standing orders might hang something more substantial than intended. And Hervé knew that with a sympathetic government in office, the Council might gain considerable leverage.[15] To imagine that councillors would not try to do so at the earliest opportunity was naïve at best and irresponsible at worst.

The supporters of a balanced bicameral system, where the two houses would engage in a legislative dialogue, were equally unconvinced. Paul Bastid, one of the Radicals' principal spokesmen on the constitution, argued that while the draft created two chambers, it read as if there were only one.[16] The Council was a parliamentary chamber, but sovereignty resided only with the National Assembly and only Deputies voted laws and ratified the appointment of the *président du conseil*. And while councillors had the right to introduce private bills, these went to the lower house first. This, he insisted, was not the right of initiative, merely of petition.[17] Bastid proposed strengthening the Council's powers of remonstrance and establishing that it represented the *collectivités*, rather than simply using them as an electoral district. His amendment was defeated by 275 votes to 273, with all but a handful of MRP deputies joining the Moderates and the RGR. The final draft passed on 30 September by 440 votes to 106, the opposition comprising 26 Radicals, 34 PRL, 12 UDSR, 22 RI and 10 assorted peasants and independents. Monnerville was the only Radical to vote in favour.

This 'bimonocaméralisme', as Jacques Georgel called it, was considerably less than the victors of the 5 May had hoped for.[18] The French were summoned to vote on 13 October 1946. The Socialists and MRP urged a 'yes'. A highly reticent PCF only offered tepid support in response to the increasing vehemence of Gaullist opposition.[19] At Épinal on 22 September, de Gaulle unreservedly condemned the constitution, but he was by no means alone: former Prime Minister Paul Reynaud described the Council of the Republic as a farce.[20] Radicals and Independents disowned the text, though they stopped short of outright rejection. In these conditions it is hardly surprising that the constitution passed by only nine million votes to a little fewer than eight, with a further eight million abstentions. It was promulgated on 27 October 1946; elections for the National Assembly were set for 10 November, with the Council of the Republic to follow on 8 December in France and over the course of the following weeks overseas.

The 'first' Council of the Republic

The next stage was to fill the Luxembourg Palace, chosen as the Council's residence despite Communist and Socialist objections. The constitution contained transitional clauses under whose terms municipal elections were to be held in the course of 1947, to be followed by a full renewal of the upper house, by freshly-elected local councillors, by the end of 1948. The 'first' Council of the Republic was therefore consciously provisional. The detail of how the *collectivités* would elect members of the upper house was left to an organic law. Radicals and Moderates argued in favour of simply making all councillors for communes and *départements* electors *ex officio*, but the PCF, SFIO and MRP all rejected this as too much like the old Senate colleges, adding that the 1945 local elections were not a reliable basis for a new chamber and insisting that any system adopted must reproduce the balance of the National Assembly. More to the point, none of the three intended to loosen what control they were able to exercise over the electoral process. Auriol proposed that for these elections only, the colleges should comprise delegates elected by universal suffrage by canton at a rate of one for every 300 electors, topped off with all Deputies and councillors for the *départements*. Technically this contravened the constitution, since cantons (groups of communes that serve as constituencies for elections to councils of the *départements*) are not *collectivités*. Nevertheless, the parties accepted and the 85,000 delegates were elected on 24 November.

Despite the Left's desire to avoid reawakening the local notables, this happened in any case. If collaboration and resistance had changed some of the personnel (as Olivier Wieviorka shows elsewhere in this book), custom and habit died hard, as voters returned mainly local *élus* to the colleges. Alfred Cobban described the delegate elections as a complicated mosaic of lists and parties that changed not only from one *département* to another but from one canton to the next.[21] In practice this was little different from what had always happened under the Third Republic, where local conditions were nearly always of far greater importance than national ones in negotiating candidatures. Cobban suggested that the confusing array of lists contributed to an average abstention rate of 25 per cent. Given understandable voter fatigue this figure does not seem excessive. Nationally, the results were much the same as the general election. More problematic, however, was the distribution of votes. The PCF received the largest national vote, as Table 3.1 shows, but concentrated in only a handful of *départements* and the SFIO were in a similar position. A distribution of seats pinned to the departmental framework would have enormously distorted the national vote. The electoral law had been drafted with this eventuality in mind.

The number of seats was fixed at 315, one more than the old Senate. Algeria (14 seats), the overseas *départements* (7) and the Union (44), accounted for one-fifth of the total, nearly twice the proportion of the lower house. Up to 214 seats were allocated to the *départements* and 50 nominated by the National

Table 3.1   Votes and distribution of departmental seats in 1946

	Delegates	Votes cast	Difference	Dept	Interdept	Total
PCF	24,544	25,780	+1,236	32	27	59
SFIO	14,939	15,710	+771	12	24	36
RGR	10,043	10,230	+187	11	12	23
MRP	24,151	27,280	+3,129	54	8	62
RI	–	4,240	–	10	0	10
PRL	–	3,723	–	6	2	8
Ind. Right	–	1,170	–	2	0	2
Total Right	11,300	–	−2,167	–	–	–
Total	84,977	88,133		127	73	200

Source: P. Smith, *A History of the French Senate*, Vol. II, *The Fourth and Fifth Republics 1945–2004* (Lampeter: Edwin Mellen Press, 2006), p. 40.

Assembly. This gave a total of 329, meaning that both categories could not be allocated in full. The final decision, however, did not have to be taken until the election results were known, leaving the parties in complete control. In the event, Nord, Seine and Seine-et-Oise did not receive their full quota. Councillors for the metropolitan *départements* were elected in two ways. First, 127 were elected directly by the colleges. The 68 *départements* with only one seat used a simple majority vote, the others proportional representation. Table 3.1 underlines strikingly that the MRP and the Moderates won the overwhelming majority of their seats in this round, among the local notables. Tactical voting among conservatives also gave the MRP seven more seats than expected.

For the next stage, the 73 remaining seats were distributed by a *commission de recensement* on a proportional, 'interdepartmental' basis based on each party's national vote. Candidates who had failed in the first ballot were ranked on their party list according to votes received individually and the successful ones were then considered to represent the department where they had stood. In most cases this meant that the next best-placed candidate was allocated the seat, but sometimes this was impossible: several Socialist councillors had come third in their *département* and one of them fourth.

The third stage, nomination by the National Assembly, took place on 19 December. But since nothing was straightforward, the parties subdivided their fifty seats into three categories. Thirty-five were distributed using the formula for electing commissions, with seven more 'national' seats to top off the parties' representation. The remaining eight were allotted to French nationals living outside the Union, principally in Tunisia and Morocco, who had been represented in the two Constituent Assemblies but were overlooked in the National Assembly. Once elections in the overseas territories were completed, the Council looked like a National Assembly *bis*. The PCF had the largest group, with 87 seats, the MRP 74 and the Socialists 63. The RGR and Moderates took 43 seats each, thanks largely to *outremer*.

The centrality of the Senate to the institutional balance of the Third Republic had been underlined by its first elections in January 1876 and the continuity among the political class. No fewer than 136 (60 per cent) of the first 225 departmental senators had sat in the National Assembly between 1871 and 1875. With the 75 life-senators, elected from within the Assembly, added in, the proportion rose above three-quarters. The contrast in 1946 could hardly have been more striking. Barely 20 had sat in the pre-1940 parliament, only 53 in the Constituent Assemblies of 1945 or 1946. The explanation lies, largely, in the place of the Council in the constitution. But numbers also played a part. The Constituent Assemblies had 586 and 619 seats respectively, the National Assembly 627. Elections still had to be fought and won, but seats were not hard to come by and seat-holders had a good chance of getting re-elected. Contrast this to the situation in 1876, where 720 members of the National Assembly were chasing 300 seats in the Senate and 535 in the Chamber of Deputies. It is also worth remembering that in 1876 the Senate had been elected first, with the election of the Chamber of Deputies acting as the *séance de rattrapage*.

A lack of parliamentary pedigree should not be mistaken, however, for political inexperience. Recent work on local elites in mid-century suggests that while the 'classic' view of the Resistance and of local *comités de libération* as the cradle of many political careers remains valid, in other cases the war pushed forward men and women (even if they did not vote) already active in local or national politics, albeit at a secondary level, before 1940.[22] Proportional representation gave parties more leverage than they had ever known, but old patterns of electoral behaviour and political culture proved surprisingly resilient. Many of the men and women elected to the first Council deserve mention, but a handful of reasonably typical cases will have to suffice as illustrations of how one became a member of the new upper house in 1946.

Nowhere was a mixture of pre-war roles in municipal politics and in the Resistance more evident than in the Seine, where the election of Georges Marrane, Max André and Léo Hamon constituted a reunion of the Comité Parisien de Libération (CPL). Mayor of Ivry-sur-Seine from 1925 until 1940, Marrane had embodied the *communiste gestionnaire* and Ivry was in all respects a classic example of municipal government in the *banlieue rouge*. Revoked in 1940, he joined the Resistance first in the Limousin, then around Lyon, before emerging as one of the principal figures in the CPL.[23] Marrane was the second of four Communists elected on a list headed by Léon Mauvais, a former trade unionist, reputed *classe contre classe* hardliner and since November 1944 the party's secretary for organisation.

Marrane's fellow CPL alumni Max André and Léo Hamon were both elected for the MRP. André was a banking expert who had spent the inter-war years in the Far East. A vice-president of the CPL, he was elected municipal and general councillor in 1945. Though not a Catholic, André was among the founders of the MRP. His knowledge of Indochina saw him accompany Bidault to Hanoi in January 1946 and he headed the French delegation at the abortive

Fontainebleau summit in July.[24] Hamon's association with Marrane pre-dated the war, when, as a young lawyer, he provided free legal advice to Communist municipalities. Born Léo Goldenberg, the son of political refugees from Tsarist Russia, Hamon kept the name he had taken in the Resistance, first in the Languedoc, and then with Ceux de la Résistance in Paris. He was a member of the Consultative Assembly and like André was elected to the city council in 1945. Despite left-wing sympathies, Hamon joined the MRP, though he remained an enigmatic figure. He lost his seat in 1958, joined the Left Gaullist Union Démocratique du Travail in the 1960s, became a Deputy in 1968 and was a minister under Chaban-Delmas in 1969. He is more usually remembered, however, as an eminent professor of constitutional law at the Sorbonne. In the Luxembourg Palace he met another jurist with a brilliant future, André Hauriou, elected for the SFIO in the Haute-Garonne.

Though the MRP was a new party, not all its councillors were new men emerging from the Resistance. The party acknowledged its roots by nominating several veterans from the pre-war standard-bearer of Christian Democracy, the Parti Démocrate Populaire (PDP). Auguste Champetier de Ribes, Paul Simon and Pierre Trémintin, had all been among the PDP's founders in 1924 and were its only members of parliament to vote against giving full powers to Pétain. A fourth nominee, Ernest Pezet, PDP deputy for Morbihan from 1928–1940, had voted for Pétain, but had soon rejected Vichy and worked with Raymond Laurent to plan the future of French Christian democracy.[25] In 1945 he became president of the Union des Français de l'Étranger and after 1948 became a senator for French nationals abroad.

Antoine Vourc'h was of a similar vintage, though less prominent and more typical of the provincial MRP *élu*. A veteran of the First World War, father of eight children and a doctor in his native Plomodiern in Finistère, he had sat on the town council since 1919. Despite the inconvenience of having a German officer billeted with his family, as many local notables did, Vourc'h ran a net-work helping resisters escape France on trawlers working out of Douarnenez and Camaret. Among them were two of his sons, Guy and Jean, the latter of whom was posthumously made a Compagnon de la Libération. Re-elected to the town council, and to that of the *département*, at the Liberation, Antoine Vourc'h represented Finistère in the first Constituent Assembly, but failed to get elected to the second. He was easily elected, however, at the head of the list for the Council of the Republic, one of three seats secured by the MRP in a heart-land of Christian Democracy: the fourth went to Hippolyte Masson, Socialist deputy for Brest from 1919 to 1936, but active in the movement from a time before 1905 when the SFIO was a distant twinkle in the eye of Jean Jaurès.

Not all pre-war Christian Democrats joined the MRP. Antoine Avinin had been active in Marc Sangnier's Jeune République. Returning to his native Lyon after the Armistice, he helped to set up France Liberté and graduated through various other organisations to become a delegate to the Conseil National de la Résistance. Avinin was among the founders of the UDSR, alongside Capitant and René Pleven. Elected to the first Constituent Assembly for the Seine, he made an unsuccessful switch to the Cantal for the second. Rather than face a second fruitless campaign, Avinin was one of two UDSR nominations for the Council, the other being Claire Saunier.

His activities in Lyons had brought Avinin into contact with Auguste Pinton, a Radical municipal councillor before the war, who by September 1944 and with the support of the *comité de libération* had emerged as the strong-man in the provisional city council. Pinton became *premier adjoint* to Justin Godart, a veteran of the Third Republic standing in as mayor for Edouard Herriot, still interned in Germany. Pinton's star rose alongside Herriot's. Like Monnerville, he was one of those figures 'venerated' by party activists but largely unknown to the public.[26] Pinton's reward was to head the RGR list in the Rhône and he represented the department for another 31 years.

The Rhône link also accounted for the election of Emile Bollaert, Herriot's *chef de cabinet* when he was prime minister in both 1924 and 1926 and prefect for the Rhône from 1934. Like fellow prefect Jean Moulin, he opposed Vichy from the outset, and following the latter's death, de Gaulle appointed him delegate-general to the CFLN, where he worked with Pierre Brossolette. The two men were arrested by the Germans in February 1944, but Bollaert was not recognised by his captors and was deported. On his return to France, he became *commissaire de la République* for Alsace. Bollaert played no role in the constitutional process in 1946, but accepted one of the RGR's nominated seats, though he spent most of his mandate in Indochina as high-commissioner.

Pierre Brossolette had not been so fortunate. Realising his cover had been blown, he leapt from the window of the fifth-storey room in which he was being held. Still, his name lived on in the Council of the Republic, through his widow Gilberte Pierre-Brossolette, who accepted the SFIO's nomination and was among 21 women councillors, a proportion (6.7 per cent) that would not be matched again in the Luxembourg Palace until the late 1990s. Eleven of the women elected were Communists, four Socialists, four MRP, two RGR and one PRL. Seven were Assembly nominees, nine others elected in *départements* using proportional representation, underlining the importance of parties in promoting women. The group included Claire Saunier, later elected chair of the assembly's education commission, Jane Vialle (Oubangui-Chari), a journalist and an outspoken critic of French colonial policy, Eugénie Eboué-Tell (Guadeloupe), and Jacqueline Thome-Patenôtre (Seine-et-Oise), mayor of Rambouillet from 1947 to 1983. Pierre-Brossolette was elected vice-president of the Council and in late 1948 she was joined by Marcelle Devaud, a PRL nominee in 1946, then senator for the Seine.

Champetier de Ribes was one of just six former senators among the intake. Throughout the 1930s Georges Pernot had been Louis Marin's great rival in the conservative Fédération Républicaine, and a *ministrable*. He had voted for Pétain in July, but in 1943 was one of a small group of senators who tried to persuade Jules Jeanneney to summon the National Assembly.[27] At the

Liberation he joined the PRL and later was one of the group of four senators behind the Centre National des Indépendants. Another of this quartet was Jean Boivin-Champeaux, who as senator for Calvados in 1940 had acted as *rapporteur* to the bill handing power to Pétain. Like many others, Boivin-Champeaux soon lost faith. One of the other returning senators was former prime minister Joseph Paul-Boncour, senator for Loir-et-Cher from 1931 to 1940. He stood there again on 8 December, but the seat went to Jacques Boisrond (PRL), a setback Paul-Boncour blamed on the local Radicals. Fortunately, the SFIO stepped in to make him one of their nominated members.

There were other 'names' from the previous regime who chose or were forced to settle for the upper house. Marc Rucart, minister responsible for the 1939 *Code de la Famille*, took a seat for Côte d'Ivoire, later switching to Haute-Volta. And after failing to get elected as deputy for the Drôme, Marius Moutet was elected for French Soudan. Gaston Monnerville was a similar case. He had embarked on an African tour in the early autumn in a bid to convince disaffected Africans to accept the second constitution. By the time he reached Guyane, Monnerville found that a seat in the National Assembly had slipped beyond him. The man who would later lead the Council and the Senate for 22 years and stand up to de Gaulle in the 1960s, returned to France in the autumn of 1946 contemplating returning to legal practice. Then, unexpected news arrived in mid-December that he had been elected member of the upper house for Guyane. Still, before the next election Monnerville took the precaution of setting himself up in the Lot, which he represented from 1948 to 1974. The man who would eventually succeed Monnerville in the presidential *fauteuil*, Alain Poher, was also among those elected in 1946.

Champetier de Ribes and Gaston Monnerville

Metropolitan Councillors of the Republic assembled for the first time on Christmas Eve 1946; most of the members for *outremer* would not be elected until mid-January. The Communists assumed that, with Socialist support, Marrane, their group chairman, would take the presidency. But the election did not go as anticipated. Robert Schuman approached Champetier de Ribes to ask him if he would accept the MRP's nomination, using his excellent relations with the other parties to form an anti-Communist bloc. Champetier was terminally ill with cancer, but accepted all the same. Informed of the date of the election he replied, 'That will do, I shall have a few weeks.'[28] Champetier won the election in the third ballot, by 124 votes to 119, thanks to half-a-dozen dissident Socialists. When the Council reconvened in January 1947 the result was tied, but Champetier took the election by virtue of the French tradition whereby, in such circumstances, the elder candidate prevails. Already, however, his illness was making its mark: absent for the election, his acceptance speech was read by Gilberte Pierre-Brossolette.[29] Champetier died two months later. Once again the Communists demanded the presidency – not least because the

Socialists held the Elysée and Matignon, and Herriot had been controversially reinstalled as speaker of the National Assembly (he had been president of the Chamber of Deputies from 1936 to 1940). With Marrane now a minister, the PCF put forward Henri Martel. To their annoyance the chair of the SFIO group, Alex Roubert, insisted on standing too.

The MRP and the Moderates had no candidate but decided to back vice-president Monnerville. The first round was evenly balanced. Martel had 83 votes, while Roubert's 96 included a handful of Christian Democrats. In first place, however, was Monnerville, whose 99 stretched across the RGR, the Moderates, and the majority of the MRP. Guy Mollet persuaded Roubert to withdraw in favour of Martel. If the SFIO voted for Martel *en bloc* he would win, but a dozen *outremer* Socialists preferred Monnerville, who won by 141 to 131.[30]

The secret of Monnerville's success was threefold. In the first place, his moderate Radical politics placed him plumb in the centre of the upper chamber. In the second, he embodied the unity of Republic and empire: overseas members regarded him as 'le père du FIDES'.[31] Thirdly, he embodied a commitment to exploiting every opportunity to promote the Council's rights as a parliamentary assembly.[32] Despite the apparent limitations, Monnerville knew that constitutions rarely play the way their authors anticipate or intend. For all its 106 articles, as Pierre Hervé had argued, the October constitution was full of spaces that could be exploited by imaginative use of standing orders. And it was Léon Blum of all people – the prime minister overthrown by the Senate in 1937 – who during his brief spell as *président du conseil* at the end of 1946 urged members of the upper house to explore every inch of their prerogatives. Monnerville knew too that much would depend on the chairs and *rapporteurs* of the permanent commissions, were willing to test the limits of their strength with minister and their counterparts in the National Assembly. With Hamon (chair of the interior commission), Roubert (finance), André Dulin (agriculture), Pernot (justice), Saunier (education) and Poher (general *rapporteur* to the finance commission), Monnerville knew he had men and women of character in the key posts.

In the early months neither the government nor the assemblies properly understood their relationship with one another. Because all legislation had to pass the National Assembly first, councillors found they spent long periods of time simply waiting. Matters were made worse by Deputies passing half of all legislation in 1947 under emergency procedures, thereby seriously restricting the Council's effectiveness. This began to change as a succession of governments, robbed of the support of the PCF after the collapse of tripartism and faced with the gathering threat of Gaullism, began to use the upper chamber as a lever in the lower.[33] In late 1947, for example, the Schuman government presented Deputies with legislation to tackle inflation drafted almost entirely by the Council's finance commission.[34] When the Council found savings of twelve billion francs in the armed forces budget in June 1948, Deputies responded with a unanimous vote of thanks.[35] And if the Council could not sink a ministry, it could keep one afloat. In July 1948 André Marie presented his ministry to the upper house for approval and a month later used the withdrawal of an amendment to the Council's standing orders as a vote of confidence in the Assembly. In the same month Monnerville complained to the Constitutional Committee that repeated use of emergency procedures made the Council's position untenable – and won. What in 1946 had looked a modest position was slowly being transformed into a viable relationship.

The next stage in the transformation of the Council from a 'façade of bicameralism'[36] would come about in 1948, when Henri Queuille took a calculated risk to revive (more or less) the electoral system put in place by Jules Ferry in 1884, in an ultimately successful attempt to dish both the Communists and the Gaullists. As a consequence, only 128 of the first Council returned for the second, with the MRP, reduced to 18 seats, the principal victim of the collateral damage. Then, in December 1948 the Council passed an amendment to its standing orders, stating that, henceforth, councillors would be known as 'senators, members of the Council of the Republic'. Not a Senate yet, perhaps, but at least a *chambre des sénateurs*.

Notes

1. J.-P. Marichy, *La deuxième chambre dans la vie politique française depuis 1875* (Paris: LDGJ, 1969), p. 139.
2. *Le Monde*, 21–22 April 1946.
3. Ibid.
4. G. Elgey, *La République des illusions, 1945–1951* (Paris: Fayard, 1965), p. 85.
5. A. Shennan, *Rethinking France. Plans for Renewal 1940–1946* (Oxford: Oxford University Press, 1990), pp. 141–68. On Brazzaville, cf. Chapter 9, pp. 142–7.
6. Elgey, *La République des illusions*, p. 187.
7. *Le Figaro*, 9 May 1946.
8. P. Smith, *A History of the French Senate*, Vol. ii, *The Fourth and Fifth Republics 1945–2004* (Lampeter: Edwin Mellen Press, 2006), p. 104.
9. *Journal Officiel de la République Française* (hereafter *JO*), *Documents de la Deuxième Assemblée Nationale Constituante*, 1946, Annexe no. 1123, p. 8.
10. T. Chafer, *The End of Empire in French West Africa: France's Successful Decolonization?* (Oxford: Berg, 2002), pp. 63–4.
11. Ibid., p. 65.
12. *JO*, *Débats de la Deuxième Assemblée Nationale Constituante*, sitting of 21 August 1946, p. 3187.
13. Ibid., p. 3244.
14. *L'Humanité*, 21 April 1946.
15. On Hervé, cf. O. Wieviorka, *Nous entrerons dans la carrière. De la Résistance à l'exercice du pouvoir* (Paris: Le Seuil, 1994), pp. 199–218.
16. *JO*, *Débats de la Deuxième Assemblée Nationale Constituante*, sitting of 21 August 1946, p. 3439.

17. F. Luchaire, 'Les radicaux et le problème constitutionnel en 1946', in G. Le Béguec and E. Duhamel (eds), *La reconstruction du parti radical* (Paris: L'Harmattan, 1993), pp. 119–30; p. 125.
18. J. Georgel, *Critiques et réforme des constitutions de la République* (Paris: Celse, 1959), p. 36.
19. *L'Humanité*, 10 September 1946.
20. *Le Monde*, 1 October 1946.
21. A. Cobban, 'The Second Chamber in France', *Political Quarterly* 19.4 (1948), pp. 323–35; p. 329.
22. G. Le Béguec and D. Peschanski (eds), *Les élites locales dans la tourmente. Du Front populaire aux années cinquante* (Paris: Éditions du CNRS, 2000).
23. N. Viet-Depaule, 'Georges Marrane, un communiste gestionnaire', in G. Le Béguec and D. Peschanski (eds), *Les élites locales dans la tourmente. Du Front populaire aux années cinquante* (Paris: Éditions du CNRS, 2000), pp. 137–44.
24. Elgey, *La République des illusions*, p. 101.
25. O. Wieviorka, *Les Orphelins de la République. Destinées des députés et sénateurs français, 1940–1945* (Paris: Le Seuil, 2001), pp. 107, 302.
26. J.-T. Nordmann, *Histoire des radicaux 1820–1973* (Paris: La Table Ronde, 1974), p. 420.
27. Wieviorka, *Les Orphelins de la République*, pp. 268–9.
28. Elgey, *La République des illusions*, p. 237.
29. M. Baroli and D. Robert, *Du Conseil de la République au Sénat 1946–1958* (Paris: Presses Universitaires de France, 2002), p. 27.
30. F. Laffaille, *Le président du Sénat* (Paris: L'Harmattan, 2003), p. 68.
31. J.-P. Brunet, *Gaston Monnerville. Le Républicain qui défia de Gaulle* (Paris, Albin Michel, 1997), p. 137.
32. Laffaille, *Le président du Sénat*, p. 313.
33. J.-D. Lassaigne, 'La compétence législative du Conseil de la République', *Politique* 45–48 (1969), pp. 157–67; p. 159.
34. J. Bruyas, 'L'évolution du Conseil de la République', *Revue du droit public* (1949), pp. 541–78; p. 547.
35. Lassaigne, 'La compétence législative', p. 160.
36. J.-P. Rioux, *La France de la Quatrième République*, Vol. I (Paris: Le Seuil, 1980), p. 153.

Bibliography

Baroli, M., and Robert, D., *Du Conseil de la République au Sénat 1946–1958* (Paris: Presses Universitaires de France, 2002).
Brunet, J.-P., *Gaston Monnerville. Le Républicain qui défia de Gaulle* (Paris, Albin Michel, 1997).
Bruyas, J., 'L'évolution du Conseil de la République', *Revue du droit public* (1949), pp. 541–78.
Chafer, T., *The End of Empire in French West Africa: France's Successful Decolonization?* (Oxford: Berg, 2002).
Cobban, A., 'The Second Chamber in France', *Political Quarterly*, 19.4 (1948), pp. 323–35.
Elgey, G., *La République des illusions, 1945–1951* (Paris: Fayard, 1965).
Georgel, J., *Critiques et réforme des constitutions de la République* (Paris: Celse, 1959).
Laffaille, F., *Le président du Sénat* (Paris: L'Harmattan, 2003).
Lassaigne, J.-D., 'La compétence législative du Conseil de la République', *Politique*, 45–48 (1969), pp. 157–67.

Le Béguec, G., and Peschanski, D. (eds), *Les élites locales dans la tourmente. Du Front populaire aux années cinquante* (Paris: Éditions du CNRS, 2000).

Luchaire, F., 'Les radicaux et le problème constitutionnel en 1946', in G. Le Béguec and E. Duhamel (eds), *La reconstruction du parti radical* (Paris: L'Harmattan, 1993), pp. 119–30.

Marichy, J.-P., *La deuxième chambre dans la vie politique française depuis 1875* (Paris: LDGJ, 1969).

Nordmann, J.-T., *Histoire des radicaux 1820–1973* (Paris: La Table Ronde, 1974).

Rioux, J.-P., *La France de la Quatrième République*, Vol. I (Paris: Le Seuil, 1980).

Shennan, A., *Rethinking France. Plans for Renewal 1940–1946* (Oxford: Oxford University Press, 1990).

Smith, P., *A History of the French Senate*, Vol. II, *The Fourth and Fifth Republics 1945–2004* (Lampeter: Edwin Mellen Press, 2006).

Viet-Depaule, N., 'Georges Marrane, un communiste gestionnaire', in G. Le Béguec and D. Peschanski (eds), *Les élites locales dans la tourmente. Du Front populaire aux années cinquante* (Paris: Éditions du CNRS, 2000), pp. 137–44.

Wieviorka, O., *Nous entrerons dans la carrière. De la Résistance à l'exercice du pouvoir* (Paris: Le Seuil, 1994).

Wieviorka, O., *Les Orphelins de la République. Destinées des députés et sénateurs français, 1940–1945* (Paris: Le Seuil, 2001).

4
De Gaulle and the Paradox of Post-War French Politics

David Goldey

The great apparent paradox of French post-war constitutional and political developments (development implying a linear, even teleological process) is that the searing experiences of defeat, occupation and liberation, from 1940 to 1945, appeared, by 1947, to have produced in the Fourth Republic merely a new edition of the Third, *revue mais peu corrigée*; whereas the grave but less all-encompassing Algerian crisis (1954–62) gave France not only another republic but a quite new semi-presidential constitution, plus – contrary to all expectation – a reformed party system and so, at last, governmental stability and greater regime acceptance. The contrast is even more striking if one compares the ambitious (if sometimes contradictory) projects for constitutional change proposed in the later Third Republic, plus the comprehensive plans for social reform nourished by the Conseil National de la Résistance during the war, with the eccentric constitutional tinkerings floated by desperate parliamentarians to bolster hapless executives in the declining years of the Fourth (some included, at the parliamentarians' behest, in 'de Gaulle's' constitution of 1958).

At both of these critical junctures – the inception of the Fourth Republic, the foundation of the Fifth – General de Gaulle played crucial roles: as restorer of the Republic from 1943 with a recognised role for the parties; as their fall guy in 1946; their hammer, 1947–51; their victim, again, 1951–3; and finally as their conqueror, between 1958 and 1962. That transformation has been explained in his own inimitable, self-serving, way by the great man himself in his *Memoirs*.[1] But de Gaulle's account does not really explain his earlier failure – if it was one – effectively to achieve political reform from 1945, as compared with (firstly) his achievements as an economic and social reformer in the same period, and (secondly) with his successes in both the political and the social and economic spheres from 1958; for de Gaulle is too reluctant ever to admit that he may have made mistakes.

In answering this question, we must take into consideration external pressures; the political impact of social and ideological (including religious) divisions, inherited and new; the party system and its constraints; and, last but not least, the General himself, his reaction to events and the availability to him of alternative choices which might have shaped a different course of events.

The international context and the Communist constraint

With the notable and dramatic exceptions of the construction of the Berlin Wall and the Cuban Missile Crisis, only admirals and air marshals seriously contemplated the likelihood of war between the Soviet Union and NATO in the last four decades of the twentieth century, a time of peaceful co-existence (in direct East–West relations) and then détente. But in the late 1940s and early 1950s, war seemed a real and present danger, and not only to de Gaulle. From before 1944, the consistent Soviet aim was to consolidate its subordination of the satellite states, to restrict American influence everywhere in Europe, and to seek advantage within the western camp. Until Stalin died in 1953, the living standards of his own people, and of the servile states controlled by him, were sacrificed to heavy industry and rearmament, an unpopular policy enforced throughout the bloc by police terror, the purges and the goulag, as before the war. The justification for this policy was the danger from capitalist encirclement, with its threat of an imperialist war against the 'motherland of socialism'; the task of the western Communist parties was to unmask and block the plots of western fascists and imperialists. Since the capitalists could not succeed if the western working class was alert and mobilised, the first enemies of the western Communist parties were the social democrats, initially often in alliances including Communists until 1947, after that in anti-communist coalitions in government and the trades unions. Their influence had to be eliminated if the Communists were to succeed. This was Stalin's brief for the Cominform, founded at the Sklarska-Poreba conference in Poland in September 1947, as it had been his policy for the pre-war organisation of the non-Soviet Communist parties, the Comintern, most explicitly for some six years after 1927.

The Cold War was not the work of France; de Gaulle and his foreign minister Georges Bidault, the equally nationalistic but more conservative leader of the Mouvement Républicain Populaire (MRP), strove mightily to insulate France from it, for obvious domestic as well as international considerations. France, they hoped, might be the bridge between Moscow and Washington – until April 1947 when Bidault returned from the abortive Moscow Conference of Foreign Ministers convinced it was impossible to do business with the Soviet Union.[2] This realisation had clear domestic implications, which French leaders had been ruminating for some time, even before the Truman Doctrine – promising American help in stopping Soviet expansionism in Europe – was expounded by the American President on 11 March 1947. Because of its strategic position in Europe and its large, well-organised Communist Party (the Parti Communiste Français, or PCF) in control of the major trade union confederation, the Confédération Générale du Travail (CGT), France risked being drawn into a cold civil war as international tensions were transmuted into domestic conflicts.

That danger was confirmed by the record of the PCF between the spring and the autumn of 1947. Increasingly restive partners in the cabinet until their expulsion from it on 5 May 1947, France's Communists then spent the summer trying to show their indispensability in government by no longer discouraging strikes for higher wages to meet rampant inflation, expecting an imminent summons to rejoin the coalition. But from late September, after Sklarska-Poreba, the PCF turned into something close to a revolutionary opposition, backing a quasi-insurrectionary wave of strikes that autumn and turning the Assembly into a bear garden.[3] The strikes of 1947 and 1948 were broken by a Socialist Minister of the Interior, Jules Moch, leaving the PCF and the Socialists (the SFIO, or Section Française de l'Internationale Ouvrière) the bitterest political enemies in the Fourth Republic. The 1947 conflict also split the CGT: the minority faction left to form (with American financial help) Force Ouvrière, an independent confederation of reformists, syndicalists and trotskyites, close but certainly not subordinate to the Socialists.[4] The CGT paid in loss of membership and militancy; and the division of the trade union base helped ensure that the sort of co-operation between Communists and Socialists that occurred in Italy was not replicated in France.

By the end of 1947, France's Communists had played their ace and lost: too far from the Red Army, too close to American and British forces to risk a coup, they had been unable, in 1945, to subordinate the Socialists by enticing them into an 'organic union'; they had been kept away from key ministries, unable to penetrate the state machine sufficiently to paralyse it. They could neither win a free election nor create a revolutionary situation, about which they were in any case ambivalent, for they had much to lose if it failed.[5] By definition the 'revolutionary party', but most successful electorally (with a consistent 25 per cent plus of the vote at national elections under the Fourth Republic and control over a growing clutch of local institutions), cocooned in their counter-society,[6] the more established and bureaucratised they became, the more they served as 'keepers of the Revolutionary Museum'. They would remain out of government in permanent opposition for the next 35 years, isolated and without electoral allies until 1962.

Even in isolation, however, the PCF exerted a powerful influence on the French party system as a whole. In the first place, the enmity between it and the Socialists wrecked any hope of a left-wing governing majority in Parliament, and with it the chance for substantive social reform that might have sapped earlier the working-class resentments that fed Communist support for the next quarter-century. Secondly, however, a fraction of the SFIO continued to yearn, despite everything, for unity of the Left. Too small to be of much use to the PCF, the left-wing Socialists were strong enough to help their party's leader from 1946, Guy Mollet, defeat an attempt to revive the party by abandoning the revolutionary verbiage which it cherished but no longer really believed in. Mollet held on to the party, like Harold Wilson in Britain, by talking Left while steering Right. In doing so he perpetuated an ambiguous attitude towards reformism and the constraints of power among France's Socialists that lasted well into the Fifth Republic.[7]

Thirdly, a strong, aggressive PCF lent credibility to the Right's anticommunism. The use of the Communist bogey, to attract voters by scaring them, was hardly new. Right-wing election posters had depicted a wild-looking Bolshevik holding a knife between his teeth from the 1920s. The founding congress of the MRP – the PCF's ally in government for two and a half years – already had a distinctly anti-Communist flavour in December 1944. But the most powerful vehicle of post-war anti-Communism, its appeal much enhanced by the international and domestic alarms and excursions of 1947 and 1948, was the Rassemblement du Peuple Français (RPF), launched by de Gaulle in April 1947 to promote the constitutional reforms he had outlined in his Bayeux speech the previous June. Anti-Communism was not at first a central RPF theme. It became so at Rennes on 27 July 1947, when de Gaulle, at the end of a month of CGT strikes, alerted the French to the creeping tide of Communism, 'only 500 kilometres – barely two stages of the *Tour de France* – from our frontier', and denounced the PCF as 'separatists', an element foreign to France's national community.[8] That line brought him much more popular support than his theses on constitutional reform, especially that autumn, with the perceived intensification of a Communist threat and the sense among many voters that de Gaulle was the only effective barrier to it. At the municipal elections of 19 and 26 October, the RPF won some 40 per cent of France's urban votes, and control of the thirteen largest cities. At the same time, however, de Gaulle's behaviour, and especially his call, directly after the poll, for immediate parliamentary elections and a new constitution,[9] reinforced suspicions among many observers – not least the Americans – of his caesarian inclinations. And, as Jean Charlot has noted, the Gaullist tide ebbed with the threat of war, with the RPF vote amounting to just 21 per cent at the 1951 parliamentary elections.[10]

A fourth effect of the PCF on the party system of the Fourth Republic concerned party structure. With the PCF in government, its organisational model inspired imitators. Both of its partners in the *tripartite* coalition, the SFIO and the MRP, at least aspired to be disciplined, mass parties, not least to avoid being overwhelmed by the PCF's organisational superiority; the RPF was fiercely authoritarian from the start, and claimed 1.5 million members in 1948.[11] The right-wing reaction after 1947, by contrast, ended up reinforcing those parties of the Centre and Right – Radicals and Conservatives – which had traditionally espoused older and looser organisational models. With the fall of the Ramadier government in November 1947, the Radicals were given more portfolios (including Finance) in the Schuman government that succeeded it. When Schuman fell in July 1948, 'the National Assembly invested the Radical André Marie, Deputy since 1928, as *Président du Conseil* with the

Independent [i.e. conservative] Paul Reynaud, Deputy since 1919, as his Minister of Finance'.[12] There were still some incentives – notably in the proportional list system used for post-war elections – for these parties to improve somewhat on their ramshackle inter-war organisation. To a considerable degree, however, they retained the old, loose, 'cadre' model, which allowed great independence for the locally-entrenched notables who made up the ranks of their parliamentarians.[13] Since many such notables had gravitated to Gaullism as the surest way to win or keep office (and, in some cases, to cover the traces of a dubious wartime record), the RPF was infected with the virus of indiscipline as early as the senatorial elections of 1948.

The importance of the Communists' dismissal from government on 5 May 1947 therefore lay not only in France's avoidance of an (admittedly fairly improbable) Czech-style Communist takeover, but also in the resulting transformation of how the regime worked. Party cohesion declined as soon as it ceased to be indispensable in defence against Communist pressure. Old individualist habits revived and profoundly affected both political behaviour and constitutional practice; and 'the fate of governments came to depend again on a handful of marginal votes – and life and uncertainty returned to the parliamentary scene'.[14] The fall of the Ramadier government, on 19 November 1947, in the midst of the general strike, was an exemplar of what was to follow: a parliamentary system without majoritarian parties or stable coalitions, encouraging a flight from responsibility, which cost the regime the support of ordinary French voters (whose electoral behaviour had left the parties little choice).

Party dynamics of the Fourth Republic, 1947–1958

Why was de Gaulle unable to take advantage of this dissatisfaction to engineer a return to power and a new constitution earlier than 1958? Part of the answer lies in the early point of the political learning curve at which the General found himself at the end of the war. A reluctant republican, he understood intellectually that only free elections could provide political legitimacy under modern conditions; but he found it difficult to accept the role this accorded to lesser men with their factious parties: 'to be a prime minister unable to act without first conciliating three strong and mutually suspicious parties, and leader of a ministry whose solidarity was little more than a mockery, would have frustrated a humbler and more patient man'.[15] While it was therefore comprehensible that he should resign, in January 1946, it was much less so that he should still refuse to organise his supporters until national elections had passed, putting off serious efforts to impose his constitutional vision until he had lost office and moved into opposition. Another part of the problem, however, lay in the extraordinarily intractable nature of the problems facing the early Fourth Republic. Some of these would decant, in a sense favourable to the Gaullists, during the late 1950s.

Three distinct cleavages divided French parties.[16] First, the ancient religious division between Catholics and anti-clericals placed the Radicals (despite their increasing conservatism on economic issues) on the Left, while excluding the more progressive elements of the MRP and even the left wing of the Gaullists. Shared by Socialists and Radicals, the secular, anticlerical tradition of *laïcité* was 'the hidden reef that wrecked the proposal for a French Labour party which Blum and his friends vainly launched at the Liberation, for only by combining Socialists and progressive Catholics in one solid organisation could the democratic Left carry weight in coalition politics and impose reforms which might loosen the communist hold on French workers'.[17] The second cleavage, class – involving at a minimum the desirability of a modicum of direct taxation and redistribution to build up France's nascent welfare state – moved the MRP (or at least its militants and most of its leaders) and the SFIO back closer, together with a progressive fringe of Radicals and Gaullists.

Class antagonisms were acute in a country where the largest union was Communist controlled, and where 'divine right employers' took an almost feudal view of their employees. Negotiating a cost of living index in 1950, employer representatives argued that the 'elementary and irrepressible' needs of an ordinary Paris worker, did not include indoor running water; that pyjamas were a needless luxury; and that one good suit counted as sumptuary expenditure, since 'a worker wore it only twice in his life, once to get married in, and once to get buried in'![18] But the largest party of the Left on this division were the Communists, and they were in parliamentary purdah. Therein lay the third cleavage, between the Third Force, those parties – Socialists, Radicals, MRP, and the conservative groupings – that (broadly) supported the Fourth Republic 'system' and those that rejected it, whether because they wanted a new constitution (the Gaullists) or because they had been told to behave as a revolutionary opposition (the Communists).

Caught between the opposition to all administrations of the Communist hammer and of the Gaullist anvil, governing coalitions had to be assembled from less than 70 per cent of the membership of the Assembly. But the pro-system 'majority' was diverse and quarrelsome. It included very conservative, often Catholic and rural interests; anti-clerical conservatives and modernisers both inhabiting the same party, the Radicals; the clerical but often economically and socially progressive MRP; and the SFIO, the party of teachers, civil servants, and an ageing working-class clientele in the north and in towns like Limoges south of the Loire. France's pressing immediate difficulties, over the economy, or colonial policy, or foreign affairs, were then superimposed on these bitter, long-standing, divisions between and within parties so allies on one set of issues were opponents on others.

If some of those divisions appeared to be frozen in a time warp, it was because French society was too. From the arrival of the depression in 1930–1, pro-cyclical economic policies (until 1936) meant that the French economy stagnated, or even regressed, for the decade before the war. Then there was the destruction consequent on the war and liberation, the pillaging of the country by the German occupiers, and their destruction of infrastructure as they retreated. Forty-five per cent rural (and with 35 per cent of the workforce still on the land) in 1939, France was still 45 per cent rural in 1945; indeed, the rural population had probably increased marginally during depression and war, for many urban French men and women were only a generation away from the farm, where at least there was something to eat in times of penury. The apparently unchanging social composition of rural France froze old political attitudes, particularly the clerical issue, immortalised in *Clochemerle*. Religious practice, where it survived, was better sustained by the social control of the village than by the anonymity of the city, particularly since the Church had historically chosen to support the crown and local country squire, and then the employer, feeding the anticlericalism of workers but also peasants around Paris, the centre, southwest, and southeast.

Meanwhile the labour movement was hobbled by the slow and incomplete character of French industrialisation. Workers were divided in outlook between the heavily industrialised north (which remained more Catholic than the south); the skilled artisans of the Paris region, radicalised by the revolutionary heritage of the capital but also by their opposition to taylorism; and the small artisanal workshops south of the Loire, drowned in a rural sea. The historical legacy of the trade union movement was secular, sometimes violently anticlerical; that divided it from potential Catholic recruits. The very different circumstances in which French workers laboured meant that it was difficult to organise at all, and certainly not in a homogeneous way. That facilitated employer opposition to unionism. At the same time, political action was hindered firstly by the minority status of the industrial working class, secondly by its dilution in rural areas, and finally by constituency malapportionment, which over-represented rural areas in the lower and especially in the indirectly elected upper house. That frustration, and the competition amongst competing socialistic parties in the late nineteenth century for union support, importing their quarrels into unions whose survival depended on solidarity, meant that the SFIO, unified in 1905, could not depend on a secure trade union base, leading to deleterious consequences for both party and the CGT, also unified in 1905, before both were split by Lenin after the First World War.

The consequences of this fragmentation for party cohesion were amplified by the lively local base of French politics, of which the *cumul des mandats*, the simultaneous holding of local and national office, was both a symptom and a reinforcement. The *cumul des mandats* allowed the lucky *cumulard* to hold office on the basis of his (practically always *his*) status as a local notable with a personal vote and personal networks, rather than on a programme dependent on a party. This was characteristic of the loosely-organised cadre party, and so, above all, of the Radicals and conservatives, who made a virtue of the liberty of vote of their parliamentarians; they would move in and out of coalitions individually or as followers of a clan leader, on the basis of issues but also on constituency or personal concerns. This was less true of the SFIO and MRP, which still aligned themselves, on most issues and with few exceptions, as blocs.[19] Even they, however, were not quite immune from the contagion; while the RPF's Deputies succumbed to it almost completely from 1953 onwards.

The range of cleavages, the divisions within as well as between parties, and the chronic indiscipline of at least some of them meant that instability was the normal expectation under the Fourth Republic. A party seeking a change of policy or orientation would aim to desert or bring down a ministry, calculating either that its successor would be more inclined to its views, or just that a spell in opposition would avoid responsibility for measures unpopular with its voters or even just its activists, and thus preserve its prospects better. As ministerial crises were unpopular with the electorate, however, parties had to try and avoid public opprobrium for their manœuvres just as they sought to avoid responsibility for unpopular policies. But with ministries deadlocked and coalitions internally divided, ministerial crises were necessary to move the system along. Under tripartism, 'there was little discipline in the government coalition. Each party claimed for its own ministers credit for any popular move and blamed the more frequent unpopular developments on the other party. At this game the Communists were less inhibited than the socialists or the MRP.'[20] After the PCF's expulsion, the others caught up.

The contortions into which the dynamics of the Fourth Republic tied its constituent parties are well illustrated by the case of the SFIO. The Liberation had presented an opportunity for the Socialists to enlarge their audience to include Resistance Catholics and become, if only it could temper its Marxist verbiage and anticlerical tropisms, a large reformist party. Guy Mollet's faction saved the SFIO from that fate by taking over the leadership at its August 1946 congress.[21] Mollet pandered to the instinctive anticlericalism of SFIO militants (who tended to prefer co-operation with a Radical, however conservative, to an MRP politician, however progressive), and to their desire for 'unity of action' (out of proletarian solidarity) with the PCF (though without the absorption by the Communists that that implied). At the same time, however, Mollet could assure Jefferson Caffery, the American ambassador, that the SFIO 'had no Communist sympathies, and desired above all to be friendly to the United States'.[22]

Mollet tried to get the SFIO deputies to support Thorez's unsuccessful bid for the premiership in December 1946, but a quarter of them defied party discipline to vote against. When SFIO premier Ramadier expelled the PCF from his government, Mollet tried (unsuccessfully) to get the party executive to order Socialist ministers to retire as well from the cabinet, thus provoking the fall of the government and risking the failure of the manœuvre that had displaced the PCF without destroying a fragile ministry. At the SFIO congress in August 1947, he engaged in the ambient anti-communist feeding frenzy – while denouncing Ramadier.[23] In November he provoked the resignation of the already lame Ramadier government, to try and move the governing coalition to the Left but also so that the Socialists might avoid heading a government responsible for crushing the strikes. But he ended up accepting Jules Moch's appointment as Interior Minister by MRP premier Robert Schuman. During the 1946–51 Parliament, Mollet found occasion to bring down six governments 'in a vain attempt to check a drift to the Right'[24] ineluctable with the PCF in permanent opposition.

Some, though only some, of these knots, were loosening from the late 1950s, rendering de Gaulle's task easier than it could have been at the Liberation. By then, the economic growth of the post-war boom years, the *trente glorieuses*, was beginning to transform France into a more prosperous, urban, salaried and secular nation, increasing the importance of the class cleavage while reducing its vehemence as religious practice declined, while the Cold War entered a phase of *relative* détente. Those changes initially best served the Gaullists, returned to power in 1958 for entirely other reasons. They also, from 1962, served the PCF, with a smaller vote than under the Fourth Republic, but still the largest, most powerful opposition party, with an unreformed SFIO in crisis, bereft of its former centrist and conservative allies, who were swallowed whole by the Gaullists in 1962. For the first decade of the Fifth Republic, the PCF – helped by the relaxation of international tensions and its own halting destalinisation – was thus strong enough to dominate the Left. But it remained frightening enough to exclude any chance of a Communist winning the presidency, or a Communist-led coalition a parliamentary majority. The Left's resulting unelectability ensured the political domination of the Gaullists and their conservative allies. Moreover, it was uncertain whether the Communists did not prefer the General, with his hostility to infringements on French sovereignty and suspicion of the United States, to their much more European and Atlantic potential allies among the Socialists and Radicals.

Asserting their hegemony over the Right as the best barrier to the Communism, de Gaulle willy-nilly, and his successors willingly, created the modern conservative majoritarian party that had eluded him in the 1940s. The interclass nature of Gaullism was already evident in the Fourth Republic; with the departure of de Gaulle in 1969, the alliance moved Right to become a more characteristically conservative party.[25] The building blocks that made majoritarian parties after 1962, then, were simpler to move about than they had been in the late 1940s and early 1950s. But if de Gaulle's task was easier, it was also because his own political skills had developed. Compare his negotiation for the margin of Socialist support he needed for a majority, and his masterful performance in the Assembly, on 2 June 1958, when he massaged the wounded sensibilities of its members while extorting full powers from them, with his dismissive retorts in cabinet and his testy responses in the assembly in the 1940s.

De Gaulle and 'the system'

De Gaulle despised the political style and the governmental instability of the Fourth Republic, yet he had himself contributed to both. Firstly (another mistake he would not repeat after 1958), he had been unwilling to encourage his own supporters to organise when he was in power or in time for proximate elections where he might have regained it. Instead, he waited until the autumn of 1947, when he remained, by his own choice, out of power and there was no national election due until 1951. More than once, in 1945, he had privately lamented that, 'the Right is outside the Nation while the Left is against the State'.[26] He appears to have regarded the latter problem as incorrigible, for he gave no encouragement to the formation of a great Resistance party of the centre-Left (he was almost as mistrustful of the Resistance as he was contemptuous of parties). The solution to the former difficulty was to be found in the transformation of the MRP – without his direct help although he hoped to be its beneficiary – into an 'intelligent conservative party' capable of uniting and organising conservatives at sea and rudderless after the discrediting of most of their pre-war leaders. But in the early Fourth Republic most of the leaders and militants of the MRP (not its conservative electorate) were closer to a 'humanist [i.e. non-Marxist] Socialism' and looked to a centre-Left alliance with the SFIO. De Gaulle had favoured the creation of the MRP, which he hoped might finally integrate the Right into the Republic as a counterweight to the Communists. But his contempt for all parties meant he would neither commit himself to leading and transforming it, nor admit that it might then have to pursue policies he disliked. Moreover, he nurtured execrable relations with the MRP leader closest to his conservative and nationalistic outlook, Georges Bidault.[27] Secondly, he rejected the painful prescriptions of Pierre Mendès France to curb inflation, restore the currency and control the black market (see below). Thirdly, he reaped what he had sown in the campaigns of October 1945: successfully supporting, at that month's referendum, an assembly with a seven-month life-span and powers to draft a new constitution which would then be submitted to referendum, he still refused, in the same day's elections to the constituent assembly, to back candidates (mostly in the MRP) who shared his positions. When he and his government lost popularity in the winter of 1945–6 because of its own incoherence, rising inflation and declining rations[28] he not surprisingly faced opposition in the Assembly, where the PCF was the largest party, and thus in his government. He resigned in January 1946 on the mistaken impression that he was indispensable and irreplaceable and would be back in power in six months on his own terms. Fourth, he repeated his mistake when he refused to campaign with MRP against the Left's first draft constitution in the referendum of 5 May 1946. Fifth, he then failed to present his own constitutional views early enough, or to support candidates committed to them for the 2 June elections to the second constituent assembly, where the MRP, with 28 per cent of the vote, emerged as the largest party, overtaking the Communists. A fortnight later, at Bayeux on 16 June, he unveiled his constitutional proposals in a speech he had been preparing for over two months.[29] No wonder, faced with such political incoherence, that the SFIO's patriarch, Léon Blum, who had floated a presidentialist regime in *À l'échelle humaine*, commented in *Le Populaire* on 21 June that 'between the General and democracy, one notes something like an incompatibility of temperament'.[30] That view seemed confirmed when, sixthly, de Gaulle opposed, at the referendum of 13 October 1946, the second draft constitution, to which the MRP was committed as the only way of holding the SFIO from the Communist embrace; but, seventh, he refused to support in the 10 November election to the first National Assembly of the Fourth Republic René Capitant's Union Gaulliste, whose foundation he had encouraged to defend the ideas of Bayeux. Finally, he announced the foundation of the RPF on 7 April 1947, to represent his ideas when he was out of power, with most of his former supporters in the institutions of the Fourth Republic now alienated from him, and most of those still loyal to him firmly outside the system.

The common thread of these errors was a wish to remain aloof from the system and to represent, not any single political force, but France. But aloofness paralysed de Gaulle, ruling out, for example, any effective use of the 40 per cent of the vote won at the October 1947 municipal elections. There may have been a brief flirtation with a *coup d'etat*; more importantly, de Gaulle and the RPF secretary-general Jacques Soustelle were so certain of the imminent collapse of the ruling parties that they did not even think to negotiate a timetable for a return to office. This although a close colleague of the General would later remark that, 'If we had had the slightest notion of how to negotiate, we would have been in power in a fortnight.'[31] Instead de Gaulle wanted unconditional surrender, to be encouraged by massive shows of popular support in the streets and running battles with the Communists. But that made him a force for disorder rather than a solution to it. In 1947, that was borne out by the wild talk of his entourage – men like André Malraux or Gaston Palewski – about assassination attempts and civil war: talk that confirmed the worst suspicions of the British and Americans.[32] In September of the following year, events rather than words confirmed the RPF's capacity for mischief-making and worse, when a Communist was killed during an RPF demonstration in Grenoble. 'Until then', recalled Charles Pasqua, young RPF cadre and future RPR eminence grise and Interior Minister, 'only the Communists really frightened people: we lost a lot of sympathy'.[33] Moreover, if the Republic governed badly, it protected itself well. Moch broke the strikes of 1947 and 1948; the Queuille government lasted a year from 1948 to 1949; France received 20 per cent of all Marshall Plan expenditure, and 50 per cent of the money spent on mutual defence – essentially NATO.[34] By 1951, when tempers had cooled, the RPF's 21 per cent of the vote could secure it only 120 Deputies – not enough to stall the system (which few of them really wanted to do anyway).

Why were so many apparent opportunities lost? Aloofness, though suited to de Gaulle's temperament, was also tactical. In truth, staying in power, or agreeing to return to it under constraint, was not an easy option since the parties were determined to hobble him. He appreciated that, and sought to keep his historic capital intact for better times. In fact, de Gaulle was not above avoiding responsibility when he thought the time unpropitious, behaving in this like a Fourth Republic politician writ large.

The time was unpropitious at the Liberation in part because the permanent penury of the immediate post-war period made all governments unpopular. 'In one form or another the economic problem destroyed most governments in the first seven years of the Fourth Republic.'[35] The situation of the French at the end of the war has been recalled by Lacouture: 'my own memories of the children of that time, so pale that they looked as if they had been dug out of the cellars in which they had so often sought refuge; of the skeleton-like old men, who, waiting for the return of men from the army or concentration camps, seemed to be stuck forever in queues, while the women worked for the whole family; of those vague crowds wandering, from an improbable train to an impossible bus.' When de Gaulle visited Lille, the city of his birth, in the spring of 1945, he was enthusiastically received, despite food rations having fallen to scarcely 900 calories a day. When he left, the Commissaire de la République recalled, life returned to normal, 'constricted, belts tightened, food tickets unhonoured, unrest skillfully maintained by opponents on both sides, demands for summary executions on the public square, rumours about the inability of the government to do better than when the Germans were here'.[36]

In circumstances where the search for sustenance dominated everyday life, it is not surprising that after the liberation of Paris, liberated France tended to forget the war that continued, leaving the French divisions fighting in Alsace bitter at their lack of support from the home front.[37] That rather recalled the observation of the non-conformist pre-war southwestern Radical deputy, Anatole de Monzie, that for rural France war was tolerable only so long as it remained confined to neighbouring departments. That sort of disabused fatalism was anathema to de Gaulle. As he was to demonstrate again in the Fifth Republic, de Gaulle was less concerned with the material circumstances of his countrymen at home than with the standing of France abroad and its impact on the morale of his fellow citizens and thus their support for an executive that could focus their latent sentiment of national unity overcoming their petty mundane concerns. Noting the stalling of the allied liberation of France in the autumn of 1944, he remarked in his *Memoirs*

> That the war was to continue was certainly tragic from the point of view of the losses, damage and expense which the French would still have to endure. But from the viewpoint of France's higher interests – which is something quite different from the immediate advantage of the French population – I did not regret it. With the war dragging on, our help would be needed in the battle of the Rhine and of the Danube . . . Our position in the world and still more, the opinion our own people would have of themselves . . . depended on this fact . . . What an opportunity this supreme phase offered for national unity, for now every Frenchman would be

subjected to the same trials, no longer be divided . . . as they had been yesterday, but henceforth living in identical conditions and governed by a single power!'[38]

It clearly had not escaped his notice that the continuation of the war helped sustain a 'style of government, in which a national hero carried out the revolutionary policies of an insurrectionary committee subject to the criticism of a parliamentary assembly'.[39] His record over the nine months between the end of hostilities in Europe and his resignation reflects the lofty view he took of his responsibilities, which were to France and History more than to his fellow citizens. Instead of expending the considerable capital he had earned from the war to restore France's economy, he and Bidault wasted resources and credit with their Anglo-American allies in a fruitless attempt to restore the French presence in the Levant, and in its bloody re-imposition in Indo-China, Algeria and Madagascar, laying the seeds of the colonial problem that was to destroy the Fourth Republic.[40]

To restore a semblance of economic normality and then prosperity to Liberation France, it was essential to stabilise the currency, control inflation and begin to master 'the only inheritance from Vichy, the mystique of the black market'.[41] Pierre Mendès France, his Minister for Economics and Finance in Algiers but only for Economics in Paris, demanded a currency reform and a severe devaluation of the franc to mop up illicit war and black market profits and reduce the money supply to match the availability of limited supplies (as in Belgium and west Germany); he also wanted the freezing of prices and wages to contain inflation (unlike Germany). Mendès' scheme presented serious difficulties. Price controls meant dismantling the black market to make rationing work; that was harder in France, which grew much of its own food on small farms where much of it was in any case consumed, than in Britain, where half the food came in through the ports. Currency reform was complicated since the American government had refused to print banknotes for the French (it had been preparing instead its own occupation currency) until it formally recognised de Gaulle's provisional government in October 1944, so the French government was short of the substitute currency needed to replace its debased paper. Whether Mendès' plan would have 'worked' in the sense of squeezing the black market, spreading the economic pain equitably, containing inflation and the price-wage spiral, and so restoring confidence in the currency, is uncertain. But it was stalled by political rather than technical obstacles. The PCF opposed the austerity programme, hoping to extend its influence further among peasants and small shopkeepers – at the expense of its urban, working-class base. Mendès France fought hard for his plan through 1944 and into January 1945, but found most members of the government, including de Gaulle, 'terrified. No one wanted to run the risk of unpopularity' or of further feeding Communist support. For Mendès to have succeeded, he would have needed all the prestige and clout of de Gaulle. Instead, the

General ceded 'to the inevitable temptation of easy solutions'.[42] French inflation continued to eat away at wage increases, the black market flourished destroying any possibility of fair shares or a reasonable wages policy, and the French remained dependent on American help with its persistent balance of payments crises, hampering the freedom of action of his successors, for example, inclining them to abandon his and Bidault's (misguided) policy of dismantling Germany and demanding reparations. The food crisis, the lack of foreign exchange, and the want of adequate American help until Marshall Aid began to flow in 1949, discouraged de Gaulle from taking power and risking unpopularity in 1947–8.

De Gaulle's touch was no surer on the class conflicts that were never far from the surface in any discussion of the economy. His talisman for these problems was the *association capital-travail*, which he outlined in a speech in the industrial city of St-Etienne on 4 January 1948. While the General had 'deplored the class struggle and urged profit-sharing', observed Val Lorwin, what the RPF had to offer was 'a hodge-podge of warmed over guild notions, the older hierarchic catholic social doctrine, scraps of Italian and Vichy corporatism, all served up with a hot sauce of anti-Communism'. Not only did most workers find this 'indigestible'; the *association* attracted few employers, who 'preferred the traditional right to the uncertainties of Gaullism, particularly as the domestic Communist tide receded'.[43] That did not bode well for success had de Gaulle returned to office at the head of the RPF.[44]

But de Gaulle's problem was more profound than that. His rich experience of palace intrigue and international politics was not the best preparation for the rough and tumble of democratic and party politics. His own conservative Catholic and military background hardly predisposed him to admire or understand them, and his time hanging about the ministerial *cabinets* of the deliquescent Third Republic reinforced that distaste. The extent of the problem was revealed in de Gaulle's difficulties in working with party politicians after the elections of 21 October 1945 had given them the legitimacy of universal suffrage. For however skilled a manœuvrer he was in and beyond diplomacy (a skill used to great effect in his containment of the PCF in 1944–5), he remained ill at ease with representative assemblies and so uncertain how to proceed more generally. Olivier Guichard, his *chef de cabinet* of RPF days and a Gaullist 'baron' of the Fifth Republic, believed 'that the General was genuinely uncertain as to what to do with the enormous fish that History had stuck on the end of his line: an elected assembly. The General manœuvred brilliantly to impose his will, but without knowing exactly what he wanted to do.'[45] For de Gaulle wished to perpetuate the disciplines of wartime politics, where the executive more easily asserts its supremacy in the overarching aim of winning the war, into peacetime politics, where differences over priorities and competing ambitions reassert themselves, unless contained by majoritarian, disciplined parties (achieved for him only in 1962). During the war, the general's strategy of unity had 'caught the parties in a trap. They were forced to accept as a leader the man whom they wished above all to see as the Symbol. Once the war was over the trap reversed its mechanism: the parties were in a position to entrap the General.'[46] His subsequent attempt, through the RPF, to envelop the parties by enlisting their Deputies and Senators to his project of constitutional change (for the RPF allowed them to retain their original party membership) ran into the same difficulty. The better-organised parties blocked dual membership, leaving the General stuck with a following composed chiefly of conservative notables – a species for which he had little sympathy and the least amenable type of politician to the fierce discipline he tried to impose on the RPF. It was they who would split the Gaullists in parliament by voting for the Pinay government in 1952, leading the General to disown the RPF and retire to Colombey in May 1953.[47]

Conclusion

De Gaulle's enormous literary talent, deployed so effectively in his *Memoirs*, is a permanent invitation to the historian to take him at his own heroic self-evaluation. For that very reason, it can be a valuable corrective to shift the focus, and view him for a moment as a politician, subject to the same constraints and responding to the same cues as any other.[48] From this perspective, his record at the Liberation displays serious shortcomings. Faced with some of the most basic tasks of a modern political leader – managing the economy and holding a coalition together – he proved no more effective than some of his humdrum successors, than, say, a Queuille or a Pinay; for his heroic view of himself and of France sometimes proved an obstacle to success. As an opposition politician at the head of the RPF, his record was almost wholly negative (and is represented in his *Memoirs* by an eloquent silence).

And yet, this extremely intelligent, prickly, determined, stiff-necked soldier, who had considered himself a man of destiny from the age of fifteen,[49] with an inveterate independence of outlook and a bleak realism saved his country three times in a decade: her honour in 1940; from American military administration and almost certain civil war in 1944; from Communist domination in 1945. That he was able to do so a fourth time, and defeat France's Algerian demons in 1958–62, was due not least to his willingness, when checked, to walk away – from the government in 1946, from the RPF in 1953 – thereby preserving his credibility for more favourable times. 'I prefer my legend to power,' he remarked to a member of his private office in 1946, unintentionally revealing the qualities of his defects. Another colleague remarked to Roger Stéphane, 'He does not cling to power, but he cannot conceive of a limited power. He's an absolutist.'[50] Often impossible, sometimes indispensable (though not as continuously as he would have liked, a misfortune he attributed to the shortcomings of his countrymen), de Gaulle, in his attachment to the 'permanent interests of France', was not without vision or foresight.

Notes

1. C. de Gaulle, *War Memoirs*, tr. Richard Howard, Vol. iii (London: Weidenfeld and Nicolson, 1960); *Memoirs of Hope* (London: Weidenfeld and Nicolson, 1971).
2. Cf. Chapter 11, pp. 197–8.
3. Cf. Chapter 10, p. 178, and G. Elgey, *La République des Illusions, 1945–1951* (Paris: Fayard, 1965), pp. 339–372.
4. V. Lorwin, *The French Labor Movement* (Cambridge, Mass.: Harvard University Press, 1954), pp. 121–9, 291–4.
5. P.M. Williams, *Crisis and Compromise: Politics in the Fourth Republic* (London: Longman, 1964), p. 24.
6. Cf. A. Kriegel, *The French Communists: Profile of a People*, tr. E. Halperin (Chicago: University of Chicago Press, 1972), pp. 183–5; R. Tiersky, *French Communism, 1920–1972* (New York and London: Columbia University Press, 1974), pp. 310–30.
7. Cf. A. Bergounioux and G. Grunberg, *Le long remords du pouvoir: Le Parti socialiste français 1905–1992* (Paris: Fayard, 1992).
8. C. de Gaulle, *Discours et messages*, Vol. ii (Paris: Plon, 1971), pp. 97–103.
9. de Gaulle, *Discours et messages*, Vol. ii, pp. 135–7.
10. J. Charlot, *Le gaullisme d'opposition, 1946–1958* (Paris: Fayard, 1983), pp. 424–5.
11. Charlot, *Le gaullisme d'opposition*, p. 88. Charlot estimates the true figure at 400,000, still considerable for France. On mass parties and their opposite, cadre parties, cf. M. Duverger, *Les Partis politiques* (Paris: Armand Colin, 1951), pp. 84–91.
12. M. Anderson, *Conservative Politics in France* (London: Allen and Unwin, 1974), p. 78.
13. On right-wing notables, cf. R. Vinen, *Bourgeois Politics in France* (Cambridge: Cambridge University Press, 1995), pp. 30–45.
14. Williams, *Crisis and Compromise*, pp. 24, 63, 71–87. This remains the best overall study of the politics of the Fourth Republic.
15. Williams, *Crisis and Compromise*, p. 133.
16. Cf. P. Converse and G. Dupeux, 'Politicization of the Electorate in France and the United States', *Public Opinion Quarterly* 26.1 (1962), pp. 1–23.
17. Williams, *Crisis and Compromise*, p. 97. *Laïcité* was just as divisive in 1964–5, defeating Defferre's attempt to promote the same union in order to contest the 1965 presidential election against de Gaulle.
18. Lorwin, *The French Labor Movement*, pp. 220–1; cf. also Vinen, *Bourgeois Politics in France*, pp. 56–81.
19. Cf. D. MacRae Jr., *Parliament, Parties and Society in France 1946–1958* (New York, St Martin's Press, 1967), p. 57.
20. Lorwin, *The French Labor Movement*, pp. 114–15.
21. P.M. Williams, *French Politicians and Elections, 1951–1969* (Cambridge: Cambridge University Press, 1970), pp. 153–6.
22. I. Wall, *The United States and the Making of Postwar France, 1945–1954* (Cambridge: Cambridge University Press, 1991), p. 59; Elgey, *La République des illusions*, pp. 217–19.
23. R.W. Johnson, *The Long March of the French Left* (London: Macmillan, 1981), p. 32; Elgey, *La République des illusions*, p. 317.
24. Williams, *Crisis and Compromise*, p. 32.
25. Charlot, *Le gaullisme d'opposition*, p. 240; Williams, *Crisis and Compromise*, p. 509; A. Knapp, *Gaullism since de Gaulle* (Aldershot: Dartmouth, 1994), pp. 167–8; Johnson, *The Long March*, pp. 82–6.
26. To the MRP minister, Pierre-Henri Teitgen: quoted in J. Lacouture, *De Gaulle*, Vol. ii (Paris: Le Seuil, 1985), p. 208.

27. Lacouture, *De Gaulle*, Vol. II, pp. 208–9; Elgey, *La République des illusions*, pp. 38–45.
28. Charlot, *Le gaullisme d'opposition*, pp. 42–4.
29. Lacouture, *De Gaulle*, Vol. II, p. 269.
30. Lacouture, *De Gaulle*, Vol. II, p. 271. For Blum's (very general) constitutional views, cf. his À *l'échelle humaine* (Paris: Gallimard, 1945), pp. 54, 129.
31. Quoted in Lacouture, *De Gaulle*, Vol. II, pp. 322–3.
32. Cf. National Archive (Kew, United Kingdom), FO371/60682/Z8619.
33. Quoted in Lacouture, *De Gaulle*, Vol. II, p. 359.
34. Cf. Chapter 11, p. 200.
35. Williams, *Crisis and Compromise*, p. 27, and pp. 25–8 for broader analysis.
36. Lacouture, *De Gaulle*, Vol. II, pp. 115–16.
37. Lacouture, *De Gaulle*, Vol. II, p. 66.
38. de Gaulle, *War Memoirs*, Vol. III, pp. 32–3.
39. Williams, *Crisis and Compromise*, p. 20.
40. Cf. Chapters 9 and 12. The same too exclusive focus on international at the expense of domestic priorities was to feed the Events of 1968, even though by then the General had learned a lot from his earlier mistakes: cf. D.B. Goldey, 'A Precarious Regime: the Events of May 1968', in P.M.Williams, *French Politicians and Elections, 1951–1969* (Cambridge: Cambridge University Press, 1970), pp. 226–60.
41. Jean Cassou, quoted in Lacouture, *De Gaulle*, Vol. II, p. 115.
42. Lacouture, *De Gaulle*, Vol. II, pp. 122–6.
43. Lorwin, *The French Labor Movement*, pp. 298–9.
44. For the failure of Gaullist industrial relations policy, cf. P. Guiol, *L'Impasse sociale du gaullisme: le RPF et l'Action Ouvrière* (Paris: Presses de la FNSP, 1985).
45. Quoted in Lacouture, *De Gaulle*, Vol. II, pp. 197–8.
46. Guichard, quoted in ibid., p. 204.
47. The notables' final victory against de Gaulle was achieved sixteen years later, with the defeat of his referendum on the reform of the Senate and his resignation from the presidency.
48. Cf. A. Moravcsik, 'Le grain et la grandeur. Les origines économiques de la politique européenne du général de Gaulle' (1ère partie), *Revue Française de Sciences Politique* 49.4–5, August–October 1999, pp. 507–43: pp. 507–11.
49. J. Lacouture, *De Gaulle*, Vol. I (Paris: Le Seuil, 1985), p. 1.
50. Lacouture, *De Gaulle*, Vol. II, p. 199.

Bibliography

Anderson, M., *Conservative Politics in France* (London: Allen and Unwin, 1974).
Bergounioux, A., and Grunberg, G., *Le long remords du pouvoir: Le Parti socialiste français 1905–1992* (Paris: Fayard, 1992).
Charlot, J., *Le gaullisme d'opposition, 1946–1958* (Paris: Fayard, 1983).
Converse, P., and Dupeux, G., 'Politicization of the Electorate in France and the United States', *Public Opinion Quarterly* 26.1 (1962), pp. 1–23.
de Gaulle, C., *War Memoirs*, Vol. III (London: Weidenfeld and Nicolson, 1960).
de Gaulle, C., *Memoirs of Hope* (London: Weidenfeld and Nicolson, 1971).
Duverger, M., *Les Partis politiques* (Paris: Armand Colin, 1951).
Elgey, G., *La République des Illusions, 1945–1951* (Paris: Fayard, 1965).
Johnson, R.W., *The Long March of the French Left* (London: Macmillan, 1981).
Knapp, A., *Gaullism since de Gaulle* (Aldershot: Dartmouth, 1994).

Kriegel, A., *The French Communists: Profile of a People*, tr. E. Halperin (Chicago: University of Chicago Press, 1972).

Lacouture, J., *De Gaulle*, Vols. I and II (Paris: Le Seuil, 1985).

Lorwin, V., *The French Labor Movement* (Cambridge, Mass.: Harvard University Press, 1954).

MacRae, D., Jr. *Parliament, Parties and Society in France 1946–1958* (New York: St Martin's Press, 1967).

Moravcsik, A., 'Le grain et la grandeur. Les origines économiques de la politique européenne du général de Gaulle' (1ère partie), *Revue Française de Science Politique* 49.4–5, August–October 1999, pp. 507–43.

Vinen, R., *Bourgeois Politics in France* (Cambridge: Cambridge University Press, 1995).

Wall, I., *The United States and the Making of Postwar France, 1945–1954* (Cambridge: Cambridge University Press, 1991).

Wright, G., *The Reshaping of French Democracy* (New York: Raynal and Hitchcock, 1948).

5
Replacement or Renewal? The French Political Élite at the Liberation

Olivier Wieviorka

Hard hit by war and Occupation, France's politicians faced three major uncertainties at the Liberation. The first, looking towards the past, concerned the reintegration into democratic politics of men who, though rarely compromised by outright collaboration, had often supported, in varying ways and to varying degrees, the Vichy regime or its leader Marshal Pétain. Could France's political élites, given their record, simply carry on without further ado, seeking the votes they had attracted before the war as if nothing had happened? Or should they be penalised for the dubious company they had kept? The settling of accounts with France's pre-war politicians remained a key question of the Liberation; its answer would depend both on the new parliament and on the judiciary. The exclusion from the system of men compromised by Vichy would encourage the emergence of new talents; an indulgent approach, on the other hand, gave the established élite every chance of remaining in post.

The second unknown was the capacity of the Resistance to make an effective entry into politics. It was clear that neither the Gaullists nor the various internal movements born of the experience of occupation expected to limit their activity to the military liberation of French territory. They readily took on an active political role, aimed both at reshaping the political landscape to their own benefit and at imposing a revolution, the broad lines of which were drawn in their various wartime sketches and programmes. 'To animate and give direction to the renewed nation of tomorrow', de Gaulle had said in a London broadcast of 20 April 1943, 'new leaders will be required. The bankruptcy of those bodies that claimed to lead the country has been only too clear, and too ruinous. France has not suffered as she has merely to return to whited sepulchres.'[1] Nine months later, the internal Resistance movement *Défense de la France* wrote that 'We think it wise to start preparing for the reconstruction of French society now, if we wish to prevent others more cunning than ourselves, who have so far stayed out of the Resistance, from taking over the country in our stead. We believe that the Resistance should dominate and lead the coming Revolution. We want the Revolution to be the extension of the Resistance.'[2] It remained, though, for these ambitions to be put into practice, and for the men charged with implementing the new order of things to win the confidence of the French. Looking forward to the future, then, the renewal of France's political élites would depend very much on the ability of internal and external Resistance groups to attract votes for their men.

Three actors would manage the process of renewal. It was up to France's legislators to fix the rules that would separate the wheat from the chaff. They might, on the one hand, consider that any citizen had the right to stand for any election he chose, whatever his attitude during the Occupation, or, on the other, exclude certain categories of Frenchmen considered unworthy to take part in democratic politics. But the application of the law would be up to the judiciary. It would be their decisions, lenient or severe, that would open or limit the range of political competition. Above all, though, it would be for the French to decide, in the last instance, whether to return yesterday's men to office or to hand it instead to relative unknowns who promised renewal. Would the voters maintain their trust in the politicians of the Third Republic, or would they reject them in disgust at their dealings with Vichy and seek to turn over a new leaf? The third and final unknown of the Liberation years, therefore, concerned the very first post-war elections, from 1945: would the Liberation, by promoting the emergence of new men, produce a real break with the Third Republic? Or would continuity prevail, as would clearly be the case if established politicians kept their jobs? This is the central question of this chapter.

The purges

Even before the Liberation had started, the Gaullist authorities gave a clear sign of what was in store. The *ordonnance* (decree) of 21 April 1944 barred from France's legislative assemblies, from the *conseils généraux* that represented the *départements*, and from the 38,000 or so municipal councils, all persons stained by collaboration or by support for the Vichy regime, unless they were able to prove a Resistance record. It was initially up to the Prefects to judge the behaviour of elected officials and, if appropriate, to annul their exclusion from public office after having consulted the local *Comités de Libération* (CDLs). But distortions were quick to appear. Some prefects were very tough – in Corrèze or Finistère, for example; others, notably in Alsace, were highly indulgent. Anxious to avoid such contrasts, the Provisional Government (GPRF) decided to standardise the process. The *ordonnance* no. 45-582 of 6 April 1945 applied a blanket ban on sitting in the National Assembly or in *conseils généraux* or municipal councils to a range of general categories: members of governments formed after 16 June 1940; persons dismissed from the civil service or suspended from their professional activities for at least two years; war profiteers; members of the Vichy National Council; sitting *conseillers généraux*, unless elected pre-war; and parliamentarians who had accepted any official post from Vichy. The same *ordonnance* created a *Jury d'honneur* with the task of clearing the names of men compromised with Vichy who had been able to show a Resistance record sufficient to compensate for their conduct. This body, whose three members were appointed by the Conseil d'État (René Cassin), the Conseil National de la Résistance (Maxime Blocq-Mascart) and the Ordre de la Libération (André Postel-Vinay), sat from 25 April 1945, but soon went back on the principles of the *ordonnance*, owing to the avalanche of cases to be dealt with.[3] Thus they took the view that *conseillers généraux* should be eligible for office, a recommendation upheld, with the single exception of councillors of the city of Paris, by an *ordonnance* of 13 September 1945.

The Liberation authorities, then, took a measured approach to the post-war purge. And 'big fish' were more severely punished than minor figures. To have served on a municipal council under Vichy did not automatically entail ineligibility from office, except for parliamentarians stripped of office for other reasons, or for *conseillers généraux* appointed under Vichy but never elected pre-war. The GPRF chose to limit the damage by distinguishing between different levels of responsibility. At the level of *communes* and *départements*, electoral competition was played out in conditions of considerable freedom; but where parliament was concerned, it remained under tight surveillance. To put it another way, the government gave priority to democratic ideals over the needs of justice at the local level, but remained uncompromising towards France's national representatives, who had, in its view, betrayed their official duties by voting full powers to Pétain on 10 July 1940.

The judiciary also intervened in this process, as it had the task of deciding whether the Resistance record of dismissed parliamentarians was sufficient to make them eligible for office. The prefects removed the ban on sixty parliamentarians, and the *Jury d'honneur* on 113. There were therefore 173 sitting Deputies and Senators who were allowed to run again at the elections of 1945 – not counting, of course, the men who on 10 July 1940 had voted No or abstained, unless the latter had actually been absent from Vichy. On the other hand, 321 elected officials, a good third of members of the two Chambers in 1939, fell under the ban. If one adds the 173 parliamentarians who had died, in various ways, under the Occupation, over half the members of the pre-war Chamber and Senate proved unable to seek the voters' support in 1945. Moreover, the parties also eliminated the black sheep within their own ranks. The Socialists SFIO (Section Française de l'Internationale Ouvrière) expelled 84 parliamentarians, the centrist Radical Socialist Party about thirty; even the very right-wing Fédération Républicaine managed to remove fifteen or so. These various expulsions created something of a vacuum likely to renew, in depth, the ranks of France's politicians and to favour newcomers. Prudence, however, remains vital in assessing the depth of this renewal.

Replacement or renewal?

The Constituent Assembly elected on 21 October 1945 confirmed the transformation of France's political élite. Of its 586 Deputies, only 121 had held seats before the war; four-fifths, therefore, were entering Parliament for the first time.[4] With the change of men went a clear political shift. The Left dominated the new landscape and held a comfortable majority, with the PCF (Parti Communiste Français) taking 5 million votes and 148 seats, just ahead of the SFIO with 4.7 million votes and 135 Deputies. While the Christian Democratic MRP (Mouvement Républicain Populaire) did well (with 4.9 million votes and 143 seats), the established parties practically collapsed. The conservatives (*modérés*) won only 2.8 million votes and 65 seats, the Radicals – France's former 'dominant' party (its position enhanced by its position at the centre of the political spectrum) just 1.7 million votes and 31 seats.

None of this was precisely unexpected, as the tide of the Liberation had already threatened to submerge both the traditional Right and the followers of Édouard Herriot (the Radical mayor of Lyons since 1905, and President of the Chamber of Deputies elected in 1936), at the municipal elections (in May 1945) and cantonal elections (in September). Of 35,307 municipalities whose political colour is clearly identifiable, the conservative *modérés*, typically well-entrenched locally, had won 15,655, against 22,685 in 1935; the Radicals' total fell from 9,162 to 6,436. The Marxist parties, by contrast, notched up substantial gains: the Socialists headed 4,115 municipal councils, against 1,376 pre-war, while the Communists' gains, in percentage if not in absolute terms, were even more impressive: 1,413 mayors against a mere 310 pre-war.[5] These elections thus legitimated changes imposed in the heady days of 1944. Men who had formed the *délégations municipales* (the provisional municipal power appointed by the GPRF)) were often returned to elective office by the voters, in proportions that varied from 40 per cent in the Bouches-du-Rhône to 74 per cent in the Eure, according to samples taken across parts of France.[6]

In September 1945, the cantonal elections (to seats on the *conseils généraux* representing France's *départements*) told a similar story. The Radicals lost 355 cantons and the independent Radicals 164 (out of a total of nearly 4,000); the centre-Right Alliance Démocratique dropped 268, and the other conservative groups 78. By contrast, the Socialists won 811 seats (outside Corsica and the Seine, the *département* of Paris), the new centrist grouping, the Union Démocratique et Socialiste de la Résistance (UDSR) took 44, the Communists 329 and the MRP 230.[7] Data at *département* level reflect these broad tendencies. In the Eure, three-quarters of the *conseillers généraux* were newly elected, as were 92 per cent of mayors of larger towns and two-thirds of those of rural municipalities. In the Indre, newcomers made up some 75–80 per cent of local elected officials. In the Sarthe, finally, 70 per cent of the mayors changed against 1935, and only eight out of 33 *conseillers généraux* elected were incumbents.[8]

The Liberation also favoured the emergence of new parties and bore down hard on old-established ones. It is true that the PCF and the SFIO were not quite new, but their effective absence from power at national level, except during the brief Popular Front period (1936–37), allowed them to appear as such. And the appearance of hitherto unknown groupings reinforced the general sense of change. The birth of the MRP in November 1944 brought Christian Democracy out of the political margins, where it had hitherto been confined, to the centre-stage of French politics. The creation of the UDSR gave the Resistance a chance to make its voice heard. By contrast, some old parties such as the Alliance Démocratique and the Fédération Républicaine were simply wiped off the map, despite (or because of) the major role they had played under the Third Republic. Moreover, the discredit of Vichy, due to its authoritarianism and commitment to collaboration, extended to the men and ideas of France's revolutionary Right. Far-Right groupings were marginalised until the Poujade movement of the mid-1950s, and then the Algerian war breathed new life into them. Similarly, political issues that had been current pre-war, reaching moderate parties as well as the extremes, disappeared because of the use of them made by Vichy and the various collaborationist parties. This was the case, to take two quite different examples, of anti-Semitism and of corporatism, both of which vanished from the scene for years to come.

Indeed, political debate moved towards new horizons, closing off cleavages which had structured politics in pre-war France. The republican regime, accepted in the aftermath of the First World War but smashed under Pétain's rule, was no longer debated, even if specific institutional questions were (as was only to be expected during the drafting of a new constitution). The place of the Catholic Church, fiercely discussed before 1914 and still controversial in the Cartel des Gauches governments of the mid-1920s, was rather less than a hot topic at the Liberation. On the other hand new issues emerged, related both to the economy (concerning notably the acceptable extent of State intervention through nationalisations) and social protection.

For all of these reasons, 1945 can be viewed as a year of sharp breaks in French politics. Old parties, worn out by the inter-war crisis and by their own dealings with (and in) Vichy disappeared. A new political generation had emerged from the Resistance both at local and at national level. Last but not least, the Right had handed over power to the Left, a quite unprecedented phenomenon. From this point of view, the Liberation appears *both* as a replacement (of the political élite) *and* as a renewal, with political debate polarised around new issues structured by new players. Nevertheless, a closer examination suggests that such a bald assessment needs qualifying.

A *trompe-l'œil* revolution?

The Resistance, in the first place, never managed to 'break the mould' of French politics. Despite the hopes entertained in the years in hiding, only one real resistance party, the UDSR, was set up. True, the MRP made the most of its Resistance origins, confirmed by the impeccable pedigree of leaders like Pierre-Henri Teitgen, François de Menthon or Maurice Schumann. But it positioned itself more as the heir to older Christian Democratic movements – the pre-1914 Sillon or the inter-war Parti Démocrate Populaire – than to

Resistance heroes like Jean Moulin or Henri Frenay. Aiming above all to reconcile Church and Republic, favourable to social reforms but hostile to any idea of revolution, the MRP's general policy thrust gave pride of place to Catholic thinking rather than to the central concerns of Resistance fighters.

De Gaulle could, it is true, have given a political expression to wartime Gaullism by creating his own party or movement. But he refused to do this, or to head the 'labour party' that Henri Frenay, leader of the *Combat* Resistance movement, wanted to see emerge. 'No, Frenay', the General answered, 'I won't do it. It's not my role. I understand your worries. The shenanigans going on inside and outside the Assembly aren't exactly calculated to calm them. But believe me, there's only one solution for men like you, and that's to go into existing parties, and bring them new life, transform them from the inside . . . All the rest is nothing but illusions.'[9] He gave the same advice to Jacques Chaban-Delmas or to Michel Debré, for example. De Gaulle's refusal is readily explained. To become a party leader would have meant going against the major pillars of Gaullist doctrine, taking up partisan positions rather than rallying the whole French people. It would have obliged him to concern himself with low-level internal party concerns, rather than placing himself above the throng. By placing the leader of the Free French at the head of a party trading on his Resistance record, finally, it would have excluded all of those French who had not joined any Resistance movement. De Gaulle also had several less high-minded reasons. Aside from the fact that he did not really believe that the Resistance had a political mission or the capacity to win votes, de Gaulle believed that he personally was sufficiently strong to break free of the tutelage of the parties and the Assembly – an illusion that would dissipate after his resignation on 20 January 1946.

So the UDSR was alone in being able to claim that it was extending the 'spirit of the Resistance' by bringing together a range of wartime underground movements. It could trace its origins back to January 1944, when the Mouvement de Libération Nationale (MLN) had succeeded in merging Franc-Tireur, Combat, and Libération-Sud in the South, and Résistance and Défense de la France in the North. In January 1945, this group refused an alliance with the Communist-led Front National, but merged instead with the Union Travailliste, an organisation which itself included both the Organisation Civile et Militaire (OCM) and Libération-Nord. It was from this combined organisation that the UDSR was born on 25 June 1945. Claiming fidelity to the ideals of the clandestine movements, the new party refused to pledge its allegiance either to the SFIO or to the PCF. But it still found itself in an awkward position. The 'unity of the Resistance' – or the myth of it – had been broken by the clear divide with Communist-linked elements. The MRP's self-appointed status as the 'party of fidelity' to the General deprived the UDSR of Gaullist patronage or support. Above all, the new party had difficulty positioning itself in relation to the population. If it remained totally true to its clandestine roots, it cut itself off from the great majority of the French who had played no Resistance role – a one-way ticket to marginal status. Throwing open its doors to all comers, on the other hand, would wreck its identity – unless, of course, it attempted a coup, a form of adventurism that most *résistants*, steadfast in their democratic beliefs, utterly rejected. To compete effectively in elections, they therefore needed allies. In fact, the MLN had envisaged 'unity of action' with the SFIO from March 1945, and the UDSR confirmed this principle at its foundation in June. This plan might, in principle, have borne fruit by bringing the old and the new together; more generally, the established parties might have used the chance of renewal by opening up to the dynamic forces of the Resistance, giving the latter, in return, a grounding of tradition and experience in politics that they generally lacked. But this benign scenario failed to materialise.

In fact, the established parties showed a certain mistrust towards *résistants*. The PCF, whose Resistance record hardly needs pointing out, nevertheless proceeded with caution. Several unimpeachable *résistants* – Charles Tillon, Georges Guingouin, or Maurice Kriegel-Valrimont – were expelled quite rapidly from the Party, as their independent-mindedness, their post-war political positions, or simply the legitimacy that their record in the dark years had won them, were viewed as a threat by the leadership. Some Communist former *résistants* did enjoy a measure of promotion at the same period – but it slowed down the higher they climbed in the hierarchy.[10] This process allowed the Thorez-Duclos tandem to remain at the head of the so-called *Parti des 75,000 fusillés* without having to fear competition from an élite born of the underground struggle. As far as doctrine was concerned, on the other hand, the Resistance played no role at all. In the eyes of the leadership, the defeat confirmed the correctness of their own pre-war analyses of the profound (and largely economic) origins of the French catastrophe. In this perspective the Resistance could add nothing from the theoretical point of view; at best it could simply be mobilised to serve Party propaganda.[11]

Similarly, the SFIO, though favourable to an alliance with the MLN and keen to renew its doctrine, returned quite rapidly to its old loyalties. True, some men of the Resistance won high positions. Gaston Defferre took over Marseille, first as president of the *délégation municipale* and then, in 1945, as mayor; Jean Badiou performed a similar feat for the SFIO in Toulouse.[12] And the proportion of *résistants* remained high among Socialist parliamentarians of both houses. But did this amount to renewal? The truth, as Castagnez observes, was that 'the Resistance was less powerful as a factor of renewal and rejuvenation than the Popular Front elections had been . . . The proportional list system [adopted in 1945] favoured activists over voters and allowed endogenous renewal. Added to rewards for long party service, this acted as a brake on rejuvenation through the promotion of young Socialist *résistants*.'[13] Moreover, the lucky few who were promoted had often joined the party before the war, like Defferre (an SFIO member since 1933) or Gérard Jacquet. Very few elected officials had had their political initiation in the years underground;

in this respect Jean-Daniel Jurgensen or Robert Salmon, Deputies in the 1945 Constituent Assembly, were the exceptions. It is true that of all the SFIO parliamentarians of the Fourth Republic, only 14 per cent had sat before 1940. It is also true, however, that only 12 per cent had joined the party after 1939.[14] The feminisation of the SFIO's parliamentary ranks, meanwhile, remained at a token level, below 3 per cent. Thus 'while the war did indeed represent a rupture, in that it led to an unprecedented purge of the SFIO's cadres and especially of its parliamentarians, it was neither the rejuvenating cure that had been hoped for, nor the opportunity for a healthy influx of new blood'.[15] Meanwhile the attempts at doctrinal renovation outlined by André Philip and Léon Blum in the essay *À l'échelle humaine*, a sketch for a modern, Europe-wide, social democracy, remained a dead letter. Badly unsettled by falling electoral support, and facing competition from the rise of the PCF, the SFIO clung to a traditional late nineteenth-century discourse, secular and *guesdiste*, 'confirmed by the arrival [at the head of the party] in August 1946 of Guy Mollet and his team, who were convinced that in doctrinal radical-isation lay the route to recovery'.[16] From June 1946 the party drew the lessons of history and chose not to constitute joint lists with the UDSR for the parliamentary elections.

This record suggests that, contrary to much received opinion, the renewal achieved at the Liberation was quite limited, because the Resistance failed to transform the political landscape. Its organisations were forced to give way to the established parties, whose interests were best served by the political system. The proportional list electoral system, in particular, gave them a decisive advantage, since only well-organised parties had the means and the experience to constitute full slates of candidates across the whole country. By contrast, Resistance organisations, making their start in politics, had far more difficulty in adopting hundreds of candidates, especially where they were relatively unknown to voters. The 1945 municipal elections, organised in haste, left them little time to organise. And however much these elections allowed the promotion of individual *résistants*, they also wrecked the structures (notably the CDLs) that had emerged from the years underground and favoured the reconstitution of established parties.[17] Individuals who emerged from clandestinity did not invariably enjoy speedy promotion, and those who did were rarely political virgins. Teitgen, Menthon, and Schumann had all been active pre-war Christian Democrats; Charles Tillon was a PCF activist and Deputy before 1939. Even the UDSR did not escape this rule: Antoine Avinin, Pierre Bourdan, Eugène Claudius-Petit and Lucien Rose came from the pre-war ranks of *Jeune République*. The same was true at local level. In the Sarthe, twelve of the 25 newly-elected post-war *conseillers généraux* had already been councillors at *arrondissement* or municipal level before 1939. The role of the Resistance, therefore, was more to ease the promotion of politicians whose rise to the top had been blocked by their elders than to bring forth new men whose political commitment dated from the Occupation.

Even the supposed 'triumph of the Left' in 1945 rests on some questionable assumptions. In the first place, the conservatives had been losing ground, and the Left gaining, since 1932, and notably in the cantonal and parliamentary elections of 1935–6; 1945 was thus less a rupture than the continuation of an established tendency. Secondly, the MRP, despite its frequent classification as a left-wing party, is more accurately placed on the Right, on the basis both of its electoral strongholds, and of its strategy, chosen from the beginning, of preventing a reconstitution of the Popular Front alliance of Communists, Socialists and Radicals.[18] Finally, the traditional Right had not disappeared altogether. As well as a significant share of power at local level, it mustered 62 Deputies in 1945, a shrunken but hardly negligible force. Supporters of Vichy, moreover, were far from being disqualified by their doubtful associations. Camille Laurent's leadership of the Corporation Paysanne from 1942 to 1944 did not prevent his election in October 1945; Jean Boivin-Champeaux, president of the Républicains Indépendants group in the upper house, had drafted a favourable report on the bill giving constituent powers to Pétain in 1940;[19] Raymond Marcellin (who would become Interior Minister under Pompidou) was elected Deputy for the Morbihan in November 1946 despite his role as no. 2 in the Institut d'Études Corporatives et Sociales under the Occupation. All of this indicates that the Left's dominance in 1945 was less complete than is often believed. Indeed, the total right-wing vote comes to 40 per cent in 1945 if the MRP is added, and to 49 if one includes the Radicals as well.

On this basis, it is arguable that the French rejected neither the élites of the Third Republic nor Vichy supporters. Local data confirm this view. At the 1945 municipal elections, no fewer than 228 incumbents were elected despite having been officially disqualified from office (77 were beaten and 23 more did not stand).[20] At the same election, in eighteen *départements* observed by the *Jury d'honneur*, an average of 58 per cent of the *conseillers généraux* who had served under Vichy won seats (the proportion varied from 40 per cent in Bouches-du-Rhône to 79 per cent in Haute-Marne).[21] Thus involvement with the Vichy state did not necessarily put voters off. In fact, the French renewed their trust in those officials who they considered had worked hard to cushion them from the worst rigours of the Occupation by representing their interests to the Germans. Rejecting collaboration, they nevertheless retained a certain attachment for Pétain and even approved of some of his policies. In that light, what would be the use of punishing élites whose behaviour had reflected the feelings of the masses? In the end, voters often preferred to keep elected officials whom they knew and trusted rather than handing over the keys to power to unknowns, however heroic. In the countryside, moreover, the survival of local networks was enough to ensure the hegemony of established notables. The authorities were sufficiently concerned by this situation to intervene directly. A law of 4 October 1945 recalled that any person condemned to national indignity under any form or motive remained disqualified from office. And the *Jury d'honneur* decided on 19 October 1945 that an election could be annulled even if it had preceded a negative verdict on the winner.

Conclusion

This rapid *tour d'horizon* underlines the ambivalent combination of continuity and ruptures that marked 1945. Of course the Liberation did provoke an earthquake. The Left won an unprecedented majority in the country and in the Assembly; the Right paid for its social conservatism and its support for Vichy. Political cleavages changed, as old quarrels, such as Church/State relations, lost their bitterness (for a while) while others, such as nationalisations, polarised political debate. On the Right, parties as important as the Alliance Démocratique and the Fédération Républicaine never recovered from the Occupation, while the Radicals experienced serious difficulties. The political élite was partially purged and substantially renewed, making room at the top for men who had hitherto been confined by their elders to second-rank posts. Thus far the Liberation signalled a major change.

Continuity with the past characterises the Liberation era in other respects. A closer look at the Right – whether the MRP or other groupings like the Parti Républicain de la Liberté – reveals its capacity to resist and to adapt to its post-war misfortunes. The Right was less decomposed as recomposed, and that with sufficient effectiveness to allow the 'Party of Order' to return to power as early as 1952. Resistance organisations, by contrast, failed to remodel the political landscape. Gaullism had no significant political outlets before the formation of the Rassemblement du Peuple Français in April 1947. The UDSR remained numerically negligible, although its position as a pivot party made its few Deputies capable of overturning a parliamentary majority. Former *résistants* were far from winning promotion on a systematic basis, thanks not only to the skill of Vichyites at maintaining many of their local positions, but also to the readiness of left-wing parties to exclude some *résistants* and to hold others back.

Yet in the social and economic domains, as Chapman's contribution to this book shows, France began an astonishing transformation – the reverse, in many ways, of the Third Republic's combination of big advances in political rights but slow social and economic progress. For a real *immobilisme* characterised post-Liberation France in many areas of politics. As the contributions by Shipway, Footitt and Cartier show, the new regime achieved slow to non-existent advances in the rights of colonised peoples or the integration of women in public affairs, while the institutions of the Fourth Republic resembled those of the former regime even though institutional reform had been a widely shared political priority since 1934. A partially-renewed political élite, then, undertook a profound economic and social renewal of the country but refused to do the same for its institutions. One explanation for this might be the political dominance of a left-wing coalition equally determined to achieve social progress and to maintain the institutional prerogatives of Parliament. Yet the economic and social reforms of the Liberation commanded a consensus including not just the Left, but the whole of the Right, for four decades: until the neo-liberal wave of the 1980s, few voices called for the privatisation of nationalised firms or for a root-and-branch reform of the Social Security system. Specifics of the extension of the public sector were discussed; but the principle in itself was not. Indeed, all actors viewed economic and social renovation as an 'ardent obligation', especially as the population, shocked by the experience of defeat and still suffering from four years of Occupation, sought better living standards and stronger social protection.

It was this (legitimate) aspiration that deprived the Resistance programme of any originality, composed as it was of a mixture of the pre-war SFIO platform and ideas developed by France's more advanced inter-war thinkers. Most of these elements became common ground, shared by practically all parties, thus depriving the *résistants* of any unique electoral selling point. Like the economic and administrative élites described by Michel Margairaz,[22] France's politicians generally converted to supporting the welfare state and the state's intervention in the economy. Conversely, the same political élite was sufficiently a prisoner of its own culture not to seek to change political rules which served it well. This was especially the case as four years of Vichy's authoritarianism had helped restore the tarnished image of the Third Republic, as well as showing the risks of a strong executive, especially combined with a personal concentration of power. In that context, there seemed little point in changing a tried and tested mode of governance, which the French, without exactly giving it overwhelming support, had not rejected either. That constraint, of course, would be lifted in 1958 with de Gaulle's return to power and the ensuing change of constitution. Then, France's political personnel would undergo what was probably a deeper renewal than in the aftermath of the Liberation.

Notes

1. C. de Gaulle, 'Discours du 20 avril 1943', *Discours et messages*, Vol. I (Paris, Plon, 1970), p. 281.
2. Défense de la France, 'Le Mouvement de la libération nationale', *Défense de la France* 43 (15 January 1944).
3. Cf. O. Wieviorka, *Les Orphelins de la République. Destinées des députés et sénateurs français, 1940–1945* (Paris: Le Seuil, 2001).
4. *Le Monde*, 1 November 1945.
5. R. Mencherini, 'Les changements des rapports de force politiques', in G. Le Béguec and D. Peschanski (eds), *Les élites locales dans la tourmente. Du Front Populaire aux années cinquante* (Paris: CNRS Éditions, 2000): pp. 33–46 for global analysis, p. 40 for figures.
6. C.-L. Foulon, *Le Pouvoir en province à la Libération* (Paris: Presses de la Fondation Nationale des Sciences Politiques, 1975), p. 224.

7. R. Mencherini, 'Les changements des rapports de force politiques', p. 40.
8. For local studies, cf. Le Béguec and Peschanski, *Les élites locales dans la tourmente*.
9. H. Frenay, *La Nuit finira*, Vol. II (Paris: Livre de Poche, 1974 (1st edn 1973)), pp. 277–8.
10. P. Buton, 'Le PCF et la Résistance sous la IVe République', in B. Lachaise (ed.), *Résistance et Politique sous la IVe République* (Bordeaux: Presses Universitaires de Bordeaux, 2004), pp. 97–110.
11. Ibid.
12. N. Castagnez, *Socialistes en République. Les parlementaires SFIO de la IVe République* (Rennes: Presses Universitaires de Rennes, 2004), p. 97.
13. Ibid., pp. 104–5.
14. N. Castagnez and G. Morin, 'Résistance et Socialisme. Brève rencontre', in Bernard Lachaise (ed.), *Résistance et Politique sous la IVe République* (Bordeaux: Presses Universitaires de Bordeaux, 2004), pp. 111–46; p. 116.
15. Ibid., p. 121.
16. Castagnez, *Socialistes en République*, p. 109.
17. G. Morin, 'Les élections locales de 1945. La normalisation de la vie politique', *La IVe République. Histoire, recherches et archives*, no. 357–358 (1997), pp. 119–33; p. 133.
18. G. Richard, 'Les droites et le Parlement, 1944–1948. Essai de mesure globale', in G. Richard and J. Sainclivier (eds), *La Recomposition des droites en France à la Libération, 1944–1948* (Rennes: Presses Universitaires de Rennes, 2004), pp. 49–59; pp. 56 ff.
19. Ibid., p. 51.
20. *Note du Jury d'Honneur*, 5 June 1945 (Archives Nationales (Paris): Archives du Jury d'honneur, carton 'généralités').
21. *Note du Jury d'Honneur*, 30 May 1945.
22. M. Margairaz, *L'Etat, les finances et l'économie. Histoire d'une conversion (1932–1952)* (Paris: Comité pour l'histoire économique et financière de la France, 1991).

Bibliography

Castagnez, N., *Socialistes en République. Les parlementaires SFIO de la IVe République* (Rennes: Presses Universitaires de Rennes, 2004).
Foulon, C.-L., *Le Pouvoir en province à la Libération* (Paris: Presses de la Fondation Nationale des Sciences Politiques, 1975).
Frenay, H., *La Nuit finira* (Paris: Livre de Poche, 1974 (1st edn 1973)).
Lachaise, Bernard (ed.), *Résistance et Politique sous la IVe République* (Bordeaux: Presses Universitaires de Bordeaux, 2004), pp. 111–46.
Le Béguec, G., and Peschanski D. (eds). *Les élites locales dans la tourmente. Du Front Populaire aux années cinquante* (Paris: CNRS Éditions, 2000).
Margairaz, M., *L'Etat, les finances et l'économie. Histoire d'une conversion (1932–1952)* (Paris: Comité pour l'histoire économique et financière de la France, 1991).
Morin, G., 'Les élections locales de 1945. La normalisation de la vie politique', *La IVe République. Histoire, recherches et archives, 357–358* (1997), pp. 119–33.
Richard, G., 'Les droites et le Parlement, 1944–1948. Essai de mesure globale', in G. Richard and J. Sainclivier (eds), *La Recomposition des droites en France à la Libération, 1944–1948* (Rennes: Presses Universitaires de Rennes, 2004), pp. 49–59.
Wieviorka, O., *Les Orphelins de la République. Destinées des députés et sénateurs français, 1940–1945* (Paris: Le Seuil, 2001).

6
'The Politics of Political Women': Reassessing the First *Députées*

Hilary Footitt

October 1945 – when women first voted in legislative elections in France, and when the first female Deputies took their seats – is something of a 'non-date' in French history. As Sian Reynolds has suggested, 'It has acquired the paradoxical status of a "fact" significant for women but not for men'.[1] In part of course this has much to do with the longstanding gender-blindness which led French historians to refer to 1848 as the date of 'universal suffrage', so that votes for women in 1945 were either presented as entirely separate from universal suffrage – 'giving the vote to women' – or as very much an incidental detail in the history of the period (as Jean-Pierre Rioux describes the referendum vote, 'The French – including 12,000,000 women – replied to the two questions.'[2]

What is a lot less clear is why this date is equally a non-date as far as most historians of women's rights are concerned. On the whole, works on women's history in France either note the date and pass swiftly on, or suggest that it was basically irrelevant to women's emancipation. In this, women's history and so-called 'mainstream' history have shared a narrative of occlusion of 1945 which serves to make suffrage, and the election of *députées*, virtually invisible to those of us in the twenty-first century who want to trace the roots of women's relationship with political power in France.

Like any radical group, the Women's Liberation Movement in the late 1960s and early 1970s espoused a kind of revolutionary 'presentism' where 1970 was represented as the 'année zéro' of women's liberation. Anything which had gone before was either of minor importance, or was reformist rather than revolutionary.[3] This radical challenging of the political in terms of the personal tended to relegate the vote, and women's political activity in the 1944–47 period, to an irrelevant, if not downright traditionalist footnote.

When later historians turned to a more measured consideration of the post-Liberation, the inheritance of the 1970s strongly marked their work. 1945 was examined in terms of the extent to which political emancipation had led to personal freedoms, and this was judged by the record of legislation passed. Thus Jane Jenson, for example, argued that whilst citizenship rights and greater access to the paid labour force were indeed delivered in the post-war period, the gains for women were strictly limited, with married women remaining without full civil rights until the mid-1960s.[4] Claire Duchen, in a later reworking of this holistic approach, examined the post-war discourses which framed women as citizens, workers and mothers, and concluded that 'The changes, which were to become visible in women's lives later, did not appear in the years after the Liberation, a period when women were invariably disappointed by the measures taken (or not taken) on their behalf.'[5]

Contemporary historians have tended to echo this narrative of disappointment, although from slightly different perspectives. Rather than the legislative failure to change the social position of women, 1945 was seen 'from the ground up' as irrelevant to the lived experience of women at that time. Thus Hanna Diamond, in a detailed study of women's lives in Toulouse, argued that, 'gaining of the vote for women was not a particularly "liberating" experience for them. For most women who were trying to keep the household going, gaining the vote was not an important event'.[6] Two studies of responses to women's enfranchisement, by Joan Tumblety and Bruno Denoyelle, concluded that the discursive context in which women voted made it extremely unlikely that the event would have any meaningful effect on their status and lives.[7] This general narrative of hopes disappointed has been only slightly modified by those who have studied women's engagement outside the strictly formal politics of the Assembly.[8]

In some senses, the 1992 *parité* movement reawakened interest in women's participation in formal politics in France, underlining Jean Pascal's conclusion that the immediate post-war period had been the highest point of women's representation in parliament (5.6 per cent in the Assembly of October 1945, 5.11 per cent in June 1946, 6.48 per cent in November 1946), until the Mitterrand era some forty years later.[9] One of the leading *parité* exponents, Françoise Gaspard, in a preface to William Guéraiche's 1999 study of women's political representation, reiterated the consensus narrative of disappointment. Women had not been elected in the post-war period in sufficient (implicitly 50 per cent) numbers to make a real difference: 'they were there, but in a strictly homeopathic dose'.[10] In the book itself, Guéraiche argued that women's accession to political power at the Liberation corresponded with a period when the normal right/left cleavages of politics had been replaced by a Resistance/Collaboration cleavage which, he concluded, had benefited women Resisters. With the restoration of a quasi-Third Republic constitutional model, normal political business could be resumed, making the Resistance, and with it, women, something of a political irrelevance. If the failure to capitalise on the election of women was a systemic failure however, Guéraiche also noted that the first women representatives themselves had to bear some of the responsibility. They were unable, he claimed, to develop a new role, and a clear view of their own female identity in politics: 'far too imprisoned by traditional representations of women, the first women in politics were unsure about affirming their differences as women'.[11]

Identifying the first *députées* so closely with the Resistance, as Guéraiche and others do, has some important consequences, I would argue, for our understanding of women and politics in France. Both in terms of personnel (19 of the first 33 *députées* had well-attested Resistance records), and in terms of tenure (the largest numbers of women in the Assembly were in 1944–47 when the discourse of Resistance was in the political ascendancy), the first wave of women elected is represented as a Resistance phenomenon. Much like the Resistance, women's activity in formal politics is implicitly constructed as 'abnormal', and doomed to be short-lived. It is something which is by definition 'provisional', and can be at least partly explained by the fact that 'real politics' has not yet resumed. Normality has not been restored.

Unlike the Resistance however, there has been no memorialising of these first women Deputies. They have disappeared from view, barely now (with the honourable exception of Guéraiche) making it into the footnotes of women's history, and appearing, if they ever do, as one composite group, 'the first women députés', 'les 33 Glorieuses',[12] apparently noticeable for the single important quality that they share, namely that they are women. In my view, this representation should be of serious concern to historians of women's history. The amnesia surrounding those women who first entered the Assembly, and their positioning as a composite and undifferentiated group – a sort of political flash in the pan, born of the abnormality of the period, and disappearing when politics gets back to normal – is arguably complicit in a general presentation of women in politics as people with no antecedents, little experience, and few political markers.

A slightly wider perspective however might show that this narrative of disappointed hopes in female representatives is neither peculiar to the 1944–47 period, nor specific to France. It has often been, and continues to be, a leitmotiv of work on women and political representation all over the democratic world. Much is hoped for, and apparently little is delivered. Joni Lovenduski, reviewing the state of contemporary research on women and political representation in Europe and North America, concluded that:

> Feminists and their opponents have consistently held unrealistic expectations of the possibilities afforded by real systems of political representation. Over the years since women were enfranchised, the meanings of their political action and of political representation changed; however reactions by both traditionalists and by many feminists did not take such changes into account . . . both the possibilities and the achievements of women's political representation have been misunderstood.[13]

Commentators have suggested that feminist agendas are inevitably coloured by contemporary party political concerns. We should thus be taking a more consciously contextualised approach to the difference women representatives can or cannot make in historically specific and gendered political environments.

As Sarah Childs argues, women may share certain 'gendered experiences', but there is no reason to suppose that they will necessarily agree on the same priorities for women, irrespective of the party political environments in which they have been elected.[14]

By this token, instead of blaming a composite group of *députées* for what was not achieved, and bemoaning their irrelevance to the history of women in France, we perhaps need to resituate these women in their political contexts, and pay them the historical courtesy of examining their careers in a little more detail. Firstly, where did they come from politically? Did they indeed emerge suddenly from the Resistance, or did they have a political life before 1940? What exactly was their political hinterland? Secondly, what did they do whilst in the Assembly? What form did substantive representation – women acting as or for women[15] – actually take in the politics of 1944–47? Finally, what happened to these *députées* after they had completed their mandates? Are there political spaces related to those of formal politics which may have been particularly propitious for women's continued political engagement at that time in French history?

This chapter takes the form of an exploratory case study of three of the first women in the Assembly. The women have been selected to include a representative from each of the major governing parties of the era – the MRP (Mouvement Républicain Populaire), the PCF (Parti Communiste Français) and the Socialist SFIO (Section Française de l'Internationale Ouvrière). The sample deliberately comprises three women whose periods of service as *députées* varied in length. The three are: Marie-Hélène Lefaucheux (MRP, one term in the Assembly, 1945–46); Madeleine Braun (PCF, three terms in the Assembly, 1945–51); and Germaine Degrond (SFIO, five terms in the Assembly, 1945–58). The aim of the chapter is not just to increase the visibility of post-war politics within the history of women in France, but also to try to reinstate this period as a vital and integral one in the long and continuous story of the political liberation of women. The ways in which women interacted with the political in the post-war years, I believe, raise issues for political history of the period, and may point to the need for new and different sorts of research in the future.

Political hinterland

'Out of this chaos, a new woman emerged', Mathilde Péri proclaimed in the Provisional Consultative Assembly on 16 May 1945,[16] and certainly, the first 33 women elected to the Constituent Assembly in October 1945 were strongly marked by the chaos of war and Resistance. The idea however that the first women politicians suddenly emerged from Resistance to take over elected office, as a new and totally inexperienced political class, is far from accurate. Like their male counterparts, there were certainly members of this group who had not been engaged in politics before the War. Marie-Hélène Lefaucheux, who became MRP *députée* for the Aisne, had been one of the first two women admitted to the École Libre des Sciences Politiques, but there is no record of her having been active in politics before the war, and it seems to have been the Resistance, in which she was a member of the (relatively conservative) Organisation Civile et Militaire (OCM), which brought her into politics.

The other two women in the sample, however, had very considerable pre-war experience in political circles. When Madeleine Braun (PCF *députée* for the Seine) was asked in 1975 how she had become involved in the Resistance, she was clear that her political education had started some years before that: 'What did I really know in 1930? That I was young and newly married, that war was threatening my country as well as my home. It was Hitler and the war in Spain which actually began the process of educating me; then it was the Resistance.'[17] In the 1930s, Braun had played a prominent role on the Comité Directeur of the Amsterdam–Pleyel Movement, the antifascist organisation of European intellectuals, and was particularly active in the pro-Spanish Republican Comité International de Coordination pour l'Aide à l'Espagne Républicaine for which she acted as secretary general. Between 1936 and 1939, she travelled extensively in Spain, and was working with Spanish Republican exiles in Paris when war was declared in 1939.[18]

Germaine Degrond (SFIO, 1945–1958, *députée* for Seine-et-Oise), the third member of the sample, also had a long pre-war political trajectory, although in her case, it was one more overtly embedded in a mainstream political party. Degrond originally started her political activity in the First World War, when she collaborated in left-wing pacifist journals like *la Voix des Femmes* and *Les Hommes du Jour*. As a member of the SFIO, she worked on three fronts. First, as a journalist, she wrote for the party's newspaper, *Le Populaire*. Second, she was involved in women's activities within the party – she edited the woman's page for *Le Populaire*, was elected as *suppléante* to the Comité National des Femmes Socialistes in 1931, and acted as assistant secretary for her Federation's Groupe des Femmes Socialistes. Finally, she was a key member in the party's pre-war organisational structure at section and federal level and, in 1937–38, became the first woman to occupy a high position in the party apparatus, in the SFIO's Commission Administrative Permanente.[19]

In 1982, when Michel Rocard gave her the Légion d'Honneur, he paid tribute to what amounted to a lifetime of service to the Socialist party, and it is significant that out of the 13 women included in the recent *100 ans. 100 socialistes* anniversary collection, she was one of only five associated politically with the pre-war period. In the party conference, held in May 2005 to celebrate its centenary, the SFIO national woman's representative, lamenting the lack of female speakers in the symposium, called upon the party to honour the women in its history, and specifically mentioned the name of Germaine Degrond in her litany of past, and apparently forgotten *militantes*.[20]

Olivier Wieviorka has suggested elsewhere in this book that many of the so-called 'new' men of 1944–5 at national level in fact had an attested pre-war history of political militancy. In looking at the first women Deputies, it is important to make the same sort of point. Whilst some of the first cohort undoubtedly received their political baptism in the Resistance, others had a clearly documented pre-war career of involvement in political parties, or in pressure groups closely associated with parties. Rather than a surprise phenomenon of 'new women', minted by the Resistance, whose presence can only be accounted for by the singularity of historical circumstance, some at least of the first women representatives assumed their seats in the Assembly as an understandable continuum of pre-war activism.

Patterns of substantive representation

A key question about *députées* at this period must be: what did they actually do when in Parliament? Is there evidence that they acted as and for women? And if so, what does this mean in the context of 1944–47 politics? I want to argue that the three women in the sample demonstrate different patterns of what we would call today the substantive representation of women.

Marie-Hélène Lefaucheux

At one end of the spectrum is Marie-Hélène Lefaucheux who was nominated to the Provisional Consultative Assembly by the OCM, served in the first Constituent Assembly as an MRP *députée*, became a party-nominated member of the first Council of the Republic (upper house of the Fourth Republic) in 1946–47, and subsequently a member of the Assembly of the French Union (1947–58).[21] For those who knew her career, Lefaucheux was an 'evangelist for women's rights',[22] consistently speaking out about the condition of women. From the beginning of her tenure, she raised the issue of women in relation to the care networks which had been established in clandestinity, and which she felt should continue to receive support post-Liberation. These networks had been largely managed by women, and it seemed to Lefaucheux to be a matter of emotional as well as political relevance to ensure that such initiatives were still supported.[23]

In a liberal/equal rights perspective, Lefaucheux concentrated on the extension of voting rights, on equality in access to public office, and on the defence of women in areas where the law appeared to be discriminating against them. From 1947 until 1958, she was a lively member (and vice president in 1950 and 1951) of the Assembly of the French Union, where she interestingly raised the issue of women's rights in the much broader context of the French Empire. She indeed accused the French authorities of failing to extend the full implications of the Declaration of Human Rights to women within the Union:

'Do we have to conclude that we are going to allow the French Government to choose whether or not it will extend the principles of the Declaration of the Rights of Man to the overseas territories of the French Republic? That is an extremely worrying idea!'[24] In terms of women's lives in the Union, Lefaucheux maintained that polygamy was banned by the Declaration of Human Rights, as were the mutilations of women practised in some states.[25] She was categorical that women should be protected no matter what opposition might come from African men: 'I think we have a fair dose of hypocrisy in our so-called desire to serve the cause of women's development. We are actually achieving nothing concrete and, more seriously still, several of our African colleagues have made it quite clear that they would not accept the principles of the Universal Declaration of the Rights of Man.'[26] It was vital, she argued, that African colleagues in the Union rejected a form of gender colonialism which had been common in France: 'They need me, so I dominate them … giving women a minor place, or rather that of a perpetual minor – we've been through that ourselves in Europe.'[27]

For Lefaucheux, the defence of women was a matter of constitutional rights, rather than of 'feminism'. No real democracy could exist in Africa, she claimed, without political rights for women. Faced with catcalls on the lines of 'It would be far better to teach them to cook!' she retorted: 'That's exactly the reaction I expected, reaction in every sense of the word … That's not a reason … for women citizens in Africa to wait as long as we have … for their most legitimate rights.'[28]

The results of Lefaucheux's work were largely concentrated in Francophone Africa, and indeed from February 1959 to August 1960, she worked in the office of the then Secrétaire d'Etat aux Affaires Musulmanes, Nafissa Sid Cara. The Conseil National des Femmes Françaises suggested that Lefaucheux's legislative efforts had been significant in several areas: she had helped to win women the right to vote in sub-Saharan Africa and Madagascar, ahead of their Anglophone African counterparts. The 1952 Code de Travail had provided *outremer* women with a structure of social laws, whilst the Jacquinot decree of 15 September 1951 had radically changed the system of forced marriages, and the status of widows.[29]

Madeleine Braun

Madeleine Braun's approach to being a *députée* was very different from that of Lefaucheux. Braun had been nominated to the Provisional Consultative Assembly as a delegate of the Communist-linked Front National Resistance organisation, and then served as a PCF *députée* from 1944–51. When she died in January 1980, her obituary and death notice in *Le Monde* put a particular emphasis on the fact that she had been the first woman to be elected as a Vice-President of the Constituent Assembly (in 1945 and 1946).[30] As a Communist, Braun refused to identify women as a particular category, outside other members of the exploited proletariat. When she remembered her time in politics, many years later, she specifically rejected attempts to divorce women's liberation from the broader liberation of all people: 'And there's no question either of a male plot against women or vice versa. Our common struggle continued: there was no freedom for one unless the others had it too.'[31] In this context, suffrage was only one part of the story, hence her reported comments on the prospect of women voting for the first time in the municipal elections of April 1945: 'Of course women should have the vote. But it hasn't made much difference in America or England, has it?'[32]

The PCF's women's movement, the Union des Femmes Françaises, was of course extremely successful in the 1944–47 period, with 620,000 members in 1945, and two press outlets, *Femmes Françaises* and *Heures Claires*. As Annie Kriegel has pointed out, PCF positioning of women distinguished between the economic 'femmes travailleuses', with women exploited in exactly the same way as men, and the 'ménagères', occupying a separate and more conventional sphere.[33]

For Braun, citizenship rights had to go hand in hand with economic rights, and these were for all workers, and not just for women. Equal pay, she argued, would therefore change the way that men and women regarded each other: 'Once it is finally agreed that women receive an equal wage for equal work, it will no longer be possible to accuse women of unfairly competing.'[34] During the referendum campaign for the first draft constitution in April–May 1946, she defended the constitutional proposals as providing a particularly good deal for women. The combination of guarantees of male/female equality, with an article (article 24) which offered social protection to women and children, was, she claimed, a major step forward: 'As citizens, workers and mothers, French women are finally going to be able to reconcile their maternal function with their own self-fulfillment, intellectually, politically and socially. It's a great victory, and a small revolution.'[35] It would then be up to women, in her view, to ensure that social legislation was passed which would support these goals, and this implied social rights relevant to all workers, whether male or female.[36]

With debates in the Assembly becoming increasingly polarised and bitter, Braun found herself under personal attack because of the position of her husband in the Communist-linked Banque Commerciale pour l'Europe du Nord.[37] Whether because of these unpalatable charges of *embourgeoisement*, or because, as Guéraiche suggests, a member of the party's Bureau Politique had started a rumour about her Resistance record,[38] Madeleine Braun did not stand as a candidate on the PCF list for the 1951 elections, and her direct involvement with Assembly-related politics ceased at that point.

Germaine Degrond

In many ways, Germaine Degrond (SFIO *députée* from 1945 to 1958) seems to be between the two extremes outlined above. Degrond's record in the Assembly suggests that she showed little interest in the type of female equality agenda pursued by Lefaucheux. On the other hand, she did not subsume questions relating to women into a broader Socialist agenda like Braun. Through her long tenure in Parliament, Degrond spoke out about issues which were undoubtedly important for many women at that time (food, the rights of children, the effects of alcoholism on family life) but which she identified as being both issues for women and mainstream issues relating to all French people.

Degrond was president of the Food Supply Committee in 1946, 1948, and 1949, and during this time, all but one of her interventions were on matters to do with food. Her first speech in December 1945 argued that food provisioning was of very particular concern to women.[39] Some seven months later, she was still maintaining that the food issue was vital, and that she, as a woman Deputy, had specific insight into it: 'It's not only as a *députée* that I want to speak about food. That wouldn't be enough. It's as a woman who is experiencing all the problems that women have in this area . . .'.[40]

As Rod Kedward suggested, it may well be that this 'gender-specific discourse was in tune with the priorities of the time, in a way that constitutional niceties, for all their necessity, appeared not to be'.[41] For Degrond at least, the standard by which the success of Government policies on food would be gauged was the ease with which the *ménagères* could find the produce they wanted at the prices they could afford and, in practice, the *ménagères* were all women in France: 'All the *ménagères*, that is all women, because it's clear that the situation of *ménagères* is not a problem for one particular class alone: every woman with a home, and the responsibility for it, is automatically affected by this issue.'[42]

By the 1950s, as the salience of the food issue receded, Degrond's principal contributions revolved around two issues which she felt particularly affected women, but which, like food, she represented as being of major importance to all voters: alcoholism and the rights of children. On the question of alcoholism, she consistently argued for clearer protections against the effect of the disease on the family unit, and noted that women in particular often bore the brunt of the problem.[43] As a woman herself, she suggested, it was especially difficult not to be able to offer other women, suffering in this situation, any kind of support: 'As a woman, I have to blush sometimes when I'm not able as a *députée* to say to mothers: "Here's what the National Assembly has done for you" . . .'.[44]

A similar issue which she felt was of major concern to all, but which had particular repercussions for women, was that of the rights of children, especially those born of adulterous relationships. She maintained that what was at stake here was basic human justice: 'It is desperately painful for the women who sit here to hear each time arguments about children which have absolutely no tenderness, no breath of humanity . . . We should try to ensure that a breath of humanity and a little justice inform our discussions.'[45]

One of Degrond's last speeches in the Assembly set out her case for a single issue (in this case alcoholism) being of both specific interest to women, and also in the general best interests of society: 'As Deputies – and incidentally I suggest that our male colleagues should never forget this – we have been elected by men and also by women who have particular situations and special interests, but they still have a common interest.'[46]

Political spaces

Like the careers of many of their male colleagues, the trajectories of these three women suggest that the spaces of politics in which they were engaged could be wider than the National Assembly itself. For Lefaucheux and Braun in particular, their activities went well beyond the business of being a *députée*. Lefaucheux, as we have seen, was a member of Assembly-related bodies like the Council of the Republic and the Assembly of the French Union. In addition, she joined the first French delegation to the United Nations in 1946, and represented France on the UN Status of Women Commission, acting as its President for five successive years (1947–51), and serving on the UN Commission of Human Rights, and on the Sub-Commission on the Prevention of Discrimination and the Protection of Minorities.

In the UN, Lefaucheux continued to argue for an end to discrimination against women: 'where discrimination was general, women suffered more than men because women were illiterate and deprived of equal status under tax and property law'.[47] As in her speeches in the Assembly of the French Union, Lefaucheux claimed that constitutional change would be needed if women were to be supported. Thus she called for UN texts on the protection of minorities to make explicit references to 'equality of rights of men and women for the right to vote, to be elected and to hold all public offices'.[48]

Outside the formal international spaces of the UN, she was also active in voluntary organisations concerned with women's rights. In 1954, she became President of the Conseil National des Femmes Françaises, whose main post-war objectives were: 'To have equality of the sexes written into the Constitution by fighting against discrimination which persists in practice as in private law. To provide political and civic education for women. To further the evolution of women in French Overseas Territories.'[49] In the 1950 and 1955 elections, the Conseil campaigned to have women included in the lists of the political parties, and urged women to study the election manifestos, and vote for women.

For Lefaucheux, who believed passionately in the link between human rights and womens' rights, the emergence and acceptance of NGOs in the 1950s and 1960s, what she called 'present forms of international life',[50] meant that bodies like the International Council of Women (which grouped together the Conseil National des Femmes Françaises and its sister organisations in other countries) could have a real role as informed interlocutors, supporting and furthering the work of intergovernmental organisations. At her funeral, one of her colleagues described Lefaucheux's political space as considerably larger than the National Assembly and France: 'she was . . . a real citizen of the world, for whom political and geographical frontiers were no obstacle'.[51]

The spaces of politics which Madeleine Braun inhabited beyond the National Assembly also crossed frontiers, but in her case these spaces were above all cultural. Throughout her time in the Assembly, Braun was on the editorial board of the *Front National* newspaper, and indeed she made regular interventions in Parliament on press-related topics: on the freedom of the press, the information budget, and the need to regulate foreign press imports which might affect children.[52] After she had completed her term in the Assembly in 1951, she continued working with the newspaper, and ten years later, moved into publishing, when she became codirector, with Louis Aragon, of the Communist-affiliated Éditeurs Français Réunis, the publisher of the well-known literary periodical, *Europe*.

Recent commentators on women and politics in France have claimed that, when reviewing the political contributions of women, it is vital to include journalism, fictional and biographical work in any account of their political lives.[53] In this perspective, all these writings, and arguably the activity of publishing itself (selecting and printing texts) can be seen as valid narratives which, when taken as a whole corpus, may provide some understanding of the ways in which knowledge about politics, and therefore power, are reframed at different periods. Arguably, the politico-cultural spaces which Madeleine Braun inhabited beyond the Assembly are of some importance in illuminating the ways in which women in politics at this period understood and negotiated the political space.

In comparison with Lefaucheux and Braun, Germaine Degrond's post-war political career was largely spent within the organisation of a political party, the SFIO. Over a twelve year continuous career, her political space was undoubtedly not just the Assembly, but also, as a very active member of the SFIO from 1916 until her death in 1991, the space of the party apparatus. After the war, she was involved (with Andrée Marty-Capgras and Emilienne Moreau) in the setting up of the new SFIO women's organisation, the Secrétariat aux Questions Féminines. Guéraiche argues that Degrond and her colleagues believed that such an organisation would only be 'temporary because its sole objective was to integrate women as quickly and completely as possible into the apparatus'.[54] In the 39th party congress in 1947, however, women delegates were still arguing that the SFIO leadership was not really interested in women. The organisational space of the party which Degrond inhabited was, and remained, a site of conflict for many women in politics, faced with party structures which were often impervious to change.

Conclusion

Far from being a non-date in the canon of women's history, 1945 should be viewed, I believe, as an important and integral part of the story of women's political liberation in France. This case study has shown that, with the election of the first *députées*, women clearly entered the discursive space of formal politics in France. At the basic level, they attained offices within the structures of the Assembly. Thus, Madeleine Braun was elected as Vice-President, Germaine Degrond chaired the important Food Supply Committee, and Marie-Hélène Lefaucheux became a Vice-President of the Assembly of the French Union.

Perhaps more tellingly, questions connected to discrimination against women were raised in the spaces of formal politics, like Lefaucheux's and Braun's concern for equality of access to the professions, and Lefaucheux's determination to extend women's rights to the French Union, and to ensure that UN texts made explicit reference to women. In addition, issues which conventional politics might have called 'women's issues' – food supply, the rights of children – were not only discussed, but were, to some extent at least, mainstreamed in the political agenda of the times, with contributions like those of Degrond. Whether any of this would have happened without the articulate presence of women representatives seems highly doubtful. Clearly, the first *députées* did not achieve the far-reaching political changes for women that later commentators might have wished. Nevertheless, from their careers, it is evident that women as a group, with specific liberal equality demands, and particular social needs, were present in the discursive space of French politics. Whilst their presence might not have changed the discourse of formal politics, it undoubtedly inflected it in new, and possibly surprising ways.

The importance of 1945 for women's history however lies not just in the effect of women's presence at the time. In the long liberation of women, the immediate post-war period tells us a great deal about the ways in which we might understand, and as historians, represent the relationship of women with political power in France. To begin with, women had *bona fide* political careers, and did not necessarily appear 'as women' suddenly, out of a political nowhere. Madeleine Braun's pre-war commitment to pacifist and pro-Spanish Republican organisations, and Germaine Degrond's long apprenticeship in the SFIO, provide markers that are perfectly comprehensible on any political map of the time. Similarly, women politicians did not simply disappear, when their mandate in the Assembly was over. Like male Deputies, many had a post-Assembly political life – Lefaucheux in the UN for example, Braun in journalism and publishing. Arguably, the expectation that women in politics will have a political trajectory, traceable in the same way as that of men, is an important one for researchers approaching this topic.

Secondly, women representatives in 1945 were not a homogeneous group. The three women in this case study exemplify ways of being a *députée* which are as different and recognisable now as they were then. There is Lefaucheux's liberal equality agenda, with its emphasis on using the law, both national and conceivably international, to change the social condition of women. There is Braun's socialist refusal to consider the claims of women as inherently separable from those of the exploited proletariat. And there is Degrond's approach, raising issues of major importance to women and arguing that these are problems for all the electorate, and not only for women – in current parlance, 'mainstreaming' women's concerns. Accepting that there are different ways of being a woman in politics, and that these are likely to be strongly influenced by contemporary political priorities, again seems to be a key perspective for those of us looking at the politics of 1944–47.

Above all, this piece of exploratory work raises further questions about women in the immediate post-war era, questions which particularly concern our definition of the spaces of politics which may be relevant to women. Perhaps it is time that we saw 'women's political spaces' in the sort of wide terms with which some commentators identify socialist spaces.[55] Perhaps we should begin to place women's political history at this period in a much broader political context, studying the relationship of women's political emancipation in France with support for women's rights in the wider Francophone world, and with the developing women's rights/human rights agenda of the nascent United Nations. Perhaps we should be looking at women's political militancy in areas beyond the conventionally political, in the parallel politico-cultural activity of women as journalists and publishers. And finally, do we need to look more critically at the histories of the political parties at this period, tracing in detail the policy parameters and organisational structures which provided the context for women's political engagement, and the political environments in which they operated? History, as Joan Scott says, is, after all, 'a participant in the production of knowledge about sexual difference'.[56] In the long liberation of women it is surely time for us to revisit our writing of the history of 1944–47, and challenge the knowledge frameworks that we, as historians, have so far produced about women and political power in France at this period.

Notes

(Translations from the original French by the author)
1. S. Reynolds, 'Marianne's citizens? Women, the Republic and universal suffrage in France', in S. Reynolds (ed.), *Women, State and Revolution* (Brighton: Wheatsheaf books, 1986), pp. 101–22: p. 103. I am also indebted to her 'Women and the Popular Front in France: the case of the three women ministers', *French History* 8.2 (June 1994), pp. 196–224.
2. J.-P. Rioux, *La France de la IVe République*, Vol. I (Paris: Le Seuil, 1980), p. 91.
3. E. Salvaresi, *Mai en heritage* (Paris: Syros, 1988), p. 135.
4. J. Jenson, 'The Liberation and new rights for French women' in M.R. Higonnet and J. Jenson (eds), *Behind the Lines. Gender and the Two World Wars* (New Haven: Yale University Press,1987), pp. 272–84.
5. C. Duchen, 'Une femme nouvelle pour une France nouvelle?' *Clio* 1 (1995), pp. 151–64. See also her *Women's Rights and Women's lives in France 1944–1968* (London: Routledge, 1994).
6. H. Diamond, 'Gaining the vote – a liberating experience?' *Modern and Contemporary France* 3.2 (1995), pp. 129–39: p. 137. See also her *Women and the Second World War in France, 1939–48: Choices and Constraints* (Harlow: Longman, 1999).
7. B. Denoyelle, 'Des corps en élections. Au rebours des universaux de la citoyenneté: les premiers votes des femmes (1945–1946)', *Genèses* 31 (June 1998), pp. 76–98; J. Tumblety, 'Responses to women's enfranchisement in France, 1944–45', *Women's Studies International Forum* 26.5 (2003), pp. 483–97.

8. See for example, D. Loiseau, *Femmes et militantismes* (Paris: l'Harmattan, 1996); S. Chaperon, *Les années Beauvoir 1945–1970* (Paris: Fayard, 2000).

9. Pascal, J., *Les Femmes députés de 1945 à 1988* (Paris: Jean Pascal, 1990).

10. W. Guéraiche, *Les Femmes et la République* (Paris: Editions de l'Atelier, 1999), p. 8.

11. Guéraiche, *Les Femmes*, p. 260.

12. See my own failure to differentiate them in H. Footitt, 'The first women députés: "les 33 glorieuses"?' in H.R. Kedward and N. Wood (eds) *The Liberation of France. Image and Event* (Oxford: Berg, 1995), pp. 129–41.

13. J. Lovenduski, *Feminizing Politics* (Cambridge: Polity, 2005), p. 10.

14. S. Childs, *New Labour's Women MPs: Women Representing Women* (London: Routledge, 2004), p. 197.

15. For a discussion of 'substantive representation', see for example A. Phillips, *The Politics of Presence* (Oxford: Clarendon Press, 1995).

16. *Journal Officiel de la République Française* (hereafter *JO*), 16 May 1945, p. 1050.

17. D. Breton (ed.), *Les Femmes dans la Résistance* (Monaco: Editions du Rocher 1977), p. 34.

18. For these details, see J. Maitron and C. Pennetier (eds), *Dictionnaire biographique du mouvement ouvrier, 1914–1939*, Vol. xx (Paris: Éditions Ouvrières, 1983), p. 227.

19. For details, see *Dictionnaire biographique*, pp. 207–8. Also J-M. Binot, D. Lefebvre, and P. Serne, *100 ans. 100 socialistes* (Paris: Éditions Leprince, 2005), pp. 102–3.

20. Binot et al., *100 ans*, p. 103; recorded in L. Rossignol, 'Centenaire du parti socialiste: où sont les femmes?' *Sisyphe* 13 May 2005, http://sisyphe.org.

21. For details, see J. Pascal, *Les Femmes députés*, pp. 226–7.

22. J.-F. de Richecour, 'Marie-Hélène Lefaucheux. Résistante et apôtre de la promotion féminine', *Lunes* 6 (January 1999), pp. 46–53.

23. *JO*, 22 March 1945, p. 666; 23 March 1945, p. 693.

24. *JO*, 9 March 1954, p. 218.

25. *JO*, 7 July 1955, p. 657; 19 February 1953, p. 243.

26. *JO*, 30 October 1956, p. 943.

27. *JO*, 26 June 1956, pp. 613–4.

28. *JO*, 29 December 1950, p. 1636.

29. Conseil National des Femmes Françaises, *Marie-Hélène Lefaucheux* (Paris: CEDIAS, 1964).

30. *Le Monde*, 24 January 1980.

31. Breton, *Les Femmes*, p. 34.

32. *Time*, 29 January 1945.

33. A. Kriegel, *Les communistes français dans leur premier demi-siècle, 1920–1970* (Paris: Le Seuil, 1985), p. 79.

34. Madeleine Braun file, unattributed press clipping, 23 November 1945, Bibliothèque Durand, Paris.

35. *Front National*, 24 April 1946.

36. Comments at a Front National/MUR rally, 29 April 1946, reported in *Front National*, 30 April 1946.

37. *JO*, 9 July 1949, p. 4502.

38. Guéraiche, *Les Femmes*, p. 132.

39. *JO*, 28 December 1945, p. 480.

40. *JO*, 30 July 1946, p. 2853.

41. H.R. Kedward, *La vie en bleu: France and the French since 1900* (London: Penguin, 2005), p. 354.

42. *JO*, 17 February 1948, p. 805.

43. *JO*, 28 October 1955, p. 5352.
44. *JO*, 6 April 1954, p. 1782.
45. *JO*, 26 June 1956, p. 3072.
46. *JO*, 13 February 1957, p. 834.
47. United Nations E/CN.SR.361, Commission on the status of women, 19 March 1962.
48. Ibid.
49. International Council of Women, *Women in a Changing World. The Dynamic Story of the International Council of Women since 1888* (London: Routledge and Kegan Paul, 1966), p. 244.
50. Ibid., p. 109.
51. Conseil National des Femmes Françaises, *Lefaucheux*, p. 12.
52. *JO*, 13 March 1946; 10 July 1947; 27 January 1949.
53. R.L. Ramsay, *French Women in Politics. Writing Power, Paternal Legitimization, and Maternal Legacies* (New York/Oxford: Berghahn, 2003).
54. Guéraiche, *Les Femmes*, p. 107.
55. G. Morin, 'Espace et réseaux socialistes après la Libération' in S. Berstein, F. Cépède, G. Morin and A. Prost (eds), *Le Parti socialiste entre Résistance et République* (Paris: Publications de la Sorbonne, 2000), pp. 307–23.
56. J. Scott, *Gender and the Politics of History* (New York: Columbia University Press, 1988), pp. 2–3.

Bibliography

Binot, J.-M., Lefebvre, D., and Serne, P., *100 ans. 100 socialistes* (Paris: Éditions Leprince, 2005).
Breton, D. (ed.), *Les Femmes dans la Résistance* (Monaco: Editions du Rocher, 1977).
Chaperon, S., *Les années Beauvoir 1945–1970* (Paris: Fayard, 2000).
Childs, S., *New Labour's Women MPs: Women Representing Women* (London: Routledge, 2004).
Conseil National des Femmes Françaises, *Marie-Hélène Lefaucheux* (Paris: CEDIAS, 1964).
de Richecour, J.-F., 'Marie-Hélène Lefaucheux. Résistante et apôtre de la promotion féminine', *Lunes* 6 (January 1999), pp. 46–53.
Denoyelle, B., 'Des corps en élections. Au rebours des universaux de la citoyenneté: les premiers votes des femmes (1945–1946)', *Genèses* 31 (June 1998), pp. 76–98.
Diamond, H., 'Gaining the vote – a liberating experience?' *Modern and Contemporary France*, 3.2 (1995), pp. 129–39.
Diamond, H., *Women and the Second World War in France, 1939–48: Choices and Constraints* (Harlow: Longman, 1999).
Duchen, C., *Women's Rights and Women's Lives in France 1944–1968* (London: Routledge, 1994).
Duchen, C., 'Une femme nouvelle pour une France nouvelle?' *Clio* 1 (1995), pp. 151–64.
Duchen, C., and Brandhauer-Schoffmann, I. (eds), *When the War was Over. Women, War and Peace in Europe, 1940–1956* (London: Leicester University Press, 2000).
Footitt, H., 'The first women députés: "les 33 glorieuses"?' in H.R. Kedward and N. Wood (eds), *The Liberation of France: Image and Event* (Oxford: Berg, 1995), pp. 129–41.
Guéraiche, W., *Les Femmes et la République* (Paris: Editions de l'Atelier, 1999).
Higonnet, M.R., and Jenson, J., *Behind the Lines. Gender and the Two World Wars* (New Haven: Yale University Press, 1987).

International Council of Women, *Women in a Changing World. The Dynamic Story of the International Council of Women since 1888* (London: Routledge and Kegan Paul, 1966).

Kedward, H.R., *La vie en bleu: France and the French since 1900* (London: Penguin, 2005).

Kriegel, A., *Les communistes français dans leur premier demi-siècle, 1920–1970* (Paris: Le Seuil, 1985).

Loiseau, D., *Femmes et militantismes* (Paris: l'Harmattan, 1996).

Lovenduski, J., *Feminizing Politics* (Cambridge: Polity, 2005).

Madeleine Braun file, unattributed press clipping, 23 November 1945, Bibliothèque Durand, Paris.

Maitron, J. and Pennetier, C. (eds), *Dictionnaire biographique du mouvement ouvrier français, 1914–1939*, Vols. xx, xxiv (Paris: Éditions Ouvrières, 1983).

Morin, G., 'Espace et réseaux socialistes après la Libération' in S. Berstein, F. Cépède, G. Morin, and A. Prost (eds), *Le Parti socialiste entre Résistance et République* (Paris: Publications de la Sorbonne, 2000), pp. 307–23.

Pascal, J., *Les Femmes députés de 1945 à 1988* (Paris: Jean Pascal, 1990).

Phillips, A., *The Politics of Presence* (Oxford: Clarendon Press, 1995).

Ramsay, R.L., *French Women in Politics. Writing Power, Paternal Legitimization, and Maternal Legacies* (New York/Oxford: Berghahn, 2003).

Reynolds, S., 'Marianne's citizens? Women, the Republic and universal suffrage in France' in S. Reynolds (ed.), *Women, State and Revolution* (Brighton: Wheatsheaf books, 1986), pp. 101–22.

Reynolds, S., 'Women and the Popular Front in France: the case of the three women ministers', *French History* 8.2 (June 1994), pp. 196–224.

Rioux, J.-P., *La France de la IVe République*, Vol. i (Paris: Le Seuil, 1980).

Rossignol, L., 'Centenaire du parti socialiste: où sont les femmes?' *Sisyphe* 13 May 2005, http://sisyphe.org.

Salvaresi, E., *Mai en heritage* (Paris: Syros, 1988).

Scott, J., *Gender and the Politics of History* (New York: Columbia University Press, 1988).

Tumblety, J., 'Responses to women's enfranchisement in France, 1944–45', *Women's Studies International Forum* 26.5 (2003), pp. 483–97.

7
France's Liberation Era, 1944–47: a Social and Economic Settlement?

Herrick Chapman

In popular memory and in textbooks, the Liberation (1944–47) was a founding moment for France's economy and social order. The first post-war governments launched a nationwide social security system and nationalised utilities, transport, and financial and industrial firms. Economic modernisation was driven by Monnet-style planning and by high-powered civil servants from the new École Nationale d'Administration, assisted by new tools such as INSEE (the national statistical institute) and INED (the demographic institute). To this list could be added economic and social democratisation. Article 1 of the Constitution of the Fourth Republic declared that 'the law guarantees to women equal rights to men in all domains'. Articles 22 to 39 proclaimed a range of new rights, including a worker's right to strike and to join (or not join) a union (Article 30), and even to 'participate, though the intermediary of his delegates, in the collective determination of working conditions and the management of enterprises' (Article 31); this last provision found practical expression in the establishment of *comités d'entreprise* in large and medium-sized firms. Contemporary protagonists from the Communists to de Gaulle viewed this as an era of bold beginnings. Even 40 years later, as governments began to sell off nationalised firms or struggled to bring social security costs under control, the image of the Liberation as a founding moment was shared both by neo-liberals who sought to reform or dismantle the post-1944 settlement and by those on the Left who struggled to preserve it.

Recent historians have been more cautious in their assessment. As in Germany, 1945 in France no longer looks like 'Year Zero'. Looking back, we can see how many of the ideas of the Liberation period (not to mention the men and women, given how many of France's business and administrative élites survived the purges) had roots in the First World War, in Léon Blum's Popular Front government of 1936–37, in Édouard Daladier's government of wartime mobilisation in 1939–40, and even in Vichy, a period no longer regarded by historians as altogether a 'parenthesis' in French history.[1] Looking forward, it can be questioned how successfully Liberation France founded a long post-war consensus on the British, West German, or American models, under which most workers won job security, social benefits, and rising living standards in return for rising productivity; the massive strikes of May 1968 testify to a continuing sense of exclusion.[2] Even concentrating on the 1944–47 period itself, it is not obvious how much the Liberation settlement settled. In particular, the tension between two central ambitions of the Resistance – economic modernisation and democratisation – found its way into France's new institutions: nationalised industries, the Commissariat au Plan, the *comités d'entreprise*, the social security apparatus. The drive to modernise invited a stronger role for experts; but many in the Resistance mistrusted technocrats for the part they had played under Vichy and feared that their empowerment would be at the expense of interest groups, legislators, and ordinary citizens.[3] If the Liberation period was a watershed, did it heighten or diminish this underlying tension? This chapter's exploration of these questions will focus on nationalisations and social security, viewed in contemporary debates, and in those of the 1980s and since, as the most contentious and far-reaching break-throughs of the Liberation era.

Nationalisation as continuity and rupture

Compared with the relatively steady pace of British post-war nationalisations under Attlee, the French process was disorderly and politicised. Each nation-alisation was undertaken by a distinct coalition of forces in a particular context. What emerged was a patchwork of public enterprises, each unique in structure, governance, company culture, and relationship to the market.[4]

Historians view the process as falling into three phases. The initial, 'insur-rectionary' wave, during which de Gaulle's provisional government used decree powers to take over Renault, Gnôme et Rhône and the Nord and Pas-de-Calais coalfields, was most directly linked to France's liberation from Germany and Vichy. Renault and Gnôme et Rhône were expropriated as punishment for collaboration, having built, respectively, vehicles and aircraft engines for the Germans. Louis Renault's convenient death in prison awaiting trial facilitated the confiscation of his firm, whose giant Boulogne–Billancourt plant had become a bastion of the Communist-led union, the Confédération Générale du Travail (CGT), in the 1930s. Renault's aero engine division was combined with Gnôme et Rhône to become SNECMA. The takeover of the northern coalfields, meanwhile, had been started on (and under) the ground by miners, who insisted on nationalisation and the removal of their collaborationist employers as a condition for extracting the coal now desperately needed to fuel war pro-duction and then recovery.

The second wave required far more planning and deliberation: more firms were involved, and the election of the first Constituent Assembly meant that it was parliamentary legislation, not decrees, that gave the takeovers force of law. The four biggest deposit banks were nationalised in December 1945, fol-lowed in spring 1946 by gas and electricity (eventually creating GDF and

EDF respectively), coal mining nationwide (producing the Charbonnages de France) and thirty-four of the largest insurance companies. The third wave, undertaken in 1948, after a two-year hiatus, by the moderate MRP-led government of Robert Schuman, was a pale reflection of the others. The state took majority shareholdings in Air France and two major maritime transport firms; the only full nationalisation converted the Paris public transport system into the RATP.

Continuities

France's post-war nationalisations had a pedigree. Nationalisation had been debated since the late nineteenth century, cautiously undertaken under the Popular Front, and accepted under Vichy. It was the very diversity of this experience that shaped the variegated fabric of what became France's public sector. Nationalisations had been central to the CGT's programme since 1919; the notion that key industries should be expropriated from the 'trusts' and put to work for the nation had been popular in left-wing circles for a generation before that.[5] Drawing on experience with state regulation and works committees during World War I, CGT moderates like Léon Jouhaux advocated nationalisations as a way to bring dynamism and rationality to the economy and democracy to the workplace. By contrast, almost no-one wanted firms to be *étatisés*, submitted to tight state control. To avoid that, Jouhaux proposed running nationalised firms through tripartite boards representing employees, consumers, and the state – a standard structure in enterprises nationalised at the Liberation. By the 1930s, 'planiste' Socialists like André Philip and Jules Moch joined forces with CGT leaders, linking nationalisations to economic planning – another key Liberation theme. Their wide-ranging ambitions featured in the Socialists' programme for the 1936 elections, but were reined in by the caution of their Communist and Radical coalition partners; only armaments and aircraft were nationalised by the Popular Front governments, with railways being amalgamated into a mixed company, the SNCF, in 1937.

Even this limited experience invited diverse, even contradictory, lessons. The record of the SNCF was anything but revolutionary, and so reassured the Right. That of the aircraft industry, by contrast, spearheaded by the (left-leaning) Radical Air Minister Pierre Cot, electrified the Left and the labour movement with new ideas about power distribution within the sector, from national co-ordinating committees to boardrooms to the factory floor. This experience, though cut short under the far more right-wing Daladier premiership after 1938, convinced many on the Left that nationalisation could both reinvigorate a stagnant industry and transform the structure of workplace authority. Even the Communists began to rethink their longstanding dogma that nationalisation was a mere palliative for capitalism.[6]

Fascination with these possibilities intensified during the war years. Though Vichy undertook no new nationalisations, it undid no existing ones. Nationalised firms offered welcome opportunities for control to technocrats like

Jean Bichelonne at the new Ministry of Industrial Production; meanwhile, the banking law of 1941 reinforced the state's control over credit and curbed bank independence in ways that were arguably more important than the nationalisations of December 1945. But it was the Resistance that made the running in its ambitions for nationalisations, which became a priority for post-war planning groups of every stripe. André Philip and the Socialists built on the CGT's inter-war agenda, calling for nationalisations in transport, banks and insurance, mines and electricity to serve national economic planning needs.[7] The much more moderate Comité Général d'Études, which had de Gaulle's backing, condemned the power of economic 'feudalities' and called for nationalisations in branches controlled by monopolies so as to prevent the renaissance of 'trusts'.[8] The charter of the Conseil National de la Résistance (CNR), which brought these diverse threads together in March 1944, avoided the politically loaded term 'nationalisation'; but the call to 'return to the nation the major means of production, the fruit of our common labour, the sources of energy, the riches underground, the insurance companies and big banks' left little doubt as to its ambitions.[9]

In that light it is plausible to argue that in this domain the Fourth Republic began in 1936 – especially with men of the Popular Front era like the Socialists André Philip and Jules Moch, or the modernising Radical Pierre Mendès-France proposing plans for de Gaulle's post-war provisional government. But it would be wrong to make too much of these continuities. The nationalisations of the Liberation marked a critical rupture. And, crucially, neither the Popular Front nor CNR Charter made them 'inevitable'. Rather, they were forged in the volatile, unpredictable balance of political forces of 1944–6.

Ruptures

The Resistance consensus for nationalisations, though real, was limited and ambiguous. Communist leaders had not quite dropped their old reservations. The Christian Democratic MRP (Mouvement Républicain Populaire), though favourable at the top (its leader Georges Bidault had headed the CNR in 1943–44) was divided at the grass roots. Conservatives like Joseph Laniel or Louis Marin had endorsed the Charter for the sake of Resistance unity, not from conviction; their future attitude remained uncertain.[10] De Gaulle's wartime pronouncements, meanwhile, had been more sympathetic than precise. 'No monopoly', he had said in a 1942 speech on the 'new democracy' to come with liberation, 'will be able to abuse men or erect barriers to the general interest.' A few months later he described a new 'economic and social régime where no monopoly or coalition can impinge on the state, nor determine the fate of individuals, and where, as a consequence, the principal sources of our common wealth will be either explicitly administered or at least overseen by the nation'.[11]

The consensus that existed was prey to ambiguities that intensified after August 1944. That pre-war French business had failed the country, many believed, even within Vichy; that private firms had done well out of collaboration, few doubted. The rhetoric of the general interest and the Republic had never been absent from the pre-war debates; now nationalisation could be viewed as a patriotic act, the logical consequence of purging traitors and 'liquidating the trusts'.[12] But how far rhetoric would be translated into a real challenge to big business, as a Liberation government faced the challenges of prosecuting the war alongside the Allies and reconstructing the country, was uncertain. Nor was it clear whether any firms that were nationalised would follow the anodyne SNCF model or open up more radical perspectives, with workplace power-sharing locally and co-ordinated investments nationally. On the eve of the Liberation, then, almost everything about a post-war nationalisation drive – its reach, its timing, its implications for French capitalism and workers' power – remained uncertain.

By late summer 1944, with four-fifths of France liberated, two countervailing forces came into play that would shape the first two waves of nationalisation. The first developed locally. As the Germans left, workers, especially in the south and the northeast, occupied mines, factories and office buildings, established management committees, and often either seized their collaborationist employers or made them flee. CGT activists, with the moral authority of their Resistance record, often led this effort to extend the political spirit of the Liberation right into the workplace. In the mines of the North, as we have seen, 'wildcat' nationalisations were confirmed willy-nilly by de Gaulle's government within weeks. In Marseille, de Gaulle's *Commissaire de la République* was forced to requisition fifteen companies under pressure from their workers; his counterpart in Toulouse had to guarantee workers in aircraft and other industries a role in management committees. Despite the insurrectionary tone of these events, local labour militants saw them as an affirmation of state authority 'from below', a grass-roots counterpart to the hoped-for expansion of the state into France's economy. They also raised expectations that future nationalisations would reinforce workers' power in the workplace.[13] By the end of 1944 the Parti Communiste Français (PCF), catching up with its own activists, had dropped its inhibitions and signed up to the CNR agenda.

A sea change in public sentiment backed the militants' acts. An IFOP poll in October 1944 revealed that 65 per cent of respondents, and 79 per cent among workers, supported workers' participation in the management of their firms; in November, 60 per cent favoured nationalising the mines; in December 68 per cent of Parisians wanted the capital's gas service publicly owned.[14] It is hard to say whether such figures reflected disillusionment with private enterprise, or a desire to punish the 'trusts' and renew the nation's economy, or to relieve anger at rare power supplies going to companies that had collaborated while the public faced blackouts.[15] That such an establishment figure as Pierre Lefaucheux, engineer and company director in the pre-war private sector, could refer to 'the bankruptcy of capitalism' that had become apparent when 'a whole fraction of the *patronat* rushed into collaboration' in 1940 indicates how far the new thinking had spread.[16] Whatever the underlying sentiments, then, IFOP's figures showed a far wider readiness than in the Popular Front era to see the public sector sharply expanded. That was reflected at the ballot-box too; the narrow Communist-Socialist majority in the Constituent Assembly of October 1945 provided the impetus for the second wave of nationalisations.

Within government, however, pressures of a second kind worked to cool the political temperature. De Gaulle sought delay, announcing that any nationalisations beyond the first, strictly punitive, wave would have to await the end of the war and the legitimation of universal suffrage. Big business, albeit much weakened, quietly counselled moderation and probably saved steel for private ownership by doing so.[17] Within the Provisional Government a battle pitted the liberal Finance Minister, businessman René Pleven, who doubted the wisdom of nationalisations, against Mendès-France, who as Minister of National Economy wanted banks, insurance, energy, machine tools, transport, and steel in public ownership, a strong economic planning bureau in his own ministry, and a tough anti-inflation policy. Only with nationalisations, he believed, would workers accept the austerity needed for a reconstruction effort that favoured investment over consumption.[18] Mendès lost the crucial monetary policy debate and resigned; de Gaulle, siding with Pleven, opted for (somewhat) fewer nationalisations, a weaker planning authority, and the politically easier path of continued inflation.

The second wave, then, fell short of what Mendès, the most ardent *dirigiste* Socialists, and the PCF wanted; the December 1945 bank nationalisation law, for example, reflected de Gaulle's refusal to bring investment banks into public ownership. But the programme still went further than Pleven and many top Finance Ministry officials had wished. This was largely thanks to the window of opportunity opened by the election of a left-wing majority in October 1945. In Spring 1946, with de Gaulle now out of office, bills nationalising energy and insurance were designed by the Communist Minister for Industrial Production, Marcel Paul, and passed after strident National Assembly debates on owners' compensation and on the balance between centralised administration and regional autonomy in the new national energy firms.

Then the window closed. It was not just that the June 1946 elections ended the overall Socialist-Communist majority and gave an (ephemeral) electoral lead to the more cautious MRP. Socialist leaders also started worrying about the growth of PCF influence, via CGT militants, within the new public sector. Nearly a year before the Communists' forced exit from office in May 1947, the constellation of forces behind the first two waves of nationalisation – grass-roots activism, popular enthusiasm, and a committed coalition of Communist and Socialist leaders with enough MRP allies to go along – was beginning to disintegrate.

Nationalisations from the inside

The CGT's ascendancy in newly-nationalised industries was part of a more complex, but wide-ranging, transformation. Air Minister Charles Tillon, a hero of the Communist armed Resistance, appointed aircraft company heads with Resistance records, ready to co-operate with CGT activists on the new tripartite boards. Marcel Paul appointed Auguste Lecœur, a Communist miner who had led a legendary coal strike in 1941, to run the new coal authority. At EDF–GDF, Renault, and the SNCF none of the new appointees, Pierre Simon, Pierre Lefaucheux, and Louis Armand respectively, were Communists;[19] all, though, were well regarded by the CGT, which quickly took an extremely high profile, with positions on tripartite boards representing not only employees but often consumers as well. The *comités d'entreprise* now required in all large firms gave union representatives authority over company benefit programmes, cafeterias, holiday camps, and social, medical and recreational services, all either instruments of paternalism or non-existent in the private-sector past. In aviation, Renault, and EDF–GDF, the CGT also acquired power through new mixed production committees, made up equally of workers and managers, set up to recommend improvements in production methods and working conditions.[20]

This organisational revolution gave unprecedented legitimacy to the trade union movement. Militants saw it as a breakthrough for the CNR Charter's vision of 'true economic and social democracy'.[21] In these early days technicians and engineers, as well as workers, at Renault, EDF–GDF, SNECMA, SNCF, or the Charbonnages, embraced the new régime and even the CGT as the chief midwife of employee power; white-collar staff saw new opportunities for meritocratic advancement.[22] Perhaps nothing signified the triumph over traditional management methods better than the labour statute Marcel Paul established by *ordonnance* for employees at EDF. It locked in pension provisions, vacation rights, paid leave for family emergencies and, most importantly, codetermination committees to deal with hiring, promotion, discipline and job descriptions. Never before had transparency in industrial management, and workers' right to have a say, been thus enshrined in law.

Proposed by the CGT in 1919, experimented in the Popular Front, popularised by the desire to punish *les patrons collaborateurs*, the real political work of taking over firms and changing power structures within them still demanded more than mere historical momentum. These transformations took place in a new, volatile political environment that gave the Left and the unions an unprecedented opportunity to reshape France's business landscape. Nationalisers, in the Constituent Assembly, in Marcel Paul's ministry, or at plant level, drew on continuity and rupture in equal measure.

Settlement or battleground?

How durable was the settlement? The Liberation years saw relative industrial peace in France, with low strike rates and rapidly rising productivity. In the short term, institutional gains helped compensate for low living standards. The Communists, anxious to establish their credentials as a responsible party of government, helped too. On May Day 1947, the PCF leader Thorez was still haranguing the Party faithful about the need for discipline to win the 'battle of production'. Four days later he was out of office, victim of a (Trotskyist-inspired) strike at Renault which had forced the PCF to turn against the government's policy of wage restraint and in turn given the Socialist Prime Minister Ramadier the chance to dismiss his Communist ministers. In September, the Szklarska Poreba conference enforced a new line for Western Communist parties: now encouraged by their Soviet masters to oppose 'bourgeois' governments by all possible means, the PCF leadership moved from restraining working-class demands to promoting them, and backing that autumn's fierce strike wave, causing the CGT to split in the process.

These events opened a battle for control of France's nationalised industries, giving 1947 every appearance of Thermidor. The Socialists, along with their MRP and Radical allies, used their ministerial power to replace company heads who had shown excessive sympathy for the CGT. New directors then reshuffled staff and cut CGT representation on tripartite boards, which themselves were marginalised as decision-making moved upwards into the director's office and the ministries. In coal, these changes provoked a protracted battle over rationalisation, wage rates, and the power of production committees, culminating (after troops and armoured cars had been sent into the coalfields) in the miners' great strike defeat of 1948. The post-1947 aircraft industry saw a new management cut the workforce by half. Anti-Communist purges became routine and erstwhile allies of the Liberation era found themselves on opposite sides. Meanwhile labour's new-won authority at the workplace was sharply curtailed; Lefaucheux liquidated Renault's production committees in 1948, while personnel boards at EDF were transformed from decision-making to consultative bodies.[23] Industrial democracy, indeed, was the main casualty of the post-1947 reaction.[24] By the 1950s, company heads had become mainly responsible for technical operations and industrial relations; investment planning and project development moved into the ministries (Renault being an exception in this respect); state auditors further enhanced ministerial authority; and the representative bodies of the Liberation era were increasingly by-passed.

What did *not* happen was a wholesale roll-back of the transformations of 1944–47. The consensus in favour of nationalisations, though battered by a handful of Senate conservatives and parts of the Conseil National du Patronat Français (CNPF), the major employers' organisation, survived into the 1950s, for several reasons. Communist and CGT power in the public sector, though not broken, had been curbed. No one outside the PCF was demanding *new* nationalisations. The Charbonnages, EDF–GDF, and the SNCF contributed to private-sector growth with cheap energy and transport. Private businessmen sat on boards of nationalised firms. The CNPF's reconciliation to nationalisations was reflected in their near-absence from the 1951 parliamentary election campaign.[25]

What also survived, albeit in modified form, was the CGT's presence in the public sector and the relatively good conditions enjoyed by workers there. True, the CGT had lost ground when Force Ouvrière split after the strikes of 1947, and lost more when many engineers and technicians switched to the more conservative Confédération Générale des Cadres in the 1950s. But it held its own against rivals (FO and the Catholic Confédération Française des Travailleurs Chrétiens) in nationalised industries, thanks to its long history of organisation in these firms, its strong links to Communist municipalities, and its support in networks of left-wing economists, academics and journalists. Not surprisingly, the PCF learned to love nationalised industries, and for a generation was the only party to want more. Meanwhile the desire of governments for social peace in firms strategic for the post-war recovery helped ensure that wages, pension rights, the unions' advisory role, and subsidies to *comités d'entreprise* and their social services tended to be better in the public than in the private sector.

Altogether more variable was the pattern of industrial relations. In the nationalised banks, they resembled the 1930s; labour relations remained paternalistic and management even stuck to traditional short-term lending practices, leaving government to finance post-war modernisation from elsewhere.[26] At EDF, by contrast, labour relations survived the conflicts of 1947 well: modernisation, the shift towards nuclear power, and a new focus on consumer services from the early 1960s all benefited from a joint commitment from CGT, engineers and management.[27] The model of the Charbonnages was altogether more confrontational. Industrial relations remained stormy after the post-1948 witch-hunt and decision-making was centralised in the Industry and Finance ministries, all against a background of the sector's steady decline. At Renault, finally, and for several firms in the aircraft industry, commercial success (with the Renault 4CV, and the Caravelle jetliner) associated nationalisation with modernisation, as at EDF, and in the case of Renault brought a unique degree of independence from government. With a strong CGT, an unsettled pattern of labour relations, but also a common willingness to embrace technology and to compromise through collective bargaining, these sectors were bellwethers for nationalised industry as a whole. Renault workers were France's first, in 1955, to win a third week of paid holiday; within a year the Mollet government had generalised this gain throughout French industry.

By the 1950s the public sector had become part of France's industrial landscape, the focus neither of romanticised hopes nor of excessive fears – nor blighted, like its British counterpart, by a reputation for low productivity and industrial decline. This 'banalisation' of nationalised industries resulted in part from how they were run: compared with the hopes, fears, and (briefly) practices of the Liberation period, they had not been democratised but subjected to the conventional hierarchies of the *État-patron*. Nevertheless, compared either to the pre-war situation or to the bulk of the post-war private sector, France's nationalised firms remained pace-setters for wages, benefits, and labour relations. That, by and large, satisfied the CGT and by extension the Communists, whose public-sector bastions secured them influence and patronage. It did not satisfy the left-wing Catholics, Socialists, and *gauchistes* who sought to revive industrial democracy in the 1960s.

Social security as continuity and rupture

When Pierre Laroque, de Gaulle's architect for social policy at the Liberation, crafted the ordinances of 4 and 19 October 1945 that created a full-fledged national social security system, he built on pre-1940 foundations. The 1928 and 1930 social insurance laws had already brought millions of French employees into a Bismarckian-style system for medical insurance and old-age pensions based on payroll taxes. Likewise, the Family Code of 1939 had catapulted France into the forefront of European pronatalist policy with an ambitious programme of family allowances (child benefits).[28] But French social protection was still woefully inadequate. Too many people remained uninsured, and health coverage and pensions were often paltry.[29] A big expansion of social protection therefore found a place on the post-war agenda of the Resistance, though far below nationalisations and workplace democracy. The main impetus for social security reform came from experts like de Gaulle's first labour minister Alexandre Parodi and the latter's protégé, Laroque, who drew inspiration from British and American models.[30] Laroque especially admired William Beveridge's post-war plans for Britain, a universal system of social welfare financed by the state through general revenues and capitalised funds. But he knew the French state was much too poor to attempt it. He chose instead to aim for Beveridge's universalistic goals by expanding and rationalising France's Bismarckian contributions-based social insurance system, hitherto corseted by the hidebound conservatism of big business and private insurers.[31]

The Left's predominance in 1945 made Laroque's reforms possible, especially because the Communists overcame their interwar contempt for social insurance and threw their weight behind the project. Laroque's *ordonnances* fused together into a single national fund, or *régime general*, what had been separate insurance programmes for death, disability, old age, health, work injuries, maternity and family allowances. Payroll taxes doubled. Employees now would contribute 6 per cent of their salaries, matched by 10 per cent from employers, with the latter also paying an additional 14 per cent to fund family allowances. Wage ceilings on eligibility disappeared, and workers acquired the right to medical benefits after only 60 hours in a job. As a result, the social insurance system became available to 20 million employees by the late 1940s, up from 7 million in 1944.[32]

Governance also changed dramatically. In keeping with a long tradition of self-governing funds and an abhorrence of 'étatisation', Laroque organised the *régime general* into some 250 local and regional *caisses* (fund bureaus) for social security and family allowances, each with a governing board. In social security *caisses*, three-quarters of the board members were to represent beneficiaries, and the rest employers; in family allowance *caisse* boards the two sides had parity. The plan at first was to have the government appoint beneficiary members from the 'most representative union,' which meant the CGT in most areas outside Alsace and Lorraine. But the CFTC and MRP fought successfully to make the board seats elected. Even so, in the first social security elections of 1947, the CGT won nearly 60 per cent of the votes and a majority of seats in 90 per cent of the *caisses*.[33] The social security system therefore represented an impressive expansion of democratic participation and just the kind of venue for CGT influence that the Communists had hoped for. What was more, on the initiative of the CGT, a Féderation Nationale des Organismes de la Sécurité Sociale (FNOSS) was established in 1946 to represent the many local and regional *caisses*. This body, too, became a site of CGT hegemony and a key authority in negotiating fees with doctors and in hiring and firing personnel in the *caisses*.[34]

Once pressure-group politics took hold, however, Laroque's efforts to bring the entire country into the *régime general* faltered. For one thing, the MRP, CFTC, Ministry of Population, and mutual aid societies fought successfully to preserve the separate status of the family allowance *caisses*, which in turn made it easier for employers, Catholics, the family lobby, and the natalists to check the influence of Communists and feminists in family policy.[35] For another, once the élan and unity of the Liberation lost its force in 1947, several key occupational groups of the self-employed – farmers, artisans and shopkeepers, liberal professionals and *cadres* (managers) – won the right to maintain their own respective insurance funds, especially for pensions. Fund autonomy was not just a matter of occupational identity; these hold-out groups believed autonomy would shield them from financing the benefits of less well-off workers. As a further blow to Laroque's design, several better-paid salaried groups – workers in mining, railways, gas and electricity, and merchant seamen – secured the survival of their separate funds. Doctors also got what they wanted: the preservation of a liberal regime (as opposed to a British-style national health system), giving patients the freedom to choose their doctors. Doctors became obliged to negotiate maximum fees with the *caisses* and the state, but until 1960 the latter lacked the capacity to enforce agreements effectively.

Social security as settlement and battleground

What emerged by 1950, then, was a compromise. Laroque's new *régime general* expanded and democratised social security to an extraordinary degree, but the system remained a mosaic of public and private funds and family policy a largely conservative preserve. This baroque structure, plus the other main attributes of the system – payroll taxes, liberal medicine, and a huge commitment to family allowances – became settled terrain by the 1950s.[36] In the Liberation era, moreover, a solidaristic ethos began to take hold, shared by Gaullists and Communists alike, that affirmed as a matter of patriotic principle the right of every citizen to social insurance and roughly equal social services.[37]

Yet if the institutional forms and governing assumptions of social security won widespread acceptance, fierce partisan conflict *within* the system endured. When Cold War politics broke apart France's governing left-wing coalition in 1947 and the anti-communist FO split off from the CGT, the FNOSS and the many governing boards of the local and regional social security *caisses* became battlegrounds. Communists saw their dominance in these bodies diminish in the face of competition from their FO and CFTC rivals. In 1950 the vote for CGT delegates to the social security *caisses* fell to 43.5 per cent.[38] Local social security and family allowance elections would thereafter remain critical contests for patronage and symbolic power in the labor movement. When Ambroise Croizat, the Communist successor to Parodi as Labour Minister, left the government in 1947, the CGT watched its influence erode in the social service administration as CFTC and FO militants found new ministerial allies. In 1949 the Communist Henri Reynaud resigned as the president of the FNOSS, and the CGT assumed a more oppositional role in what had become a crucial institution in the social security system.[39]

As in the nationalised sector, the state administration in the new Social Security system also countered CGT influence (and the inefficiencies of the highly decentralised network of *caisses*) by expanding its bureaucratic authority.[40] From the late 1940s on, Labour and Finance ministry officials demanded administrative approval of local board decisions and enhanced the role of the Cour des Comptes, the powerful state auditing authority, over the *caisses*.[41] De Gaulle would extend this process further under the Fifth Republic. Reform decrees in 1960 reduced the power of local boards over personnel decisions, eradicated the FNOSS's hiring and firing authority, and gave local social service administrators greater autonomy from boards. Decrees in 1967 restructured boards to give employers 50 per cent of the seats, a move much resented by workers that helped pack the powder that exploded in May '68.[42]

Conclusion

The nationalisations and social security reform proceeded through the same great arch of innovation, Cold War crisis, and conservative recalibration. A temporary eclipse of employer power and right-wing parties at the Liberation made reform possible. A fractious post-Resistance coalition of opposites shared enough of a common stake in economic renovation and a restoration of France's international standing to implement much of the CNR agenda. Cold-war division then ushered in a protracted battle for political predominance within nationalised firms, the social security boards, and the economic ministries. What emerged by the early 1950s was a both a political settlement over the legitimacy of these new institutional forms and continuing competition over how they would evolve and who would control them. The settlement, paradoxically, owed as much to conflict as consensus, since the efforts at anti-Communist purge gave moderates, big business, and eventually a revived political Right a greater sense of ownership of these new institutions, even though the Left could claim original patrimony.

By the same token, left-wing innovation and conservative recalibration also produced an enduring ambiguity over how nationalisations and social security would be regarded thereafter. The Left, especially Communists, clung to the notion that nationalisations remained a meaningful instrument for challenging capitalism and expanding working-class power – hence their centrality in the Left's Common Programme of the 1970s and the early Mitterrand presidency. The Right, especially Gaullists, regarded state ownership as a practical tool for nationalist industrial policy – hence the intensity of the debates in France over privatisation in the 1980s and the leeriness with which even right-wing governments in recent decades have responded to foreign investment in French firms. In the case of social security, which the CGT liked to regard as a workers' conquest, the politics of anti-Communist purge and the compromises forced upon Laroque's programme made it easier for the Right to embrace the system, and all the more so in the 1960s when self-employed groups found it financially wise to abandon their separatist strategies.[43] When heady post-war growth gave way to long-term crisis and high unemployment after 1974, the weaknesses of an insurance system anchored in the payroll tax became exposed for all to see. But by then the public's investment in the system's benefits and its solidaristic ethos, as well as the trade unions' stake in the governing boards as a *raison d'être*, made it very difficult indeed to emulate the flexibilities of either Scandinavia's progressive social democracy or Britain's neo-liberalism.[44]

What of the promise that nationalisations and social security would democratise France? These reforms, to be sure, did a great deal to integrate the working-class, the CGT, and the Communist party into the Fourth Republic and a modernising economy. Yet two ironies also emerged by the early 1950s. First, the CGT, which after its reunification in 1943 could make a plausible claim in 1945 to represent most blue-collar employees and many white-collar as well and which swept into the participatory apparatus of workplace committees and *caisses* boards accordingly, saw its democratic image badly tarnished by the political poison of the Cold War. Battered by the FO schism and the tightening strictures of the PCF's Stalinist leadership, this erstwhile champion of Liberation-era democracy watched its moral and political capital decline. By 1950 trade union pluralism, though in many ways the bane of the labour movement, became the chief guarantor of participatory democracy in public enterprise and social security. Ironically, too, some of the very groups that worried most about 'étatisation' in nationalised industry and in social security in 1945 – political moderates, business people, Catholics – found themselves, in the interest of checking the Communists, tolerating an expansion of state authority in public enterprise and in the supervision of the *caisses*. The Liberation settlement, then, for all its democratic achievements, played its part in setting the stage for a renewal of conflict over bureaucratic authority, be it Gaullist technocracy or Communist 'bureaucratic centralism', in the 1960s.

Notes

1. Cf. for example, R.F. Kuisel, *Capitalism and the State in Modern France, Renovation and Economic Management in the Twentieth Century* (New York: Cambridge University Press, 1981); A. Shennan, *Rethinking France, Plans for Renewal, 1940–1946* (Oxford: Clarendon Press, 1989); R.O. Paxton, *Vichy France, Old Guard and New Order, 1940–1944* (New York: Knopf, 1972); R. Lenoir, *Généalogie de la morale familiale* (Paris: Le Seuil, 2003); and P. Dutton, *Origins of the French Welfare State: the Struggle for Social Reform in France, 1914–1947* (New York: Cambridge University Press, 2002).
2. P. Fridenson, 'Could Postwar France Become a Middle-Class Society?' in O. Zunz, L. Schoppa, and N. Hiwatari (eds), *Social Contracts Under Stress* (New York: Russell Sage Foundation, 2002), pp. 89–107.
3. A. Williams, 'France and the new world order, 1940–1947,' *Modern and Contemporary France* 8.2 (May 2000), pp. 191–202: p. 196.
4. For descriptions of the several waves of nationalisation, see especially A. Prost, 'Une pièce en trois actes,' in C. Andrieu, L. Le Van, and A. Prost (eds), *Les Nationalisations de la libération, De l'utopie au compromis* (Paris: Presses de la FNSP, 1987), pp. 236–46; and J.-C. Asselain, 'Les nationalisations, 1944–45,' in *Études sur la France de 1939 à nos jours* (Paris: Le Seuil, 1985), pp. 180–207. On the comparison with Britain, see A. Sturmthal, 'The structure of nationalized enterprises in France,' *Political Science Quarterly* 67 (1952), pp. 357–77; A. Sturmthal, 'Nationalization and workers' control in Britain and France,' *Journal of Political Economy* 61.1 (1953), pp. 43–79; and M. Einaudi, M. Byé, and E. Rossi, *Nationalization in France and Italy* (Ithaca: Cornell University Press, 1955), pp. 33–44.
5. D. Holter, 'Mineworkers and nationalization in France, insights in concepts of state theory,' *Politics and Society* 11.1 (1982), pp. 29–49: p. 32.
6. On the aircraft industry, see H. Chapman, *State Capitalism and Working-Class Radicalism in the French Aircraft Industry* (Berkeley: University of California Press, 1991).
7. On Philip's plan, see Kuisel, *Capitalism and the State*, pp. 177–9.
8. R. Courtin, *Rapport sur la politique économique d'après guerre* (Algiers: Éditions 'Combat', 1944), pp. 17, 21.
9. C. Andrieu, 'Comment la nationalisation entra dans le programme du CNR,' in Andrieu et al., *Les Nationalisations de la libération*, pp. 52–61, especially p. 58.
10. Ibid., pp. 59–60.
11. C. Andrieu, 'De Gaulle,' in *Les Nationalisations de la libération*, pp. 230–5, especially p. 233.
12. Andrieu, 'Comment la nationalisation entra dans le programme du CNR', pp. 59–60.
13. See H. Chapman, 'The Liberation as a moment in state-making,' in K. Mouré and M.S. Alexander (eds), *Crisis and Renewal in France, 1918–1962* (New York: Berghahn Books, 2002), pp. 174–98: p. 188.
14. Prost, 'Une pièce en trois actes,' p. 237.
15. H. Morsel, 'Paul Ramadier et l'électricité,' in S. Berstein (ed.) *Paul Ramadier, la République et le Socialisme* (Brussels: Éditions Complexe, 1988), pp. 309–35: p. 327.
16. Quoted in Asselain, 'Les nationalisations', p. 184.

17. P. Fridenson, 'La puissance publique et les nationalisations,' unpublished paper given at the *colloque* of 4 and 5 December 1981 on 'La France en voie de modernisation, 1944–52', Fondation Nationale des Sciences Politiques; J. Bouvier, 'Sur la politique économique en 1944–1946,' in *La Libération de la France*, Actes du Colloque International tenu à Paris du 28 au 31 octobre 1974 (Paris: Édition du CNRS, 1976).
18. Shennan, *Rethinking France*, p. 244.
19. For aircraft, see Chapman, *State Capitalism*; for coal see D. Holter, *The Battle for Coal, Miners and the Politics of Nationalization in France, 1940–50* (DeKalb: Northern Illinois University Press, 1992); for EDF see R.L. Frost, *Alternating Currents, Nationalized Power in France, 1946–1970* (Ithaca: Cornell University Press, 1991).
20. Frost, *Alternating Currents*, p. 72.
21. C. Andrieu, *Le Programme commun de la résistance, Des idées dans la guerre* (Paris: Les Éditions de l'Érudit, 1984), p. 173. On workers' participation in management in this period, see also A. Steinhouse, *Workers' Participation in Post-Liberation France* (Lanham, MD: Lexington Books, 2001).
22. Fridenson, 'La puissance publique'; Fridenson, 'Renault,' in *Les Nationalisations de la liberation*, pp. 279–93, especially pp. 292–3; F. Bloch-Lainé and J. Bouvier, *La France restaurée, 1944–1954, Dialogue sur les choix d'une modernisation* (Paris: Fayard, 1986), p. 116.
23. C. Andrieu, L. Le Van, and A. Prost, 'Des nationalisations de 1946 à celles de 1981,' in *Les Nationalisations de la libération*, pp. 359–74, especially p. 363.
24. On shared power as a basis for post-war settlement see I. Wall, 'The French social contract: conflict and cooperation,' *International Labor and Working-Class History* 50 (Fall 1996), pp. 116–24, especially p. 117; on conflict in nationalised industry from 1947 to the early 1950s, see on coal D. Holter, *The Battle for Coal, Miners and the Politics of Nationalization in France, 1940–50* (DeKalb: Northern Illinois University Press, 1992), and R. Trempé, 'Les Charbonnages, un cas social,' in *Les Nationalisations de la liberation*, pp. 294–309; on aviation, Chapman, *State Capitalism*, 256–316; on EDF, see Frost, *Alternating Currents*.
25. On the process of adaptation of private business to nationalization, see P. Uri, 'La Querelle des nationalisations,' *Les Temps Modernes* 45 (July 1949), pp. 165–70; H. Ehrmann, *Organized Business in France* (Princeton: Princeton University Press, 1957), pp. 344–54; Chapman, *State Capitalism*, 289–94.
26. On Société Générale and bank nationalisations generally, see L. Maguire, 'Contingent obligations: Société Générale and the French state, 1945–1981' (Ph.D. dissertation, New York University, 2003).
27. Bloch-Lainé and Bouvier, *La France restaurée*, pp. 193–4; Frost, *Alternating Currents*.
28. On social policy in the interwar period, see especially Dutton, *Origins*; Susan Pedersen, *Family, Dependence, and the Origins of the Welfare State: Britain and France, 1914–1945* (Cambridge, Cambridge University Press, 1993); H. Hatzfeld, *Du paupérisme à la sécurite sociale, 1850–1940* (Paris: Armand Colin, 1971); and D. Ashford, *The Emergence of the Welfare States* (Oxford: Basil Blackwell, 1986).
29. B. Valat, *Histoire de la sécurité sociale (1945–1970): L'État, l'institution et la santé* (Paris: Economica, 2001), p. 20.
30. Shennan, *Rethinking France*, pp. 214–15.
31. B. Palier, *Governer la sécurité sociale: Les réformes du système français de protection sociale depuis 1945* (Paris: Presses Universitaires de France, 2002), pp. 100–6. On the reforms of 1945 and the compromises that followed, see also Valat, *Histoire*, pp. 10–165; Dutton, *Origins*, pp. 184–225; Shennan, *Rethinking France*, pp. 210–23; H. Chapman, 'French democracy and the welfare state', in G.R. Andrews and H. Chapman (eds), *The Social Construction of Democracy, 1870–1990* (New York: New York University

Press, 1995), pp. 291–314; P. Laroque, *Au service de l'homme et du droit: Souvenirs et réflexions* (Paris: Association pour l'Étude de l'Histoire de la Sécurité Sociale, 1993), pp. 197–245; Henry C. Galant, *Histoire politique de la sécurité sociale française, 1945–1952* (Paris: Armand Colin, 1955); and P. Baldwin, *The Politics of Social Solidarity: Class Bases of the European Welfare State, 1875–1975* (Cambridge: Cambridge University Press, 1990), pp. 158–207.

32. Valat, *Histoire*, p. 85.
33. Ibid., p. 243; Dutton, *Origins*, pp. 216–17.
34. On the FNOSS, see A. Catrice-Lorey, *Dynamique interne de la sécurité sociale*, 2nd edition (Paris: Economica, 1982), pp. 220–30, and Valat, *Histoire*, pp. 225–70.
35. On political conflict over family allocations, see Lenoir, *Généalogie*; Dominique Ceccaldi, *Histoire des prestations familiales en France* (Paris: Union nationale des caisses* d'allocations familiales, 1957); Valat, *Histoire*, pp. 75–83.
36. A big missing piece in this scheme, unemployment insurance, was added in 1958.
37. S. Cohen and C. Goldfinger, 'From permacrisis to real crisis in French social security: the limits to normal politics', in L.N. Lindberg et al. (eds), *Stress and Contradiction in Modern Capitalism: Public Policy and the Theory of the State* (Lexington, Mass.: Lexington Books, 1975), pp. 57–98: pp. 59–61, 76–77.
38. Valat, *Histoire*, p. 243.
39. Catrice-Lorey, *Dynamique*, p. 38.
40. Valat, *Histoire*, p. 342.
41. Catrice-Lorey, *Dynamique*, pp. 40–8.
42. D. Schnapper, J. Brody, and R. Kastoryano, 'Les français et la sécurité sociale: sondage d'opinion, 1945–1982,' *Vingtième siècle* 10 (April 1986), pp. 71–6.
43. Baldwin, *Social Solidarity*, pp. 253–68.
44. On obstacles to changing social security, see T.B. Smith, *France in Crisis: Welfare, Inequality and Globalization since 1980* (Cambridge: Cambridge University Press, 2004), and Palier, *Governer*.

Bibliography

Andrieu, C., *Le Programme commun de la résistance, Des idées dans la guerre* (Paris: Les Éditions de l'Érudit, 1984).

Andrieu, C., Le Van, L., and Prost, A. (eds), *Les Nationalisations de la libération, De l'utopie au compromis* (Paris: Presses de la FNSP, 1987).

Ashford, Douglas, *The Emergence of the Welfare States* (Oxford, Basil Blackwell, 1986).

Asselain, J.-C., 'Les nationalisations, 1944–45,' in *Études sur la France de 1939 à nos jours* (Paris: Le Seuil, 1985), pp. 180–207.

Baldwin, P., *The Politics of Social Solidarity: Class Bases of the European Welfare State, 1875–1975* (Cambridge: Cambridge University Press, 1990), pp. 158–207.

Bloch-Lainé, François and Bouvier, Jean, *La France restaurée, 1944–1954, Dialogue sur les choix d'une modernisation* (Paris: Fayard, 1986).

Bouvier, Jean, 'Sur la politique économique en 1944–1946,' in *La Libération de la France*, Actes du Colloque International tenu à Paris du 28 au 31 octobre 1974 (Paris: Éditions du CNRS, 1976).

Catrice-Lorey, A., *Dynamique interne de la sécurité sociale*, 2nd edn. (Paris: Economica, 1982).

Ceccaldi, D., *Histoire des prestations familiales en France* (Paris: Union nationale des caisses d'allocations familiales, 1957).

Chapman, H., *State Capitalism and Working-Class Radicalism in the French Aircraft Industry* (Berkeley: University of California Press, 1991).

Chapman, H., 'French democracy and the welfare state,' in George Reid Andrews and Herrick Chapman (eds), *The Social Construction of Democracy, 1870–1990* (New York: New York University Press, 1995), pp. 291–314.

Chapman, H., 'The Liberation as a moment in state-making,' in Kenneth Mouré and Martin S. Alexander (eds), *Crisis and Renewal in France, 1918–1962* (New York: Berghahn Books, 2002), pp. 174–98.

Cohen, S., and Goldfinger, C., 'From permacrisis to real crisis in French social security: the limits to normal politics,' in L.N. Lindberg et al. (eds), *Stress and Contradiction in Modern Capitalism: Public Policy and the Theory of the State* (Lexington, Mass.: Lexington Books, 1975), pp. 57–98.

Courtin, René, *Rapport sur la politique économique d'après guerre* (Algiers: Éditions 'Combat', 1944).

Dutton, P.V., *Origins of the French Welfare State: the Struggle for Social Reform in France, 1914–1947* (New York: Cambridge University Press, 2002).

Einaudi, M., Byé, M., and Rossi, E., *Nationalization in France and Italy* (Ithaca: Cornell University Press, 1955).

Ehrmann, Henry, *Organized Business in France* (Princeton: Princeton University Press, 1957).

Fridenson, P., 'Could Postwar France Become a Middle-Class Society?' in O. Zunz, L. Schoppa, and N. Hiwatari (eds), *Social Contracts Under Stress* (New York: Russell Sage Foundation, 2002), pp. 89–107.

Frost, Robert L., *Alternating Currents: Nationalized Power in France, 1946–1970* (Ithaca: Cornell University Press, 1991).

Galant, H.C., *Histoire politique de la sécurité sociale française, 1945–1952* (Paris: Armand Colin, 1955).

Hatzfeld, H., *Du paupérisme à la sécurite sociale, 1850–1940* (Paris: Armand Colin, 1971).

Holter, D., 'Mineworkers and nationalization in France: Insights in concepts of state theory,' *Politics and Society* 11.1 (1982), pp. 29–49.

Holter, Darryl, *The Battle for Coal, Miners and the Politics of Nationalization in France, 1940–50* (DeKalb: Northern Illinois University Press, 1992).

Kuisel, R.F., *Capitalism and the State in Modern France, Renovation and Economic Management in the Twentieth Century* (New York: Cambridge University Press, 1981).

Laroque, Pierre, *Au service de l'homme et du droit, Souvenirs et réflexions* (Paris: Association pour l'Étude de l'histoire de la sécurité sociale, 1993), pp. 197–245.

Lenoir, Rémi, *Généalogie de la morale familiale* (Paris: Le Seuil, 2003).

Maguire, L., 'Contingent obligations: Société Générale and the French state, 1945–1981', Ph.D. dissertation, New York University, 2003.

Morsel, H., 'Paul Ramadier et l'électricité,' in S. Berstein (ed.) *Paul Ramadier, la République et le Socialisme* (Brussels: Éditions Complexe, 1988), pp. 309–35.

Palier, B., *Governer la sécurité sociale, Les réformes du système français de protection sociale depuis 1945* (Paris: Presses Universitaires de France, 2002).

Paxton, R.O., *Vichy France, Old Guard and New Order, 1940–1944* (New York: Knopf, 1972).

Pedersen, S., *Family, Dependence, and the Origins of the Welfare State: Britain and France, 1914–1945* (Cambridge: Cambridge University Press, 1993).

Schnapper, D., Brody, J., and Kastoryano, R., 'Les français et la sécurité sociale: sondage d'opinion, 1945–1982,' *Vingtième siècle* 10 (April 1986), pp. 71–6.

Shennan, Andrew, *Rethinking France, Plans for Renewal, 1940–1946* (Oxford: Clarendon Press, 1989).

Smith, T.B., *France in Crisis, Welfare, Inequality and Globalization since 1980* (Cambridge: Cambridge University Press, 2004).

Steinhouse, A., *Workers' Participation in Post-Liberation France* (Lanham, MD: Lexington Books, 2001).

Sturmthal, A., 'The structure of nationalized enterprises in France,' *Political Science Quarterly* 67 (1952), pp. 357–77.

Sturmthal, A., 'Nationalization and workers' control in Britain and France,' *Journal of Political Economy* 61.1 (1953), pp. 43–79.

Uri, P., 'La Querelle des nationalisations,' *Les Temps Modernes* 45 (July 1949), pp. 165–70.

Valat, B., *Histoire de la sécurité sociale (1945–1970), L'État, l'institution et la santé* (Paris: Economica, 2001).

Wall, I., 'The French social contract: conflict and cooperation,' *International Labor and Working-Class History* 50 (Fall 1996), pp. 116–24.

Williams, A., 'France and the new world order, 1940–1947,' *Modern and Contemporary France* 8.2 (2000), pp. 191–202.

8
Catholics and the Long Liberation: the Progressive Moment

Nicholas Atkin

By and large, historians of religion have not lingered on the Liberation. They have focused instead on the Occupation, providing several excellent studies of Catholicism under Vichy, though there are still areas deserving of investigation, not least the attitudes of the lower clergy towards the regime. The continuing reluctance of the Church to disclose fully its wartime archives has hampered research, and has done more harm than good by giving rise to unfounded speculation about clerical behaviour during the 'dark years'.[1]

When historians of religion have studied the Liberation, their interests have been eclectic but predictable. A perennial concern has been the *épuration*, which proved a mild shake-out of high-ranking ecclesiastics who compromised themselves with the Germans and Vichy.[2] A further interest has been the ways in which the Liberation contributed to the growth of Christian Democracy, embodied in the Mouvement Républicain Populaire (MRP).[3] More recently, historians have studied the fate of those Jewish children, sheltered by Catholic institutions during the war, who, it is alleged, were not allowed to rejoin their families in 1945. On 28 December 2004, the *Corriere della Sera* published a document of 23 October 1946, purportedly authored by the Vatican but discovered in a church archive outside Paris, instructing Antonio Roncalli, the papal nuncio in France and future John XXIII, not to assist Jewish organisations in attempts to reunite families if the children had received a Christian baptism.[4] As the *New York Times* observed, its disclosure touched on 'the raw debate' over the role of Pius XII during the Holocaust, and has cast a shadow on the reputation of Roncalli, who is on the way to sainthood.[5]

In these enquiries, the Liberation has been treated as a discrete episode, more or less a coda to the Occupation, making it difficult to grasp its importance in the wider religious history of France. This chapter argues that this significance may be gleaned by employing the notion of the 'long liberation' which historians have applied more generally to the *après guerre*. This begs questions of periodisation. When did the Liberation begin; when did it end? To answer these questions, writers have reflected on how individuals, communities and institutions responded to wartime. For a small minority, it began in June 1940;

"

for rather more, sometime during the Occupation itself, when they rejected Vichy, the Germans and the Armistice. What is clear is that liberation did not end with the expulsion of the occupier and coming of the Fourth Republic.[6] In the course of the 'dark years', aspirations grew for the future, which drew on hopes from the past. Not all of these aspirations would be realised in 1944–46, despite the spirit of a 'New Jerusalem' which prevailed. For certain groups – for instance, Jews, women, and above all the peoples of colonial France – liberation remained incomplete.[7]

Viewed in this perspective, liberation is a fluid concept, something especially true for Catholics. On one level, the expulsion of the occupier was obviously a liberation. Whatever position Catholics had adopted towards Vichy, only a minority threw in their lot with the Nazis, and they were wholly discredited in 1944. On another level, that of the *longue durée*, a more complicated picture emerges, a picture that can only be understood by reference to the contest for authority which had long troubled the French Church. Ever since the 1830s, the hierarchy had been struggling to direct the activities of the lower clergy and laity. Some of these activities, to do with stemming dechristianisation, were welcome; others, especially in the political domain, were not; all had the potential for undermining authority. In 1940, a moment when Pétain called for restraint, there was an opportunity to reassert discipline, in particular, says W.D. Halls, through an insistence on obedience to the 'teachings dispensed by the bishops'.[8] This call for discipline was one of the many reasons why the hierarchy lent support to Pétain's government. Though that support was subsequently nuanced, the episcopacy compromised itself with the regime with the result that its reputation in 1944 was tarnished, and its authority questioned.

In this situation, as René Rémond indicated, progressive Catholics had their chance.[9] Straining at the leash in the final years of the Third Republic, in 1940 they initially heeded the hierarchy's advice, but at varying points under Vichy came to think and act for themselves. Whereas the Occupation proved an unpropitious environment to realise their dreams, in 1944 it seemed that their moment had arrived. Swept along by the joy of liberation, they took advantage of the eclipse of episcopal power to undertake several initiatives: an attempted *rapprochement* with the Left; a renaissance of Christian democracy; a renewal of religious practices; and a process of deconfessionalisation of Catholic institutions so as to reach out to the popular classes. Thanks to these *démarches*, Catholicism reasserted itself as an important presence in national life at the Liberation and, as Maurice Larkin states, avoided the backlash it had received at other moments of national upheaval, notably 1830 and 1871.[10] It did not endure. The freezing over of the Cold War in 1947 enabled an ungracious hierarchy to re-establish discipline. For progressives, therefore, liberation, in terms of realising spiritual and clerical freedoms, was only briefly glimpsed in 1944–47, and would not truly happen until Vatican Two and the spirit of *aggiornamento*, though there are those who bemoan the discipline imposed by the recent cardinals of Paris, Lustiger and Vingt-Trois.[11]

The background: the growing questioning of authority

The French hierarchy had always prided itself on its organisational capacity. In the eighteenth century, the French Church was alone in Europe in possessing a single representative body, the General Assembly of the Clergy, which regulated relations with the state and maintained internal discipline. The Revolution of 1789 and the Napoleonic Concordat of 1801 destroyed that apparatus, but strengthened the wish of the hierarchy to retain control of its flock. Bishops were not only frightened by new revolutionary concepts of citizenship; they were concerned that, in the Terror, members of the laity had either lost their faith or had practised it without a priest present, especially women. A process of laicisation of religion had begun. There were those who welcomed this. In the 1830s, a small group of intellectual Catholics, huddled around Lammenais, Lacordaire and Ozanam, appreciated the ways in which the Revolution had intentionally and unintentionally empowered the laity. They thus argued that the lay members and lower clergy should be more involved in the day-to-day activities of the Church so as to defend clerical freedoms, resist state encroachments, and combat secularisation. There ensued a proliferation of diverse lay initiatives designed to halt the spread of dechristianisation: Albert de Mun's Cercles Catholiques d'Ouvriers (1871), Léon Harmel's Union Fraternelle du Commerce et de l'Industrie (1889), and the Association Catholique de la Jeunesse Française (ACJF) (1910).

Despite these initiatives, authority remained above. The *Ralliement* notwithstanding, particular watch was kept on lay involvement in politics; hence the official discouragement of Jacques Piou's Action Libérale Populaire (ALP) and Marc Sangnier's Sillon, which was banned by the papacy in 1910. Christian democracy subsisted in France, but historians suggest that it was represented most eloquently in a newspaper, the Rennes daily, *Ouest-Éclair*. Tellingly, the same discouragement was not extended to those integralist Catholics who gravitated to the far right Action Française, a movement admired by the Church in France (despite its having been officially condemned by Pope Pius XI in 1926), not for its spirituality but for its commitment to order.

In this battle to retain discipline, the hierarchy was assisted by a number of factors: the unpropitious Catholic intellectual world of the late nineteenth century, dominated by a neo-Thomism which was intolerant of dissent; a widely acknowledged need among the faithful to maintain discipline in the face of the anticlerical assaults of the 1880s and 1900s; and the support of the papacy itself, though the suspicions of Pius X even applied to the French episcopacy.

After 1918, there was a different environment. The 'second ralliement' of the 1920s eased Church–state relations and, aside from the Herriot cabinet of 1924, no government, not even the Popular Front, thought of imposing the anticlerical legislation of the past.[12] With no threat on the horizon, Catholics relaxed their defences. Moreover, in the interwar years long-standing concerns about dechristianisation became ever more urgent, encouraging lay initiatives.

At hand, Catholics had the first detailed sociological analyses of the situation, notably those undertaken by Gabriel Le Bras.[13] Something had to be done if France was not to become a *pays de mission*, and lay Catholics seemed well equipped to take action. In the aftermath of the 1905 Separation, and during the mobilisation of 1914–18, Catholics at 'grass-roots level' learned the lessons of organisation.[14] And had not the Vatican itself encouraged greater lay engagement, notably in the 1922 encyclical, *Ubi Arcano Dei*?

There thus evolved in the interwar years a multiplicity of Catholic organisations. They never had a unified programme, but possessed some common characteristics. They all supported the further empowerment of the laity; they were all receptive to new ideas; and, with the exception of the Fédération Nationale Catholique (FNC), they were movements of the Centre, occasionally of the Left, thus breaking the French Church's traditional alliance with the Right, though many progressives had not yet wholeheartedly embraced liberal democracy.[15] Those who had done so gravitated to the fledgling Christian Democrat Parti Démocrate Populaire (PDP), and the more forward-looking Jeune République (JR), though neither was very popular. More successful in terms of recruitment were the 'socio-occupational' organisations of Action Catholique founded in the 1930s and designed to promote the apostolic tasks of the Church, notably the Jeunesse Ouvrière Chrétienne (JOC), the Jeunesse Étudiante Chrétienne (JEC), and the Jeunesse Agricole Chrétienne (JAC). Members of these movements, especially Jocistes, graduated to the Ligue Ouvrière Chétienne (LOC), established in 1935, and the Christian trade union movement, the Confédération Française des Travailleurs Chrétiens (CFTC), founded in 1919, and half a million strong in 1940, though not as well supported as the Left-dominated Confédération Générale du Travail (CGT). Lastly, the 1930s saw the rise of numerous intellectual journals: the Dominican *La Vie Intellectuelle*, Emmanuel Mounier's *Esprit*, and the Christian Democrat *L'Aube*.

The French hierarchy did not necessarily disapprove of these initiatives, especially those tackling the 'Social Question'. Yet there was an expectation that these activities would be under episcopal control. As Pius XI stipulated in his 1925 encyclical *Quas primas*, hitherto Catholics had 'neither that social position nor that influence which those really should have who hold high the truth . . . but if only the faithful understand that they must fight under the standard of Christ the King with courage and perseverance, then they will strive with apostolic zeal to lead the alienated and ignorant souls back to the Lord'.[16] Read carefully, this was an injunction to the laity to channel their enthusiasms through their bishops, but it is not difficult to see how it could be interpreted differently, and it is not difficult to believe how prelates feared they were losing their grip, especially at the time of the Popular Front.[17] In his speech of 17 April 1936, the Communist leader Maurice Thorez famously offered a *main tendue* to Catholic workers. As David Curtis has shown, while a small group of theologians welcomed a dialogue with the Left, if only to signal the error of its ways,[18] it was a worrying development for Church leaders who supported the Vatican's subsequent intervention into French affairs. In 1937, Rome banned *La Terre nouvelle*, a fringe interdenominational review, and the more influential *Sept*. Only an intervention by Cardinal Verdier of Paris, fearful of the Church being portrayed as hopelessly reactionary, prevented a suppression of Mounier's *Esprit*.

The hierarchy and Vichy: broad collaboration, mild retribution

In June 1940, the hierarchy had no such qualms. This eagerness has been explained in a variety of ways. Apologists argue that it was customary for the Church to recognise a *de facto* government, one accepted by everyone save the Free French and the British. Even de Gaulle admitted that the hierarchy had little choice but to accept the 'established order'.[19] It is also argued that that the Vatican failed to give a clear lead; even in 1942, it dithered in its condemnation of the Jewish round-ups in France. Analysis of the four leading Cardinals – Liénart, Suhard, Gerlier and Baudrillart – has revealed politically naïve men.[20] That naivety was compounded by an admiration for Pétain's National Revolution and a desire to benefit from Vichy's early wish to grant religious freedoms. Although these concessions dried up, as the Catholic presence at Vichy faded, there was always Pétain. Though his own spirituality was lukewarm – his marriage to a divorcee was widely known[21] – this was excused, for he at least professed an outward Catholicism. He was, additionally, the 'Victor of Verdun', important given that most prelates had fought in the First World War, a point stressed by Halls. Above all, he was venerated for his concern for order, and in 1940 discipline was everything. According to Church leaders, a moral laxity had contributed to the defeat and without discipline, by which they meant without Pétain, there lurked civil war or a takeover by either collaborationists or Germans. It was thus the duty of Catholics to rally, as they had done in the 1880s and 1900s. It did not go unnoticed that this new-found discipline would also enable the Church to rein-in progressives.

This desire for order was constant. Episcopal pronouncements repeatedly called for discipline, and became shriller as the Occupation endured and fears grew of civil war. Admittedly, in 1940 only a small number of prelates made the undiplomatic move of calling Vichy the *autorité légitime*. In 1941, worried at the repressive direction of Darlan's Vichy, the Assembly of Cardinals and Archbishops (ACA) attempted to clarify its position by calling for 'un loyalisme sincère et complet' towards 'le pouvoir établi'.[22] If further amplification had followed, which distanced the hierarchy further from the regime, something of the episcopacy's integrity might have stood intact in 1944. Similarly, as Édouard Daladier observed, this credibility would have been further enhanced if the Church had relinquished 'certain overly spectacular favours' it had received from Vichy.[23] Instead, the hierarchy clung to these gains, especially state subsidies to confessional schools, and the 1941 declaration remained the official line, refined in late February 1944 in a statement which mixed praise for the Marshal with condemnation of Allied bombing, which some prelates termed 'acts of terrorism'. These words, plus the episcopal criticisms of the Resistance, were gleefully replayed by anticlericals in 1944.[24] The Church replied with Mgr Guerry's *L'Eglise catholique en France sous l'occupation*, a collection of contemporary documents highlighting Catholic doubts about Vichy, and printed by a lay publisher so as to lend weight to its supposed impartiality, though it could not be ignored that Guerry was permanent secretary of the ACA.[25] It was not until 1997, however, that the Church formally distanced itself from the Pétain regime when Archbishop de Berranger of St Denis made a public apology for the Church's behaviour during Occupation, especially its 'silence' over the Jews.[26]

Against this background, the loss of confidence on the part of the episcopacy in 1944 is understandable. Evidence to support this comes from the *Semaines Religieuses*, the weekly diocesan bulletins published under the authority of the bishops. In July 1940, these were full of comment, regret for the defeat undoubtedly, but condemnation too of the laicism of the past and hope for the future.[27] Though in 1945–46 the bulletins became more forthcoming, in autumn 1944 they are bereft of analysis, containing little except details of diocesan events. For instance, the *Semaine Religieuse de Montpellier* reported, in early September, that the area had been liberated, as did the *Semaine Religieuse de Limoges*, yet neither offered any commentary.[28] There is virtually no reference to political goings-on, all of which suggests a fear, on the part of the bishops, of putting themselves forward.

That fear was tangible. In the words of Gerlier, the Resistance in 1944 had subjected the bishops to a type of 'persecution'.[29] The episode of 26 August where Suhard was prevented from participating at the *Te Deum* at Notre Dame cathedral, in thanks for the Liberation, is well documented. Other prelates, notably Du Bois de la Villerabel at Aix-en-Provence, Auvity at Mende, Dutoit at Arras, fled their dioceses for fear of reprisal. It was these three, together with Beaussart at Paris, plus a trio of apostolic vicars, who were forced to resign. Three bishops, in turn, were promoted to cardinal: Saliège, Petit de Julleville and Rocques. It was a gentle purge, even judged by the standards of the *épuration*, but, as André Latreille demonstrated, it would have been fiercer had it not been for a series of factors.[30] The Provisional Government was never united over what course of action to pursue. While Bidault had a long 'blacklist' of bishops to demote and a 'white list' of those to promote, not all agreed with his choices. The government also lacked evidence against individual clerics. Most critically, it was hampered by the Vatican, which temporised, and which did not restore full diplomatic relations until late 1944.

Laity and regulars under Vichy: distance, resistance, renewal

Whereas members of the hierarchy displayed an indulgence towards Vichy, lay Catholics, or at least the politically motivated among them, were ambivalent.

On one level, there was admiration for Pétain and the changes he augured. On another level, there was concern that Vichy was authoritarian, overly dependent on and imitative of Germany. Such ambiguity could be found in almost all branches of Catholicism from Mounier's *Esprit*, through the youth movements of Action Catholique, to include the unionists of the CFTC and PDP and JR deputies, as well as the leading Catholic newspaper, *La Croix*.[31] As Halls comments, Catholic dilemmas were best articulated by the Jesuit Père Dillard, who stated that the Vichy enterprise was 'a magnificent adventure to be resisted'.[32]

And resist they did, albeit at varying stages. The protests of figures such as Edmond Michelet, François de Menthon and Henri Frenay are well documented. Deserving of greater acknowledgement are the activities of Catholic charitable organisations, youth groups, and regular orders. In her study of the churches of occupied Paris, Vesna Drapac has illustrated how the charitable initiatives of the *confrères* of Saint Vincent de Paul embraced a 'spiritual resistance', though claims that regular religious observance by members of the laity constituted a similar form of resistance should perhaps be treated with caution.[33] As to the young, the activities of Jocistes are acknowledged, but the archives heave with examples of 'ordinary' young men and women who took matters into their own hands, for instance the pupils at the Institution Saint-Jean in Saint-Quentin who, in June 1943, distributed resistance tracts.[34] In June 1945, the *Bulletin des Écoles Libres du Diocèse de Viviers* recounted the exploits of young Catholic *résistants* from the region: eighteen year-old Louis Rivier, shot by the Germans for liaising with the *maquis*; Claudius Brunier, killed in action fighting for the FFI; and the students of an unnamed secondary school, requisitioned by the Germans, who held regular study circles in which they reflected on the anti-Nazi encyclical *Mit Brennender Sorge*.[35]

Special mention, too, should be made of the regulars. While grateful to Vichy for revising the associations law of 1901 and revoking the teaching ban of 1904, they were innately suspicious of government, perhaps because they were accustomed to living an illegal existence, and also because they considered that Vichy had not gone far enough in restoring freedoms. Even the most Pétainist of monks, congregated in the veterans' organisation, the Ligue des Droits des Religieux Anciens Combattants (DRAC), regarded the Marshal's government as a disappointment.[36] An independent spirit further sprang from the fact that the orders enjoyed, to varying degrees, a closed life and could carry out clandestine acts unnoticed, something especially true of nuns who often hid Jewish children. In the case of male orders, the fact that they were answerable to Rome, not to their local bishop, further facilitated free thought.

In any case, it was widely rumoured in 1941 that the Dominicans and Jesuits were Gaullist in sympathy and critical of the ACA's position towards Vichy, a charge the chief Dominican at Lyon was keen to refute.[37] The evidence points elsewhere. The Jesuit periodical *Études*, which reappeared in December 1940 as *Temps présent*, was suppressed by Vichy for its outspokenness; and, of course, it was the Jesuit fathers, Chaillet and Fessard, who launched *Témoignage Chrétien*, *the* Catholic resistance journal. It was Fessard too who, in 1943, authored *Le Prince-Esclave*, in which he argued that Vichy had lost legitimacy through its failure to promote and defend the moral and material welfare of its citizens.[38] Such indiscipline exasperated conservatives. In early 1944, Canon Polimann, the former right-wing deputy, chastised the regulars, singling out the Marists for particular blame.[39] It is only a pity that we do not know more about the secular clergy. Some local insight is provided in a report of October 1942 by the *responsable culturel* of the Parti Populaire Français (PPF) in Rodez and sent to the party headquarters.[40] Through regional contacts, he discovered that the *vieux clergé*, veterans of 1914–18, were for the marshal. Younger clergy were for the English. As to trainee priests, at the Grand Séminaire de Rodez, there reigned a 'Gaullisme à outrance'.

Even if Catholics did not actively join the Resistance, the circumstances of the Occupation and the ambivalent response of their bishops forced them to act independently. This was especially true when confronted with big issues of conscience: the persecution of Jews and the obligatory work service to Germany, the Service du Travail Obligatoire (STO). Much has been written about Catholics and Jews, and it is well documented that a majority of the laity were initially unconcerned by Vichy's discriminatory measures, partially because these were seen as necessary for the common good and partly because people were preoccupied with other matters. With the intensification of the round-ups in 1942, it was not easy to stand idly by; and we know that Catholics provided much assistance to Jews, through such organisations as Père Chaillet's Amitié Chrétienne. This was in spite of the fact that most bishops said so little.[41] Much, too, has been written about Catholics and STO. Prelates had no liking for this measure and Saliège, the independent-minded archbishop of Toulouse, pressed for a collective protest, yet others did not want to be seen counselling disobedience. The solution was a fudge, articulated by Liénart in a speech of 21 March 1943 when he spelt out the importance of compliance, but acknowledged it was not a 'sin' to refuse STO, a position repeated by the ACA. Mgr Guerry later remarked that this was the first time in the Occupation that the hierarchy had advised refusal of Vichy legislation, and made much of this 'liberation'. It was hardly a 'liberation' for the thousands of Jecistes and Jocistes drafted into German factories, and it was a mealy-mouthed message compared to the forthright denunciations of STO made by Catholic Resistance movements.

Though refusal of STO was not, in practical terms, the 'liberation' later suggested, the gruelling circumstances of the Occupation did imply a liberation in other respects by offering Catholics the possibility of sloughing off episcopal oversight to pursue their own agendas. Catholics were as active as other parts of French society in orchestrating 'plans for renewal'. In the social domain, the CFTC, traditionally respectful of ecclesiastical wishes, moved independently. Working alongside CGT members in the Conseil National de la Résistance (CNR), it developed an ambitious social programme, calling for nationalisations, trade union freedoms and social welfare schemes. In the political arena, Christian Democrats discovered, especially within the Resistance, that they could work alongside other Republicans, even those on the far Left, and envisaged a non-confessional party. In the religious sphere, there was opportunity to take advantage of the upsurge in religious observance, produced by the shock of defeat, to overcome dechristianisation, a challenge highlighted by the publication of Père Lhande's *Le Christ dans la banlieue* (1927), in its 131st printing by 1931, and Abbé Godin's *La France, pays de mission?* (1943), which quickly sold out its initial run of 100,000 copies.[42] There ensued countless evangelising initiatives: the remodeling of the LOC to become the Mouvement Populaire des Familles (MPF), concerned with families of all backgrounds; the beginnings of the worker-priest movement; and the rural campaign of Père Epagneul's Frères Missionaries des Campagnes. What these initiatives had in common was a readiness to act outside episcopal strictures, a willingness to engage with a pluralistic society, and a desire to build a new society on earth based on Christian values. The problem was that the Occupation militated against the realisation of these aims. 1944, it was hoped, would be different.

Renewal and redemption? The progressive moment

It is widely acknowledged that had the hierarchy's position been typical of Catholics, then the Church as a whole could have expected hostility. Instead, Catholicism's place in national life was redeemed by lay members and lower clergy who had disobeyed their superiors. As André Mandouze, editor of *Cahiers de notre jeunesse*, stated to the bishop of Marseille, '*Monseigneur*, humble yourself and admit your errors. If some of your sons, among priests and laity alike, had not had the courage to disobey you and follow their own consciences for four years, neither you nor most of your peers would still be sitting in your bishops' palaces.'[43] Whether all bishops understood this is a moot point but, as remarked, they were apprehensive of the future and, at the Liberation, suffered a loss of confidence.

This was in contrast to the laity and lower clergy, who enjoyed new-found empowerment. The German presence had been removed and with it the Vichy government, though some retained a residual admiration for Pétain. There was always de Gaulle, who was known to be a practising Catholic and who was surrounded by prominent Christian Democrats, notably Bidault and Maurice Schumann. A strong Catholic presence could also be identified in the local *comités de libération*, some of them dominated by Jocistes and Jecistes. As to government more generally, Larkin has shown how, at the Liberation, many middle-class officials openly advertised their faith, something which would have been an obstacle to promotion under the Third Republic.[44] Additional signs of Catholic confidence were evidenced in the re-emergence of a powerful press, magazines such as *La Vie catholique illustrée*, and the Christian-Democrat newspapers *L'Echo-Liberté* (Lyon), *Le Réveil* (Isère) and *Ouest-France* (Rennes).

As to intellectual reviews, *Esprit* reappeared, alongside such new titles as the interdenominational *Dieu Vivant*, the left-leaning *Etudes Carmélitaines* and the Personalist/Marxist *La Quinzaine*.

Christian democracy was, of course, reborn with the MRP, launched in November 1944. Here is not the place to rehearse the origins of the MRP, but to remark on certain of its early characteristics which point to the sense of freedom enjoyed by its leadership. Larkin has stressed that, unlike its pre-1914 counterparts, neither the Vatican nor the French episcopacy were consulted about its founding. The MRP grew out of the Resistance, and initially had little to fear from clerical intrusions. The episcopate had no wish to be seen meddling, lest this invited more criticism of its indulgence of Vichy. The Vatican, too, remained at a distance. While the eventual publication of Roncalli's post-war diaries might tell a different story, the 1963 collection of his diplomatic papers, admittedly a rather saccharine collection designed to present the then Pope in the best possible light, contains no reference to Rome's links with French parties.[45] It has been speculated that, as nuncio, Roncalli knew of the distaste in France for Pius XII, both for his record in the 1930s, when he had been equivocal in the face of Nazism, and for his failure to speak out against the wartime persecution of Jews. For their part, MRP leaders knew that to have involved the Vatican at the outset of their venture would have courted enormous unpopularity.

The hope of the party's leadership was to project a form of Christian democracy which lacked close associations with the Church. Whether this aim was ever realised is a moot point, yet the early independence of the MRP at least allowed for a centrist agenda, and one left of centre in social matters. The natural instinct of the prelates would have been to have called for a programme which represented the interests of *bourgeois* France. Instead, the party championed nationalisations, state planning, the extension of social security schemes, and even the promotion of women's civil rights, though this last issue was pressed most energetically by women themselves, notably the charismatic deputy, Marie-Hélène Lefaucheux.[46] Eventually the party drifted in a rightwards direction thanks to the Cold War and pressure from the episcopacy and Rome, both of which were recovering their nerve. As discussed below, these factors generally put a brake on the activities of lay Catholics. An additional factor undermining the MRP's radicalism was its reliance on conservative voters who, in the early years of the Fourth Republic, had few alternatives to support, thanks to the general discrediting of the Right. The MRP's structure exacerbated this trend. The party's founders had hoped that their creation would resemble not 'an electoral machine' but, in the words of Irving, 'a great *rassemblement* of ordinary men and women, inspired by their political doctrine and humanitarian idealism to bring about a new and genuinely democratic republican regime'.[47] In the event, this *rassemblement*, which placed stress on local organisation, proved a weakness as there were insufficient 'transmission belts' to communicate the views of party activists to the leadership, leaving the MRP reliant on a right-wing electoral base and badly placed to face the challenge from de Gaulle's Rassemblement du Peuple Français (RPF) and the recovery of the mainstream Right in the form of the Centre National des Indépendants et des Paysans (CNIP).

Already in electoral difficulties by 1951, the MRP might also have fared better if it had not devoted so much of its energies to rechristianising the working classes. This was, of course, the other great concern of the rejuvenated Catholicism of the Liberation period. Again, initiatives were launched without episcopal approval, though the best known, the worker-priest movement, began under the auspices of Suhard. Alongside those one hundred or so priests sent in mufti to accompany workers conscripted into STO, Suhard was so troubled by the findings of Godin's *Pays de mission* that, in 1943, he established the Mission de Paris whereby trainee priests were encouraged to devote at least part of their time to living the life of the working classes.[48] One of the most famous of these 'missionaries', Henri Perrin, enrolled in a factory in the 13th arrondissement, close to the deprived parish of Notre Dame de la Garde where the Jesuits were active. It was his intention to gain the confidence of his peers, urging them to reflect on spiritual matters, before revealing his true identity, though in practice most priests were easily spotted.[49] It was a technique emulated elsewhere as the Mission de France established outposts in Lyon and Marseille. The danger always was that priests would go native as *cégétiste* activists – as nearly did Perrin himself who, in 1949, became the CGT secretary at the Isère-Arc factory. As we shall see, this involvement in left-wing politics sealed the fate of the worker-priest movement.

In 1944–45, there were other disparate initiatives designed to counter secularisation. Notable were the efforts to revitalise the institution of the parish as the key building block in the missionary life of the Church. All too often, parish structures had failed to stay abreast of huge demographic increases which were accompanied by social inequalities. Yet the experiences of overcrowded POW and concentration camps had shown how a community could be reforged and how individuals could rediscover their spiritual self. So it was that Abbé Remilleux attempted to overhaul his parish of St-Alban in the suburbs of Lyon.[50] Similar efforts were made by Abbé Michonneau at Sacré-Coeur du Petit-Colombes in the outreaches of Paris, where he believed a 'pagan mentality' had seized hold of the working classes thanks to the inability of the Church to keep abreast of materialism and demographic growth.[51] Debates over how best to proselytise were also undertaken by the MPF and the Jeunesse de l'Église, loosely tied to the ACJF, which argued that traditional church structures were insufficient to meet the modern challenge.

As Halls has shown, two communities remained beyond the reach of progressive Catholics: Jews and Protestants. In the case of the former, it is perhaps no surprise that Jewish leaders were lukewarm to offers of friendship, despite the best efforts of Amitié Chrétienne, *Témoignage Chrétien* and Resistance leaders such as Père Glasberg. The case of Protestants is more intriguing, especially given the way in which the Reformed Church had cultivated ecumenicalism within the Resistance and Oflags. Part of the failure to build bridges was the Catholic preoccupation with rechristianisation, which had led to a long-standing neglect of interdenominational links. Besides, these were frowned upon by the Vatican, at least before the Second Vatican Council. As Halls observes, the repeated failure of Rome to partake in ecumenical councils was remembered by French Protestant leaders in 1945, and there remained long-standing religious differences, especially over the place of the Bible.[52] Such debates were regularly played out in the pages of the Protestant weekly *Réforme* in 1945. Lurking behind these discussions was the fear that what Catholics really wanted was nothing less than the conversion of Protestants and the disappearance of the Reformed Church.

The other relationship which some progressives wished to build was that with Communists, a relationship extensively explored by Michael Kelly.[53] It will be recalled that a handful of intellectuals had struck up a dialogue with the extreme Left at the time of the Popular Front. The shared experience of Resistance enabled Catholics and Communists to recognise that they possessed a set of common values, especially in their desire to build a new society. With little to fear, in the Liberation period, from episcopal censure, theologians readily engaged with Communist thinkers in a stimulating dialogue.[54] It could not last, nor did it.

What has been less commented upon, and was more significant, was the leftward drift of some Catholic organisations. This trend included not just new movements, such as the Marxist-leaning Union des Chrétiens Progressistes (UCP), but other organisations such as the MPF, which in 1950 changed its name yet again to become the Mouvement de Libération du Peuple (MLP), adopting a more political stance towards social issues.[55] A similar change of perspective overcame the JOC and, in the process, it loosened ties with the bishops. Yet it was the CFTC which underwent the greatest changes. Before 1940, it had displayed a firm loyalty towards the episcopacy and had hesitated to enter the political arena. As its president declared in 1936, to justify its Christian credentials the organisation needed to be faithful 'to the doctrine of the Gospel and the teachings that clarify it'.[56] The war changed its outlook. Disturbed by Vichy's brand of economic corporatism, CFTC members built links with the CGT and were appointed to the CNR, where they were beyond the watchful eyes of the bishops. At the Liberation, a lively debate ensued as to whether the CFTC should secularise itself so as to concentrate more on social rights and less on confessional ones. Historians agree that this had effectively happened by 1947, though it was not until 1964 that the organisation discarded its religious image by renaming itself the Confédération Française Démocratique du Travail (CFDT). At the time of the 1968 protests, it was the CFDT, rather than the CGT, that proved more troublesome, partly because it was not beholden to the Communist party, but also because it had a stronger appreciation of the individual condition and the way in which this had been affected by material inequalities.

Deconfessionalisation of the CFTC had become ever more likely thanks to the more general changes that overtook the Church in 1947. At this point, the freedoms anticipated in the 1930s and Occupation years, and experimented with at the Liberation, began to fizzle out, as they did for non-Catholics. In the wider context, the Cold War was taking hold. In France, this was reflected, in May 1947, in the expulsion of the Communists from government, ending the Socialist–MRP–Communist coalition which had governed France since de Gaulle's resignation in January 1946. In the new 'Third Force' governing coalition, the Socialists and MRP drew on conservative support in parliament. And as noted, by then the MRP was coming under increasing episcopal pressure to tone down its programme, signifying a recovery of nerve on the part of the prelates. That recovery was also true of Pius XII, whose confidence had been restored by the success of the Christian Democrats in Italy. A natural conservative, he was alarmed at what was happening within western European politics, especially France. To stamp his authority, in 1949 he excommunicated all Catholics who engaged in Communist politics.

There followed other strictures. In 1951, ecclesiastical pressure ended the UCP. In 1953, the *Jeunesse de l'Eglise* was condemned by the ACA, which reimposed its authority over the JOC. That same year, the Curia's Cardinal Pizzardo wrote to the French hierarchy stipulating that seminarians could no longer work in factories. Cardinals Liénart, Suhard and Feltin, who valued the work of the Mission de France, despite its dangers, attempted a compromise, but the Vatican's obduracy terminated the worker-priest movement in 1954–5. At the same time, Rome condemned *La Quinzaine*, dismissed a number of French Dominicans involved in the worker-priest project, and silenced the order of its more independent-minded members, for instance the distinguished medieval scholar Père Chenu, who had advised on the social question, and Père Boisselot, editor-in-chief of the Dominican publishing house, Les Editions du Cerf. In 1957 the ACJF, which had been strongly critical of the Algerian war, was dissolved, though its various branches continued to function. It was as well that the MPF and CFTC had effectively flown the coop by deconfessionalising themselves at an earlier stage, as they too would have come under similar pressure.

Conclusion

The Liberation is one of those moments in history, similar to 1848 or 1968, when the surface is rolled back, and it is possible momentarily to view the goings-on underneath. This is especially true of French Catholicism. Since the early nineteenth century, this had been involved in a power struggle between the centre, the hierarchy and Rome, and elements of the periphery, progressive lay members and clerics. Until the 1930s, the centrifugal forces within the Church remained firm, but were faltering. Paradoxically, the Occupation, a time when bishops called for restraint, was the moment when indiscipline flourished as Catholics questioned the decisions of the hierarchy, and highlighted their own agendas. Essentially these schemes looked to an acceptance of a pluralistic society, the promotion of Christian democracy, the rechristianisation of the popular classes and the deconfessionalisation of certain movements. Not everything was addressed. Ecumenicalism was largely left to one side, and was not tackled until the Second Vatican Council in the 1960s.

It would be misleading to believe all these initiatives disappeared in 1947, but the start of the Cold War sounded their death knell. What progressives found depressing was that their leaders seemed to have learned little from the Vichy experience. In the 1950s bishops maintained an agenda which would not have been out of place in 1940: hopes for a concordat, the reintroduction of the catechism into state schools, and rights for religious orders. Only in the 1960s, in the spirit of *aggiornamento*, did this wish-list change as the laity again recovered its confidence and a new generation of bishops came to power. It had been the men raised in the anticlerical battles of the 1900s who had ruled France to that point and, in a sense, it was their gradual disappearance that marked another liberation for French Catholicism.

Notes

1. See J. Duquesne, *Les Catholiques français sous l'occupation* (Paris: Grasset, 1966); R. Bédarida, *Les Catholiques dans la guerre* (Paris: Hachette, 1998); M. Cointet, *L'Eglise sous Vichy* (Paris: Perrin, 1998); E. Fouilloux, *Les Chrétiens français entre crise et libération, 1937–1947* (Paris: Le Seuil, 1997); and W.D. Halls, *Politics, Society and Christianity in Vichy France* (Oxford: Berg, 1995).
2. A. Latreille, *De Gaulle, la libération et l'Eglise catholique* (Paris: Cerf, 1978).
3. M. Larkin, *Religion, Politics and Preferment in France since 1890* (Cambridge: Cambridge University Press, 1995), p. 185.
4. *Corriere della Sera*, 28 December 2004.
5. *New York Times*, 9 January 2005.
6. K. Adler, *Jews and Gender in Liberation France* (Cambridge: Cambridge University Press, 2003), pp. 5–6.
7. See the essays on France overseas in H.R. Kedward and N. Wood (eds), *The Liberation of France* (Oxford: Berg, 1995), pp. 227–82.
8. W.D. Halls, 'Catholics, the Vichy interlude and after', in S. Fishman et al. (eds), *France at War. Vichy and the Historians* (Oxford: Berg, 2000), pp. 231–45 (p. 234 for this quotation), a thought-provoking essay which greatly informed this piece.
9. R. Rémond, 'Les Catholiques français pendant la seconde guerre mondiale', *Revue d'Histoire de l'Eglise de France*, July–December 1978, pp. 203–13.
10. Larkin, *Religion, Politics and Preferment*, p. 174.
11. See L. Frölich, *Les Catholiques intransigeants en France* (Paris: L'Harmattan, 2002).
12. See H.W. Paul, *The Second Ralliement. The Rapprochement between Church and State in the Twentieth Century* (Washington: Catholic University of America Press, 1967).
13. G. Le Bras, 'Statistique et histoire religieuse: pour un examen détaillé et pour une explication historique de l'état de catholicisme dans les diverses régions de France,' *Revue d'Histoire de l'Eglise de France* xvii (1931), pp. 425–49.
14. E. Weber, *The Hollow Years. France in the 1930s* (New York: Norton, 1994), p. 188.

15. This point is made in J. McMillan, 'France', in T. Buchanan and M. Conway (eds), *Political Catholicism in Europe, 1918–1945* (Oxford: Oxford University Press, 1996), pp. 34–68.

16. N. Atkin and F. Tallett, *Priests, Prelates and People. A History of European Catholicism since 1750* (London: Tauris, 2003), p. 234.

17. See M. Darbon, *Le Conflit entre la droite et la gauche dans le catholicisme français, 1830–1953* (Toulouse: Privat, 1953).

18. See D. Curtis, 'True and false modernity: Catholicism and Communist Marxism in 1930s France', in K. Chadwick (ed.), *Catholicism, Politics and Society in Twentieth-Century France* (Liverpool: Liverpool University Press, 2000), pp. 73–96.

19. C. de Gaulle, *Mémoires de Guerre*, Vol. II, (Paris: Plon, 1956), p. 314.

20. See W.D. Halls, 'Catholicism under Vichy. A study in diversity and ambiguity', in H.R. Kedward and R. Austin (eds), *Vichy France and the Resistance. Culture and Ideology* (London: Croom Helm, 1985), pp. 133–46.

21. Even in Britain. National Archives, Kew (UK) FO/1055/1, letter of father M . . . to Lady Peel, September 1940.

22. *La Vie catholique. Documents et actes de la hiérarchie catholique, années 1940–1941* (Paris: La Bonne Presse, 1942), p. 65.

23. E. Daladier, *Prison Journal, 1940–1945* (Boulder: Westview Press, 1995), p. 190.

24. See J. Cottereau, *L'Eglise et Pétain* (Paris: Editions de l'Idée Libre, 1947) and his 'L'Eglise a-t-elle collaboré?', *Problèmes Actuels*, mai 1946, no. 65.

25. Mgr Guerry, *L'Eglise catholique en France sous l'occupation* (Paris: Flammarion, 1947).

26. *Le Monde*, 1 October 1997.

27. See C. Langlois, 'Le Régime de Vichy et le clergé d'après les *Semaines Religieuses* des diocèses de la zone libre', *Revue Française de Science Politique* (22) 4, 1972, pp. 750–73.

28. Bibliothèque Nationale (hereafter BN), *SR de Montpellier* 2/9 September 1944, *SR de Limoges* 18 August/8 September 1944.

29. J. Verlhac, 'La jeune génération catholique en 1944 et le parti communiste', in X. Montclos (ed.), *Eglises et Chrétiens dans la IIe guerre mondiale* (Lyon: Presses Universitaires de Lyon, 1978), p. 504.

30. P. Bolle, 'Les Chrétiens dans la France libérée, 1944–1945', in ibid, pp. 463–4.

31. R.F. Crane, '*La Croix* and the Swastika. The ambiguities of Catholic responses to the fall of France,' *Catholic Historical Review* 90.1 (2004), pp. 45–66.

32. Halls, *Politics, Society and Christianity*, p. 49.

33. V. Drapac, *War and Religion. Catholics in the Churches of Occupied Paris* (Washington: Catholic University of America Press, 1998). See, too, T. Kselman, 'Catholicism, Christianity and Vichy', *French Historical Studies*, 23.3 (2000), pp. 513–30.

34. AN F¹⁷ 13365, letter of the superior of the school to the secrétaire général de la Société Générale d'Education et d'Enseignement, 12 June 1943.

35. BN, *Bulletin des Ecoles Libres du Diocèse de Viviers*, no. 5, June 1945, pp. 153–4.

36. AN 2 AG 493 CC75 B, 'Histoire succincte de la Question des Congrégations depuis l'Armistice', 18 July 1941.

37. AN 2 AG 492 CC72 A, Letter of the Prieur Provincial de la Province de Lyon to the Prieur des Dominicains, 23 August 1941.

38. W.D. Halls, 'Church and state: prelates, theologians and the Vichy regime' in N. Atkin and F. Tallett (eds), *Religion, Society and Politics in France since 1789* (London: Hambledon, 1991), pp. 167–86.

39. AN F¹⁷ 13346, Annexe du Rapport de M. le Chanoine Polimann sur son séjour à Barcelone, 28 mai–5 juin 1944.

40. AN 2 AG 492 CC72 A, 'Politique religieuse du PPF', 20 February 1943.
41. M. Marrus and R.O. Paxton, *Vichy France and the Jews* (New York: Basic Books, 1981), p. 273.
42. Père Lhande, *Le Christ dans la banlieue* (Paris: Plon, 1927) and H. Godin and Y. Daniel, *La France, pays de mission?* (Lyon: Editions de l'Abeille, 1943).
43. Duquesne, *Les Catholiques français*, pp. 443–4.
44. Larkin, *Religion, Politics and Preferment in France*.
45. *Souvenirs d'un Nonce. Cahiers de France, 1944–1953* (Rome: Edizioni di Storia e Letteratura, 1963).
46. See pp. 92–4.
47. R.E.M. Irving, *The Christian Democratic Parties of Western Europe* (London: Allen and Unwin, 1979), p. 21.
48. O. Cole-Arnal, 'The *Témoignage* of the worker priests. Contextual layers of the pioneer epoch, 1941–1955', in G.R. Horn and E. Gerard (eds), *Left Catholicism, 1943–1955. Catholics and Society in Western Europe at the Point of Liberation* (Leuven: Leuven University Press, 2001), pp. 118–41.
49. B. Wall (ed.), *Priest and Worker. The Autobiography of Henri Perrin* (London: Macmillan, 1965), pp. 99–130.
50. Bolle, 'Les Chrétiens dans la France libérée', in Montclos, *Eglises*, p. 467, and A. Dansette, *Destin du catholicisme français* (Paris: Flammarion, 1957), pp. 306–7.
51. G. Michonneau, *Revolution in a City Parish* (Oxford: Blackfriars, 1949), p. 1.
52. Halls, 'Catholics, the Vichy interlude, and after', in Fishman, *France at War*, pp. 233–4.
53. M. Kelly, 'Catholics and Communism in Liberation France', in Atkin and Tallett (eds), *Religion, Society and Politics*, pp. 187–202.
54. E. Fouilloux, *Une Eglise en quête de liberté. La pensée catholique français entre modernisme et Vatican II, 1914–1962* (Paris: Desclée de Brouwer, 1998).
55. Halls, 'Catholics, the Vichy interlude, and after', in Fishman, *France at War*, pp. 241–2, for much that follows here.
56. W. Bosworth, *Catholicism and Crisis in Modern France* (Princeton, NJ: Princeton University Press, 1962), p. 267.

Bibliography

Adler, K., *Jews and Gender in Liberation France* (Cambridge: Cambridge University Press, 2003).
Atkin, N. and Tallett, F., *Priests, Prelates and People. A History of European Catholicism since 1750* (London: Tauris, 2003).
Bédarida, F., *Les Catholiques dans la guerre* (Paris: Hachette, 1998).
Bolle, P., 'Les Chrétiens dans la France libérée, 1944–1945', in X. Montclos (ed.), *Eglises et Chrétiens dans la IIe guerre mondiale* (Lyon: Presses Universitaires de Lyon, 1978).
Bosworth, W., *Catholicism and Crisis in Modern France* (Princeton NJ: Princeton University Press, 1962).
Cointet, M., *L'Eglise sous Vichy* (Paris: Perrin, 1998).
Cole-Arnal, O., 'The *Témoignage* of the worker priests. Contextual layers of the pioneer epoch, 1941–1955', in G.R. Horn and E. Gerard (eds), *Left Catholicism, 1943–1955. Catholics and Society in Western Europe at the Point of Liberation* (Leuven: Leuven University Press, 2001), pp. 118–41.

Cottereau, J., 'L'Eglise a-t-elle collaboré?', *Problèmes Actuels* mai 1946, no. 65.

Cottereau, J., *L'Eglise et Pétain* (Paris: Editions de l'Idée Libre, 1947).

Crane, R.F., '*La Croix* and the Swastika. The ambiguities of Catholic responses to the fall of France,' *Catholic Historical Review* 90.1 (2004), pp. 45–66.

Curtis, D., 'True and false modernity: Catholicism and Communist Marxism in 1930s France', in K. Chadwick (ed.), *Catholicism, Politics and Society in Twentieth-Century France* (Liverpool: Liverpool University Press, 2000), pp. 73–96.

Daladier, E., *Prison Journal, 1940–1945* (Boulder: Westview, 1995).

Dansette, A., *Destin du catholicisme français* (Paris: Flammarion, 1957).

Darbon, M., *Le Conflit entre la droite et la gauche dans le Catholicisme français, 1830–1953* (Toulouse: Privat, 1953).

de Gaulle, C., *Mémoires de Guerre*, 3 vols (Paris: Plon, 1954–59).

Drapac, V., *War and Religion. Catholics in the Churches of Occupied Paris* (Washington: Catholic University of America Press, 1998).

Duquesne, J., *Les Catholiques français sous l'occupation* (Paris: Grasset, 1966).

Fouilloux, E., *Les Chrétiens français entre crise et libération, 1937–1947* (Paris: Seuil, 1997).

Fouilloux, E., *Une Eglise en quête de liberté. La pensée catholique français entre modernisme et Vatican II, 1914–1962* (Paris: Desclée de Brouwer, 1998).

Frölich, L., *Les Catholiques intransigeants en France* (Paris: L'Harmattan, 2002).

Godin, H., and Daniel, Y., *La France, pays de mission?* (Lyon: Editions de l'Abeille, 1943).

Guerry, Mgr, *L'Église catholique en France sous l'occupation* (Paris: Flammarion, 1947).

Halls, W.D., 'Catholicism under Vichy. A study in diversity and ambiguity', in H. R. Kedward and R. Austin (eds), *Vichy France and the Resistance. Culture and Ideology* (London: Croom Helm, 1985), pp. 133–46.

Halls, W.D., 'Church and state: prelates, theologians and the Vichy regime' in N. Atkin and F. Tallett (eds), *Religion, Society and Politics in France since 1789* (London: Hambledon, 1991), pp. 167–86.

Halls, W.D., *Politics, Society and Christianity in Vichy France* (Oxford: Berg, 1995).

Halls, W.D., 'Catholics, the Vichy interlude and after', in S. Fishman et al. (eds), *France at War. Vichy and the Historians* (Oxford: Berg, 2000), pp. 231–45.

Irving, R.E.M., *The Christian Democratic Parties of Western Europe* (London: Allen and Unwin, 1979).

John XXIII, *Souvenirs d'un Nonce. Cahiers de France, 1944–1953* (Rome: Edizioni di Storia e Letteratura, 1963).

Kedward, H.R., and Wood, N. (eds), *The Liberation of France* (Oxford: Berg, 1995).

Kelly, M., 'Catholics and Communism in Liberation France,' in N. Atkin and F. Tallett (eds), *Religion, Society and Politics in France since 1789* (London: Hambledon, 1991), pp. 167–86.

Kselman, T., 'Catholicism, Christianity and Vichy', *French Historical Studies* 23.3 (2000), pp. 513–30.

Langlois, C., 'Le Régime de Vichy et le clergé d'après les *Semaines Religieuses* des diocèses de la zone libre', *Revue Française de Science Politique* 22.4 (1972), pp. 750–73.

Larkin, M., *Religion, Politics and Preferment in France since 1890* (Cambridge: Cambridge University Press, 1995).

Latreille, A., *De Gaulle, la libération et l'Eglise catholique* (Paris: Cerf, 1978).

Le Bras, G., 'Statistique et histoire religieuse: pour un examen détaillé et pour une explication historique de l'état de catholicisme dans les diverses régions de France,' *Revue d'Histoire de l'Église de France* xvii (1931), pp. 425–49.

Lhande, Père, *Le Christ dans la banlieue* (Paris: Plon, 1927).

Marrus, M., and Paxton, R.O., *Vichy France and the Jews* (New York: Basic Books, 1981).

McMillan, J., 'France', in T. Buchanan and M. Conway (eds), *Political Catholicism in Europe, 1918–1945* (Oxford: Oxford University Press, 1996), pp. 34–68.

Michonneau, G., *Revolution in a City Parish* (Oxford: Blackfriars, 1949).

Paul, H.W., *The Second Ralliement. The Rapprochement between Church and State in the Twentieth Century* (Washington: Catholic University of America Press, 1967).

Rémond, R., 'Les Catholiques français pendant la seconde guerre mondiale', *Revue d'Histoire de l'Eglise de France*, July–December 1978, pp. 203–13.

Verlhac, J., 'La jeune génération catholique en 1944 et le parti communiste', in X. Montclos (ed.), *Eglises et Chrétiens dans la IIe guerre mondiale* (Lyon: Presses Universitaires de Lyon, 1978).

Wall, B. (ed.), *Priest and Worker. The Autobiography of Henri Perrin* (London: Macmillan, 1965).

Weber, E., *The Hollow Years. France in the 1930s* (New York: Norton, 1994).

9
Whose Liberation? Confronting the Problem of the French Empire, 1944–47

Martin Shipway

Tuesday, 8 May 1945 . . . In all the succession of significant dates which have been commemorated from the history of the twentieth century, surely none has more ironically and symbolically divergent meanings invested in it, marking as it did *both* the end of the war in Europe, the culmination of France's and occupied Europe's struggle for Liberation, *and* the date on which VE-day celebrations in the Eastern Algerian towns of Sétif and Guelma turned to violent disorder, to the deaths of some hundred European settlers, and then to the wholesale massacre – 'genocide' even, according to recent Algerian claims – of a still disputed number of Algerians (but certainly many thousands), and thus constituted the effective start of the Algerian struggle for national liberation.[1]

The ironic contrast between metropolitan Liberation and the deferral of colonial liberation may both illuminate and obscure the post-war history of French decolonisation. Certainly the events of 8 May 1945 prefigured the almost continuous violence and trauma of France's retreat from colonial empire. Within weeks of the Algerian risings, the French airforce was bombing Damascus and other Syrian cities in a vain attempt to head off France's withdrawal from its League of Nations Mandate in Syria and Lebanon.[2] And the 'long' Liberation over the following two years culminated, in Indochina, in the definitive outbreak in December 1946 of France's eight-year war against the revolutionary Vietnamese regime of Ho Chi Minh. Still less than two years after VE-day, from the end of March 1947, French forces again found themselves repressing nationalist insurrection, this time in Madagascar, and again inflicted massive casualties on the local population.

Decolonisation *was* violent, of course, and arguably the comparative perspective of war and disorder in the French, Dutch, Belgian and Portuguese decolonising endgames offsets the somewhat misleading received idea of a 'peaceful' British decolonisation. Conversely, a comparative approach may help us to recognise what French policy makers thought they were doing in the period of Liberation, and perhaps even to understand what went wrong. The problem with decolonisation is that 'we know the end of the story', and therefore tend to read the history backwards from the moment of independence.[3]

In the French case, two partly complementary narratives tend to be read backwards to their beginnings in our period. According to the first of these, which might be labelled '*Enfin Roosevelt vint*', decolonisation was 'inevitable', at the latest from the moment of the Atlantic Charter signed by Roosevelt and Churchill in August 1941, which proclaimed the 'rights of all peoples to choose their form of government under which they will live'. By this view, French policy makers were merely resisting a global process of change. As one historian puts it:

> The fundamental deficiency of [the Fourth Republic] and its leaders was an inability to recognise and adapt to the fact that the age of colonial empires was coming to a close. The endless parliamentary and party disputes over overseas policy that accompanied successive colonial crises were in reality struggles over the details of a single, fundamentally unsound policy of preserving colonial-style hegemony over the dependencies.[4]

This is a humbling perspective indeed for those historians who seek to engage with the record of such futile 'struggles' over insignificant 'details'.

Secondly, however, the thesis of 'inevitable' decolonisation also squares roughly with a version of French post-war history which projects backwards from the Algerian endgame, and from the return to power in 1958 of France's towering *homme providentiel*, and which might therefore be labelled '*Enfin de Gaulle vint*'. We may readily set aside an earlier myth of a prophetic '*homme de Brazzaville*', who, at the eponymous 1944 Conference, had already mapped out French disengagement from empire.[5] Addressing a more persuasive Gaullist myth, historians and political scientists have long recognised the unloved Fourth Republic's achievements as well as its failures, not least in facilitating eventual French retreat from Indochina, Morocco and Tunisia, if not from Algeria, and in setting up the structures which led to decolonisation in sub-Saharan Africa.[6] Nonetheless, the impression is unavoidable that French decision-making, particularly in colonial policy, was kept 'on hold' for much of the period from the Liberation until the advent of the Fifth Republic.

In the historiography of decolonisation, especially of British decolonisation, a better understanding of the perspective and purpose of an imperial 'official mind' can displace more determinist narratives. A key paradigm in the British literature traces the 'decline, revival and fall' of empire, where the second part of this process is associated with the reinvigoration of imperial purpose following the Second World War.[7] Broadly speaking, empire assumed greater importance for Britain because of the war, and British post-war reconstruction was in part projected on the back of a 'second colonial occupation' of British-held territories, particularly in Africa.[8] Crucially, the *quid pro quo* for this more intensive exploitation of imperial resources was the funding of colonial development, under the 1945 Colonial Development and Welfare Act, and the institution of political reform conceived in terms of gradual evolution towards self-government. Both these processes were imagined as stretching into a distant future under continuing British imperial control.[9] This long-term imperial vista soon proved to be an illusion, but in the mid-1940s it filled the horizon. Though Britain transferred power to India in 1947, and to Ceylon and Burma in 1948, also the year of Britain's humiliating retreat from Palestine, it did so partly through weakness, but also because the Labour government persuaded itself and a metropolitan audience that this was a 'last act' of imperial generosity that would preserve British influence within a new-minted British Commonwealth; that optimism, however, needs to be set against the near-anarchy of the final months of British rule in India, and the violence of Indian Partition. (There was even a brief moment, in 1946, when French officials could reasonably believe they were faring better in Vietnam than the British in India.)

French policy-makers also staged an attempted post-war imperial revival coupled with reform. In this chapter, we explore the rationales for the reformist component of this revival, and seek the reasons for its failure. A starting point may be found in the confidential views of a key colonial official at the Liberation, writing to his Minister in June 1945 in response to the events in Algeria and Syria. Governor Henri Laurentie was a *'gaulliste de la première heure'* who had played a courageous role in rallying Afrique Équatoriale Française (AEF) to de Gaulle in August 1940; three years later, he was appointed Director of Political Affairs in the Commissariat for the Colonies, in de Gaulle's makeshift 'Resistance State' at Algiers, and in this capacity organised the Brazzaville Conference in January–February 1944. Still only 43 years old at the Liberation, Laurentie retained the job in liberated Paris until March 1947, in the Ministry of Colonies (Ministry of Overseas France from January 1946), and thus found himself at the forefront of French colonial policy making, exerting considerable influence on policy in Indochina, sub-Saharan Africa and Madagascar. He may be considered the principal architect of French reformist colonial policy in the Liberation period, the so-called *'politique de Brazzaville'*. In June 1945, that policy was already being undermined, as he saw it, in the aftermath of the Algerian and Syrian crises, from which he extrapolated a more general 'colonial crisis':

> Feelings of disillusionment, disaffection, defiance, and hatred are so general as to be dangerous. Our counterweight is a feeble one: the apathy of the colonial masses can never offset the nationalism which is being born or proclaimed across the empire.
>
> This nationalism is finding expression at the exact moment when our only hope of keeping the Empire was to undertake a massive operation to capture hearts and minds. Providing we made substantial sacrifices here and there, we could hope to reaffirm through renewal the bonds which unite France to her overseas territories. For want of real power we had to deploy different weapons.

> . . . The arguments which we thus allow the nationalists to use against us, including the appearance of weakness which clings to us with the repeated use of force, are such that we now run the risk of being dragged into a chain of events which we can no longer control. One more 'incident', if we are unlucky, would be enough to set off the final avalanche.[10]

This very personal document, typed on plain, unheaded paper, and suggestive of the burning of midnight oil, offers a way into the perspective of the French 'official mind' at this key juncture, and Laurentie's 'liberal' reformism provides the focus for much of what follows.

Three aspects of this reformism will be studied here. First, part of Laurentie's frustration came from the fact that, notwithstanding the rhetoric of 'Overseas France' and the centralising impulses of the French Republic, the empire was not a homogeneous monolith. Imperial administration was divided between several ministries, and Algeria and Syria fell outside the responsibility of the Ministry of Colonies. Imperial unity was indeed a priority for the Gaullists going back to 1940, and we explore the background to the Brazzaville Conference in this light. Secondly, however, the core of Laurentie's message was the 'operation to capture hearts and minds', and we may consider the discussions at Brazzaville in this light, and the reasons why the reforms emerging the conference fell so far short of this ideal. Thirdly, May–June 1945 was a pivotal moment, and Laurentie's memorandum, with its slightly odd use of the imperfect tense (*'avions . . . pouvions . . . faisions . . .'*, in the French version of the second paragraph quoted above), suggested that the so-called 'spirit of Brazzaville' was already flagging. The remainder of the Chapter thus traces the fortunes of the 'Brazzaville policy' over the following two years in Indochina, Black Africa and Madagascar: in the first and last of these cases, Laurentie's striking equation between French weakness and the repeated use of force was to prove prophetic indeed.

The search for imperial unity

The Brazzaville Conference was in part intended to celebrate the uniting of the French empire under the authority of de Gaulle's Comité Français de la Libération Nationale (CFLN) at Algiers. This process stretched back to 1940 and, with one crucial piece missing, was completed on Bastille Day 1943, when the French Antilles (West Indies) rallied to de Gaulle. The exception was Indochina, still under Japanese suzerainty, and under the Vichyite authority of Governor-General Jean Decoux, who remained in place even after the effective end of the Vichy regime, until overthrown by the Japanese on 9 March 1945.

Those Governors and Governors-General who deliberated at Brazzaville were thus defined by their loyalty to de Gaulle. Officials of the four constituent colonies of AEF and Cameroun had all undergone the 'palace revolutions' involved in rallying to de Gaulle in July–August 1940 (slightly later in

Gabon, where Gaullists faced a brief but bloody stand-off with Pétainists).[11] Félix Eboué, then Governor of Chad, a Guyanese of African descent nearing the end of a career stretching back to the early 1900s, became Governor-General of '*Afrique Française Libre*' at Brazzaville, where de Gaulle established a makeshift capital. Laurentie, Éboué's Secretary-General at Fort-Lamy, moved with him to Brazzaville. The Governor-General of Afrique Occidentale Française (AOF), Pierre Boisson, resisted de Gaulle's appeals and repelled the disastrous Anglo-Gaullist Dakar expedition of September 1940. AOF thus came under complete Gaullist authority only in July 1943, and even then personnel changes were limited: at senior levels only Boisson and four out of seven Governors were replaced; a fifth Governor, Croccichia of Guinée, failed to attend at Brazzaville, and was relieved of his post; in all, only about twenty officials in AOF were purged. Similarly, when the CFLN moved from Algiers to Paris, a *Commission d'Epuration* was established at the Ministry of Colonies, but even quite senior officials kept their jobs.[12]

Loyalty to de Gaulle did not equate with reformist dynamism, and in many cases wartime Gaullism revived flagging careers, or simply delayed retirement; this was arguably the case for the new Governors-General of AOF, Pierre Cournarie, and Madagascar, Pierre de Saint-Mart. An ailing Éboué, whose chairmanship at Brazzaville was hindered by poor health and poor hearing, died a few months later in Cairo.[13] A more significant characteristic of the Governors was that eighteen of twenty-one deliberative members at Brazzaville were graduates of the École Nationale de la France d'Outre-Mer (ENFOM), and thus members of France's newest *grand corps d'État*, the Corps Colonial. Although it could be charged with imposing an unthinking conformism, ENFOM was nonetheless the only *grande école*, before the foundation of the École Nationale de l'Administration in 1947, which specifically trained administrators, as opposed to engineers, army officers, teachers, *et al.*[14] Given that ENFOM's rise dated from the 1920s, this was the first time that such a majority of senior ranking 'Colo' graduates was mustered. Brazzaville was thus a defining moment for the French colonial service's *esprit de corps*.[15] Significantly, perhaps, given his subsequent maverick role, Laurentie was one of the three non-ENFOM graduates.

If *esprit de corps* was a crucial factor at Brazzaville and subsequently, so too, indirectly, were inter-service rivalries. The Empire was divided into a number of discrete components, reflecting the pattern of conquest and acquisition. Two of the three French North African territories, Tunisia and Morocco, were protectorates under international treaties signed at Le Bardo (in 1881), and Fez (in 1912), which preserved the sovereignty of the Bey of Tunis and of the Sultan of Morocco, but in practice did not prevent the establishment of substantial settler minorities in both countries. Algeria, meanwhile, had been governed since 1848 according to the constitutional fiction that it was part of French national territory. Algeria's coastal plains and mountains were thus divided into *départements* on the metropolitan model, while the Southern Territories of the Sahara were the province of the Army (and attained civil status as *départements* only in the late 1950s). This facilitated European settlement, and by the 1940s a settler community numbering some 800,000 consigned the eight million indigenous Algerians to 'second-class' status within their own country. Syria and Lebanon, as League of Nations 'A'-Class Mandated Territories, were destined for eventual independence (although the Popular Front's promise of independence had been deferred), and were thus not classed as 'colonial' territories either.

Imperial policy thus had to be co-ordinated between three rival ministries: Colonies, Foreign Affairs (responsible for the North African protectorates and the Levant Mandates), and Interior (which oversaw the Algerian *départements*). Within the latter two ministries, whose central attention was 'directed elsewhere',[16] a powerful and entrenched *Direction* acted as an effective screen blocking out ministerial or parliamentary interference: the *Direction de l'Afrique-Levant* at the Foreign Ministry and the *Sous-direction de l'Algérie* at the Interior. Although disrupted by the war, this informal system of 'sealed partitions' was fully operational by the time of Brazzaville. Indeed, the original plan had been for a grand imperial conference at Brazzaville, and Laurentie vigorously argued the case for coordinating policy between the different parts of the empire.[17] However, caution prevailed, presumably with de Gaulle's approval, and, given that Indochina was necessarily excluded from the debate, Brazzaville's agenda was restricted to sub-Saharan Africa and the Indian Ocean (Madagascar and dependencies, Réunion). Officials of the Rabat, Tunis and Algiers administrations attended Brazzaville as observers, intervening only to curb the reformist impulses of Laurentie and others. Moreover, where the Conference addressed themes of relevance to North Africa, relating, for example, to Islam or the use of Arabic in schools, passages were struck from the record; this was a customary, but nonetheless striking, instance of official discretion.[18]

The limits of imperial reform at the Liberation

The Brazzaville Conference failed, in large measure because too much was invested in it. Aside from celebrating imperial unity, it was staged as an international propaganda event, as de Gaulle was keen to counter American hostility, including President Roosevelt's personal animosity, towards the post-war revival of French colonialism.[19] Brazzaville, and in particular de Gaulle's famous *'discours de Brazzaville'*, his opening address to the Conference whose proceedings he did not attend, was thus the equivalent of Churchill's affirmation in October 1942 that he had 'not become the King's First Minister in order to preside over the liquidation of the British Empire'. There was a parallel too with the aim of liberating French metropolitan territory without undue American involvement. It was also crucial to match the policy declarations made by British spokesmen and the exiled Queen of the Netherlands since the signing of the Atlantic Charter in October 1941. One official captured the ambiguity of all this, identifying two distinct questions to be answered at the Conference:

1. What is our imperial policy?
2. What is the French imperial policy that we should declare to be ours before a foreign audience?

It was the second question, however, which he considered the more significant:

We should immediately adopt the noblest definition. We should make it our solemn wish to grant the most generous settlement to our possessions. In every international conference we should show ourselves to be the most liberal, the least imperialist of nations. But we should take every opportunity to proclaim, with the same fervour as General Smuts, that our national sovereignty over our colonies must remain intact, and that those nations which have been solely responsible for their colonies in the past should retain sole responsibility for them in future.[20]

Simply on its own terms, as a ten-day conference of colonial practitioners held behind closed doors, the Conference achieved its objectives, and covered a wide agenda ranging from technical issues to sometimes abstruse discussions of the largely sophistical distinction between Assimilation and Association as guiding principles of French colonialism. In a modest way it set down guidelines for future colonial policy in Africa, including recommending long overdue reforms such as abolishing forced labour (banned in a 1930 convention, to which France was a signatory), and ending the *indigénat*, the system of arbitrary administrative justice. The first of these measures, championed by Félix Houphouët-Boigny (whose political career it helped launch), and made law by the First Constituent Assembly in April 1946, was of huge symbolic significance, although the issue was scarcely debated, since 'merely reminding the world that a system akin to slavery existed in French Africa rendered it indefensible'.[21]

Where the Conference backfired most seriously was in Laurentie's attempt to steer debate towards an ambitious proposal to re-organise the Empire along federal lines, a far wider question than the Conference was competent to discuss, but by the same token too big a question simply to go away. The idea was more or less ruled *ultra vires*, but it seems to have provoked the Conference's most infamous statement:

Before examining this [political] part of the agenda, the French African Conference at Brazzaville decided to establish the following principle: 'The ends of the civilising mission accomplished in the colonies exclude any idea of autonomy, all possibility of evolution outside the French bloc;

> also excluded is the eventual establishment of *self governments* [*sic*] in the colonies, even in a distant future.'[22]

This is often taken as evidence that the Governors missed, or were deliberately eschewing, a 'chance for a serious debate on independence',[23] but that was simply unthinkable in the context of 1944. A more plausible interpretation is that they were engaged in a virtual debate with their British counterparts – hence the awkward *franglais* formulation – and were rejecting the alien concept of self-government, since on the whole even the most liberal officials believed they have something better to offer. However, this was hardly a bold proclamation of colonial liberalism, which partly explains Brazzaville's anti-climactic aftermath.

Brazzaville was the first, faltering stage in a wider, and necessarily complex, debate directed towards rethinking the Empire, which was common to the two major colonial powers, and indeed to the Dutch and Belgians as well (although it would be more difficult to fit the Salazarist or Francoist empires within this paradigm). This was largely an internal debate, not least because it gave rise to the sorts of disagreements aired at Brazzaville. However, there was a broad point of agreement, on which French, British and other officials would have concurred, which was that Empire *had* a future. The aim was to set colonial rule on a proper footing, to engineer the late colonial state on surer foundations than the circumstances of conquest and colonial consolidation had allowed. The intended method, at least on the 'liberal' side of the argument, was not simply to maintain the colonial state through minimal reform, but rather to transform it into a more effective instrument for development, while at the same time anchoring and legitimating its activities through as extensive a system of political representation as was consistent with continuing colonial control.[24]

Laurentie's federal vision may be fitted into this broad imperial project. Although rejected at Brazzaville, de Gaulle took up the idea, announcing in a speech in New York, in July 1944, his belief 'that every territory over which the French flag flies must be represented within a federal system which includes the *Métropole* and where the interests of each party may be heard'.[25] The constitutional project went through a series of iterations, but the essential principle remained fairly constant, which, broadly speaking, was to pull the threads of Empire together into what came to be called the French Union: the name was first used publicly in the Declaration on Indochina of 24 March 1945 (see below), and was apparently chosen in sentimental homage to France's new ally, the Soviet Union (while the term 'Federation' evoked the wrong anti-Republican resonances). This is how Laurentie summed up the scheme in March 1945:

> All French territories are destined to attain their political majority. Some have already achieved this: Morocco, Tunisia, Indochina, New Caledonia. Others have some way to go, and they will remain under the control (*en tutelle*) of the French executive, which will also retain some measure of

legislative control. But this executive control will be provisional: the United Territories will evolve as is appropriate in each case, either towards the assimilated status of Overseas Departments (*Départements d'Outre-Mer*), or towards the status of Associated States.[26]

There is a high level of abstraction here, and key terms such as 'political majority' (or, in other texts, 'political personality') are never adequately defined. Moreover, the categories were unstable, so that, for example, Madagascar was sometimes judged to have attained its majority – a judgement which certainly squared with that of Malagasy nationalists – and sometimes grouped with the African Federations.[27] Laurentie exceeded the limits of his official competence by proposing the North African protectorates as candidates for the status of 'Associated State': the proposal was readily deflected by the 'sealed partitions', and was never realised. However, even Laurentie avoided the anathema of including Algeria in his schemes. There was nonetheless considerable novelty in the idea of bifurcating development towards *either* autonomy within the overarching framework of French control, *or* complete assimilation into the French Republic. The latter option was exercised as early as April 1946, with the Loi Aimé Césaire creating the four *Départements d'Outre-Mer* of Martinique, Guadeloupe, Guyane and Réunion.[28]

Laurentie's scheme was an ideal which needed to be tested against imperial realities. In this it had much in common with the planning, also conducted in a political vacuum, which characterised much British colonial policy, or that of the Dutch for their ill-fated 'return' to Indonesia. In the French case, it may also be set alongside wartime planning by the metropolitan Resistance, which was comparably limited both in political perspective and in later applicability.[29] After the Liberation, colonial policy was quickly exposed to the turbulence generated by rapidly moving events, and to the oxygen of Parisian politics. We now assess how the principles of the French Union came to be applied, and more particularly misapplied, in the period to early 1947, when France and the French Union moved into the post-lapsarian world of the Fourth Republic.

Indochina, 1945–47: missed opportunities, lost initiatives

The Declaration of 24 March 1945 was intended as a major policy statement regarding not only Indochina, but also the eventual status of Associated States throughout the French Union. However, it had already been outpaced by the Japanese takeover in Indochina on 9 March 1945, which installed 'independent' nationalist governments in Hanoi, Phnom Penh and Vientiane. The French declaration, presented two weeks later by the Minister of Colonies, Paul Giacobbi, thus seemed merely a reaction to events, although it had been drafted over several months.[30] It was nonetheless a striking statement of imperial intent, providing a framework for French actions in Indochina.

Indochina was to have a federal government, within the French Union, representing all national communities including settlers, an elected assembly and a nominated Council of State, a dual system of Indochinese and French Union citizenship allowing access to administrative posts within Indochina and across the French Union, 'compulsory and effective' primary education, and economic autonomy in which industrialisation would be encouraged. Conversely, French control was to be assured by a Governor-General. Of key significance for the future, the Federation was divided into five 'countries . . . distinguished by civilisation, race and traditions'. There were sound reasons for imposing this model. Whereas pre-war Indochina was a patchwork of kingdoms, protectorates, concessions (Hanoi and Haiphong) and one actual colony (Cochinchina), the five federal units would now each have equal status; and a better demographic balance would be achieved between Laos, Cambodia and the three highly populous regions (or *ky*) of Vietnam: Tonkin, Annam and Cochinchina.[31] But the tripartite division of Vietnam was historically dubious, and was contradicted by facts on the ground: even Decoux had referred to 'Vietnam'; and by August 1945, Emperor Bao Dai's rule had been asserted over all three regions of a (re-)united Vietnam.[32]

A gulf widened between the March Declaration and the intelligence picture that was pieced together over the summer. Colonial Ministry officials, first and foremost Laurentie, sought to move away from the restrictive provisions of the Declaration. In September, Laurentie came close to 'going public' in favour of recognising some limited form of independence for Vietnam, but was overruled by a furious de Gaulle.[33] By contrast, the new High Commissioner's primary mission, combining the roles of Governor-General and Commander-in-Chief, was 'to restore French sovereignty over the territory of the Indochinese Union'; to ensure compliance, de Gaulle appointed an unswervingly loyal member of his entourage, the aristocratic former Carmelite monk, Admiral Georges Thierry d'Argenlieu.

French policy-makers were again wrong-footed by a momentous sequence of events. First, at Potsdam in July 1945, the Allies (not including de Gaulle) agreed that, to receive the Japanese surrender, Indochina would be temporarily occupied north of the 16th Parallel by Chinese Nationalist troops within the American China Command, and by Indian Army troops of Mountbatten's South-East Asia Command South of that line. Secondly, the bombing of Hiroshima and Nagasaki, followed by the Japanese surrender on 15 August, left the French completely unprepared for their planned 'return'. And thirdly, in late August, the Viet Minh (League for the Independence of Vietnam), a broad front of nationalist groups spearheaded by the clandestine Indochinese Communist Party, and led by a former Comintern agent now calling himself Ho Chi Minh ('He who Enlightens'), descended from the mountains, overthrew the government in Hanoi, and prompted Bao Dai's abdication from the imperial throne; on 2 September, Ho declared independence for the Democratic Republic of Vietnam.

These events dictated French actions over the following six months. In the South, the British commander, General Gracey, assisted the French Expeditionary Corps commanded by General Leclerc, who concluded a brilliant campaign of 'pacification' across Cochinchina and Cambodia in early 1946. In the North, troops of the Yunnanese General Lu Han blocked both French and Vietnamese designs, and seemed to be settling in indefinitely, awakening secular Vietnamese fears of Chinese imperialism. So although the Potsdam partition barred the North to French officials, apart from a beleaguered emissary in Hanoi, Jean Sainteny, it provided a lever in negotiations with Ho. In February 1946, French diplomats secured an agreement for Chinese withdrawal in return for the cession of all French extraterritorial and transit rights in China. This then paved the way for Sainteny's agreement with Ho on 6 March 1946, which allowed French troops and officials into Hanoi. However, Sainteny had been pushed to the wall by a last-minute confrontation between French and Chinese forces: Leclerc urged Sainteny to do anything to secure agreement, in order to avoid further bloodshed and a military fiasco.[34]

The March 1946 Accords marked a brief moment when French officials might reflect positively on their achievements within the competitive arena of Asian colonialism, as Laurentie argued:

> We must consider that opinion in Asia is generally hostile to the colonial powers. Britain's difficulties in India, and those of the Dutch in Indonesia, are ample proof of this. It is therefore remarkable that our country should by amicable means have arrived at a definition of common ground with [Vietnamese] nationalism.[35]

France recognised the Democratic Republic of Vietnam (DRV) as 'a Free State with its own government, parliament, army, and finances, forming a part of the Indochinese Federation and of the French Union'; the question of the three *ky* was to be put to a referendum. Thus far, the Accords were within the bounds (just) of the structures envisaged in the March 1945 Declaration. The idea of containing a Vietnamese state ('free', but not independent) within the double casing of Indochina and the French Union was even imitated by Dutch officials confronting Sukarno's Indonesia.[36] However, Sainteny had also agreed, in an Annex to the Accords, to progressive French troop withdrawals over five years, which would leave Vietnam in Ho's hands. It was this agreement which enabled Ho Chi Minh to 'sell' the Accords to his more intransigent lieutenants, but it ensured that the Accords were never accepted, either by d'Argenlieu, who had remained aloof from negotiations, and was steeling himself for a showdown following de Gaulle's ill-tempered resignation in January 1946, or by the Gouin government (on the verge of presenting the first constitutional text in the referendum of 5 May 1946).

The Accords thus amounted to a purely tactical agreement, allowing a French foothold in northern Indochina, and ostensibly restoring French sovereignty, but only marginally slowing the descent into the violence which more accurately reflected the distance between French and Viet Minh objectives. Ho Chi Minh presented himself as a head of state in his dealings with French officials, and during his protracted visit to France from June to September 1946. Meanwhile, the Viet Minh consolidated its regime, sidelining or liquidating supporters and leaders of Chinese-backed (and now isolated) parties, and re-establishing links with the South. But against a backdrop of growing anti-Communism in Paris, French officials based in Saigon were unremittingly hostile towards the 'brutal and puerile' Viet Minh, and interpreted the Accords as a purely local agreement with 'Tonkin', to be set alongside the agreements signed with the sovereigns of Cambodia (7 January 1946) and Laos (7 May 1946). Similar agreements were envisaged with Annam and, crucially, Cochinchina, where a provisional government of pro-French notables was assembled. The Franco-Vietnamese conference envisaged in the Accords, held at Fontainebleau, almost inevitably failed, but Ho returned to Vietnam with an eleventh-hour *modus vivendi* agreed with the Minister of Overseas France, Marius Moutet (SFIO), in mid-September, which held out hopes – as it turned out vain hopes – of a ceasefire and a referendum on Cochinchina.

Events leading to the violent breakdown of relations between the French and the Viet Minh have been amply covered elsewhere. Given the sense of doom which attaches to the first of France's long wars of decolonisation, it is striking that French officials and soldiers felt no sense of failure at this crucial juncture, much less of insoluble colonial conflict. This was partly a question of military over-confidence. Although the initial French riposte to the Viet Minh attacks of 19 December was disappointing, the 'hawks' who had plotted for action remained convinced that a quick military victory could be achieved. Indeed, French military leaders remained intermittently so convinced until the bitter end. But already in late 1946, officials had a plan to sidestep Ho Chi Minh altogether, and to recognise a State of Vietnam conforming more closely to French interests.[37] This involved reinstating Bao Dai, still under a cloud following, first, his collaboration with the Japanese and, second, his role as Ho's 'Supreme Counsellor', and in refuge in Hong Kong. It took two years for this 'Bao Dai solution' to be implemented. However, by the time the 'Associated State' of Vietnam was created, in July 1949, the Dutch were negotiating their withdrawal from Indonesia, and Southeast Asia was about to be transformed by Mao Zedong's victory in China. The concept of an 'independent' Vietnam freely associating with the French Union was thus even less plausible that it had appeared in 1945.

Black Africa and Madagascar: the impossible calculus of overseas representation

The pressure of events substantially beyond France's control had thus compromised Indochina's role as a model for relations between *métropole* and periphery within the brand new French Union. Black Africa and Madagascar offer in many ways the opposite scenario. French control was never in doubt, even when it came to suppressing nationalist revolt in Madagascar. And the defeat of federalism at Brazzaville already pointed towards a more traditional approach to colonial reform. The tradition in question was that of Assimilation, which allowed parliamentary representation for the citizens of Overseas France, mostly settlers but including assimilated *colonisés*; indeed, this was implied in the constitutional status of a colony (as opposed to a protectorate, etc). Amongst French colonies in this strict sense were the 'Four Communes' of coastal Senegal, notably Dakar, which had been represented by an African *député* since 1914. Almost as an afterthought, the Brazzaville Conference recommended the representation of '*territoires d'outre-mer*' (the term 'colony' was considered politically incorrect) in an eventual Constituent Assembly. A quirk of colonial history was thus extended to the whole of AOF, AEF, Madagascar, Algeria, and various smaller dependencies, which all sent representatives to the two Constituent Assemblies (1945–46) and eventually to both Chambers of the National Assembly. Tradition by itself did not rule out innovation, and the presence of colonial Deputies in the metropolitan capital (unthinkable in British imperial and parliamentary practice) was a striking feature of French late colonial politics. However, it did raise significant points of principle: what would constitute equitable representation? How was that to be squared with local representative structures? And what of those who yet resisted the French Republican embrace?

Although Assimilation was at odds with the federal principle, Laurentie backed the proposals made by a Commission set up in early 1945 to devise a scheme for colonial elections. Chaired by the Guyanese ACP member and future Senate leader, Gaston Monnerville, this Commission brought together African notables (including future Deputies Léopold Sédar Senghor of Senegal and the Dahomeyan, Sourou Migan Apithy), colonial 'experts' and officials. The Commission recommended universal suffrage, with no distinction between 'citizens' and 'non-citizens'. The Commission also established one persistent feature of the system, which was that each constituency would include approximately 800,000 inhabitants (i.e. about ten times more than in metropolitan France). Laurentie's Minister, Giacobbi, preferring the advice of the African Governors and Governors-General to Laurentie's urgent lobbying, overturned these bold but coherent recommendations. A double college system was imposed, guaranteeing a voice for the tiny settler communities in the sub-Saharan territories (although in Senegal, the African mayor of Dakar, Lamine Guèye of the Socialist Section Française de l'Internationale Ouvrière (SFIO), was elected). Limited suffrage was introduced for non-citizens, based on criteria such as military service, literacy or post-holding (e.g. appointed village chiefs). As Laurentie commented, 'This is a failure with regard to our principles, and in political terms it is dangerous.'[38] For the 1945 elections, constituencies were composed of two neighbouring (but otherwise disparate) territories, so that, in AOF, while Côte d'Ivoire stood alone, Senegal was fused with Mauritania, Dahomey with Togo, Soudan with Niger, and were in each case to be represented by one 'citizen' Deputy and one 'non-citizen' Deputy. Subsequently, constituencies were realigned with individual territories – in effect, the future independent states of francophone Africa.

Although compromised from the start, and although the October 1945 elections came within a hair's breadth of administrative fiasco, the parliamentary presence of African and other colonial Deputies ensured a hearing for colonial issues. This was due not least to the alliances (*apparentements*) forged between the Overseas Deputies and the SFIO and Parti Communiste Français (PCF) (and subsequently the Christian Democratic Mouvement Républicain Populaire (MRP) and other parties). In late 1946, the group split between SFIO Deputies and those who joined the new Rassemblement Démocratique Africain (RDA), which allied with the PCF. Towards its end, the first Constituent Assembly passed several laws fleshing out some of the Brazzaville recommendations, including those abolishing forced labour and the *indigénat*, already mentioned, and the Law of 30 April 1946, introducing the principle of a Fonds d'Investissement pour le Développement Economique et Social (FIDES), a counterpart to the British Colonial Development and Welfare Fund. The landmark Law of 7 May 1946, presented by Lamine Guèye, created a common citizenship of the French Union, which, although only vaguely defined, provided 'a reference point for future campaigns for equality between Africans and Europeans'.[39] This made the double-college system untenable, in AOF at least, though it was retained until 1956 in AEF and Cameroun. Local assemblies also maintained a double college until 1956, most notoriously the Algerian Assembly created by the 1947 Algerian Statute. Algerian, African and Malagasy Deputies' numbers increased from their October 1945 base, but they remained a small minority in the Assembly. For if the number of overseas Deputies ever reflected the demographic balance of the French Union, France would become, as Edouard Herriot famously put it, 'a colony of her former colonies'.[40] Although Senghor condemned this 'racism', Herriot was merely stating the obvious limits of French assimilation. So for the duration of the Fourth Republic, one metropolitan French citizen equated with approximately ten Africans. Universal suffrage was introduced in 1956, when Gaston Defferre's Loi-Cadre extended real powers to local assemblies, and thus transformed the system.[41] Meanwhile, the Overseas Deputies, who 'naturally took a detached view of much French parliamentary business', exercised an influence disproportionate (thanks to the always uncertain majorities of Fourth Republic governments) to their number and 'colonial' status, and 'behaved, with growing effect, like territorial spokesmen in a federal senate'.[42]

The Overseas Deputies quickly learned the rules of the parliamentary game, albeit the hard way. In return for their support of the Communist/Socialist unicameral constitutional model, they received majority backing for the French Union articles in the constitutional draft. These stated that France formed a 'freely consented Union' with the Overseas Territories and the Associated States; substantial powers were to be devolved to territorial assemblies, elected by universal suffrage; and Under-Secretaries of State replaced colonial Governors. This 'Constitution Senghor' has rightly been seen as a blueprint for radical reform, but less plausibly as a 'missed opportunity' for decolonisation.[43] Fear of an all-powerful Communist-dominated Assembly, rather than popular disapproval of the French Union articles, led to the 'No' vote in the May referendum. On 16 June 1946, de Gaulle broke his silence following his resignation in January, and in his speech at Bayeux, *inter alia*, he denounced the French Union articles. Although officials initially reassured Overseas Deputies that the French Union articles would remain intact, their objections to the draft stemmed not only from anti-Communism, but were also from organisational considerations: as the elections had demonstrated, the political and administrative infrastructure of the African Federations was still embryonic and fragile, and would scarcely sustain the kind of demands that would thus be placed upon it.[44] Laurentie's Minister, Marius Moutet, was in any case carried along by the growing conservative consensus in favour of revision, led by the MRP leader, Georges Bidault. Following some stormy debates in the Chamber, and the decisive intervention of Ministry officials, led by Laurentie, the draft approved in the October 1946 referendum was much less radical in its implications both for the Republic and for the French Union. Although the legislative advances of the first Assembly were retained, 'Overseas Territories' now effectively differed from colonies in name only. A few months later, the outbreak of the Malagasy insurrection seemed to confirm the conservative drift in overseas policy.

The Malagasy exception

In Laurentie's federal schemes, Madagascar was sometimes identified as belonging in the category of territories which might in time become an Associated State.[45] It was perceived as having a continuous indigenous tradition of political activity, and dissent, and a strong national identity based on its pre-colonial statehood, which, it was believed, could nonetheless be accommodated within a French-oriented framework. Certainly, Malagasy nationalists placed themselves explicitly in a long line of resistance to colonial rule, going back to the French annexation of 1895–96 (an anniversary marked in August 1946 by a 'day of national mourning'), and defined their goal as national liberation and restoration of national sovereignty. When the Insurrection came in March 1947, insurgents fought under the red-and-white flag of the Malagasy monarchy, emblazoned with eighteen stars representing the united 'peoples' of Madagascar. Conversely, French officials discounted the thesis of national unity, preferring their official history, according to which France had liberated the oppressed 'coastal peoples' of Madagascar from the 'imperialism' of the Merina kingdom; this counter-argument found political expression, against the background of worsening political disorder in Madagascar up to March 1947, in official suspicion of the Deputies' party, the Mouvement pour la Rénovation Malgache (MDRM), against which they favoured a new Parti des Déshérités Malgaches (PADESM).[46]

The relationship between insurgents and the 'legitimate' nationalist movement was crucial, but ambiguous. The lifting of the three Malagasy Deputies' parliamentary immunity, and their conviction after a virtual show trial in Tananarive in 1948, rested on the evidence of a telegram sent on 27 March 1947 by two of the three, Joseph Ravoahangy and Jacques Rabemananjara, warning MDRM members against precipitate action: although they had got wind of the planned attacks, the telegram was almost certainly not, as the French authorities alleged, a coded message launching the insurrection. The Deputies were arguably 'guilty', but not as charged. Quite apart from the fact that the MDRM, quickly banned, was heavily infiltrated by the secret societies which launched the insurrection (and which were also banned), the three Deputies two of whom, Raseta and Ravoahangy, were veterans of the national cause enjoying immense prestige at home, could be seen as playing a risky double political game. As Deputies, they were participating in the already somewhat tarnished imperial project of the French Union. However by portraying themselves to their electorates as ambassadors, consorting with Ho Chi Minh during his stay in Paris over the Summer 1946,[47] and pleading the justice of the Malagasy national cause, they exhausted the limited reserves of French official liberalism, but also risked raising unrealistic political expectations at home. The insurrection may partly be seen in this light as encouragement for the Deputies' Parisian campaign, and the articulation of disappointment that they were achieving so little.

More than other episodes of late colonial violence, our understanding of the Malagasy insurrection suffers from inadequate access to the historical record, which has tended to be augmented by myth. This may partly be due to the close association between the insurrection, events in Indochina, and the expulsion of Communist ministers from the Ramadier government in May 1947, which helped create a partisan *cause célèbre*. Reports of torture and atrocities, including the aerial defenestration of prisoners, and of the violence of Foreign Legionnaires and *tirailleurs sénégalais*, have all been reliably documented, but at the time these reports, exaggerated by rumour, generated an inchoate impression of generalised French brutality. This was apparently confirmed by a later, largely unfounded, *official* death toll of around 80,000 (typically amplified to 100,000): as Jean Fremigacci has commented, for once the Communists were happy to take their adversaries at their word.[48] A more plausible estimate, nearer 10,000, is appalling enough, especially given a further 20,000–30,000 deaths attributable to malnutrition and disease amongst refugees; but it places the Malagasy insurrection more in line with post-war insurgencies in British-held territories such as Malaya, Kenya and Cyprus. As in Malaya and Kenya, the colonial military campaign easily crushed a poorly armed insurgency, and also achieved its immediate political goals, in that the 'separatist' MDRM was destroyed. But the political costs were high indeed, not least the long-term cost of France's lost reputation as a would-be 'liberal' colonial power, as Madagascar, along with Sétif and Guelma, became a by-word for 'colonial massacre'.

Conclusion

The Malagasy insurrection delivered the *coup de grâce* to the 'Brazzaville policy', and further exposed the contradictions inherent in the federal idea. The Malagasy *députés* were arguably condemned for claiming what federalism might have offered them: some measure of independence within the parameters of a continuing relationship with France. In Indochina, conversely, French forces were ostensibly fighting not so much over a principle as over the likely beneficiary of that principle: the core of the March 1946 Accords (if not the contentious Annex) conformed to both Vietnamese and French designs, but by the end of 1946 Ho Chi Minh had put himself almost irremediably beyond the pale. Curiously, a further short-term defeat for federalism was reflected in the presence of African *députés* in the Palais Bourbon, which ironically confirmed the Brazzaville Conference's interdiction of 'self governments', and it would take ten years for a viable system of local assemblies to emerge in the wake of Defferre's Loi-Cadre of 1956.

At Brazzaville, de Gaulle had given few hostages to fortune, resting his case for imperial reform on the unanswerable argument that the war had wrought irreversible changes; that France would act on those changes 'because she is France, [whose] immortal genius is destined to raise men gradually towards the summits of dignity and fraternity where they can one day unite'; that imperial reform flowed from France's gratitude to her overseas territories for their fidelity in war; and that France was 'animated . . . by an ardent and practical will to renewal'.[49] By early 1947, the provisional limits of French imperial renewal had been reached. In this, and despite French forces' serial violent encounters with resurgent anti-colonial nationalism, those limits were comparable with those established by other European colonial powers. But de Gaulle had also enunciated a more hazardous principle, that it was France's sole prerogative to 'proceed at the right moment to the reforms of imperial structure which she will decide in her sovereignty'. It would take the seventeen tumultuous years of France's post-war withdrawal from empire for French statesmen, including de Gaulle, to absorb the lesson that such reforms were not in France's gift.

Notes

1. J.-C. Jauffret, 'The origins of the Algerian War: the reaction of France and its army to the emergencies of 8 May 1945 and 1 November 1954', in R. Holland (ed.),

Emergencies and Disorder in the European empires after 1945 (London: Frank Cass, 1994), pp. 17–29; M. Harbi, 'La guerre d'Algérie a commencé à Sétif', *Le Monde Diplomatique*, May 2005.

2. M. Thomas, 'Divisive decolonization: the Anglo-French withdrawal from Syria and Lebanon, 1944–46', *Journal of Imperial and Commonwealth Studies* 28 (2000), pp. 71–93.

3. F. Cooper, *Decolonization and African Society: the Labor question in French and British Africa* (Cambridge: CUP, 1996), p. 6.

4. J.I. Lewis, 'The MRP and the genesis of the French Union, 1944–1948', *French History* 12/3 (1998), pp. 276–314: p. 276.

5. Institut Charles de Gaulle and IHTP, *Brazzaville, aux sources de la decolonisation* (Paris: IHTP and Plon, 1988), hereafter cited as *Brazzaville*.

6. V. Wright, *The Government and Politics of France*, 3rd edn (London: Unwin Hyman, 1989), p. 1.

7. J. Gallagher, *The Decline, Revival and Fall of the British Empire* (Cambridge: Cambridge University Press, 1982).

8. See e.g. J. Hargreaves, *Decolonization in Africa*, 2nd edn (Harlow: Longman, 1996).

9. R. Hyam (ed.), *The Labour Government and the End of Empire*, British Documents on the End of Empire, A/2 (London: HMSO, 1992).

10. Archives Nationales (AN), 72AJ535 (Papiers Henri Laurentie), *Note*, 20/21 June 1945.

11. M. Thomas, *The French Empire at War, 1940–1945* (Manchester: Manchester University Press, 1998), pp. 56ff.

12. W.B. Cohen, *Rulers of Empire: the French Colonial Service in Africa* (Stanford: Stanford UP, 1971), pp. 169–70; P. Novick, *The Resistance versus Vichy: the Purge of Collaborators in Liberated France* (London: Chatto and Windus, 1968), pp. 86–93.

13. B.Weinstein, *Eboué* (New York: Oxford University Press, 1972), pp. 310–12.

14. Cohen, *Rulers of Empire*; for a critical view, see an ex-Governor's memoir, Louis Sanmarco, *Le colonial colonisé* (Paris: ABC, 1983).

15. M. Shipway, 'Reformism and the French "Official Mind": the 1944 Brazzaville Conference and the legacy of the Popular Front', in T. Chafer and A. Sackur (eds), *French Colonial Empire and the Popular Front: Hope and Disillusion* (Basingstoke: Macmillan – now Palgrave Macmillan, 1999), pp. 131–51.

16. Laurentie, *Note*, 20/21 June 1945, loc.cit.

17. *Note*, Laurentie to Gaston Palewski, Directeur du Cabinet du Général de Gaulle, 8 December 1943, AN, 3AG1-279 (papiers de Gaulle).

18. *Brazzaville*.

19. W.R. Louis, *Imperialism at Bay: the United States and The Decolonization of the British Empire* (Oxford: Oxford University Press, 1977).

20. Notes sur le programme général de la conférence de Brazzaville, DE CURTON, 20 Oct. 1943, AOM, AP/2288/4. The South African wartime leader had declared, somewhat improbably, that the British Commonwealth was the 'greatest organised system of human freedom in history'.

21. F. Cooper, *Africa since 1940* (Cambridge: Cambridge University Press, 2002), p. 42.

22. Ministère des Colonies, *La Conférence Africaine Française* (Paris, 1945), p. 32.

23. R. Kedward, *La Vie en bleu: France and the French since 1900* (London: Penguin, 2005), p. 318.

24. This argument is developed in M. Shipway, *Decolonization and its Impact: a Comparative Approach to the end of Colonial Rule* (Oxford: Blackwell, 2007, forthcoming).

25. 10 July 1944, Charles de Gaulle, *Discours et messages*, Vol. I (Paris: Plon, 1970), pp. 418–19.

26. Henri Laurentie, Bureau d'Etudes Constitutionelles, 3rd session, 20 March 1945, AOM, AP/214bis.
27. M. Shipway, 'Madagascar on the eve of insurrection, 1944–1947: the impasse of a liberal colonial policy', *Journal of Imperial and Commonwealth History* 24/1 (1996), pp. 72–100, repr. in J. Le Sueur (ed.), *A Decolonization Reader* (London: Routledge, 2003), pp. 80–102.
28. H. Hintjens, 'Constitutional and political change in the French Caribbean', in R. Burton and F. Reno (eds), *French and West Indian: Martinique, Guadeloupe and Guiana Today* (Basingstoke: Macmillan – now Palgrave Macmillan, 1995), pp. 21–33.
29. A. Shennan, *Rethinking France, Plans for Renewal 1940–1946* (Oxford: Oxford University Press, 1989), pp. 288–9.
30. M. Shipway, *The Road to War: France and Vietnam, 1944–1947* (Oxford and Providence RI: Berghahn, 1996), p. 123.
31. Population in 1945: Laos, 1.5 m; Cambodia, 4.6 m; Annam, 6 m; Tonkin, 10 m; Cochinchina, 4.6 m: M. Chamberlain, *European Decolonisation in the Twentieth Century* (London: Longman, 1998), p. 9.
32. D.G. Marr, *Vietnam 1945: the Quest for Power* (Berkeley: University of California Press, 1995).
33. Shipway, *Road to War*, pp. 132–47.
34. Ibid., pp. 170–1.
35. Tel. no. 262 Circ/AP, ref.HL/bp, Secret, 8 Mar. 1946. AN, 72AJ535, in ibid., 174.
36. Yong Mung Cheong, *H.J. van Mook and Indonesian Independence: a Study of his Role in Dutch–Indonesian Relations, 1945–48* (The Hague: Nijhoff, 1982), pp. 76ff.
37. Shipway, *Road to War*, pp. 230–1, 270–1.
38. 'NOTE au MINISTRE au sujet des élections coloniales', 4 Aug. 1945, AOM, Cab.10.
39. T. Chafer, *The End of Empire in French West Africa: France's Successful Decolonization?* (Oxford and New York: Berg, 2002), pp. 63–4.
40. *JOANC*, Débats, 27 Aug. 1946, 3334.
41. See Chafer, *End of Empire*; Shipway, *Decolonization and its Impact*.
42. Philip Williams, *Crisis and Compromise: Politics in the Fourth Republic*, 3rd edition (London: Longman, 1964), p. 181.
43. See e.g. J.I. Lewis, 'The French Colonial Service and the issues of reform, 1944–8', *Contemporary European History* 4/2 (1995), pp. 153–88.
44. See e.g., Laurentie, Note personnelle pour Monsieur le Ministre, 'Situation politique des colonies au début de juin 1946', 4 June 1946, AOM, AP/214bis.
45. See e.g. a Conférence de presse (Directeurs de Journaux), 14 Sep. 1945, AN, 72AJ539 (the same occasion on which Laurentie spoke most openly of independence for Indochina).
46. Shipway, 'Madagascar . . .'; J. Tronchon, *L'Insurrection malgache de 1947* (Paris and Fianarantsoa, Ambozontany/Karthala, 1974/1986).
47. Tronchon, *L'Insurrection malgache*, pp. 335–7.
48. See J. Fremigacci, '1947: L'insurrection à Madagascar', in *Marianne*, 25–31 December 2004.
49. de Gaulle, *Discours et messages*, Vol. I, pp. 370–3.

Bibliography

Brocheux, P., and Hémery, D., *L'Indochine: Une Colonisation ambiguë* (Paris: La Découverte, 1995).

Chafer, T., *The End of Empire in French West Africa: France's Successful Decolonization?* (Oxford and New York: Berg, 2002).

Chamberlain, M., *European Decolonisation in the Twentieth Century* (London: Longman, 1998).

Clayton, A., *The Wars of French Decolonization* (Harlow: Longman, 1994).

Cohen, W.B., *Rulers of Empire: the French Colonial Service in Africa* (Stanford: Stanford University Press, 1971).

Cooper, F., *Decolonization and African Society: The Labor Question in French and British Africa* (Cambridge: Cambridge University Press, 1996).

Cooper, F., *Africa since 1940* (Cambridge: Cambridge University Press, 2002).

Dalloz, J., *La guerre d'Indochine 1945–1954* (Paris: Le Seuil, 1987).

de Gaulle, C., *Discours et messages*, Vol. I (Paris: Plon, 1970).

Fremigacci, J., '1947: L'insurrection à Madagascar', *Marianne* 25–31 Dec. 2004.

Gallagher, J., *The Decline, Revival and Fall of the British Empire* (Cambridge: Cambridge University Press, 1982).

Harbi, M., 'La guerre d'Algérie a commencé à Sétif', *Le Monde Diplomatique*, May 2005.

Hargreaves, John, *Decolonization in Africa*, 2nd edn (Harlow: Longman, 1996).

Hintjens, H., 'Constitutional and political change in the French Caribbean', in R. Burton and F. Reno (eds), *French and West Indian: Martinique, Guadeloupe and Guiana Today* (Basingstoke: Macmillan – now Palgrave Macmillan, 1995), pp. 21–33.

Hyam, R. (ed.), *The Labour Government and the End of Empire*, British Documents on the End of Empire, A/2 (London: HMSO, 1992).

Institut Charles de Gaulle and IHTP, *Brazzaville, aux sources de la décolonisation* (Paris: IHTP and Plon, 1988).

Jauffret, J.-C., 'The origins of the Algerian War: the reaction of France and its army to the emergencies of 8 May 1945 and 1 November 1954', in R. Holland (ed.), *Emergencies and Disorder in the European Empires after 1945* (London: Frank Cass, 1994), pp. 17–29.

Kedward, R., *La Vie en bleu: France and the French since 1900* (London: Penguin, 2005).

Lewis, J.I., 'The French Colonial Service and the issues of reform, 1944–8', *Contemporary European History* 4/2 (1995), pp. 153–88.

Lewis, J.I., 'The MRP and the genesis of the French Union, 1944–1948', *French History* 12/3 (1998), pp. 276–314.

Louis, W.R., *Imperialism at Bay: the United States and The Decolonization of the British Empire* (Oxford: Oxford University Press, 1977).

Marr, D.G., *Vietnam 1945: the Quest for Power* (Berkeley: University of California Press, 1995).

Ministère des Colonies, *La Conférence Africaine Française* (Paris, 1945).

Novick, P., *The Resistance versus Vichy: the Purge of Collaborators in Liberated France* (London: Chatto and Windus, 1968).

Sanmarco, L., *Le colonial colonisé* (Paris: ABC, 1983).

Shennan, A., *Rethinking France, Plans for Renewal 1940–1946* (Oxford: Oxford University Press, 1989).

Shipway, M., *The Road to War: France and Vietnam, 1944–1947* (Oxford and Providence, RI: Berghahn, 1996).

Shipway, M., 'Reformism and the French "official mind": the 1944 Brazzaville Conference and the legacy of the Popular Front', in T. Chafer and A. Sackur (eds), *French Colonial Empire and the Popular Front: Hope and Disillusion* (Basingstoke: Macmillan – now Palgrave Macmillan, 1999), pp. 131–51.

Shipway, M., 'Madagascar on the eve of insurrection, 1944–1947: the impasse of a liberal colonial policy', *Journal of Imperial and Commonwealth History* 24/1 (1996), pp. 72–100, repr. in J. Le Sueur (ed.), *A Decolonization Reader* (London: Routledge, 2003), pp. 80–102.

Shipway, M., *Decolonization and its Impact: a Comparative Approach to the End of Colonial Rule* (Oxford: Blackwell, 2007, forthcoming).

Thomas, M., *The French Empire at War, 1940–1945* (Manchester: Manchester University Press, 1998).

Thomas, M., 'Divisive decolonization: the Anglo-French withdrawal from Syria and Lebanon, 1944–46', *Journal of Imperial and Commonwealth Studies* 28 (2000), pp. 71–93.

Tronchon, J., *L'Insurrection malgache de 1947* (Paris and Fianarantsoa: Ambozontany/ Karthala, 1974/1986).

Weinstein, Brian, *Eboué* (New York: Oxford University Press, 1972).

Williams, P., *Crisis and Compromise: Politics in the Fourth Republic*, 3rd edition (London: Longman, 1964), p. 181.

Wright, V., *The Government and Politics of France*, 3rd edn (London: Unwin Hyman, 1989).

Yong Mung Cheong, *H.J. van Mook and Indonesian Independence: a Study of his Role in Dutch–Indonesian Relations, 1945–48* (The Hague: Nijhoff, 1982).

10
Moscow, the Parti Communiste Français, and France's Political Recovery

Natalia Naoumova

Moscow's view of France at the Liberation differed from those of Washington or London in four significant ways. First, France's importance, though not negligible, was secondary. No Soviet leader or diplomat thought of France as a major power. Stalin opposed both French participation at the Yalta conference of February 1945 and a French zone of occupation in Germany. On 9 May 1945, only Eisenhower's pressing request allowed the French to be included at the Soviet-organised surrender ceremony outside Berlin.[1] Moreover, whatever Europe's medium-term future, securing a defensive glacis through the installation of pro-Soviet regimes in the East took priority, for Soviet leaders, over designs for Communist revolution in the West. If good behaviour there – holding back any revolutionary aspirations – ensured Anglo-American acceptance of Soviet hegemony in the East, the price was well worth paying.

Secondly, however, the Soviet Union, unlike the other two major allies, possessed a powerful client party in France, in the Parti Communiste Français. On one level, the PCF pursued the conventional aims of a party in a democratic system – policy achievements, office, and votes. At the same time the Soviet archives of the period testify to Moscow's enormous influence on the PCF's strategy and tactics, even during the period between the dissolution of the first Communist international organisation, the Comintern, in May 1943, and the foundation of its successor, the Cominform, in September 1947. Inevitably this influence was used in accordance with Soviet foreign policy goals.

Thirdly, France's post-war economic predicament, of increasing concern to the British and Americans, was of marginal importance to Franco-Soviet relations. True, shipments of Soviet wheat reached France, and were made much of by the PCF, in the approach to the elections of June 1946. But the French traded relatively little with the Soviet Union, and looked to Washington not Moscow for economic aid.

The fourth difference lies in the Soviet attitude to de Gaulle, which was almost a mirror image of the British and American views. In Anglo-American eyes, the General's major quality was his ability to contain the Communists; for the Soviets, whatever the accommodations of the moment, he belonged to the 'reactionary' camp. On the other hand, his prickly independence from the western allies was a clear recommendation for Moscow. Stalin had been a better 'Gaullist', at least since 1943, than either Roosevelt or Churchill: readier to recognise the Comité Français de Libération Nationale, set up in Algiers in June 1943, as a government-in-waiting, and willing to accommodate the CFLN in Moscow in case of further difficulties with the 'Anglo-Saxons'.[2] His signature of the Franco-Soviet pact in December 1944 should be viewed in this light.

The making of that alliance is the first focus of this chapter. Its significance, however, proved largely symbolic, especially after the end of hostilities in Europe. A more important aspect of Franco-Soviet relations, at least over the 'long' Liberation period, was the relationship between Moscow, the PCF, and the French political system. The vicissitudes of this relationship, from co-operation to Cold War, are covered in the remainder of this study, which approaches both questions from a Moscow perspective, using both official archives and the Soviet press.

The Franco-Soviet alliance

On 30 August 1944, *Pravda* published a message from Stalin to de Gaulle, president of the Gouvernement Provisoire de la République Française (GPRF): 'On the occasion of the liberation of Paris, capital of France, we address to you . . . in the name of the peoples of the Soviet Union and of myself, friendly congratulations to the French people and our wishes for the most speedy liberation of France from the German yoke.'[3] The warmth of Stalin's greeting was returned on 2 December, as de Gaulle's arrived in Moscow in the company of his Foreign Minister Georges Bidault: 'I am happy and flattered', said the General, 'to be in the capital of the Soviet Union and to offer the homage of France, ally of the Soviet Union, with a view to victory and a beneficial peace for the whole of humanity.'[4] De Gaulle's stay, which lasted over a week, saw an impressive round of cultural events and diplomatic receptions, but above all substantive talks with Stalin, Foreign Minister Vyacheslav Molotov, and other Soviet leaders.

That de Gaulle wanted a treaty of alliance was clear from his first contacts with Stalin and Molotov. 'France', he told the Russians, 'understands that for the problem of the German danger to be settled it is not enough to resolve frontier issues. To prevent a new attack from Hitler an alliance of anti-German powers will be needed.' When the Soviet leaders observed that a Franco-Soviet mutual assistance pact had been signed with the Laval government in 1935, de Gaulle remarked with some bitterness that he was not Laval, and expressed a strong wish to conclude an improved pact 'which would include additional points'.[5] At his first formal talks with Stalin, he added that 'The French know what Soviet Russia has done for them, and that Soviet Russia played the chief role in their liberation . . . The origin of France's recent misfortunes lay in the fact that France did not have Russia at her side and lacked an effective treaty.'[6]

For de Gaulle, the attractions of a treaty with Moscow were both symbolic and practical. It would mark France's return to great-power status, able to deal on equal terms with the Soviet Union, and thus by implication the British and Americans. It revived the Franco-Russian alliance of 1893, which had always been directed against Germany: the heart of the new treaty was a commitment to fight together to the final defeat of Germany and to prevent any resurgence of the German threat. Both de Gaulle and Bidault also hoped for Soviet help in pressing France's aims for Germany, above all the detachment of the Rhineland from the rest of the country, the internationalisation of the Ruhr, and the economic linkage of the Saar to France. For the Soviets, an alliance offered three possible benefits. France's commitment to fight on until final victory would hinder any realisation of Stalin's nightmare – a separate Anglo-American peace with Germany. A treaty would reinforce the position, within France, of a leader who had shown both independence from Washington and London and a willingness, however circumstantial, to govern with Communists. And it would, Stalin hoped, further his Eastern European plans if de Gaulle could be persuaded to support the displacement of Germany's Eastern border to the Oder–Neisse line, and the claims of the Soviet-backed National Liberation Committee (the 'Lublin Committee') to rule Poland rather than the Polish government in exile in London.

The Moscow talks of December 1944 form one of the great set-pieces of de Gaulle's *War Memoirs*.[7] The account centres on de Gaulle's own refusal to bow to pressure from the Soviets, especially on the Polish issue. His willingness to break off negotiations won him Stalin's respect, and an alliance that did not compromise France's honour by selling out Poland – a country where, in 1920, he had acted as a military advisor to a government at war with the newborn Soviet Union. Other authors are more sceptical. Werth, for example, claims on his reading of Soviet archives that de Gaulle had asked for an invitation to Moscow – rather than, as de Gaulle argues, responding to pressing offers from the Soviet ambassador to the GPRF, Alexander Bogomolov – and has Stalin embarrassing the General with probing questions on France's economic and military recovery, which had hardly begun.[8] Even Lacouture, a more sympathetic biographer, takes some of the gloss off de Gaulle's account.[9]

Compared with the protracted negotiations on an Anglo-French treaty, however, the drafting process in Moscow was speedy. Bidault had passed a draft to Bogomolov, who had accompanied the French party, on 3 December; Stalin gave de Gaulle a favourable response in principle on 6 December; and Molotov passed the Soviet draft 'Treaty of alliance and mutual assistance between the USSR and the French Republic' to Bidault on the same day.[10] The core of both drafts was a common commitment to pursue the war to final victory, to refuse any separate peace, and to provide mutual assistance in any future conflict with Germany.

There remained, however, two potential stumbling-blocks. The first was the issue of Poland and the Lublin committee. The second concerned the extension of the alliance to the United Kingdom. Stalin had kept Churchill informed of de Gaulle's visit since 20 November, and had asked for British views on a Franco-Soviet pact by telegram on 2 December, the day of de Gaulle's arrival. The British Cabinet had discussed the issue two days later, and backed Foreign Secretary Anthony Eden's preference for a tripartite Anglo-Franco-Soviet alliance. Churchill's telegram to Stalin of 5 December supported such a treaty, as well as the inclusion of de Gaulle in any Big Three talks affecting France. Stalin's reply, dated 7 December, agreed to propose a tripartite pact to de Gaulle.[11]

The two questions came together at the de Gaulle–Stalin meeting of 8 December. To de Gaulle's direct question as to 'whether Marshal Stalin considered closer relations between our two countries were necessary', Stalin again agreed to the principle of a Franco-Soviet pact but added that 'there are good pacts and there are better pacts. A tripartite pact onto which Britain was coupled would be better.'[12] De Gaulle refused the proposal, with some irritation, for three reasons. It appeared as an unacceptable intervention by Churchill in the sovereign conduct of French foreign policy; France's position in a triple pact would inevitably appear less important than in a bilateral treaty; and de Gaulle viewed France's differences with the Soviet Union – despite the Polish question – as less fundamental than the unresolved issues with the United Kingdom, notably over the Levant and Germany. Those differences, for de Gaulle, could be settled only in the 'second stage' of France's construction of alliances – the third being the future United Nations pact with the United States and other powers.[13]

The Soviet records suggest that Stalin then used the tripartite idea as a bargaining counter to secure recognition of the Lublin Committee. 'Now the British propose a tripartite pact', he told de Gaulle. 'Let the French do us a service and we will do the same for them. Poland is an element of our security. We have been talking with the French about this question for two days. Let the French receive the Paris representative of the Polish National Liberation Committee. We will sign a bilateral agreement. If Churchill doesn't like it, too bad.' When de Gaulle observed that 'Stalin had won this game', Stalin replied that 'Winning is the purpose of playing – but France will win more.'[14] This account is sharply at variance with that of de Gaulle, who describes Stalin as a 'good loser' over the Polish issue.[15]

The pact signed on 10 December was a minimal text centred on Germany. Stalin secured no French support for the Oder–Neisse line within the treaty (though ultimately none of the western allies objected to it); de Gaulle won no Soviet backing for *his* German plans. Britain was left out, to no great regret on Churchill's part.[16] France limited relations with the Lublin committee to an exchange of unofficial representatives to deal with practical issues, notably prisoners of war; but the identity of de Gaulle's representative – Christian Fouchet, a trusted young Gaullist of 1940 pedigree – and the fact that the French, along with the British and Americans, effectively recognised the Lublin

Committee as the government of Poland in August 1945, somewhat limits the real importance of France's refusal to concede on this issue.

Pravda reported the meetings on 11 December in largely conventional terms, referring to 'the many manifestations of sympathy, reinforced by the shared hardships of war, between the peoples of France and the Soviet Union', and the talks between the French delegation, Stalin, and Molotov, on 'the full range of problems relating to the continuation of the war and the organisation of the world'.[17] Of more interest are de Gaulle's and Bidault's official letters to Stalin, reproduced on 15 December. De Gaulle observed that the alliance would serve 'to co-ordinate the military efforts of Russia and France with those of the United Nations with a view to safeguarding our two peoples from a similar catastrophe in the future', while Bidault underlined the 'close and permanent community of interests between our two countries' which would 'reinforce our will to win and guarantee peace in the future'.[18] In general, however, *Pravda*'s reports were relatively low-key: while the outward events of the French visit were covered, there was no analysis of the treaty's content, and little interruption to the paper's staple diet of (victorious) war news, considered more important. Privately, Stalin told Averell Harriman, the American ambassador to Moscow, that he had found de Gaulle 'awkward and stubborn', as well as unrealistic in his aims for Germany.[19] French coverage, by contrast, was altogether more fulsome. The treaty dominated the first-ever issue of *Le Monde*, whose editorialist observed that 'barely a few months after her liberation, France's co-operation has been sought out by one of the clearest victors of the war', that the alliance was 'a further proof of the skill and farsightedness of the head of the Provisional Government', and that it would no doubt pave the way for a tripartite pact with Britain.[20] What neither side mentioned, finally, was the stake of the alliance for French internal politics. For the Soviets, it would enhance the status of the PCF; for de Gaulle, it would help keep the same party in check.

The Stalin–Thorez conversations

De Gaulle's BBC broadcast of 6 June 1944, inviting the French to 'fight the enemy with all the means at their disposal' in the wake of the D-day landings, was echoed by a call to 'national insurrection' from the PCF's Central Committee. In a few days the overall number of partisan units, grouped under the umbrella of the Forces Françaises de l'Intérieur (FFI), multiplied several times over, reaching nearly half a million men, very many of them Communists. Militarily, the results of the insurrection varied from the tragic (premature risings, provoking ferocious reprisals, in Tulle and other provincial towns) to the dashing and successful (in Lille, Marseilles, Limoges, Thiers and above all Paris). It remained to be seen which authority the FFI would recognise. Officially, the answer was clear: since April 1944, two Communists had sat on the CFLN and then the GPRF, as part of a unified Resistance movement headed by de Gaulle (who gave a ministry to Charles Tillon, commander of the main Communist Francs-Tireurs et Partisans, on 9 September). Officially again, from 9 June the FFI were under the command of the French army, and de Gaulle ordered the dissolution of their senior command structure on 28 August. On the ground, things were less simple. The FFI sought to maintain their autonomy from the regular army, while the *comités de libération*, often drawn from their ranks, disputed control over localities with the prefects and special commissioners appointed by the GPRF: hence de Gaulle's extensive provincial tours in autumn 1944, aimed at reinforcing the GPRF's authority across France.[21]

These two competing authorities could not coexist for long. On 28 October de Gaulle ordered, by a decree of the GPRF, the disarmament and dissolution of all armed groups other than the army and the police. The two Communist ministers accepted the decree; criticism of it within the PCF was initially muted; but the Conseil National de la Résistance (CNR), dominated by Communists, attacked it. So did many of the militias directly concerned, with growing support from the PCF press. The Communist leadership, indeed, talked as if it was preparing a revolution: on 15 November Jacques Duclos, the party's acting leader in the absence of its secretary-general Maurice Thorez, called for the summoning of 'estates general' (a reference to 1789), locally and then nationally, for the exercise of local power by 'elected and not appointed bodies', and for a regime in which the people's representatives could 'be dismissed at any moment'.[22] De Gaulle's decree remained 'a dead letter' a month after its promulgation.[23] But the logical corollary of this – a full insurrection against the GPRF – never took place. De Gaulle, supported by the majority of the population, and on the Left by the Socialists of the SFIO (Section Française de l'Internationale Ouvrière), was obviously disinclined to play the role of Kerensky. Tens of thousands of Allied troops remained in France. And no instructions for a rising had come from Moscow, either from the Kremlin or from Thorez.

Thorez had deserted from the French army in 1939 and been exfiltrated to the Soviet Union, where he had resided since. His return, decided in Paris and Moscow, testifies both to the extremely close relations between the Kremlin and the PCF and to the exceptional sensitivity of the contemporary French political situation.

In the autumn of 1944, Thorez had twice requested de Gaulle's authorisation to return to France, but the General had ignored his messages.[24] On 21 October Georgy Dimitrov, former Comintern secretary-general and future head of Bulgaria's first post-war government, then also in exile in the USSR, wrote to Molotov about this one-sided correspondence. While a campaign for Thorez's return had started in France, said Dimitrov, 'hostile elements' were spreading the 'myth' of his desertion in 1939 and claiming that he had had links with the Germans. Meanwhile, Dimitrov claimed, Thorez continued to enjoy Soviet hospitality, while the Soviet press remained 'totally silent' on the problem, creating 'a very embarrassing situation not only for Thorez but also for ourselves', which could best be remedied via an article on the subject (which Dimitrov submitted for Molotov's approval) in *Pravda*. Molotov's comments, handwritten on the draft, indicate a clear intention to apply gentle pressure on de Gaulle: 'The article does not explain clearly where the problem lies. *Why* can Thorez not return? *Who* is refusing him entry?'[25]

This form of indirect influence – and, no doubt, the situation in France – produced results within a week. On 28 October – the same day as the decree dissolving the militias in France – de Gaulle wired Roger Garreau, France's ambassador in Moscow, to say that 'The government has decided to quash the verdicts of French courts-martial reached before 18 June 1940 and relating to persons who subsequently took part in the national Resistance movement. This decision gives M. Maurice Thorez the right of re-entry into France. You may inform him of it. However, before a visa can be delivered a few days' wait will be necessary until the decree is published in the *Journal Officiel*.'[26]

During this wait, on 19 November, Thorez had a long conversation with Stalin. The length of their meeting, the detail of Stalin's instructions on how the Communists were to behave in liberated France, and the presence of both Molotov and Lavrenti Beria all indicate the extreme importance placed in Moscow on the PCF's activities – as well as the strengths and limitations of Stalin's view of French politics under the GPRF.[27] For Stalin, 'the most important question was how to get through the current difficult period when the Communists were not masters in France, and counted enemies as well as friends; and how to rally their own forces while preventing the forces of reaction from rallying theirs.' Stalin punctuated the conversation with questions to Thorez, whose answers he used as the basis for his own orders. At first, he simply asked Thorez how he viewed the French situation, while expressing a revealing perplexity that former prisoners of war (such as Bidault or Juin) had been given important posts in the GPRF. Thorez's answer focused on the PCF's relations with the French Socialists, and noted the SFIO leadership's refusal to co-operate with the PCF despite the Communists' success in winning working-class Socialists to their cause and despite Socialist commitments to 'unity of action'. The Socialists, complained Thorez, were denigrating the PCF's war record by suggesting that their heroic role in the struggle against the Germans dated only from 1941.

Stalin's reply broached the central theme of his advice to Thorez by stressing the PCF's continuing need for allies against the 'forces of reaction' and warning against excessive criticism of the SFIO. De Gaulle, Stalin argued, might well try to isolate the PCF and to act against the Communists; even if personally unwilling, 'he will be pressed to do so by the Americans and the British, who want to create a reactionary government in France, as they do everywhere they can'. The Communists, he stressed, 'are not strong enough to take on the struggle against the reactionary forces on their own', and should therefore seek allies among Radicals, Socialists and 'other elements' to form a 'bloc against the forces of reaction', allowing the PCF to 'defend itself now and, when the situation had changed, to go onto the attack'. For that reason, they 'should not seek to identify who, among the Socialists, said what and when against the Soviet Union'. Even if 'we know the Socialists well' as 'the left wing of the bourgeoisie', the overriding need now was to avoid the PCF's isolation. The bloc should also create close but discreet links with trade unions and with youth movements. 'The youth movement', added Stalin, 'should not be called the Communist youth. Some people are frightened of flags, and this should be taken into consideration.'

Perhaps the most remarkable moment in the conversation came when Thorez mentioned that 'the patriotic militias that had formed the main force of the Resistance under the Occupation' had, for the moment, kept their arms. In reply, Stalin warned Thorez to:

> take account of the fact that there now existed in France a government recognised by the Allied powers. In these conditions it was difficult for the Communists to have their own armed forces alongside those of the regular army, as their need for such detachments was now open to question. As long as there was no Provisional Government, and as long as no zones to the rear of the battle-front fell under the authority of such a government, there was some point in the existence of such units. But what was their use now that there was a government with an army? Such arguments could be used by the Communists' enemies, and would seem convincing to the average Frenchman. The position of the Communist Party was therefore weak and would continue to be so as long as it kept its armed forces; its position was simply hard to defend. That was why the armed units needed to be transformed into a more political organisation; as for the weapons, they should be hidden.'[28]

Stalin added that he had mentioned this point because he felt the PCF had not understood how the situation in France had changed, and accused them of pursuing their old policies, notably in attacking the Socialists and trying to hold on to their weapons, oblivious of the new context in which de Gaulle headed a government recognised by Britain, the Soviet Union, the United States, and other powers. Because the PCF was not strong enough to 'strike at the head' of this government, it would need to change strategy, gather its forces, and seek allies so as to be able to claim, in the event of an offensive from reactionary forces, that it was not just the Communists who were under attack, but the whole people. Such allies would also be of use if the situation allowed the Communists to go onto the offensive. To attract them, the PCF needed a broad platform including industrial reconstruction, jobs for the unemployed, the defence of democracy, and punishment for the Vichyites who had acted to suppress it.

Stalin returned again and again to the need for the PCF to be both strong in itself and, crucially, to be surrounded by allies, to thwart its enemies' attempts to isolate it. He was equally cautious on foreign policy issues, and advised against the French Communists' adopting the dismemberment of Germany as a slogan, at least unless public opinion and the French intelligentsia clearly favoured it. Outwardly at least, Stalin justified his caution in relation to domestic politics: advocating such a policy without a broad supportive consensus could place the PCF 'in the same camp as the worst reactionaries', and in danger of condemnation by association. Hence the need to take careful soundings before moving in this direction. It might be added in passing that the Soviets themselves, while wanting the Oder–Neisse line, had no wish for a divided Germany, and gave rather little support to the GPRF's positions on this point.

The relationship between the two men was clearly indicated by the close of their conversation. Asked if he had any further questions, Thorez replied in the negative but assured Stalin that he 'would always need his advice'. Returning to Paris, Thorez immediately called on the French to unite their forces for victory and to 'struggle for a free, democratic and independent France'. By the end of January 1945, he had become the clear and effective advocate of the disbanding of the militias in accordance with the GPRF decree, and of the subordination of the CDLs to the GPRF.[29]

Thorez had received a brief mention during de Gaulle's visit to Moscow, when Stalin recommended him to the General as 'a good Frenchman', adding 'In your place, I would not put him in prison . . . at least, not right away!'[30] But Thorez's return to Paris on 27 November, and the orders Stalin had given him, proved in many ways more significant than the Franco-Soviet alliance. Stalin had ensured that the PCF would be led by his own hand-picked chief; and for the moment at least, France's Communists would work within the 'bourgeois' political system. The importance of this was not lost on de Gaulle. On Thorez's death in 1964, he wrote to the Communist leader's son that 'whatever he may have done before and after, Maurice Thorez answered my call and, as a member of my government, contributed to the maintenance of national unity'.[31]

Communists in government, 1944–46

Throughout the existence of the GPRF, France's Communists did their utmost to implement Stalin's directives of November 1944. They remained within government in order, as they said, to 'bring the war to a victorious conclusion' and to ensure 'the co-operation of all the patriotic forces towards France's democratic renaissance'. On one level, they were extremely successful. The PCF established itself as France's premier political party, heading the poll at two out of the three national elections (of October 1945 and June and November 1946) with over a quarter of the vote – ahead of their Socialist rivals and over 10 points above their own best pre-war result of March 1936. Progress at the ballot-box was paralleled by an explosion in membership. Out of a pre-war total of some 300,000, the PCF had counted barely 5,000 members in the winter of 1939–40. Their numbers had risen to 60,000 by August 1944, to over 200,000 the following month, and to nearly 544,000 by April 1945; they would exceed 785,000 by the year's end.[32] This was, to a degree, part of a wider international movement. The prestige of the USSR, as the country which had made the greatest sacrifices to defeat Nazi Germany, was at its peak.[33] Communist ideas had won widespread popularity, not least because state control and egalitarianism were readily associated with the wartime mobilisation which had secured victory. In nine countries of Western Europe, including Italy, Belgium, Finland and France, as well as in four Latin American countries, Communists were in government. And in central, eastern, and south-eastern Europe the Communists had won power on the heels of the Red Army. Within France, meanwhile, the influence of the Resistance and of the democratic and antifascist forces linked to it were at their height; the PCF, as one of the principal forces of the Resistance, could not but reap the benefits. Its leading role within the main trade union, the Confédération Générale du Travail (CGT), itself experiencing a membership boom (with close to four million members), also helped the party put down deep roots in French society.

But France's Communists were less successful in implementing the central thrust of Stalin's directives – the construction, under their leadership, of a broad-based left-wing alliance. Parallel to the string of electoral victories ran a series of battles over the new constitution and over the formation of governments; in these, the PCF often faced a stark choice between the isolation that Stalin had warned against and substantial concessions to its 'weaker' partners of the SFIO and the third major governing party of the Liberation era, the Christian Democrat Mouvement Républicain Populaire (MRP).

The divided Left, 1945

The alliance strategy won an initial success at the municipal elections of April–May 1945. Here the PCF ran broad-based lists labelled 'republican, democratic, and anti-fascist union'. After the first round of voting it called for 'a bloc of all the republican, democratic and secular forces' for the second ballot.[34] The pre-election Communist–Socialist alliance secured victories in over 5,500 municipalities, over three times more than the pre-war total (cf. Chapter 5); Communist mayors headed 1,462 municipalities, including, for the first time, big towns such as Toulon, Nantes, Limoges and Reims.[35] *Pravda* took note with satisfaction, underlining that the victorious 'anti-fascist' lists consisted of candidates proposed jointly by the PCF and the SFIO, as well as Resistance organisations and, in some areas, the Radical Party.[36]

At the same time, the PCF leadership heeded Stalin's counsels of moderation and his instruction to build a left-wing bloc. The party's watchwords were national economic reconstruction, the punishment of traitors, real guarantees of democratic rights and freedoms, and the drafting of a new constitution – all of which would require a broad union of national forces around the programme of the CNR. Speaking at the PCF's first post-war congress (the Tenth Congress, held in Paris from 26–30 June 1945), Thorez declared that 'the renaissance of France is not the business of a single party or of a few statesmen, but a problem to be solved by millions of French men and women, by the whole nation'.[37] Three weeks later he offered proof of his party's commitment to workplace discipline when he told France's miners that their first 'duty as a class' was to 'produce, produce, and again produce'; the CGT did not hesitate to break strikes where they occurred.[38]

In party terms, the leadership counted primarily on the Socialists to avoid the isolation that Stalin had warned against. At the Tenth Congress, Thorez underlined 'the urgent need to create a strong French Labour party which would bring together Socialists and Communists and constitute the basis of a union between all republicans and all true Frenchmen'.[39] Shortly afterwards, a PCF delegation made merger proposals to the SFIO leadership. But the Socialists were in no hurry. Many feared that their party would be weakened or (as in some East European countries) simply swallowed up by the Communists in a united structure. Léon Blum, the former prime minister, whom Stalin had called a 'charlatan' even in 1936, during the Popular Front era, and who now returned the compliment by referring to the PCF as a 'foreign nationalist party', reinforced these concerns after returning from deportation in Germany at the end of hostilities.[40] His growing influence within the SFIO leadership helped tip the balance at the SFIO's Congress of August 1945: favourable to 'unity of action' with the PCF, the Socialists voted against a merger. Such a union might not have produced comparable results to those obtained in Eastern Europe. But the decision was a setback for the PCF's strategy as set out by Stalin; and from that summer, relations between the two parties began to deteriorate.

Partial isolation: the referendum of 21 October 1945

The same balance of electoral success with political setbacks was discernible at the referendum and elections of 21 October 1945, the first vote at national level since the war. With 26.2 per cent of the vote (against the MRP's 24.9 and the SFIO's 23.8), and the largest parliamentary group, the PCF was France's leading party. *Pravda* again noted the result with satisfaction, explaining that 'the French people know very well the role played by the Communist party in the Resistance organisations, in the struggle against the Hitlerite occupation, and in the restoration of democratic principles'.[41]

The double referendum held concurrently with the elections, by contrast, produced a less welcome result for the PCF. The referendum (itself a break with tradition, since no referendum had been held in France since the fall of the Second Empire in 1870) concerned the powers of the new legislature, and specifically its right to draft a new constitution and the limitations, if any, to be placed on its mandate. Only the Radicals opposed any attribution of constituent powers: they preferred a straight return to the Third Republic, under which they had held a pivotal position. The PCF and the CGT took the opposite position, seeking open-ended and constituent powers for the new assembly. De Gaulle, however, proposed, in the name of the GPRF, that those powers be limited. The new assembly would have normal powers of a parliament; it would draft a new constitution; but its mandate would last just seven months and its constitutional draft would be submitted to a new referendum.[42] 'De Gaulle has openly thrown his gauntlet into the balance', noted *Pravda*, apparently quoting from the French press.[43] Supported by the SFIO, the MRP, and other 'bourgeois' groups from the Resistance, this project was opposed, unsuccessfully, by the Communists and the Radicals, as well as the CGT. At the referendum, 95 per cent of the voters backed constituent powers for the new assembly, revealing the Radicals' extreme weakness; but two-thirds also approved de Gaulle's proposal to limit its powers, showing – in line with Stalin's warnings – the *relative* weakness of the PCF when isolated.

A sense of isolation was aggravated by the behaviour of the SFIO during the campaign. *Pravda* noted gloomily that 'The Socialist Party's campaign was almost entirely directed against the PCF. The Socialist Party rejected . . . the hand held out to it, and preferred an unnatural alliance with the MRP. The outcome was more than unfavourable for the Socialists.'[44] Three days later, the main culprit was identified by name: 'Léon Blum has repeatedly spoken in favour of working-class unity and co-operation with the Communists, but every act of the election campaign was directed against the PCF. At the same time, the organisations within the Socialist Party that really pursued working-class unity and co-operation with the Communists were punished by the Socialist leadership.'[45]

The strains of tripartisme, 1945–46

A further occasion for frustration with the SFIO came with the formation of a new government. The 1945 elections had given the PCF and the SFIO together an absolute majority in the Constituent Assembly. Following parliamentary tradition, under which the majority parties form a government headed by a leader of the strongest party, the PCF's *Bureau politique* proposed a PCF–SFIO coalition government with Thorez as Prime Minister, or even – as a fall-back position – with a Socialist at its head. The Socialist leadership refused on both counts, insisting that they would only take part in a tripartite (PCF–SFIO–MRP) government headed by de Gaulle. Mindful of the Kremlin's advice not to fight the Socialists openly, the PCF withdrew its proposal; the Constituent Assembly duly (and unanimously) invited de Gaulle to form a government. The General proposed to include representatives of the three biggest parties, but refused to appoint PCF ministers to the three most sensitive posts – Foreign Affairs, Defence, and the Interior – provoking a serious conflict. In the ensuing compromise, the Communists made major concessions, settling for the ministries of Arms Production, Labour, National Economy and Industrial Production, and sat in government alongside the SFIO and the MRP as well as de Gaulle's non-party supporters. Thorez had no portfolio but the rank of *Ministre d'État*, second in the government's order of protocol. This tripartite coalition would be the model for almost all French governments until May 1947.

Within weeks, however, a new conflict had erupted – between the Left and de Gaulle in the first instance, but then between the PCF and its partners. The Socialist–Communist majority demanded cuts in military spending; de Gaulle, resenting any interference by the Assembly in the government's day-to-day business, resigned on 20 January, condemning himself to a twelve-year crossing of the desert, and the regime to a new crisis. Again the PCF proposed Thorez as Prime Minister at the head of a Socialist–Communist government, *Pravda* observing that if the Socialists stood by their pact with the PCF, the conflict would be quickly resolved.[46] Again the Socialists refused the Thorez candidacy, which was also rejected categorically by the MRP. And again the Communists conceded, agreeing to participate in a tripartite government under the Socialist Félix Gouin.

In principle, Socialist–Communist unity fared better when it came to drafting the new constitution. Their agreed project proposed a parliamentary system with wide-ranging powers for a unicameral National Assembly, largely formal functions for the president, and guarantees of political and social rights as well as a secular state. Approved by the Socialist–Communist majority over the MRP's opposition, the draft was put to referendum on 5 May 1946. Opposed in the country by the MRP as well as the Radicals and conservative groupings, it went down to defeat by 53 per cent of the voters to 47. This was a setback for the PCF, which had also still failed to create the united left-wing bloc Stalin desired. For the Communist press in Moscow and Paris, the blame, again, lay with the Socialists. *Pravda* reported that the PCF had 'carried practically the whole burden of the campaign', with Socialist support for the new constitution remaining 'soft'; it noted that the PCF daily *L'Humanité* had attributed the result to 'the Socialists' refusal to accept Communist proposals for union and unity of action between the two parties.'[47]

Similar complaints marked the campaign for elections to the second Constituent Assembly, held on 2 June 1946. The PCF's political isolation was now noted openly by *Pravda* and illustrated with a claim that when the Interior Minister had ordered the removal of election posters from unauthorised sites, only the PCF's posters had been taken down, leaving those of other parties, including the fiercely anti-communist Parti Républicain de la Liberté (PRL), intact.[48] Such practices were cited to explain the PCF's descent into second place at the elections, with 25.9 per cent of the vote to the MRP's 28.2. But *Pravda* also dwelt on losses by the Socialists (who fell back to 21.1 per cent), seen as resulting from 'the anti-communism of the Socialist leadership', which had 'sown confusion among the party's leaders and local organisations'. *L'Humanité*, it added, had underlined the 'need for the union of workers and democratic forces in France against the reactionaries, who have not disarmed'.[49]

That summer's events in France worried the Soviet press. The MRP used its electoral success to propose its leader Georges Bidault for the premiership. *Izvestia* saw the hand of Blum in the post-election manoeuvring, oddly claiming that he sought a single-party MRP government, able to 'back the anti-communist campaign that certain political parties are currently leading'.[50] Commenting on the signs of anti-communism appearing within French society against the background of the developing Cold War, *Pravda* observed that on the day before the vote on the premiership, 'a group of young Fascist sympathisers attacked the offices of the PCF Central Committee in Paris, looting the bookshop in the same building and burning its stock', and added that 'the police showed complete negligence' in the matter.[51]

The Constituent Assembly voted Bidault into the premiership on 19 June 1946 by 384 votes. The 161 Communist Deputies abstained, neither welcoming Bidault as premier nor wishing to move into opposition. It was 'a pity', Duclos observed (and *Pravda* agreed), that France had foresworn the opportunity of ending the provisional regime by rejecting the first draft constitution, but the Communists, as good republicans, respected the people's will. The new government could only be provisional. On the constitution, the PCF was open to concessions, except on two issues: the secular character of the state (a reference to the MRP's Catholic loyalties) and the powers of the second chamber (a reference to the MRP's intention to revive the Senate in some form).[52]

This relative self-restraint allowed the PCF to join the Bidault government, which was approved by an overwhelming majority in the Constituent Assembly on 26 June: Thorez and Gouin both became vice-premiers. But the government's composition, with nine MRP ministers, seven Communists, six Socialists, one member of the UDSR and one with no party allegiance, reflected a weakening in the positions of the PCF and the SFIO, which now controlled only slightly over half the portfolios between them. Meanwhile de Gaulle had joined in the constitutional debate: his Bayeux speech of 16 June called for strong leadership at the top in what resembled a presidentialised republic. France's anti-communist forces were now divided between Gaullists, mainstream conservatives, and the right wing of the MRP. Yet de Gaulle was always the PCF's most formidable opponent; his return to the political scene inevitably gave the leadership pause for thought.

For the PCF, the two years since the liberation of Paris presented a mixed picture. Its membership and electorate had grown to levels unimaginable before 1939; ministerial office had won it respectability, plus the chance to place Communists in key administrative posts. But its wooing of the Socialists had been rebuffed; its claims to lead the government, however democratically legitimate, had been vetoed by the Socialists and the MRP; its preferred constitutional project – whose lack of checks and balances offered the best opportunity for any party that dominated the National Assembly to install itself durably in power – had been rejected by the voters; and the MRP had overtaken it (briefly, as it would turn out) at the ballot-box. Above all, perhaps, the 'left-wing bloc' was no nearer being achieved than in 1944. It was against this background of setbacks that the PCF received further advice from Moscow.

Stepping back: the Frachon–Suslov meeting and the October 1946 referendum

Within the ongoing contacts between the PCF and Moscow, the meeting of 19 June 1946 between Mikhail Suslov, a member of the CPSU's Central Committee, and Benoît Frachon, joint secretary of the CGT and an unofficial member of the PCF's *Bureau politique*, is especially important. Suslov sent a record of the conversation, marked 'Top Secret', to Molotov, stressing that Frachon had asked, in the name of the PCF leadership, for advice from the CPSU, though without raising any specific questions.[53]

Suslov's record is chiefly remarkable for Frachon's self-criticism over the PCF's implementation of Stalin's directives. The referendum campaign, he said, had seen a bitter struggle between the forces of 'democracy' and those of 'reaction', which had gone onto the offensive. But the PCF had run ahead of events, notably by demanding the premiership for Thorez. Intended to rally the largest possible number of Communist sympathisers, and ultimately to give 'the masses' a practical demonstration of Communist-led government, the slogan *'Thorez au pouvoir'* 'failed to take account of the fact that there are millions of Frenchmen who vote for the Communists but who don't yet want them leading the government'. The PCF had also underestimated the forces of reaction, who, with the 'profascist' PRL at their head, had used *'Thorez au pouvoir'* to play on hesitant voters' fears. Although the Party had 'taken a step back' after the referendum, it had still faced an unprecedented anti-communist campaign at the June elections, led not only by the Right but by the Socialists, MRP and Radicals as well, which had left the PCF isolated. Even though Frachon talked of the PCF's 'victorious' electoral campaign, his closing statement still leaves the impression that the Party was seeking to recognise its errors and its failure to heed Stalin's warnings of November 1944. 'Avoiding the isolation of the Party, holding on to positions gained, and surviving the difficulties of the current period' were the bases of the PCF's line. 'Avoiding isolation' meant seeking to extend the Party's influence with the peasants, working with the petty bourgeoisie, continuing to work for the 'unity of the working class' (presumably a reference to competitive co-operation with the Socialists) and establishing relations with 'democratic elements' in the Radical Party and the MRP.

The PCF's behaviour at the referendum of 12 October 1946 on the second (and definitive) draft Constitution corresponded to the strategy outlined by Frachon. The MRP, despite its former self-definition as the party of 'fidelity' to de Gaulle, sealed a lasting split with the General by refusing to back the strong presidential regime he had advocated at Bayeux. It was then obliged to reach an agreement with the Communists and Socialists. The second draft included the upper chamber the MRP had always wanted. But its powers (and the president's) would be limited, and the state's secular character would be guaranteed.[54] This compromise was backed by all three of the *tripartite* parties, and the PCF threw itself into the Yes campaign. On 7 October the Central Committee issued a text, reproduced in *Pravda*, calling on 'all French patriots' to ensure 'the triumph of the Constitution of the French Republic', against the 'murky forces of reaction' backed by 'the trusts' who opposed the restoration of republican principles in the Constitution now, as they had betrayed French democracy in the past. *Pravda* also, significantly, underlined the common ground between the PCF and the SFIO, reporting a speech by Vincent Auriol, the Socialist president of the Assembly, underlining the need to end the provisional regime and the dangers of a No vote.[55]

A similar theme – the PCF's alignment with France's 'democratic forces' against the 'reactionaries' who opposed the constitutional draft – is found in the treatment of de Gaulle during the campaign. Thus *Pravda* reported Thorez's carefully-worded attack on the General, who, 'whatever the respect owed him for past services to the country', had now lined up with a 'reactionary coalition' including former supporters of the 1938 Munich agreements with Hitler, and of the Vichy regime.[56] After polling day, *Pravda* again underlined that by supporting a strong executive and warning of 'disorder and anarchy' if the constitution were approved, de Gaulle had provoked negative reactions not only from the PCF (which now branded him 'the representative of the reactionary forces') but also from former supporters in the MRP and in newspapers like *Le Monde* and *Le Figaro*.[57]

The referendum result, in which the constitution was approved by 53.5 per cent of those voting (or 36.2 per cent of the registered electorate) was hailed in *Pravda* as a 'victory for democratic forces' in France, and a 'double defeat' for 'the reactionaries'. The 'democratic forces', the PCF chief among them, had first, at the price of significant concessions during the drafting, successfully defended articles defining the 'republican and democratic' nature of the regime, and had then prevailed in the 'intense political struggle' of the campaign. The three parties – PCF, SFIO, and MRP – that had backed the constitution now faced a further 'fierce struggle' at the parliamentary elections against the 'reactionary camp' – the PRL, the right wing of the Radicals, the UDSR, and the Union Gaulliste – which had opposed the text. A 'hard and important test', requiring 'the union of all the truly democratic forces of the country', awaited France's renascent democracy, especially as 'outside influences' were encouraging the reactionaries.[58] It would be hard to find a better exegesis of Stalin's instructions to the PCF of two years earlier. In the short term at least, the Party's behaviour in the autumn 1946 appeared to pay off. It had played a significant role in drafting the constitution, with several clauses bearing its mark. And at the November 1946 elections it regained its leading position, winning a historical record score of 28.2 per cent. Yet the PCF had still not managed to implement the core of Stalin's instructions – to unite the Left under its leadership, ready to move onto the offensive and take power in due course. Indeed, a final Thorez candidacy for the premiership failed – not, this time, because it was refused by the Socialist leadership, but only because the SFIO was unable to enforce voting discipline on its own Deputies, 23 of whom opposed the PCF leader. The PCF was again forced to fall in behind Socialist prime ministers (Blum in December 1946, and Ramadier in January 1947) and, with the constitution ratified, a Socialist president (Auriol). Despite these concessions, within a year the Party would find itself more isolated than ever, out of government and backing a fierce wave of strikes that shook, but did not topple, the new regime.

Into the 'ghetto', 1947

The PCF's displacement from the seat of government to the political 'ghetto', where it would remain through (and beyond) the remaining life of the Fourth Republic, was played out in five main locations: the scenes of armed colonial conflict in Madagascar and Indochina; the shopfloor of Renault's Boulogne–Billancourt works; the heart of political Paris, the Chamber and the Council of Ministers; the founding conference of the Cominform at Sklarska-Poreba, in Poland; and finally, in November–December 1947, across the whole of urban and industrial France.

Colonial conflicts, analysed in this book by Martin Shipway, undermined the Communists' position in the Ramadier government from the moment it took office on 22 January 1947. War had broken out in Indochina a month earlier; it was a Communist Defence Minister, François Billoux, who was now responsible, at least nominally, for the armies fighting Ho Chi-Minh's Communist-dominated nationalist movement.[59] By the early spring of 1947 the PCF was mobilising public opposition within France to the war; Billoux refused to stand up in the Chamber in homage to France's troops fighting there; and when Ramadier sought a vote of confidence on his Indochina policy on 22 March, he was supported by the PCF's ministers, but not by its other Deputies, who abstained. A week later an insurrection broke out in Madagascar; its savage repression led the PCF ministers to walk out of the Council of Ministers on 16 April.

But it was wages policy that provoked the final break. Whatever the benefits of some policy initiatives backed by the PCF – the greater security enjoyed by public-sector workers after nationalisations, and the foundation of France's welfare state – the PCF's support for wage restraint alienated workers. That was already visible in the slow rate of party membership renewals that spring, as well as in the CGT's disappointing results in elections to governing bodies of the social security system.[60] A strike over wages at Renault, organised by a small Trotskyist group from 25 April, left the CGT, after four days, with little choice but to join in. And when Ramadier, by now resolved to force the issue, asked for a vote of confidence over wages policy on 4 May, all of the Communist Deputies, including the ministers, voted against the government of which they were a part. It is likely that they expected Ramadier to resign; in the ensuing negotiations to form a government, they could demonstrate the impossibility of ruling the country without Communist co-operation. Instead, Ramadier found non-Communist replacements for the PCF ministers, and carried on governing with the support of Socialists, MRP and Radicals.[61]

With the dismissal of Thorez and his colleagues on 5 May 1947, the PCF was out of office and friendless: Stalin's strategy of November 1944 had clearly failed. The PCF leaders, however, went on trying to implement it for five more months. On the international scene, the PCF evoked the 'division of the world into two blocs', but as a danger to be avoided rather than a *fait accompli* – even if the summer saw increasingly hostile statements towards 'American imperialism', especially after the Soviets had finally withdrawn from negotiations over the Marshall Plan, as well as (unsubstantiated) claims that the Americans had engineered the Party's removal from government. In domestic politics, the Communists now did nothing to restrain outbreaks of industrial unrest; the aim was to prove how necessary their participation in government was. Thus the emphasis at the Eleventh Congress, held from 25 to 29 June, remained the PCF's status as a 'party of government' and the need to bring the Socialists (if not the MRP) back to a left-wing alliance. Even on 22 September, Thorez was still calling for the PCF's return to office within a 'government of democratic union'.[62]

Just as *L'Humanité* was carrying Thorez's message to thousands of Communist readers, Duclos was gathering with leading figures from the Italian and East European Communist parties in Sklarska-Poreba. What they heard from the Soviet Politburo member Andreï Zhdanov could leave them in no doubt that Moscow's line had changed radically. The world, said Zhdanov, was now divided into 'two camps' – the 'imperialist and anti-democratic' camp aimed at the 'world domination of American imperialism', and the 'anti-imperialist and democratic' camp, led by the Soviet Union, which sought the 'undermining of imperialism, the consolidation of democracy and the eradication of the remnants of fascism'. Particularly dangerous in this confrontation was the 'treacherous policy of right-wing Socialists like Blum in France, Attlee and Bevin in England, Schumacher in Germany', who, as the imperialists' 'faithful accomplices', were 'sowing dissension in the ranks of the working class and poisoning its mind'.[63] It followed that alliances with such traitors, as practised until May by the French and Italian parties, were a crass error. The French and Italian comrades now stood accused of legalism, opportunism, and parliamentarianism, as well as a soft line towards the Marshall Plan, and were forced to make a thoroughgoing self-criticism before going home.

The PCF digested the Zhdanov line within a month. Thorez reproduced it at length in his report to the Central Committee on 29 October, regretting the Party's 'slowness' in analysing the new international situation. No longer were the SFIO and MRP placed, as a year earlier, in the 'democratic' camp: now *all* non-Communist forces, from Socialists to Gaullists, belonged to 'the American party'.[64] The new line was translated into action in France's workplaces and streets, on the back of rising working-class discontent resulting from falling living standards. Now the PCF proposed to lead industrial action, through its CGT majority, and to add political demands to wage claims. On 12 November the CGT's Central Committee linked a virulent attack on the Marshall Plan (henceforth an 'attempt by war-mongering American capitalists to enslave Europe')[65] to calls for strikes in support of a 25 per cent wage rise. The strike wave that gripped France for the next four weeks involved some 2.5 million workers and an exceptional level of violence. Marseilles and other southern towns fell, albeit briefly, into a state of quasi-insurrection; CGT militants derailed the Paris–Lille express with the loss of sixteen lives. The Ramadier government fell on 22 November. But its successor, headed by Robert Schuman, held firm; the Socialist Interior Minister Jules Moch proved ferocious in his use of police and armed forces against strikers, adding further poison to his party's now execrable relations with the PCF; the moderates in the CGT drifted back to work after three weeks; and the strike formally ended on 10 December. The PCF had made a significant demonstration of force; but it ended the year more isolated than ever, with the CGT now split by the defection of its moderates to form a new union, Force Ouvrière. In conventional political terms, the policy pursued since the Liberation was in tatters. But the autumn U-turn had returned the Party to Moscow's good graces. A meeting with Stalin in Moscow on 18 November – three years almost to the day since their conversation of 1944 – confirmed Thorez as the leader who would take the PCF into its long crossing of the Fourth Republic desert.[66]

Conclusion: policy, office, votes – and Moscow

A conventional political party in a democratic system faces continual and difficult choices between 'policy, office, or votes'.[67] Office is attractive to party leaders for the opportunities it offers to achieve policy goals, as well as for party patronage and personal advantage.[68] But the realisation of policy goals is always subject to constraints, whether political (for example, in relation to coalition partners) or economic and financial. In the long run, to dilute or sacrifice policy goals in the face of constraints simply to remain in office may lose votes, temporarily or permanently; a spell out of office may serve to revitalise a party (through the revision or reaffirmation of policies) and win back electoral support.

The PCF's record in the Liberation era can be analysed from this perspective. On the one hand, it was inevitable that a party openly committed to the transformation of French society in the interests of the working class would have difficulty keeping working-class support indefinitely when governing at a time of great economic hardship. In that sense, the PCF's departure from government in May 1947 was decided at Billancourt rather than Washington or Moscow. At the same time, the PCF drew important benefits from its time in office. Building on its Resistance record, it established a status – not held hitherto – as a party of government. It claimed credit for major policy achieve-ments: many of the social transformations of the Liberation era, outlined in this book by Herrick Chapman, owed something to the activities of Communist activists, Deputies, and ministers, and earned the party a durable capital of goodwill among workers. The new nationalised industries became strong-holds of CGT and PCF activists; local elections – despite setbacks in October 1947 – gave the party a network of municipalities, especially in the sub-urbs of major cities; both lasted for decades. The PCF's roots within French society, even at the dawn of the twenty-first century, owed much to the Liberation era.[69]

But the PCF was not a conventional left-wing party; it was defined by its relationship to Moscow. This had two consequences. First, as is clear from the Soviet archives, it took orders from the Kremlin. These orders did not coincide with the party's spontaneous preferences; several weeks might be required to assimilate them; but obedience always prevailed. In 1944–45, the PCF aspired to a strategy of confrontation and even revolution; Stalin, through Thorez, made it behave like a conventional party. In 1947–48 the PCF lead-ership, at least, had grown rather attached to their mainstream status; Moscow obliged them to undertake 'mass actions' (especially political strikes). Secondly, the Soviet link, and the suspicions it provoked among non-Communists, inevitably shaped the PCF's position in the French political system. Even with the wartime alliance surviving – uneasily – on the world stage, and the tripar-tite PCF–SFIO–MRP coalition governing France, the Soviet link, more than any-thing else, disqualified the leader of France's largest party from the premiership, on three separate occasions. And as the world slipped into Cold War it ensured that the PCF's exclusion from office, far from being the brief absence hoped for by Thorez, would last thirty-four years.

Notes

1. C. Cogan, *Forced to Choose: France, the Atlantic Alliance, and NATO – Then and Now* (London: Praeger, 1997), p. 6; J. Young, *France, the Cold War and the Western Alliance, 1944–1949* (Leicester: Leicester University Press, 1990), pp. 33–5; R.C. Raack, *Stalin's Drive to the West, 1938–1945* (Stanford, Stanford University Press, 1995), p. 116.
2. Young, *France, the Cold War and the Western Alliance*, p. 6.
3. *Pravda*, 30 August 1944.
4. *Izvestia*, 3 December 1944.
5. Russian state archives of social and political history (hereafter RSASPH), 45/1/392, pp. 11–12. This part of the Soviet record corresponds to de Gaulle's account of the talks.
6. RSASPH, 82/2/1353, p. 4.
7. C. de Gaulle, *War Memoirs*, Vol. III, tr. Richard Howard (London: Weidenfeld and Nicolson, 1960), pp. 62–82.
8. A. Werth, *De Gaulle* (Harmondsworth: Penguin Books, 1965), pp. 181–6.

9. J. Lacouture, *De Gaulle*, Vol. II (Paris: Le Seuil, 1985), pp. 85–96.

10. RSASPH, 45/1/391, pp. 30–7.

11. United Kingdom, National Archives, Kew (NA): CAB 120/524/T.2153/4; CAB 120/524/T.2233/4; CAB65/48, pp. 60–1; CAB 120/524/T.2258/4; CAB 120/524/T.2287/4.

12. RSASPH, 45/1/391, p. 76.

13. de Gaulle, *War Memoirs*, Vol. III, pp. 71–2.

14. RSASPH, 45/1/391, p. 78.

15. de Gaulle, *War Memoirs*, Vol. III, p. 81.

16. 'I do not understand why it was that you wished to put this triple pact into my telegram', Churchill wrote, somewhat disingenuously, to Eden on 11 December, a week after the Cabinet had agreed to do precisely that. UK National Archives, CAB 120/524/T.2342/4.

17. *Pravda*, 11 December 1944.

18. *Pravda*, 15 December 1944.

19. Young, *France, the Cold War and the Western Alliance*, p. 32.

20. *Le Monde*, 19 December 1944.

21. The essential French account of the PCF in this period is P. Buton, *Les Lendemains qui déchantent. Le Parti communiste français à la Libération* (Paris: Presses de la Fondation Nationale des Sciences Politiques, 1993). Cf. also S. Courtois and M. Lazar, *Histoire du Parti communiste français*, 2nd edn (Paris: Presses Universitaires de France, 2000), pp. 204–15.

22. Quoted in Courtois and Lazar, *Histoire du Parti communiste français*, p. 213.

23. P. Robrieux, *Histoire intérieure du Parti communiste*, Vol. II, 1945–1972 (Paris: Fayard, 1981), p. 77.

24. RSASPH, 82/2/1353, pp. 52–3.

25. RSASPH, 82/2/1353, p. 54. Original italics.

26. RSASPH, 82/2/1353, p. 58.

27. The record of this conversation, from which the ensuing quotations are taken, is in RSASPH, 45/1/390, pp. 85–93. A French translation may be found in *Communisme* 45–6 (1996).

28. Some arms were hidden, though there is no evidence that this was done systematically. Cf. A. Harris and A. de Sédouy, *Qui n'est pas de droite?* (Paris: Le Seuil, 1978), pp. 212–3.

29. Buton, *Les Lendemains*, p. 188.

30. De Gaulle, *War Memoirs*, Vol. III, p. 67.

31. Quoted in A. Grosser, *Politique extérieure* (Paris: Flammarion, 1984), p. 26.

32. Cf. Buton, *Les Lendemains*, pp. 269–70.

33. In September 1944, 61 per cent of respondents to an IFOP poll conducted in Paris considered that the USSR was making the greatest contribution to Germany's defeat (quoted in Courtois and Lazar, *Histoire du Parti communiste*, p. 226).

34. *L'Humanité*, 4 May 1945.

35. P. Martin, *Les élections municipales en France depuis 1945* (Paris: La Documentation Française, 2001), pp. 20–1.

36. *Pravda*, 16 May 1945.

37. M. Thorez, *Articles et discours choisis* (Moscow: Politicheskaya Literatura, 1966), p. 254.

38. Thorez in a speech to mineworkers on 21 July 1945, quoted in Buton, *Les Lendemains*, p. 196.

39. M. Thorez, *Œuvres*, Vol. XXI (Paris, Éditions Sociales, 1963), pp. 126–7; *Pravda*, 1 June 1945.

40. *Documents on the Foreign Policy of the USSR*, Vol. xx, Moscow, 1973, p. 613; Courtois and Lazar, *Histoire du PCF*, p. 229.
41. *Pravda*, 28 October 1945.
42. Cf. Chapter 2.
43. *Pravda*, 19 October 1945.
44. *Pravda*, 25 October 1945.
45. *Pravda*, 28 October 1945.
46. *Pravda*, 22 January 1946.
47. *Pravda*, 8 May 1946.
48. *Pravda*, 3 June 1946.
49. *Pravda*, 6 June 1946.
50. *Izvestia*, 19 June 1946.
51. *Pravda*, 20 June 1946.
52. *Pravda*, 16 June 1946.
53. The following account is taken from RSASPH, 82/2/1353, pp. 64–9. A French translation may be found in *Communisme* 35–7 (1994).
54. Cf. Chapters 2 and 3.
55. *Pravda*, 9 October 1946.
56. *Pravda*, 9 October 1946.
57. *Pravda*, 13 October 1946.
58. *Pravda*, 16 October 1946.
59. Ramadier, unlike de Gaulle, had allowed a Communist into the Defence Ministry – but not before creating a separate ministry under him for each of the three armed services: these were headed by non-Communists.
60. Buton, *Les Lendemains*, pp. 295–302; Courtois and Lazar, *Histoire du PCF*, p. 259.
61. The best account of this episode remains G. Elgey, *La République des illusions, 1945–1951* (Paris: Fayard, 1965), pp. 288–91.
62. Courtois and Lazar, *Histoire du PCF*, pp. 260–2; Robrieux, *Histoire intérieure du Parti communiste*, Vol. ii, pp. 198–204.
63. Royal Institute of International Affairs, *Documents on International Affairs, 1947–48* (London: RIIA, 1952), pp. 122–46.
64. Courtois and Lazar, *Histoire du PCF*, p. 278. For a contemporary reaction, cf. Duff Cooper to Ernest Bevin, 13 November 1947, NA/FO/371/67683; Duff Cooper, Britain's ambassador to Paris, viewed the speech as a 'complete reversal' of policy imposed by Zhdanov.
65. V. Lorwin, *The French Labor Movement* (Cambridge, Mass.: Harvard University Press, 1954), pp. 119–20.
66. Courtois and Lazar, *Histoire du PCF*, p. 282.
67. W. Müller and K. Strøm (eds), *Policy, Office or Votes? How Political Parties in Western Europe Make Hard Decisions* (Cambridge, Cambridge University Press, 1999).
68. The top PCF leadership also enjoyed a particularly lavish lifestyle in the Liberation years: cf. Robrieux, *Histoire intérieure du Parti communiste*, Vol. ii, pp. 154–7.
69. Cf. M.-C. Lavabre and F. Platone, *Que reste-t-il du PCF?* (Paris: CEVIPOF/ Autrement, 2003).

Bibliography

Auriol, V., *Journal du Septennat*, Vols. i, 1947 and ii, 1948 (Paris: Armand Colin, 1974).
Buton, P., *Les Lendemains qui déchantent. Le Parti communiste français à la Libération* (Paris: Presses de la Fondation Nationale des Sciences Politiques, 1993).

Cogan, C., *Forced to Choose: France, the Atlantic Alliance, and NATO – Then and Now* (London: Praeger, 1997).

Courtois, S., and Lazar, M., *Histoire du Parti communiste français*, 2nd edn (Paris: Presses Universitaires de France, 2000).

de Gaulle, C., *War Memoirs*, Vol. III, tr. Richard Howard (London: Weidenfeld and Nicolson, 1960).

Elgey, G., *La République des illusions, 1945–1951* (Paris: Fayard, 1965).

Grosser, A., *Politique extérieure* (Paris: Flammarion, 1984).

Harris, A., and de Sédouy, A., *Qui n'est pas de droite?* (Paris: Le Seuil, 1978).

Lacouture, J., *De Gaulle*, Vol. II (Paris: Le Seuil, 1985).

Lavabre, M.-C., and Platone, F., *Que reste-t-il du PCF?* (Paris: CEVIPOF/Autrement, 2003).

Lorwin, V., *The French Labor Movement* (Cambridge, Mass.: Harvard University Press, 1954).

Martin, P., *Les élections municipales en France depuis 1945* (Paris: La Documentation Française, 2001).

Müller, W., and Strøm, K. (eds), *Policy, Office or Votes? How Political Parties in Western Europe Make Hard Decisions* (Cambridge, Cambridge University Press, 1999).

Raack, R.C., *Stalin's Drive to the West, 1938–1945* (Stanford, Stanford University Press, 1995).

Robrieux, P., *Histoire intérieure du Parti communiste*, Vol. II, 1945–1972 (Paris: Fayard, 1981).

Royal Institute of International Affairs, *Documents on International Affairs, 1947–48* (London: RIIA, 1952).

Thorez, M., *Œuvres*, Vol. XXI (Paris: Éditions Sociales, 1963).

Thorez, M., *Articles et discours choisis* (Moscow: Éditions du Progrès 1966).

Werth, A., *De Gaulle* (Harmondsworth: Penguin Books, 1965).

Young, J., *France, the Cold War and the Western Alliance, 1944–1949* (Leicester: Leicester University Press, 1990).

11
Washington at the Liberation, 1944–47

Charles Cogan and Andrew Knapp

France at the close of 1944 presented an unpromising prospect for the United States. De Gaulle, now firmly in harness at the head of the Gouvernement Provisoire de la République Française (GPRF), enjoyed famously poor relations with President Roosevelt, who had recognised the GPRF late and reluctantly. The knowledge that the main alternative to de Gaulle was Western Europe's strongest Communist Party (whose representatives sat in the GPRF) hardly improved matters. For his part, de Gaulle longed to break free from his country's state of forced dependence on his British and American allies, and had already undertaken the first diplomatic step in this direction by signing a treaty of alliance with the Soviet Union; France had no such treaty with either Britain or the United States.

Three years later, the political outlook was radically improved from the American viewpoint. Both de Gaulle and the Communists were out of power. The 'Third Force' government of Socialists, Christian Democrats (the Mouvement Republicain Populaire, or MRP) and Radicals had aligned France firmly within the American camp in the nascent Cold War, and faced down Communist attempts to disrupt the regime on the back of the November 1947 strike wave. While neither political nor economic stability had been restored – governments were no more long-lived under the Fourth Republic than under the Third, and France remained in dire need of American economic aid – the foundations had been laid for a period of unusually close Franco-American relations. In Cold War parlance, France had not been 'lost'.

This chapter explores the development of that relationship. The first section considers the particular difficulties experienced by de Gaulle in winning recognition and support from the United States. There follows an analysis of the three key issues that shaped the Franco-American relationship in the early post-war years: France's need for economic aid, the American assessment of France's internal politics, and the German question. These came together in the crucial and fraught year 1947, which is given separate consideration. A concluding section considers the issue of France's dependence – military at first, then economic above all – on the United States and the extent to which the Americans used this dependence to shape French politics and policy.

The General and the Presidents, 1940–45

It is one of the oddities of history that de Gaulle – described by François Furet as (with Churchill) one of the two great anti-fascists to emerge at the head of the post-war anti-Communist struggle in Europe[1] – was regarded in the United States less as a bulwark against Communism than as a quasi-Fascist or Caesarist figure liable, as were the Communists, to undermine French democracy. From the Fall of France in 1940 till the end of hostilities in Europe, relations between the American administration and the Free French remained execrable. Part of the explanation lies in personalities: however disputed it may be by what may be called the number-crunching school of American political science, the role of the individual in history is germane to any account of the relationship. Roosevelt described himself as a 'stubborn Dutchman'; his resolve that 'I will not let that impostor [impostor being one of his kindlier expressions for de Gaulle] take over the government of France'[2] was only abandoned with extreme reluctance. Episodes such as the Dakar fiasco (when a joint Free French/British force was obliged to withdraw under fire after failing to take control of France's African colony of Senegal in September 1940) or the St-Pierre et Miquelon incident (when Free French forces freed these Atlantic colonies close to the Canadian coast from Vichy control, in December 1941, without consulting the Americans) enhanced the worst impressions of de Gaulle as neither trustworthy nor even very competent.

But the gulf between the Free French and the American Administration transcended personal chemistry or unhappy incidents. To begin with, neither Roosevelt nor others in the Administration understood what both Jean Lacouture and Stanley Hoffmann have called the 'element of mysticism in de Gaulle'.[3] It was de Gaulle's gift first to combine his own Free French troops with both the Forces Françaises de l'Intérieur (the internal Resistance) and France's North African forces, and second to make this assortment look like a victorious army committed from first to last to the defeat of Germany – despite the fact that the third (and largest) of the three groups had previously been loyal to Vichy, as de Gaulle himself indirectly admitted in June 1945.[4] To Gaullists, this was alchemy. To a sympathetic British observer like Duff Cooper, aware of the desperate starting-point of June 1940, it remained impressive. To Americans, it too readily looked like a case of smoke and mirrors.

For the United States, the shock of 1940 was brutal: accustomed to regarding the French Army as the most powerful in the world, and after seeing this power reduced to ashes within a few weeks, the political class in the United States concluded that France was finished as a major power. This was the a-historical attitude of a young nation that had broken with its European past and lacked a long view of the Old Continent and the vicissitudes and comebacks of its powers. Few in 1945, for example, would have predicted that over half a century later a German Foreign Minister, Joschka Fischer, would observe that 'France is politically stronger than Germany for historical reasons and will remain so'.[5] Within this perspective, the contrast is striking between, on the one hand, the Gaullist *Weltanschauung*, in which Europe meant essentially continental Europe, with Britain rarely included, and on the other Roosevelt's casual dismissal of France. According to Henry Kissinger (a confirmed admirer of de Gaulle), it was his 'deep disdain for France' that led the American President to overestimate Britain's capacity to organise Europe's post-war reconstruction and defence.[6] Paradoxically, the British, including Churchill and especially Anthony Eden, took a more modest view and saw France as critical to post-war European recovery and security.

A third reason for Roosevelt's mistrust of de Gaulle applied to Churchill as well; he sought the end of colonial empires, the British and French chief among them. This issue was so sensitive that in June 1944, a week before de Gaulle's visit to the United States, the GPRF representative in Washington warned the General by telegram to stay off the subject of French overseas territories and bases in his conversations with the President (the telegram was intercepted by US military intelligence and passed to Roosevelt).[7]

A fourth source of friction concerned men. De Gaulle's wartime emissaries to Washington were mediocrities, at least compared to the non-Gaullist competition. The latter included Alexis Leger, the former secretary-general of the Quai d'Orsay (the French Foreign Ministry), and Jean Monnet, the great co-ordinator of American military supplies to Europe and future founding father of European integration. Leger, whose modest role as 'consultant' to the Library of Congress belied his influence, described de Gaulle's methods as 'similar to those of Hitler';[8] Monnet, initially in British employ, was not far behind (though he did convert to a pragmatic support for the General after being sent to Algiers, initially to keep him under restraint).

Perhaps most importantly, the incompatibility between the United States and the Free French movement was shaped by the position of the United States at the moment of the French defeat in June 1940. Still a neutral power then, the United States established (or rather, continued) relations with Vichy, as the surviving regime to which the French Parliament had delegated full powers on 10 July 1940. It suited the pragmatic Americans to deal with the government in place, and besides, Vichy, unlike de Gaulle (at the start), disposed (with German permission) of an army of 100,000 men. American diplomats at Vichy (Robert Murphy, Freeman Matthews, Admiral William Leahy) proceeded to relay to Washington the regime's hostile view of de Gaulle, whom they readily termed a 'Fascist' (an assessment that the behaviour of Colonel Passy, the Gaullist intelligence chief, and other members of the General's entourage tended to bear out). Relations with Vichy personalities could become positively friendly, as when Roosevelt arranged for Admiral Darlan's polio-stricken son to be treated at his own preferred resort of Warm Springs, Georgia.[9] Nor did the end of American neutrality in December 1941 change much: the United States maintained relations with their German enemy's client for a further eleven months. Only after the North African ('Torch') landings had taken place, in November 1942, did Washington finally break with Vichy.

That did not, however, entail any rehabilitation of de Gaulle. When, with the Torch operation agreed in summer 1942, the Americans began searching for a suitable French figurehead to rally the French territories to the Allies, de Gaulle was not considered. Possible candidates included both politicians (Albert Lebrun, the last President of the Third Republic, Édouard Herriot, President of the Chamber of Deputies elected in 1936, neither of whom had officially resigned their posts) and generals (Weygand, de Laurencie and de Lattre de Tassigny), as well as Alexis Leger. The front-runners, however, were Admiral Darlan and General Henri Giraud. Darlan was considered capable of bringing the French fleet over to the Allied cause, but his obvious Vichy connections (he had headed the government in Vichy from April to December 1941) were a liability even for the Americans. In October, they chose Giraud, whose spectacular escape from a German prisoner-of-war camp had caught Roosevelt's imagination.[10] But when, as soon as the landings took place, Giraud demanded supreme command of all Allied forces in North Africa, the Allies switched to Darlan, who was fortuitously present in Algiers, before reverting to Giraud after Darlan's assassination at Christmas 1942. Even after de Gaulle had arrived in Algiers six months later, installed himself as joint head with Giraud of the Comité Français de Libération Nationale (CFLN), and then eased the politically inept Giraud into a subordinate position in the course of 1943, the Americans tried to use Lebrun as a symbol of the restored legitimacy of France – and as yet another way to block de Gaulle. Lebrun refused.[11]

Nor were these difficulties resolved when the war moved to France; indeed, the D-day landings placed de Gaulle and the Administration on diametrically opposed courses. Three days before the landings, on 3 June 1944, de Gaulle had transformed the CFLN into the GPRF, with the clear intention of taking over the government of French territory as it was liberated. His claim to do this rested on arguments developed by Gaullist constitutionalists and outlined elsewhere in this book by Emmanuel Cartier. Roosevelt rejected such claims to legitimacy. The Administration had avoided any meaningful discussions with de Gaulle on the organisation of civil affairs during planning for D-Day; as Commander-in-Chief of the Allied expeditionary force, General Eisenhower was instructed to deal with whichever French authorities he saw fit. A new French currency had been printed by the Allies without consulting de Gaulle. And Free French troops were kept out of initial land operations.

Officially, Roosevelt's justification for keeping the Free French at arm's length was a democratic one. As he put it to General George Marshall four days before D-Day,

> I have a moral duty which transcends 'an easy way.' It is to see to it that the people of France have nothing foisted on them by outside powers.

It must be a French choice – and that means, as far as possible, forty million people. It carries with it a very deep principle in human affairs.[12]

For de Gaulle, the re-establishment of the French State, under the GPRF, would precede the re-establishment of democracy via elections. Roosevelt's view was that free elections should precede the re-establishment of a French State – and that in the meantime France should be administered, like Italy, by an Allied Military Government of Occupied Territories (AMGOT).

For Gaullists, Roosevelt's institutional arguments, never very persuasive, were all the less credible because after D-Day the Americans continued to seek – or appeared to seek – the same formula they had attempted in Algiers: a non-Gaullist figurehead and even a smooth transition with Vichy. One possible choice, according to de Gaulle, was Herriot, brought out of detention by Pierre Laval on 12 August for a meeting with Otto Abetz, Germany's ambassador in Paris. The plan quickly collapsed: neither Herriot, nor, for that matter, Hitler countenanced it. But de Gaulle would claim in his memoirs that Laval had used an intermediary named Enfière (a pseudonym for Enfieropoulos) to contact Allen Dulles, then station chief for the American Office of Strategic Services (OSS: predecessor of the CIA) in Berne, in order to secure American support for the operation.[13] André Kaspi's account of the Liberation has Enfière delivering a message from Dulles to Laval to the effect that 'if you arrange for Herriot to be liberated, Roosevelt [who numbered Herriot among his personal acquaintances] will take this into account.'[14]

An OSS dossier on Enfière, still not available in full, survives from his Berne days, and includes a report from him, dated 14 July 1944, on Herriot's political activities. Herriot's view, according to Enfière, was that while de Gaulle had saved France's military honour and Vichy was null and void, he bore a danger of Bonapartism which made it all the more necessary to follow the Constitutional Law of 1875 to the letter and give the National Assembly the task of reconstituting the French state – an unremarkable view for the President of the Chamber of Deputies.[15] It is clear from the dossier that the Administration was interested both in Herriot's conditions of detention and in his activities. From there to stating that the Americans were supporting a manœuvre, led by Laval, to thwart the Gaullist march to power by using the National Assembly and its president is a step too far, in view of the present limited knowledge of the facts.

It is significant in itself, though, that de Gaulle believed that such manœuvres were taking place, and that Herriot was not the only candidate under consideration. The briefing papers drawn up for Roosevelt's meeting with de Gaulle in Washington in July 1944 indicate a concern to reassure de Gaulle on this point, and in particular on any question of continued Vichy links:

There are persistent rumors coming out of Algiers, according to which the United States maintains a kind of link between Marshal Pétain and Vichy. According to one of these rumors, the United States favored the formation, under Pétain's aegis, of a government headed by M. Camille Chautemps, and in which M. Jean Fabry would be a member. We can assure you that there is no agreement of any kind between the United States and Marshal Pétain or Vichy. There is no secret agreement between the United States and anyone in particular [in France]. The United States Government believes that a democratic-type government would be the best for France and hopes that, once the Nazis are defeated and thrown out of France, the French will choose themselves, without foreign help or influence, a government that best responds to their needs.[16]

It should be noted that Jean Fabry was known as a violent anti-Gaullist. The fact that these rumours should circulate, and above all that de Gaulle should give at least one of them formal credibility in his memoirs, speaks volumes about the state of Franco-American relations.

De Gaulle's behaviour in the summer of 1944 should be understood in that context. His concern for a speedy re-establishment of republican legality in France under the GPRF was motivated by a wish to pre-empt, not only the Communists (as he states in his memoirs),[17] but also the Americans. He disposed of four main assets for this undertaking. The first was his own undoubted popularity. Clear from his first foray onto French soil, at Bayeux on 14 June, this was reinforced, according to Wall, as the possible alternative of an AMGOT in France became known to the public.[18] The second lay in the *de facto* (but still not *de jure*) recognition given the GPRF by Roosevelt during the Washington visit of July 1944. The third lay in his gift for judiciously-timed declarations, in particular the *ordonnance* of 9 August annulling the constitutional and many other acts of the Vichy period. The fourth was French military force, notably Leclerc's famed 2nd Armoured Division, in France since 1 August. Last but not least was Eisenhower, whose knowledge of de Gaulle and of the situation on the ground made him far more sympathetic to the General than Roosevelt was. Eisenhower's agreement greatly facilitated Leclerc's dash to Paris, the timely liberation of the capital, and de Gaulle's grand return there on 25 August which, more than any other single event, marked the General out as France's inevitable post-war leader.

None of this was enough to bring Roosevelt round to the principle of *de jure* recognition, which he was still resisting as late as 18 October. But by this time he was being pressed not only by Eisenhower, who needed to hand over the burden of administering civilian areas away from the front, but also by two of his own closest advisors, Cordell Hull and John McCloy, who argued that non-recognition could spell trouble with France's population at the war's end. Hull's credibility in the matter was all the greater in that he had been a fierce anti-Gaullist from 1941 before coming round to the General in 1943 and persuading Roosevelt to grant *de facto* recognition in July 1944.

The tardy American recognition of the GPRF on 23 October (*after* a postwar government had been recognised in Italy, an ally of more recent vintage) did little to dispel the mutual mistrust between Washington and the General. The President delayed signing a new Lend-Lease agreement with the French from September 1944 till 28 February 1945.[19] He kept de Gaulle away from Yalta, telling Churchill that 'any attempt to include de Gaulle in the meeting of the three of us would merely introduce a complicating and undesirable factor'.[20] He dismissed the French armed forces, telling his Secretary of State, Cordell Hull, that 'they have very little to contribute for the moment' either by land or by sea, and then ensured that this would continue to be the case by refusing to equip a further eight French divisions to take part in the war's finishing stages.[21] France's military revival by the war's end (with 1.3 million men under arms and a place at the surrender ceremonies, to the Germans' surprise and chagrin) was hardly fostered with enthusiasm by the Americans. France's diplomatic revival (with an occupation zone in Germany plus full veto-carrying membership both of the United Nations Security Council and of the Allied Control Commission, set up in Berlin to shape the future of Germany) owed more to Churchill than to either of the other Big Three leaders.

Meanwhile three incidents, relatively minor in themselves but magnified by the context of mutual mistrust, continued to plague Franco-American relations. The first was de Gaulle's response to orders from the Allied Supreme Command to evacuate Strasbourg during the German offensive of December 1944. Mindful of Strasbourg's immense symbolic and political importance, de Gaulle refused to obey and threatened to withdraw Free French troops from the Allied command before persuading Eisenhower to rescind the order.[22] A second incident concerned de Gaulle's refusal, in April 1945, to remove French troops from Stuttgart to make way for American forces until the formal establishment of France's occupation zone. The third, and perhaps the most serious, arose from the French occupation of the Val d'Aosta in Italy early in June, provoking a fierce reaction from Truman against 'the unbelievable threat that French soldiers bearing American arms will combat American and allied soldiers whose efforts and sacrifices have so recently and successfully contributed to the liberation of France itself', and suspending all military aid to France pending withdrawal (the French troops duly left, but France held on to two other French-speaking localities, Tende and La Brigue, which had not been inside the French frontier in 1939).[23]

None of these confrontations was as serious as the Syrian affair was in relation to Franco-British relations.[24] Equally, though, there had been no compensating public displays of warmth such as took place during Churchill's November 1944 visit to Paris. And Truman's intense irritation over the Val d'Aosta incident shows that American antipathy to de Gaulle did not die with Roosevelt. In August 1945 the new President and the General held talks in Washington. Before their meeting, Truman spoke to a senior member of the British Embassy staff of his disappointment at France's progress over the past year, which he ascribed to an excessive preoccupation with politics. He was resolved to tell de Gaulle, 'like a Dutch uncle', that he 'expected France to pay her full part in promoting her own economic recovery'. The General he referred to as a 'pinhead'.[25] The record of the talks suggests that little happened to break the ice.[26] It was scarcely an auspicious opening to the post-war era.

Dollars, Germany, and Communism, 1945–46

Yet Franco-American relations there had to be, of whatever sort. Truman would soon discover that a shattered France, like other European countries, desperately needed the economic aid that only the United States could supply. Both countries, along with the British and Russians, were to administer Germany now and, in principle, settle its future in the medium term. And as Europe began to slide towards the Cold War, American observers took a growing interest in France's internal politics, and particularly in the possibility of a Communist election victory or even a *coup d'état*.

The aid question

France's desperate post-war economic state has been outlined in the Introduction to this book. At the end of 1944, industrial production was at a mere 40 per cent of its 1938 levels. Recovery would require heavy investment both in transport (two-thirds of the merchant fleet and 60 per cent of all rail lines were out of action) and in plant: the average age of French machine tools in 1945 was 29 years, compared to 8 in the UK and 5 in the United States, the newest articles having been taken by the Germans. But France also desperately needed raw materials and the most basic consumer goods. Wheat output stood at 78 per cent of its pre-war level in 1944, at a mere 52 per cent in 1945 and at 83 per cent in 1946; immediate post-war food rations were well below (already modest) British levels, at barely a third for meat and less than two-thirds for fats and sugar.

In short, France, like other European countries, needed imports in huge quantities – but lacked the short-term capacity to pay for them. Exports stood at a mere 10 per cent of imports in 1945, at 28 per cent in 1946, and at 48 per cent in 1947. In the short term, the deficit could be made up out of existing gold and foreign currency reserves, but these had already shrunk from $3,185 million at the end of 1939 to $1,818 million in 1945 – about enough to cover just one of the big post-war trade deficits.[27] The problem was compounded by the wider disruption of world trade, which meant that major trading partners, especially Britain and Germany, were often unable to supply the imports France needed or to accept the exports France offered. In the short term at least, then, France (like other European countries) would have to import more from the United States – and to pay for it in dollars. When Jean Monnet first drew up a French import programme in November 1944, he expected the United States to supply half of French food imports, a quarter of coal and other raw materials, and between 80 and 90 per cent of industrial goods; a French Supply Council came to employ a staff of 1,200 in New York.[28]

In principle, as Frances Lynch argues, there were three ways to finance France's recovery – but two were barely realistic.[29] One was through German reparations, but the Allied co-operation needed for this was not forthcoming: as early as May 1945, Secretary of State James Byrnes was warning Georges Bidault, de Gaulle's Foreign Minister, against expecting anything in this area.[30] A second means, supported by Pierre Mendès-France as Minister for National Economy, would be to put investment first and delay consumption. This would have condemned France to a generation of austerity, a political impossibility given the strength of the Parti Communiste Français (PCF) and the expectations for social reform raised at the Liberation. De Gaulle refused the plan, and Mendès resigned in April 1945. The one remaining possibility was to finance recovery by borrowing from the United States. An essential component of post-war relations between the two countries was the steady demand for dollars emanating from Paris, from the wartime Lend-Lease programme to the large and regular payments made from Spring 1948 under the Marshall Plan.

It was paradoxical, given the poor personal relations between Roosevelt and de Gaulle noted above, that the Administration extended Lend-Lease provisions, initially conceived for Britain, to the Free French as early as September 1942, and confirmed them with the CFLN in Algiers a year later. An extension to the agreement was signed for France by Monnet on 28 February 1945; under its conditions France undertook to end discrimination in trade and to reduce tariffs after the war. Lend-Lease ended, for France as for Britain, with hostilities on 14 August; but the United States was able to agree a further loan of $550 million, payable over 30 years at just over 3 per cent, from the Export-Import Bank, which was used as a provisional supplier of world credit pending the launch, under the Bretton Woods agreements, of the International Bank for Reconstruction and Development (IBRD). France's acceptance of this loan was again subject to general conditions about entering a more liberal post-war trading system, and France's National Assembly duly ratified Bretton Woods in December 1945 – but not without provision for a transitional period of five years, during which the French economy was expected to recover sufficiently to face the rigours of currency convertibility.

This loan was almost immediately considered insufficient in the light both of short-term French economic forecasts and of the ambitious projects of Monnet and the Commissariat au Plan, created in January 1946. An early step of the Félix Gouin government, which took office after de Gaulle's resignation on 20 January, was to despatch Monnet and the Socialist former Prime Minister Léon Blum to Washington to negotiate further credits. Congress, after all, had just voted an aid package worth $3.75 billion to Britain, and the more optimistic French leaders hoped for something comparable. Monnet was less sanguine, and correctly told Blum on reaching Washington in March that 'we have arrived at the worst possible moment'.[31] Byrnes had already told Jefferson Caffery, the US ambassador in Paris, on 4 February that 'An approach to Congress for a credit comparable to the British loan would not be practicable', while the under-secretary of State for economic affairs, William Clayton, delivered the same message to the French ambassador in Washington, stressing that Britain was a 'special case'. France, in Clayton's view, should seek further help from the Export-Import Bank in the first instance and thereafter from the IBRD, expected to be operational late in 1946 or early in 1947.[32] But the resources of the Export-Import Bank were limited, and big loans were already planned to the Soviet Union and China; France was unlikely to get much more than $500 million, instead of the $2 billion hoped for.[33] Moreover, the Americans now sought more concrete commitments in return: a devalued franc, an end to what were viewed as restrictive trade practices, and movement to free currency exchange, as well as the free export of American films to France, a more liberal policy on American investments, a way to dispose of American war surplus materials in France, and commercial access to the French Empire; politically, they hoped for a change in French attitudes to Germany.[34]

The Blum–Byrnes agreements, which emerged from these unpromising positions on 28 May 1946, were frustrating to both sides.[35] France obtained a loan of $720 million, payable at 2 per cent over 35 years, to pay for American goods already being delivered plus war surplus materials; the write-off of outstanding Lend-Lease debts; plus a further $650 million of new money from the Export-Import Bank and the promise of support for a further loan of $500 million from the IBRD (in the event, France applied for the IBRD loan on 8 October 1946 and received half of the expected sum – $250 million – on 7 May 1947).[36] The package helped France through another winter, but failed to resolve the longer-term dollar shortage and appeared stingy compared with what the British had obtained. The Americans, for their part, won no concessions on Germany. Interestingly, the really explosive aspect of the agreements in France related to improved access of American films to French cinemas. This was almost immediately attacked (especially, but not exclusively, by the Communists) as American cultural imperialism. In fact, the cinema agreement was fundamentally misunderstood by its critics, honoured more in the breach than in the observance, and completely renegotiated within two years.[37] But the controversy surrounding it was an indication of how the conditions linked to a necessary loan could be attacked within France as representing a loss of national sovereignty.

For the Americans, France's position in the post-war as in the wartime world was ambiguous: neither a special case like Britain, nor a minor European power like Norway or the Benelux countries. If a more liberal international economic order was to be created then France, with its empire, had a crucial role to play. At the same time economic aid to France depended above all on the political priorities of the Administration, and these were evolving all the time. On one key issue, however, French concerns increasingly stood in the way of American policy.

Germany

In the closing months of the war, the future of Germany might have seemed a consensus issue between France and the United States. The so-called Morgenthau Plan, formulated by the US Treasury Secretary and endorsed by Roosevelt, proposed the complete dismantling of Ruhr industry and the 'pastoralisation' of Germany.[38] De Gaulle, for his part, sought to ensure that Germany should never again pose a military threat to France; that France should assure the security of its eastern frontier with Germany; and that Germany should not be allowed to re-establish itself economically faster than France. There was little in these two projects that could not be reconciled.

Consensus, however, did not outlast hostilities. On the French side, de Gaulle's broad objectives crystallised into a set of precise aims. These included the economic incorporation of the coal-rich Saar region into France; the perpetuation of a highly decentralised Germany, at the very least until a peace treaty was drawn up; the detachment from Germany of the Ruhr, which would be placed under international control with a view to using its industrial resources for the benefit of the victorious powers; and the permanent military occupation of a string of garrisons along the Rhine.[39] Both de Gaulle and then Bidault (who remained as Foreign Minister, with a brief gap, until 1948) pursued these goals with great consistency into 1947. Nor did they hesitate to seek Soviet support for their aims at the periodic meetings of the Council of Foreign Ministers and the Allied Control Commission: the Soviet Union was, after all, France's only formal ally, it shared some (though far from all) of France's priorities for Germany, and de Gaulle and Bidault both tried to maintain France's freedom of manœuvre between the two emerging superpowers. American policy, by contrast, was radically reversed after 1945. The Morgenthau plan, never formal policy, died with Roosevelt. The reconstruction of Germany was soon accepted as a necessity, because of the costs and practicalities of military occupation, and because a Germany that was politically and economically weakened would represent a vacuum at the heart of Europe – a vacuum which the emerging pattern of the Cold War suggested the Soviets would be all too willing to fill. As early as 22 August 1945, de Gaulle's insistence, during his meeting with Truman, on the amputation of the Ruhr from Germany had been countered by Truman's reply that the Russians were also keen to internationalise the Ruhr, and to send troops there.[40] The French position, though, remained clear and inflexible, and in November 1945 the French on the Allied Control Commission vetoed the creation of all-German transport, telecommunications, and postal services decided by the Big Three (but not France) at Potsdam the previous August. The following year, American acceptance of the perspective of a Germany divided for many years, and with US troops still present, moved two steps closer when Secretary of State Byrnes first (in July 1946) invited any country that wished to merge their zone with the American one, and then indicated (in September) that US troops might have to remain in Germany for longer than the two years initially expected. The British responded favourably to the first initiative (which they had encouraged), and the Anglo-American 'bizone' came into being in January 1947. The French stayed out.

The German issue was complicated, for the French, by that of coal. Before 1939, France had imported nearly one-third of consumption, and a higher proportion of coking coal used for steel manufacture. Britain and Germany had each supplied about a tenth of the total consumption, or some 7 million tons; but the French steel industry had imported nearer two-thirds of its coke and coking coal from Germany. With Britain's export capacity vastly reduced, France naturally looked to Germany, both to supply established needs and to fuel ambitions for industrial expansion: Monnet told the first meeting of the Council for the Plan on 16 March 1946 that France would need an annual 20 million tons from Germany.[41]

In principle there was potential for convergence between French and American policy on coal. In June 1945 Truman had ordered 25 million tons of coal exported from Germany (though not all to France) in the next year, whatever the consequences. In the event, however, little more than 12 million tons were exported, to France and the Benelux countries, over the whole of 1946 and 1947, and France received barely a third of that total.[42] One opponent of Truman's plan had been General Lucius Clay, Commander-in-Chief of US forces in Germany, on the grounds that to export what amounted to nearly half of Germany's total production would hamper the most basic German recovery.[43] More important, however, were the British, in sole control of the Ruhr mines (which lay in their zone and accounted for four-fifths of German production) from 17 July 1945. Their reluctance to export massively was shaped partly by a concern not to lose traditional coal markets (which they still thought they would soon be able to supply again) to Germany; partly by a growing wish to rebuild Ruhr industry to ensure that their zone paid for its occupation costs; partly, too, by a readiness to use their position in the Ruhr as a bargaining tool with the other Allies.[44] Moreover, weak British management of the Ruhr mines (and physically weak miners) meant that production there rose more slowly than in the (smaller) mines in the French zone. It is true that the export and distribution of German coal was a matter not for the British alone, but for the inter-Allied European Coal Organisation, and less directly for the Allied Control Commission. But when Hervé Alphand, France's representative on the Control Commission, protested in November 1945 against the reduction of monthly German coal exports to France from 1.2 million tons to 900,000 tons, he was met with the American argument that a major difficulty was transport, and that the French would accordingly do well to reverse their recent vetos on central German services.[45] Six months later further cuts, and further French protests, produced broadly the same results.[46]

In this context it was hardly surprising that the French should focus on the major coal-producing region of their zone, the Saar, with which they unilaterally announced a customs union in December 1946. The British and Americans, without openly supporting the move, turned a blind eye. In every other respect, however, the German question in Franco-American relations had reached deadlock by the end of 1946, with the French clinging to the German policy set by de Gaulle as they watched their share of German coal production dwindle to barely a tenth of what Monnet had hoped for the previous March.

Anticommunism and anxiety: Americans view French politics

A French government dominated by the PCF was feared by virtually all official American observers of French politics in the Liberation period, and their concern grew more intense as Europe's Cold War divisions took shape. However, they differed in their assessments of the PCF's intentions; of the viability of the available alternatives; and of what, if anything, the United States could do to prevent the worst case becoming reality.

One argument in de Gaulle's favour in autumn 1944 was precisely that he was the best available barrier against the PCF. This was explicitly stated in an OSS report the written on the very day the GPRF was recognised.[47] Caffery, meanwhile, argued on 27 October that 'As France goes, the Continent of Europe will probably go and it is not in our interest to have the continent . . . dominated by any single power – friend or enemy.'[48] His worries about Communism in France found a growing echo within the State Department during 1945. They were reinforced by the PCF's strong showing at the elections of 21 October 1945; de Gaulle's formation of a government including the PCF but excluding it from the most sensitive ministries receiving general approval in Washington. It is significant that de Gaulle's entourage kept the Americans fully informed (more so than the British) of the process of government formation, as they did two months later of his impending resignation (and of his intention to return to power on his own terms).

From the American viewpoint, therefore, de Gaulle's departure removed a difficult partner but also an obstacle to the PCF. The State Department soon took a pessimistic view of future prospects, seeing the PCF as a disciplined machine ready to seize power on the word from Moscow. Officials in the Paris embassy, by contrast, were sceptical of this view, and more respectful (inspired, in part, by memories of the New Deal) of the PCF's record in government. Caffery was somewhere between the two. He (correctly) disbelieved military intelligence reports that the PCF planned a coup in the event of the first draft constitution, which the Communists and Socialists backed, being rejected at the referendum of 5 May 1946 (it is interesting to note that the PCF leader Maurice Thorez went out of his way to reassure Caffery on this point).[49] But he was no friend to the PCF, and strongly supported a large American loan during the Blum mission precisely in order to reinforce moderate elements in France's governing coalition at the June 1946 elections.[50]

To a degree, the results of these elections, by raising the MRP (temporarily) to the position of France's leading party, appeared to bear out Caffery's approach.

Yet any resulting optimism was short-lived. By 29 October 1946, just before the referendum on the second draft constitution, Caffery could write to Washington that, while he did not wish to be alarmist, many Frenchmen now saw 'only two possibilities – a dictatorship by the Communist Party or an authoritarian regime under de Gaulle' – and that, whatever their misgivings about the General, they would prefer him to the PCF.[51] There was not, however, a sense in this despatch that the United States could or should do anything to intervene. Indeed, the only direct American intervention in French politics at this time appears to have come, not from government at all, but from the American Federation of Labor (AFL), which had sent emissaries to Europe in 1945 to help organise non-Communist unions. Their financial support, however, was very small in these early stages.

By the end of 1946, therefore, there were few reasons for satisfaction in Washington with France's post-war record. French policy on Germany was a source of continual irritation; Lend-Lease, the Export-Import Bank credit of December 1945, and the Blum–Byrnes agreements had secured neither political nor economic nor financial stability; and it was no consolation at all that the most promising alternative to the PCF was still de Gaulle. But things scarcely looked better from Paris. Here, the Americans' lack of sympathy to French security concerns in Germany, or to France's needs for Ruhr coal, were a constant source of frustration, while American credits, however welcome, were viewed as insufficient by comparison both with French needs and with what had been granted to the British. It was to take the multiple crises of 1947 – economic, financial, diplomatic, social, and political – to force a degree of convergence between the two countries.

The United States and the crises of 1947

At the heart of the crises of 1947 were France's unsatisfied needs for the most basic of commodities, wheat and coal. The wheat shortage that loomed at the New Year arose both from poor weather conditions and from the dysfunctions of France's agricultural pricing policy; where the harvest of 1946 had exceeded four-fifths of pre-war levels, that of 1947 would be barely half. Imports, under these conditions, were not enough to stop the French bread ration from falling to 250 grammes in May 1947, and to a mere 200 grammes in August.[52] The coal crisis was even more immediate. While French production in 1946, at 49.3 million tons, was rather higher than the level of 1938, imports had collapsed. Only 0.7 million tons of coal reached France from Britain in 1946, against 6.5 million in 1938; only 3.4 million tons from Germany, against 7.2 million in 1938; only 1.1 million tons from other sources (chiefly Belgium, Holland, and Poland), against 9.1 million in 1938. Even with 5.2 million tons imported from the United States (against zero pre-war), that left less than 60 million tons of coal available to France in 1946, over 10 million down on 1938 levels – hardly enough to cover current consumption, let alone to fuel the ambitions of the Monnet Plan. Worse, the start of 1947 saw cutbacks of coal exports from Britain and from the British zone; just 100 tons of British coal reached France in January, and a mere 1,000 tons from the Ruhr in February.[53] The obvious supplier for both coal and wheat was the United States, but quite aside from considerations of price (German coal sold into France at $14 a ton in 1946, American at $22), purchases from America would widen France's already yawning dollar shortage.[54]

Securing supplies of German coal was a prime concern of Bidault at the Moscow Foreign Ministers' conference of Spring 1947. In this aim he was reasonably successful: the four powers agreed a sliding scale linking exports of Ruhr coal to anticipated rises in production and fixed France's share of exports at 28 per cent when production had reached 370,000 tons per day. France also obtained broad British and American support for the principle of an international authority to oversee Ruhr industrial production.

This, however, was the limit of French success. The wider importance of Moscow for French policy was twofold: it saw the end both of the German policy that de Gaulle and then Bidault had pursued since 1944, and of Bidault's attempts to position France at a mid-point between the 'Anglo-Americans' and the Soviet Union.

On the German question, while George Marshall, the new US Secretary of State, had promoted the sliding scale agreement, he was to prove quite uncompromising when it came to the economic and political organisation of the Anglo-American bizone. This would henceforth be done without consulting either of the other two occupying powers. A first indication of this was the July 1947 agreement to raise levels of industry there. French protests (on the ground that Germany's recovery was being promoted at the expense of the rest of Europe) were met with a clear statement that, to have any voice in decisions relating to the bizone, the French would have to merge their own zone of occupation with it.[55] By late September, Bidault would conclude that, in view of British and American behaviour and France's reliance on American aid, the punitive German policy formulated under de Gaulle was a 'lost cause' and that France had no choice but to follow the more conciliatory line proposed by the British and Americans.[56] This did not produce an overnight policy U-turn; the advisability, and above all the timing, of a French decision to join the bizone were matters of lively debate within the French elite through 1948, and the French still tried to slow down Anglo-American initiatives on Germany's political organisation.[57] But it signalled the start of a slower turnaround that would lead France to participate in the creation of the Federal Republic of Germany and would culminate, in 1950, in the European Coal and Steel Community (ECSC) – a successful French initiative, but one based (as the Americans desired) on co-operation not confrontation with the old enemy.

Before the Moscow conference, Caffery – thinking chiefly of the German question – had encouraged Bidault to think in terms of a choice between East and West.[58] But France's broader Cold War alignment also dates from the

Moscow conference, for as Georges-Henri Soutou has observed, France's attitude to the German question and the French understanding of Cold War issues
were intimately linked.[59] British and American support for France's call for
an international authority in the Ruhr had been given with the proviso that
the Soviets fulfilled their commitment to treat the whole of Germany as a single economic unit. This requirement amounted to a demand – unacceptable
to the Soviets – that the construction of Communism in the East be reversed.
France's association with it provoked the Soviet delegation into opposing French
demands for the economic integration of the Saar with France – a core French
demand at the conference, and one to which the Anglo-Americans were
more sympathetic. In effect, without setting out to side with the British and
Americans at Moscow, Bidault, faced with Soviet hostility on almost every
issue, found himself placed willy-nilly in what was becoming the Western
camp.[60] At the next Foreign Ministers' conference, held at London in
December 1947, Bidault would deliberately line up with the West and isolate
the Soviets, even at the price of leaving French demands on the Ruhr out of
the discussion.[61]

France's progressive identification with the Western camp during 1947
had its obvious internal counterpart in the removal of the Communist ministers from the Ramadier government on 4 May. On this episode, authors close
to the PCF have constructed a durable myth – that the United States provoked the departure of Communists from government, and rewarded it, and
France's international alignment with the West, with aid.[62] What is certain,
and unsurprising, is that Washington continued to follow French internal
politics with intense interest. By late March, Caffery was telling the State
Department that he now feared a Communist takeover less than a year previously, and that the removal of the Communist ministers might now, therefore, be accomplished more safely.[63] In the aftermath of 4 May, he wrote that
'the present government is the best we could hope for', notably because it
'excludes the Communists on the extreme left and the reactionary elements
on the right, and combines the essentially democratic elements of the centre
and the left'.[64] But these words are far from proving direct American involvement. As Irwin Wall observes, the government crisis itself was in any case
'overdetermined' by internal political factors, in particular the deep split sep-
arating Communists from their Socialist and MRP colleagues on colonial issues
(notably Indochina and Madagascar) as well as the Renault strike; indeed,
France's more anticommunist ministers had already been purging their ministries of PCF sympathisers without any prompting from the Americans.
Moreover, the events of 4 May produced no immediate 'reward' of American
aid; the IBRD loan of $250 million announced that month was half what the
French had been hoping for, and Prime Minister Ramadier reproached the
Americans with cutting back on wheat shipments. More generally, historians
have searched over nearly six decades for the 'smoking gun' of direct American
intervention – in vain.[65]

More credible, on the other hand, is the link between American aid and American anxiety over French internal politics during the crisis of autumn 1947. The leading cause for concern was the PCF's newly militant line, expressed in the strikes of November–December. But a close second place was taken by de Gaulle, whose launch of the Rassemblement du Peuple Français (RPF) in the spring had been rewarded by a surge in membership and Gaullist activism and spectacular victories in the municipal elections of 27 October – all of which the Americans viewed with all the ambiguity they had traditionally shown towards the General. For a brief period in the autumn, indeed, Americans again believed themselves faced with the stark alternative of the Communists or de Gaulle. For the Embassy and the State Department, de Gaulle's return, though seen in October and November as both inevitable and preferable to a Communist takeover, remained far from welcome. Shortly after the municipal elections, when de Gaulle's *directeur de cabinet* Gaston Palewski told one of the American Embassy staff that de Gaulle aimed to return to power, as he did in 1958, with full powers to undertake major institutional reforms, the State Department's reaction was categorical: 'We are deeply worried by Palewski's remarks. . . . Press commentaries in this country, although they welcome the polarisation of anti-Communist forces in France, indicate extreme concern lest de Gaulle's supposed methods lead to the substitution of a dictatorship for parliamentary procedures.'[66] An armed confrontation between Gaullists and Communists was also an eventuality freely suggested by members of de Gaulle's entourage, and noted with alarm by Caffery.[67] It was not until a new government under Robert Schuman, with Jules Moch as Interior Minister, had successfully faced down the strikes in December that Caffery and the State Department were persuaded of the viability of the Third Force. They were further reassured by the split of the Communist-led trade union, the CGT. The role of the CIA in financing, via the AFL, the foundation of an anticommunist trade union, Force Ouvrière, which then played a key role in breaking the strikes, has also gone down in Communist mythology. Although CIA money was certainly employed, its importance in precipitating a split that had deeper long-term causes has been questioned by more recent research.[68]

Underlying American assessments of French internal politics during 1947, however, were the relentless round of bad economic news and the question of aid. The aid issue surfaced in spring 1947 from a variety of sources. One was the French themselves; Bidault had stressed to Marshall that the IBRD loan of $250 million would not meet French needs. His arguments fell on sympathetic ears, for Marshall left the Moscow conference convinced of the Russians' 'cold determination to exploit the powerlessness of Europe so as to spread Communism, instead of co-operating with the rest of the world' and resolved to counter it.[69] Meanwhile C. Tyler Wood, economic adviser in the State Department, was arguing that France was a 'critical region that may need aid in the coming months', and the State, War and Navy Co-ordinating Committee, precursor of the National Security Council, placed France fifth among world problems facing the US, behind Greece and Turkey, Iran, Italy, and Korea, and considered France as a country justifying aid 'for political and not economic reasons'.[70] That aid, judiciously applied, could promote recovery was indicated by the Monnet Plan: indeed, as Stewart Patrick has argued, 'The Monnet Plan's approach, including the definition of total dollar needs and the identification of economic targets, provided Washington with a small-scale model for a coordinated, continentwide scheme for recovery and modernisation that became known as the Marshall Plan.'[71]

France, then, was politically and intellectually central to the conception of the European Recovery Programme, announced by Marshall at his Harvard speech of June 1947. Later the same month, it was the French who hosted the European conference to define the future shape of the programme. When the Soviet delegation tried to lay down its own conditions for the plan, and then walked out of the talks, it was the French, with British encouragement, who chose not to try and salvage them, ensuring that Marshall aid became, *de facto*, a Western programme. France, with the United Kingdom, would become its largest beneficiary, receiving some $2.6 billion between 1948 and 1951; even the more sceptical accounts of the programme's effectiveness across Europe that have emerged since the mid-1980s concede that in the French case, in conjunction with the Monnet Plan, it proved remarkably helpful.[72]

Yet Marshall Aid, even once agreed by Congress, would only come into force on 1 April 1948 – too late to address the crisis of late 1947. The Quai d'Orsay announced the gathering storm in September by informing Washington that France's foreign currency reserves would be exhausted within seven weeks, preventing any imports of raw materials including wheat, coal and cotton.[73] The potential consequences, especially at a time of rising PCF militancy, were extremely grave: not only the adjournment *sine die* of any long-term plans for economic modernisation, but also food shortages and mass lay-offs as firms ran out of raw materials. Caffery echoed French concerns and called for an interim aid package to see France through the winter, arguing that 'the present government has steadily moved its policy toward that of the United States and continues to resist strong pressure from the Communists to return to office . . . [The government counts] on the Marshall Plan and on interim aid until the Marshall Plan comes into operation next spring.'[74] Reactions at the highest level made a more or less explicit link between the need for aid and the Communist threat. Thus President Truman declared that 'If the programme of economic recovery [for Western Europe] is to succeed a way must be found to help France and Italy to survive as free and independent nations over the coming critical winter. Available funds from Executive sources are insufficient to provide help beyond December. Assistance this winter at a much higher level . . . is essential. This aid can only come from Congress.'[75] Two months later, with $328 million now requested by the administration for France to cover the period from December 1947 to March 1948, Marshall told his British counterpart Ernest Bevin that immediate congressional agreement to an interim aid package was vital 'so as not to run the risk of losing France'.[76] The Foreign Aid Act 1947, voted by Congress in December, provided $522 million of interim aid, in the form of grants not loans, to France, Italy, and Austria, with France receiving $284 million and a further $28 million in March 1948.

Whether or not it 'saved' France, the package certainly helped the Schuman government through a perilous social, economic, and political situation. It also prompted and made possible the Mayer Stabilisation Plan of January 1948, widely credited with creating the financial and monetary conditions for France's recovery.[77] A single month had seen the defeat of the autumn 1947 strikes (and with them of any immediate prospect of a Communist return to power), the split of the CGT, the alignment of France on Western positions at the London conference, and the vote of an aid package which, in conjunction with the more substantial Marshall Plan, showed a level of American commitment to European recovery, and a linkage of that commitment to the Communist threat, that would have been unthinkable a year earlier.

Conclusion

The three post-war years demonstrated the elusiveness of the national independence that de Gaulle had so ardently sought to regain for his country. France's German policy, with neither British nor American (nor, really, Soviet) support, was an abject failure. Economic reconstruction, though impressive in some areas, remained heavily dependent on American aid; so, indeed, did current consumption. And as Wall has observed, 'the French found it increasingly difficult to pursue German weakness and American credits simultaneously'.[78]

It is tempting to link this dependence to the series of policy outcomes, all highly welcome to the Americans, seen in the course of 1947. These included the removal of the PCF from government and the firm stand taken against Communist-led strikes, France's alignment on Western positions at the London conference, the beginnings of a changed German policy, and, at the year's end, the drawing-up of an economic stabilisation plan aimed at balancing the budget, controlling inflation, and finding a realistic exchange rate for the franc on international markets. There is no doubt that the Americans were intense and anxious observers of French domestic politics; that they designed the aid programmes of 1947 in part to save France from Communism; that they linked aid packages (notably the Blum–Byrnes agreements) to agreements to France's integration into a liberal, multilateral, world economic order; or that they put pressure on the French to alter their German policy. But a simple relationship of cause (American pressure) and effect (French integration into an American-led political and economic system) is hard to establish in detail. Too many alternative explanations are readily available. The domestic sources of the PCF's exclusion from government are well established; the evidence of direct US intervention is not. American demands for France's integration into a more liberal post-war trading order found ready support among the French political and administrative elites, men like Monnet and Alphand, who had been developing plans to modernise the French economy on this basis since the war years. Even on the international issues, French positions were dictated as much by the increasing hostility of the Soviet Union (notably at the Moscow conference) as by American demands; and by the year's end, French policy-makers were convinced that the autumn strikes had been directed from Moscow in order to sabotage the economic recovery of Western Europe.[79]

The 'empire by invitation' thesis – that French policy-makers, conscious of a convergence of interests with the United States, voluntarily placed their country under American economic (and later military) protection at the price of a partial loss of sovereignty – is rather more attractive.[80] Yet it ignores France's highly imperfect alignment on the policy preferences of the United States after 1947. If the French never returned to the German policy of de Gaulle, they still pursued a relatively independent line on the German issue through 1948, obtaining important concessions from their allies, such as the International Authority for the Ruhr, as the price of merging with the bizone. And the successful ECSC initiative was designed to contain Germany, economically and politically, by other means. Meanwhile Marshall Aid was used, in the first instance, to further French (rather than European) modernisation through the Plan, before significant amounts were diverted to finance France's war in Indochina. France's integration into a multilateral world economic order proceeded at a pace dictated in Paris, not Washington; the most striking initiative to end trade restrictions, the European Economic Community, also entailed getting France's European partners to pay for a Europe-wide agricultural protectionism that has lasted half a century, much to the irritation of the Americans. Even the political stabilisation discernible at the end of 1947 did not last, and within barely a decade the Fourth Republic had given way to de Gaulle and the Fifth – a less dictatorial regime than the State Department had feared, but hardly more amenable to American concerns than the GPRF of 1944.

If France could afford to remain an awkward partner for the United States, it was not least because the state of dependence that developed in the post-war years was mutual. For most of the post-war decade, the French relied on American aid, first economic and then, with the spread of colonial wars, military. Equally, though, Washington depended on France for the success of the Marshall Plan, and for the wider consolidation of capitalist democracy in Western Europe: as a CIA report warned starkly in December 1947, 'if France is lost, Europe is lost'.[81] In that context, no American administration could afford to have a French government appear as Washington's poodle; the risk was too great that pressure on Paris would merely push France into the arms of de Gaulle or, worse, the Communists. It was not the least paradox of France's regime as it emerged from the Liberation that political and economic fragility at home could be used as a lever to extract American aid, and that any strings attached were to prove tenuous indeed.

Notes

1. F. Furet, *Le passé d'une illusion: essai sur l'idée communiste au XXe siècle* (Paris: Robert Laffont/Calmann-Lévy, 1995), p. 475.
2. J.M. Blum (ed.), *From the Morgenthau Diaries: Years of War, 1941–45* (Boston: Houghton Mifflin, 1967), p. 174.
3. S. Hoffmann, 'The man who would be France', *The New Republic*, 17 December 1990, p. 34.
4. Cf. J. Planchais, *Une Histoire Politique de l'Armée*, Vol. II (Paris, Le Seuil, 1967), p. 108.
5. *Le Monde*, 13 January 2001, p. 1.
6. H. Kissinger, *Diplomacy* (New York: Simon and Schuster, 1994), p. 396.
7. Franklin D. Roosevelt Library (hereafter FDRL), PSF (Box 31, Diplomatic Correspondence: France: Charles de Gaulle, 1944–45).
8. I. Wall, *The United States and the Making of Postwar France, 1945–1954* (Cambridge: Cambridge University Press, 1991), p. 25.
9. Ibid., pp. 21–2.
10. M. Ferro, *Pétain* (Paris: Fayard, 1987), pp. 421–2.
11. C. de Gaulle, *War Memoirs*, Vol. II, tr. Richard Howard (New York: Simon and Schuster, 1959), pp. 485–6.
12. 'The view from Hyde Park', *The Franklin and Eleanor Roosevelt Newsletter*, Winter 1989, p. 8.
13. C. de Gaulle, *War Memoirs*, Vol. II, pp. 290–3.
14. A. Kaspi, *La Libération de la France, juin 1944–janvier 1946* (Paris: Perrin, 1995), p. 103.
15. OSS Dossier 'Lamballe', National Archives II, College Park, MD. 'Lamballe' was another pseudonym for Enfieropoulos.
16. FDRL, PSF (Box 31, Diplomatic Correspondence: France: Charles de Gaulle, 1944–45): memorandum of 4 July 1944, p. 1.
17. C. de Gaulle, *War Memoirs*, Vol. I, tr. Jonathan Griffin (New York: Simon and Schuster, 1955), p. 269.
18. Wall, *The United States*, p. 25.
19. F.M.B. Lynch, *France and the International Economy: From Vichy to the Treaty of Rome* (London: Routledge, 1997), pp. 28–9.
20. National Archives, Kew (UK), CAB 120/524/T.2275/4: Roosevelt to Churchill, 6 December 1944.
21. Frankin D. Roosevelt Library, Map Room (FOF), Box 31, France Civil Affairs (1), FDR to Cordell Hull, 18 October 1944; J. Lacouture, *De Gaulle*, Vol. II (Paris: Seuil, 1985), p. 66.
22. C. de Gaulle, *War Memoirs*, Vol. III, tr. Richard Howard (New York: Simon and Schuster, 1960), pp. 165–71.
23. Ibid., pp. 194–5, 206–9. For Truman's reaction, cf. Wall, *The United States*, p. 32.
24. Cf. Chapter 12, pp. 208–9.
25. National Archives, Kew (UK), FO800/464: John Balfour, British Minister at Washington embassy to Foreign Office, 16 August 1945.
26. Cf. I.M. Wall, 'Harry S. Truman and Charles de Gaulle', in R.O. Paxton and N. Wahl (eds), *De Gaulle and the United States: a Centennial Reappraisal* (Oxford: Berg, 1994), pp. 117–39.
27. The above figures are taken from Lynch, *France and the International Economy*, pp. 7, 31, 49, 98, and 155.
28. Wall, *The United States*, pp. 35–6.
29. Lynch, *France and the International Economy*, pp. 24–5.

30. Wall, *The United States*, p. 39.
31. J. Monnet, *Mémoires* (Paris: Fayard, 1976), p. 295.
32. *Foreign Relations of the United States (FRUS)*, 1946, Vol. v, pp. 410, 416
33. Lynch, *France and the International Economy*, p. 38.
34. Wall, *The United States*, pp. 38–9.
35. The text of the agreements is in *FRUS*, 1946, Vol. v, pp. 463–4.
36. *FRUS*, 1947, Vol. iii, p. 708.
37. Wall, *The United States*, pp. 56, 113–21.
38. P. Pulzer, *German Politics, 1945–1995* (Oxford: Oxford University Press, 1995), pp. 24–5.
39. J. Young, *France, the Cold War and the Western Alliance 1944–49*, Leicester, Leicester University Press, 1990), pp. 14–15.
40. Harry S. Truman Library, PSF, Foreign Affairs File, Box 178, France–Germany: memorandum of Truman–de Gaulle conversation, 22 August 1945.
41. Lynch, *France and the International Economy*, pp. 40, 54, 59.
42. A. Milward, *The Reconstruction of Western Europe, 1945–51* (London: Routledge, 1992 (original edition 1984)), p. 133.
43. Lynch, *France and the International Economy*, p. 34.
44. Sir Ll. Woodward, *British Foreign Policy in the Second World War*, Vol. v (London: HMSO, 1976), p. 341.
45. Wall, *The United States*, p. 40.
46. National Archives, Kew (UK): FO371/58403/UR5273: Allied Control Authority, Economic Directorate, meeting of 29 May 1946.
47. FDRL, Map Room (FOF), PSF-OSS, Box 171, OSS reports, memorandum from General William Donovan (head of OSS) to President Roosevelt, 25 October 1944.
48. Quoted in Young, *France, the Cold War and the Western Alliance*, p. 39.
49. Wall, *The United States*, pp. 42–7, 53.
50. W.I. Hitchcock, *France Restored: Cold War Diplomacy and the Quest for Leadership in Europe, 1944–1954* (Chapel Hill and London: University of North Carolina Press, 1998), p. 35.
51. *FRUS*, 1946, Vol. v, pp. 469–70.
52. Wall, *The United States*, p. 64; Lynch, *France and the International Economy*, pp. 54, 57, 163; Hitchcock, *France Restored*, p. 72.
53. Lynch, *France and the International Economy*, pp. 52–4.
54. Ibid., pp. 56–7; Hitchcock, *France Restored*, p. 67.
55. Hitchcock, *France Restored*, pp. 78–9.
56. Wall, *The United States*, p. 89.
57. Hitchcock, *France Restored*, pp. 80–2, 87–92.
58. Wall, *The United States*, pp. 65–7.
59. G.-H. Soutou, 'La sécurité de la France dans l'après-guerre', in M. Vaïsse, P. Mélandri, and F. Bozo (eds), *La France et l'OTAN, 1949–1996* (Brussels: Complexe, 1996), p. 24.
60. Wall, *The United States*, p. 66; Young, *France, the Cold War and the Western Alliance*, p. 144; Hitchcock, *France Restored*, p. 71.
61. Hitchcock, *France Restored*, p. 89.
62. A. Lacroix-Riz, *Le Choix de Marianne: les relations franco-américaines, 1944–1948* (Paris: Messidor/Éditions Sociales, 1985).
63. Wall, *The United States*, p. 68.
64. *FRUS*, 1947, Vol. iii, pp. 709–10.

65. Cf. Wall, *The United States*, pp. 68–70; and I. Wall, 'The Marshall Plan and French politics', in M. Schain (ed.), *The Marshall Plan: Fifty Years After* (New York: Palgrave, 2001), pp. 167–83; p. 170.
66. *FRUS*, 1947, Vol. III, pp. 791–2.
67. 'Conversations between M. Malraux and Foreign Correspondents', 30 September 1947, National Archives, Kew (UK), FO371/67682/Z8619; Wall, *The United States*, p. 70.
68. Cf. the account of the senior CIA officer responsible, T. Braden, in the *Saturday Evening Post*, 20 May 1967, p. 4, and J. Ranelagh, *The Agency: the Rise and Decline of the CIA* (New York: Simon and Shuster, 1986), p. 246. For a more sceptical view, see D. MacShane, *International Labour and the Origins of the Cold War* (Oxford: Oxford University Press, 1992).
69. H. Truman, *Memoirs*, Vol. II (Garden City, NY: Doubleday, 1956), p. 112.
70. Wall, *The United States*, p. 75; *FRUS*, 1947, Vol. III, pp. 203, 206.
71. S. Patrick, 'Embedded Liberalism in France? American hegemony, the Monnet Plan, and postwar multilateralism', in M. Schain (ed.), *The Marshall Plan: Fifty Years After* (New York: Palgrave, 2001), pp. 205–45: p. 238.
72. Lynch, *France and the International Economy*, p. 58; Hitchcock, *France Restored*, p. 206; Wall, 'The Marshall Plan and French Politics', p. 168.
73. Wall, *The United States*, p. 88.
74. *FRUS*, 1947, Vol. III, p. 761; Hitchcock, *France Restored*, p. 83.
75. Harry S. Truman Library, presidential declaration of 29 September 1947.
76. *FRUS*, 1947, Vol. III, pp. 807–8.
77. Lynch, *France and the International Economy*, p. 88.
78. Wall, *The United States*, p. 35.
79. Hitchcock, *France Restored*, p. 93.
80. Cf. G. Lundestad, *The American 'Empire' and Other Studies of U.S. Foreign Policy in Comparative Perspective* (Oslo: Norwegian University Press, 1990).
81. Hitchcock, *France Restored*, p. 84.

Bibliography

Acheson, D., *Present at the Creation: My Years in the State Department* (New York: W.W. Norton, 1969).

Alphand, H., *L'étonnement d'être: journal 1939–1973* (Paris: Fayard, 1977).

Auriol, V., *Journal du Septennat, 1947–1954*, 7 volumes (Paris: Armand Colin, 1974).

Azéma, J.-P., *From Munich to the Liberation, 1938–1944* (Cambridge: Cambridge University Press, 1984).

Blum, J.M. (ed.), *From the Morgenthau Diaries: Years of War, 1941–45* (Boston: Houghton Mifflin, 1967).

de Gaulle, C., *War Memoirs*, Vol. I, tr. Jonathan Griffin (New York: Simon and Schuster, 1955).

de Gaulle, C., *War Memoirs*, Vol. II, tr. Richard Howard (New York: Simon and Schuster, 1959).

de Gaulle, C. *War Memoirs*, Vol. III, tr. Richard Howard (New York: Simon and Schuster, 1960).

Eisenhower, D., *The Papers of Dwight David Eisenhower*, ed. Alfred D. Chandler, Jr. (Baltimore: Johns Hopkins University Press, 1970).

Ferro, M., *Pétain* (Paris: Fayard, 1987).

Fondation Charles de Gaulle, *De Gaulle et la Nation face aux problèmes de defense* (Paris: Plon, Collection Espoir, 1983).

Furet, F., *Le passé d'une illusion: essai sur l'idée communiste au XXe siècle* (Paris: Robert Laffont/Calmann-Lévy, 1995).

Hitchcock, W.I., *France Restored: Cold War Diplomacy and the Quest for Leadership in Europe, 1944–1954* (Chapel Hill and London: University of North Carolina Press, 1998).

Hoffmann, S., 'The man who would be France', *The New Republic*, 17 December 1990.

Kaspi, A., *La Libération de la France, juin 1944–janvier 1946* (Paris: Perrin, 1995).

Kissinger, H., *Diplomacy* (New York: Simon and Schuster, 1994).

Lacouture, J., *De Gaulle*, 3 volumes (Paris: Le Seuil, 1984–6), (English edition tr. Alan Sheridan, 2 volumes, London: HarperCollins, 1991–2).

Lacroix-Riz, A., *Le Choix de Marianne: les relations franco-américaines, 1944–1948* (Paris: Messidor/Éditions Sociales, 1985).

Lundestad, G., *The American 'Empire' and Other Studies of U.S. Foreign Policy in Comparative Perspective* (Oslo: Norwegian University Press, 1990).

Lynch, F.M.B., *France and the International Economy: From Vichy to the Treaty of Rome* (London: Routledge, 1997).

MacShane, D., *International Labour and the Origins of the Cold War* (Oxford: Oxford University Press, 1992).

Milward, A., *The Reconstruction of Western Europe, 1945–51* (London: Routledge, 1992 (original edition 1984)).

Monnet, J., *Mémoires* (Paris: Fayard, 1976).

Murphy, R., *Diplomat among Warriors* (Garden City, NY: Doubleday, 1964).

Patrick, S., 'Embedded liberalism in France? American hegemony, the Monnet Plan, and postwar multilateralism', in M. Schain (ed.), *The Marshall Plan: Fifty Years After* (New York: Palgrave – now Palgrave Macmillan, 2001), pp. 205–45.

Planchais, J., *Une Histoire Politique de l'Armée*, Vol. ii (Paris: Le Seuil, 1967).

Pulzer, P., *German Politics, 1945–1995* (Oxford: Oxford University Press, 1995).

Ranelagh, J., *The Agency: the Rise and Decline of the CIA* (New York: Simon and Shuster, 1986).

Rousso, H., *Le Syndrome de Vichy de 1944 à nos jours* (Paris: Le Seuil, 1987).

Soutou, G.-H., 'La sécurité de la France dans l'après-guerre', in M. Vaïsse, P. Mélandri, and F. Bozo (eds), *La France et l'OTAN, 1949–1996* (Brussels: Complexe, 1996).

Truman, H., *Memoirs*, Vol. ii (Garden City, NY: Doubleday, 1956).

Wall, I., *The United States and the Making of Postwar France, 1945–1954* (Cambridge: Cambridge University Press, 1991).

Wall, I., 'Harry S. Truman and Charles de Gaulle', in R.O. Paxton and N. Wahl (eds), *De Gaulle and the United States: a Centennial Reappraisal* (Oxford: Berg, 1994).

Wall, I., 'The Marshall Plan and French politics', in M. Schain (ed.), *The Marshall Plan: Fifty Years After* (New York: Palgrave – now Palgrave Macmillan, 2001), pp. 167–83.

Woodward, Sir Ll., *British Foreign Policy in the Second World War*, Vol. v (London: HMSO, 1976).

Young, J., *France, the Cold War and the Western Alliance 1944–49* (Leicester: Leicester University Press, 1990).

12
The Half-open Window: France and Britain, 1944–47

Andrew Knapp

If there was a window for the development of a special Anglo-French relationship, it was surely in 1944–47. Britain and France emerged from the Second World War as the strongest, or least weak, West European powers. Both were democracies, but each sought to maintain great-power status through a traditional empire. Both could draw lessons from failures to build a European security system before 1939. Although 1940, Dunkirk, and Mers-el-Kebir had provoked intense anti-British feeling in France, the *de facto* habit of wartime co-operation thereafter ensured widespread popular and élite support for a post-war Anglo-French alliance. This could only be reinforced by Roosevelt's statement, at the Yalta conference in February 1945, that the United States planned to withdraw troops from Europe within two years.[1]

A treaty was indeed signed (symbolically, at Dunkirk), on 4 March 1947. But it proved an empty shell, its promises of mutual assistance against a German 'policy of aggression' over a decade too late. Attempts at economic and military follow-up came to little; it was superseded more than consolidated by the Brussels Treaty of 17 March 1948 and the NATO Treaty of 4 April 1949. The closest example of Anglo-French co-operation in the post-war generation was the disastrous Suez operation. France's 'privileged partner' in Europe proved to be, not a reluctant Britain, but West Germany.[2] For Anglo-French relations, the Liberation period was a moment where the high hopes of (some) élites and peoples alike gave way to the more familiar twentieth-century pattern of uneasy alliance.

Personality clashes between leaders contributed to, but did not determine, this outcome. On each side, other priorities too often took precedence over a close alliance during the world's complex transition from war to Cold War. Neither France's internal situation nor British perceptions of it eased negotiations. Post-war penury hindered closer economic relations. And differing views on the future of Germany encapsulated wider economic and strategic differences.

The impact of personalities

Far more than their successors, Churchill and de Gaulle personally shaped Anglo-French relations until their departures on, respectively, 26 July 1945 and 20 January 1946. Their stormy wartime partnership was structured around de Gaulle's sometimes quixotic insistence on France's great-power status; Churchill's overriding concern for good relations with the United States, which always trumped his abiding sense that Britain still needed France and de Gaulle; and Roosevelt's antipathy for the General.[3] Relations reached breaking-point in the autumn of 1942, in January and June 1943, in early June 1944, and in May 1945, to name but five occasions. Even during the (real) interludes of goodwill, each mistrusted the other's motives. De Gaulle's account of Churchill's Paris visit of November 1944, for example, stated that while seeking 'a formal alliance', Churchill wished to exclude France from dealings between the great powers and to consolidate Britain's position in the Mediterranean at French expense.[4] When de Gaulle favoured an alliance five months later, Churchill regretted 'that this man has another opportunity of inflicting another slight upon the Western allies and of lulling himself with the feeling that they are suitors for his favour'.[5] Even with Churchill gone, Jean Chauvel, the post-war secretary-general of the Quai d'Orsay (the French foreign ministry), could write that by the time of de Gaulle's resignation, 'all diplomatic activity was completely blocked', and 'whatever the issue concerned, our agreement was conditional on the settlement according to our requirements of the problems of the Levant and Germany' – without any prospect of such conditions being fulfilled.[6]

The most serious Anglo-French conflict of the period broke out in France's two League of Nations-mandated territories, Syria and Lebanon, where both Free French and British troops were stationed by the Liberation. In each country a nationalist movement, legitimated by elections in summer 1943, had formed a government pending fulfilment of an Anglo-French promise of post-war independence. But de Gaulle showed no hurry to cede sovereignty, suspecting that the British aimed to supplant France in the Levant. The British concern, meanwhile, was that French heavy-handedness in Syria and Lebanon could fan the flames of Arab nationalism, which could easily spread to British Middle Eastern mandates and protectorates.[7]

The arrival of French military reinforcements in May 1945 provoked rioting in several cities, which the French then shelled. The British commander reacted by ordering French soldiers, and their officers, to barracks under threat of force. Only lack of resources, an incensed de Gaulle told Britain's ambassador Alfred Duff Cooper, held France back from war with Britain; Churchill informed Truman that he considered de Gaulle 'one of the greatest dangers to European peace'.[8] The Levant soured Anglo-French relations until early 1946, with an agreement on mutual withdrawal of December 1945 breaking down over implementation difficulties. But de Gaulle's position lacked supporters in the Quai, the press, and the political élite; his departure greatly eased a settlement. A workable withdrawal agreement was reached after a UN Security Council resolution in February 1946, with the British leaving in June and the French at the year's end.[9]

Explosive, but not vital to either country's interests, the Levant was the extreme example of damage that personalities could do. Yet behind the principals, élites in both London and Paris probably wanted closer relations more than at any time since the Entente Cordiale. British supporters of the alliance had already backed de Gaulle's wartime leadership against American opposition. Both Harold Macmillan, British Minister Resident in Algiers through 1943, and his successor Duff Cooper supported the General as France's inevitable – and necessary – future leader.[10] Both were heavyweight political appointments: Duff Cooper used the four critical years of his ambassadorial post – *de facto* in Algiers and *de jure* in Paris, from January 1944 to December 1947 – to argue first for recognising de Gaulle and then for a close Anglo-French alliance.[11] Meanwhile Foreign Office officials were 'still anxious to bring about an Anglo-French alliance' even in the unpromising conditions of June 1945. Figures such as Sir Alexander Cadogan, the Permanent Under-Secretary from 1938 to 1946; Sir Orme Sargent, his successor; Sir William Strang, head of the German section of the Foreign Office and British representative on the European Advisory Commission; and Sir Oliver Harvey, Duff Cooper's successor in Paris, all supported de Gaulle during the war and closer Anglo-French relations from 1944.[12] Of their political chiefs, Churchill's Foreign Secretary, Anthony Eden, believed that French opinion was 'overwhelmingly behind de Gaulle', that de Gaulle's provisional government deserved speedy recognition, that 'in dealing with European problems of the future we are likely to have to work more closely with France even than with the United States' and therefore that British policy 'must aim at the restoration of the independence of the smaller European Allies and of the greatness of France'.[13] Ernest Bevin, Foreign Secretary after Labour's election victory on 26 July 1945, consulted closely with Eden, implemented 'virtually a bipartisan foreign policy', and started work on improving relations with France within two weeks of taking office.[14] Meanwhile Bevin's own party, from the Keep Left group to the moderate Fabians, supported closer relations with France as consistent with a 'Socialist foreign policy'. The British press, from the left-wing *New Statesman* to the *Economist* via the *Manchester Guardian* and the *Times*, took a similarly positive view.[15]

So did many in France. Like Duff Cooper, France's Ambassador to London from 1944 to 1954, René Massigli, was more than a simple career diplomat. A leading pre-war anti-appeaser, dismissed from the Quai d'Orsay by Vichy in 1940, Massigli was the Commissioner for Foreign Affairs in the Comité Français de Libération Nationale (CFLN) from June 1943 until his appointment to London; he ended his career as Secretary-General of the Quai.[16] Massigli viewed a British alliance not only as a vital counterweight to the

Franco-Soviet treaty of December 1944, but 'the condition for a real autonomy of French policy'.[17] Views in the Quai were, it is true, more mixed: Maurice Couve de Murville, the director of its political section (and future Foreign Minister), took a cooler view than Massigli, while Massigli himself mentions ex-Vichyites and men with antique grudges for ancestors killed at Trafalgar.[18] But he did have allies in Jean Chauvel, secretary-general of the Quai from January 1945, and (to a lesser extent) in Hervé Alphand, director of its economic section.

The leading political supporters of a British alliance were the Socialists, whose August 1945 congress called for such a treaty as the centrepiece of the world's future peace and collective security.[19] Léon Blum, France's first Socialist Prime Minister from June 1936 to June 1937, had placed close relations with Britain at the centre of his foreign policy. His return to the premiership at the head of an all-Socialist government from December 1946 to January 1947 was decisive in moving alliance negotiations forward, despite its brevity (determined by Blum's age and physical frailty, and the interregnum between the November 1946 elections and the inauguration of the Fourth Republic). For Vincent Auriol, president of the second Constituent Assembly and then first president of the Fourth Republic, a Franco-British treaty lay at the heart of any post-war project for Western Europe.[20] Several leading Socialists, such as André Philip, Finance Minister and then Economics Minister in 1946–47, had spent part of the war in London; the Beveridge Report had helped inspire the programme of the Conseil National de la Résistance.[21] Labour's July 1945 election victory naturally reinforced the Socialists' regard for Britain. In the Assembly, they could often rally much of the Radical Party to their Anglophile views, as well as a minority of the Christian Democratic MRP (Mouvement Républicain Populaire) and some conservatives of the Briand tradition. *No* parliamentary group, not even the Communists, opposed the Dunkirk Treaty.

Somewhat distant from the general climate of support for a British alliance was the MRP leader Georges Bidault. The Blum interlude aside, Bidault was Foreign Minister for four years from September 1944 and chief foreign policy-maker after de Gaulle's departure on 20 January 1946. A less obsessive nationalist than the General, Bidault shared some of the same susceptibilities; his interest in an Anglo-French alliance was more pragmatic than instinctive or emotional. Having sought unsuccessfully for two years to give substance to the Soviet alliance of 1944, Bidault gradually came to believe that 'An Anglo-French alliance would provide an essential basis for other agreements, if the worst came to the worst and we had to organize a system of defence.'[22]

After January 1946, the personal focus of Anglo-French relations shifted to the foreign ministers: summit talks were rare, the Attlee–Blum conversations of early 1947 being a major exception. On Massigli's account, personal relations between Bevin and Bidault – both susceptible men – varied from the warm (as during the London Conference of Foreign Ministers in September 1945, or when working on the European Recovery Plan in 1947) to the stormy;

but Bevin's irritation at Bidault's reluctance to anchor France to the West, or Bidault's annoyance at being called a 'dear little man' by Bevin, were barely comparable to the epic de Gaulle–Churchill clashes.

Algiers to Dunkirk, 1943–47

De Gaulle and Bidault had concluded the Soviet alliance in barely a week during December 1944; negotiating the Dunkirk treaty, despite the support for an Anglo-French alliance on either side of the Channel, took vastly longer – and it was scarcely more operational once signed.

An alliance, of course, required a recognised French government. But the Americans explicitly denied the CFLN any governmental status. So, officially, did the British, even if Macmillan had personally viewed the CFLN as 'in effect the provisional Government of France' as early as the summer of 1943.[23] As D-Day approached, Roosevelt gave Eisenhower, as Supreme Commander of Allied forces in Europe, responsibility for law and order in liberated territories. Roosevelt's plans for the administration of France, viewed in the Foreign Office as 'insulting' to the CFLN, were not even shown to de Gaulle. The General retaliated by unilaterally transforming the CFLN into the Gouvernement Provisoire de la République Française (GPRF) on 3 June 1944.[24] No agreement on the administration of France was reached before D-day. For Roosevelt, elections, and the liberation of all French territory, should precede the recognition of any French government;[25] for Eden and the Foreign Office, de Gaulle could be trusted to organise free elections in due course, while failure to recognise the GPRF would play into the hands of the Communist-dominated internal Resistance. Churchill backed Roosevelt, telling the Cabinet on 4 September – ten days after the liberation of Paris – that 'there should be no change in our relations with the French National Committee until he had had the opportunity of discussion with President Roosevelt' and that 'we should encourage the French to put themselves to the country as soon as might be'.[26]

Four factors led to a change of policy and recognition. First, reports from British and American intelligence agents from mid-June on confirmed de Gaulle's high level of support in liberated France.[27] Second, the General made a gesture to Allied opinion as well as the internal Resistance by broadening the GPRF on 9 September and the Consultative Assembly that underpinned it in October. Third, as Eisenhower's Supreme Headquarters Allied Expeditionary Force (SHAEF) admitted, Allied troops could not maintain order in the liberated zones, amounting to over four-fifths of French territory, while simultaneously fighting a war against stiffening German resistance in the East.[28] Fourth, worries about the strength of the Parti Communiste Français (PCF), discreetly encouraged by de Gaulle but also confirmed by intelligence reports from France, played a part in rallying the Allies to the General. If the British in France did not yet view the PCF through a Cold War mindset, both

Eisenhower and Jefferson Caffery, the United States emissary (and soon ambassador) to the GPRF urged recognition partly on these grounds.[29] When Roosevelt gave way, on 21 October, Allied recognition, and with it the official handover of the greater part of France from Allied to French control as an 'interior zone' away from the battlefront, followed within 48 hours.[30]

Less than three weeks later (10–12 November), Churchill made a triumphant visit to Paris. De Gaulle called it 'the practical manifestation of an alliance that cruel vicissitudes have made more necessary than ever'.[31] The war's last months gave concrete expression to the British policy of 'building up France'. Unable to secure French representation at Yalta or Potsdam, the British still 'fought like tigers' at both conferences to secure (in addition to the permanent seat on the United Nations Security Council, agreed at Dumbarton Oaks in August–September 1944) France's entry into the European Advisory Commission set up in 1943 to decide the future of post-war Europe, and particularly Germany; a French occupation zone in Germany; and seats both on the Reparations Commission and on the inter-Allied Council of Foreign Ministers created to settle peace agreements with the Axis powers.[32] Bevin struggled to ensure a French role in negotiating all European peace treaties, allowing the first Council of Foreign Ministers, held at London in September 1945, to break down when the Russians refused it.[33]

Yet for nearly two-and-a-half years the Anglo-French treaty was *l'Arlésienne* of West European diplomacy: often talked of, never seen. Before signing the Soviet alliance in December, Bidault had told the Foreign Office that France planned a similar treaty with Britain.[34] In answer to telegrams from Stalin requesting advice on the impending Franco-Soviet pact, Churchill, with the Cabinet's support, told Stalin on 5 December that he welcomed the Franco-Soviet initiative but would prefer a tripartite pact. De Gaulle rejected this initiative, with some irritation, but still claimed to favour an alliance with 'la vieille et brave Angleterre' – under conditions – in a radio broadcast on 5 February 1945.[35] Bidault and Eden discussed a treaty later that month in London. Duff Cooper and de Gaulle did the same in April 1945; both Chauvel and Bidault followed up with messages to the British Ambassador. By the war's end the British had a draft treaty prepared.[36] Duff Cooper and Bidault held further talks in August 1945, while de Gaulle's *Times* interview of 10 September stressed the community of interest between Britain and France and the need for them to concert their actions.[37] Félix Gouin, de Gaulle's Socialist successor as head of the GPRF from 26 January 1946, used both the National Assembly (on 29 January) and the Socialist party congress (on 30 March) to call for a Franco-British alliance. Sir Oliver Harvey was sent to Paris to negotiate it in April 1946, only to find the Gouin government too divided to agree. Bidault again offered Bevin a treaty in the autumn of 1946, but preferred to wait until after the elections before concluding it. Only with the brief Blum government was significant progress made, first during Duff Cooper's talks with the veteran premier on 26 December 1946, then at Blum's successful London visit of 13–14 January 1947, when the official communiqué specifically mentioned

an alliance. Bidault, who returned to office on 22 January after Blum's departure, completed negotiations within a month.

The treaty was signed at Dunkirk on 4 March 1947 – just eight days before
President Truman spoke to Congress and launched both the 'doctrine' bearing his name and, on one reading, the Cold War. But like the earlier Anglo-
Soviet and Franco-Soviet pacts, the Dunkirk Treaty still looked back to the
wartime alliance. Explicitly directed at Germany, as Bevin confirmed to the
House of Commons on 15 May, it promised 'all military and other [mutual]
assistance' in any war with the old enemy, as well as 'such agreed action . . .
as is best calculated to put an end' to any German 'policy of aggression'.[38] As
this threat proved unreal, the alliance offered, at best, a general framework
for a close future understanding between the signatories. Such an understanding could be strategic, economic, or diplomatic. But strategic co-operation,
in the form of staff talks, though sought by the French and supported by Duff
Cooper, was blocked by London until December 1947. In the economy, at
least in bilateral terms, the record was limited, despite the creation, in
September 1946, of an Anglo-French Economic Committee 'to avoid unneces-
sary trade competition and to study the Anglo-French balance of payments
problem'.[39] The project of a customs union, envisaged in the Attlee–Blum
talks of January, came to nothing; in October Duff Cooper was complaining
that follow-up to the previous month's Bevin–Ramadier talks on economic
co-operation had been scuppered by officials.[40] The major collaboration
between the two powers had been the establishment of the Committee for
European Economic Co-Operation (the CEEC, including sixteen European
countries) and its preparation, between July and September 1947, of a European
recovery plan; and that had been in reaction to Secretary of State George
Marshall's speech of 5 June offering American aid. In diplomatic terms, the
two countries converged somewhat on the critical issue of Germany, and made
joint preparations for the December Conference of Foreign Ministers in
London. But by the end of 1947 the Anglo-French alliance had been practically superseded by the multilateralism that would find expression in the
Brussels treaty and, in 1949, in NATO. Rather than an accretion of further countries around an Anglo-French core, envisaged by Duff Cooper or the French
Socialists, the two further treaties integrated Britain and France as two individual nations in a wider partnership, with the Benelux countries and then
the United States and other NATO members.

What explains this fairly meagre record, long after the exit of Churchill
and de Gaulle? The obstacles to a close alliance sprang, in the first place,
from fundamentals in the Anglo-French relationship in the context of a
rapid and unpredictable transition to Cold War.

Anglo-French relations and the transition to Cold War

Three possible futures could be foreseen for Europe as the war ended: a continuation of the wartime Grand Alliance between the Soviet Union, the United

States, Britain, and (now) France (Scenario A); a breakdown of that alliance, with the United States disengaging from Europe and the Western democracies facing the threat of a resurgent Germany, a hostile Soviet Union, or, in the worst case, both together (Scenario B); and finally, what happened – a breakdown of the alliance but with continued American engagement, resulting in a divided Europe, and a divided Germany, at the centre of the worldwide Cold War (Scenario C). Uncertainty about the continent's future, plus the speed of events, made foreign policy-making in the immediate post-war years exceptionally fluid and complex. For example, in June 1947 Auriol agreed with General de Lattre, Inspector General of France's armed forces, that in a war between the United States and the Soviet Union, France might join either side, or remain neutral.[41] British and French perspectives on the unfolding situation differed in important ways, shaped by distinct views of national interest and domestic political constraints. The British reacted more strongly to Soviet actions in Greece, Turkey, or Iran; the French were more worried for longer about a resurgent Germany. Similarly, the presence of Communists in the French government until 5 May 1947, and their continued parliamentary strength thereafter, affected both French behaviour towards the Soviet Union and British perceptions of France as a potential ally. This was not a simple environment within which to build a new bilateral relationship.

Scenario A had a particular status, at least till early 1948, as the framework that no one in government could openly abandon. Any power that did so would risk wrecking any remaining chances of great power co-operation, and appearing as an aggressor before allies, coalition partners, and domestic and international opinion. Publicly, Truman denied advance knowledge of the contents of Churchill's March 1946 Iron Curtain speech; privately, he had read and endorsed it.[42] Bevin expressed his growing worries about the Soviet threat in Cabinet that May; shared since 1944 by the Foreign Office and Britain's Chiefs of Staff, they were still too pessimistic for the Labour Left, for Prime Minister Attlee – and for the public.[43] By Autumn 1946, Bevin and the Foreign Office expected the division of Germany – a defining feature of the Cold War – but wanted a chance to blame the Soviets for it.[44] This need to maintain a public commitment to four-power co-operation helps explain why, even nine months later, the Dunkirk Treaty was drafted, by both sides, as directed against Germany, and why Belgian approaches to join it the same spring were stalled by Bevin.[45] Even in December 1947, in talks with Bidault on co-operation with the United States after the failure of the last Conference of Foreign Ministers, in London in December 1947, Bevin sought to 'avoid, if possible, giving the Russians a slogan or a plan with which to come out against the Western Powers and embarrass all three of them'.[46] The French had additional reasons to be attached to Scenario A: the Soviet alliance of December 1944 had been intended to counterbalance relations with the British and Americans, especially over the German question, and there was a widespread and genuine sympathy for the Soviet Union in the country, within and beyond the confines of the PCF.

Conversely, Scenario B – a worst case, but a credible one – was discussed behind closed doors. Churchill's worries about Russia dated at least from the Tehran conference late in 1943.[47] Meanwhile Roosevelt's stated intention to bring American troops home within two years of the war's end, the abrupt end of Lend-Lease in August 1945, and the opposition of American opinion that autumn to further military or economic assistance to Europe, all pointed towards American disengagement.[48] The Truman administration's toughening stance towards the Soviet Union from early 1946 entailed no speedy material commitments; even by early 1948, the US army was only 554,000 strong, less than half of it in Europe.[49] And there appeared little chance of West European forces alone, with Germany disarmed, resisting a Soviet attack. Indeed, memories of the Rappallo Treaty of 1922 or the Nazi–Soviet pact of 1939 suggested the possibility of a German–Soviet *entente* confronting the West. Two options were open to escape Scenario B. Bidault's was to cling to Scenario A and keep working with the Soviet Union, with France playing a role as a 'bridge' between East and West, reflecting the domestic consensus he sought between the three partners of France's *tripartite* governing coalition.[50] By the end of the Moscow Conference of Foreign Ministers in Spring 1947, however, a disabused Bidault was convinced that 'any agreement with the Russians is impossible'.[51] The second option, pursued with some consistency by the Foreign Office and Bevin, was to seek to (re-)engage the Americans, switching from Scenario B to C: as Bevin told Bidault in December 1947, the Americans 'had to be persuaded that we were all in this together as Allies and that was the goal towards which we should all strive'.[52]

An Anglo-French alliance had an ambiguous place in each scenario. The alliance, it should be noted, was widely conceived as the hard core of a wider 'Western bloc'. Both inter-war experience, political and economic, and wartime discussions with governments in exile, suggested the need to include at least the Benelux countries in planning for Western Europe. In Britain, the Post-Hostilities Planning Sub-Committee, a group created by the War Cabinet linking the Foreign Office and the Chiefs of Staff, had adopted the 'Western bloc' idea by late 1944, at least as an insurance policy; Eden had set it out to Massigli on 14 December.[53] Duff Cooper, more grandly, conceived 'a federation of the western seaboard of Europe together with the principal Powers of the Mediterranean', and their empires; Bevin's conception was equally ambitious, and extended to economic and cultural co-operation.[54]

During the war, the Western bloc might possibly be presented as a sort of diplomatic second front; Stalin had approved the idea early in 1944.[55] But in a context of post-war great power co-operation (Scenario A), it was harder to justify, even with the economic and cultural spin given by Bevin. Hence, for example, Eden's fear that a Western bloc might either 'provoke the Soviets or encourage isolationists in the United States by casting doubt on European support for the United Nations', or de Gaulle's reluctance to compromise France's new alliance with the Soviets, increasingly hostile to a Western bloc from 1945.[56] During negotiations for the Dunkirk Treaty in February 1947, Harvey had to assuage the concerns of the Chiefs of Staff, who 'regard collaboration with the Americans as the keystone on which our major strategy and planning are based, and consider that any risk of impairing these relations would be too great a price to pay for such a treaty'.[57] These concerns are echoed in Bevin's report to Cabinet on the February 1947 negotiations for the Dunkirk Treaty. While both allies would engage 'all the means at their disposal' if war broke out with Germany, Bevin stressed that Britain had avoided any 'automatic commitment' in the lesser emergency of a German 'policy of aggression'; and, crucially, the alliance would 'safeguard the proposed Four-Power treaty [the so-called 'Byrnes Treaty'] for the disarmament of Germany', thereby reassuring the superpowers.[58] Nor were these anxieties about Soviet and American reactions misplaced. The Moscow press had reacted fiercely to news of the talks.[59] The Dunkirk Treaty had hardly been signed when Bogomolov, the Soviet ambassador in Paris, made clear to Auriol that he would have preferred a tripartite Anglo-Franco-Soviet pact, while Secretary of State Marshall stressed to him the wider context of four-power co-operation.[60] Within Scenario A, then, an Anglo-French alliance was just acceptable to the emerging superpowers if limited to two countries and directed against Germany – what Bidault had termed 'a battle order against an army of ghosts'.[61]

Within Scenario B, by contrast, an alliance appeared vital for both British and French security, whether the threat was German, Soviet, or both. The Post-Hostilities Planning Staff in general and Orme Sargent in particular had stressed France's importance, typically as part of a Western bloc, in the event of the Grand Alliance breaking down.[62] Bevin would regularly come back to the same point between 1945 and 1947.[63] But as soon as either British or French policy-makers contemplated a serious breakdown in relations with the Soviet Union, their understandable first reflex was to secure American help. That was a central concern of Churchill's late in the war. It was reinforced by the view of the Chiefs of Staff that West European forces would be 'wholly inadequate' to stop a Soviet advance into Western Europe, and that the United States was 'the only country which possesses sufficient manpower and reserves to stabilise the situation'.[64] 'It cannot be too often repeated that the continuance of American interest in Europe is vital to the peace of Europe', Bevin told the House of Commons on 22 October 1946, stating Britain's most consistent aim for the continent in the immediate post-war era.[65] For the French, the full implications of a breakdown with the Soviets were not seriously discussed until 1947, when the failure of the Moscow Conference of Foreign Ministers, the removal of Communist ministers from the Ramadier government, Anglo-French acceptance of Marshall Aid, and finally the failure of the London Conference in December all signalled a decisive alignment within the Western camp. But it was clear during Chauvel's and Bidault's London visits in October and December 1947 that the French immediately started thinking, in a context of heightened tension with the Soviet Union, of reinforcing relations with the Americans as well as the British.[66]

Under Scenario C, finally, the Anglo-French alliance was subordinate to the larger Atlantic alignment: necessary as the basis of the wider Western union that would be realised in Brussels in 1948, itself an assurance of Western Europe's will to defend itself, but in the end secondary to each country's relationship with the United States. For the British, this order of priorities was clear from Bevin's conversation with Marshall on 17 December 1947. Announcing plans for informal military talks with the French, Bevin 'was doubtful whether we could go so far with the French as we were able to do with the Americans, with whom our military conversations were like those between members of one country'. Bevin and Marshall agreed that Anglo-French talks should be kept separate from planned Anglo-American conversations.[67] The Chiefs of Staff took an even more restrictive view, arguing that 'military conversations with France and the other countries should, until we have discussed the larger issue with the Americans, be confined to this Service Department level' – such as 'supply of great coats and clothing to the French Army, and aircraft spares for the French Air Force'.[68] Meanwhile Bidault, once aligned with the 'Anglo-Saxons' (a commitment confirmed by the French Cabinet on 19 December), preferred his contacts with the Americans to be direct rather than via British intermediaries.[69]

The Alliance, then, was a critical Anglo-French priority under Scenario B – the worst case for both powers. But it was a potential threat, especially in the form of a Western bloc, to great-power co-operation under Scenario A. The Cold War scenario that finally materialised was certainly no block on such an alliance, as its enlargement in the 1948 Brussels Treaty confirmed. Indeed, it has been argued that an opportunity was lost to construct a real Western European defence pole, able to complement the Atlantic links that both allies sought.[70] It is understandable, though, that in the context of late 1947 the vastly greater military capacity of the United States should make the Anglo-French alliance appear a less viable security guarantee, for each country, than the continued American engagement that both sought.

French internal politics and the London view

The scope of the alliance was also limited by British worries about political instability and Communist influence in France. At first, the Paris embassy had viewed the PCF with patronising sympathy. 'The presence of Communists in Government Councils makes for a steadying and educative influence', Holman, the British Minister, wrote in January 1945; 'it provides them with experience and opens their eyes to the responsibilities attaching to office'.[71] London was always more sceptical; the Paris embassy soon followed.

British worries about Communists in government could point three ways. One, albeit short-lived, was panic. When de Gaulle resigned in January 1946, Bevin anticipated 'civil war within a year' and the Channel ports 'virtually in Russian hands.'[72] A second view, in the Embassy and the Foreign Office, was that an Anglo-French alliance could help reinforce non-Communist forces.[73]

This was, in part, behind the despatch of Oliver Harvey to Paris following Gouin's encouraging speeches.[74] But Gouin could not carry a majority which included, not only his own Socialists, but Communists (hostile to anything resembling a western bloc) and the pro-Gaullist wing of the MRP (opposed to any alliance before a settlement of German differences). The failure of Harvey's visit suggested a third conclusion: that France was an unreliable ally.[75] Bevin concluded that Gouin had 'been speaking only for his own party and was not speaking for the French government as a whole'; later he would add concerns about Communists in government as a reason to delay military conversations with the French.[76]

The Dunkirk treaty appears as an absolutely logical outcome to these conflicting perspectives. The breakthrough with Blum after Christmas 1946 came under France's first post-war government without Communist ministers; the encouragement of non-Communists in government was rarely far from the British negotiators' perspectives; and the alliance once signed was of limited scope.[77] This was particularly true of military questions, which the British (still blissfully unaware of Communist spies in their own diplomatic service) kept at arm's length for months. In October 1947, in the midst of rumours of a Gaullist *coup*, and dispatches from Duff Cooper underlining the PCF's complete change towards a more aggressive strategy since the formation of the Cominform, Orme Sargent was stressing to Chauvel that 'it would be unwise in the extreme to frighten the public by staging Anglo-French military talks prematurely and without reference to the Americans'. Misgivings were also voiced about General Revers, the chief of the French staff, considered right-wing, naïve, and dangerous.[78] Only on 23 December 1947, after Bidault had given reassurances on the Communist issue,[79] did Bevin instruct Montgomery, the Chief of the Imperial General Staff, to initiate talks with Revers.[80]

The paradox of France's internal politics for the British (and the Americans) was that de Gaulle was both the best post-war barrier to Communism and the most difficult prospective ally. His departure removed obstacles to closer relations, but reinforced British worries about Communism and more general political stability. The removal of Communist ministers in May 1947 answered the former objection; but it laid the foundations for the Fourth Republic's endemic instability, and was also a reflection of the slide to Cold War that would place the alliance under American sponsorship.

France, Britain, and the economics of penury

If Anglo-French diplomatic and strategic co-operation was constrained by the emerging Cold War and the two countries' relationships with the superpowers, slow progress in economic relations had other reasons. Bevin's ideas in this area were very ambitious. In the late summer both of 1946 and 1947 he tried to promote an Anglo-French customs union – responding, in the second instance, to an invitation from Alphand.[81] Europe's post-war history would clearly have been very different had a major customs union been successfully launched in 1947 with Britain as a founding member, rather than in 1957 with Britain outside. What was achieved was far less: the simplification of France's debt obligations to Britain and the creation of an Anglo-French Economic Committee in September 1946, undertakings of economic consultation in the Dunkirk Treaty (Article 4), and Anglo-French leadership in the creation of the Organisation for European Economic Co-Operation to co-ordinate Marshall Aid through the European Recovery Programme a year later.

Three contexts defined the customs union project. The first was the general post-war commitment to freer international trade made by Britain and France when they accepted Lend-Lease, post-war American loans, and the Bretton Woods monetary agreements. Bevin saw in freer trade an opportunity to break 'the vicious circle whereby between the wars trade could not flourish because of lack of security, while security was endangered through lack of trade';[82] for Alphand and above all for Monnet, France's first *Commissaire au Plan*, it was a lever for the modernisation of France. But both countries, desperately short of dollars to pay for imports, hesitated to lift trade restrictions too rapidly. Moreover, it was not clear, at least until mid-1947, that the Americans would not view a European customs union as a regional arrangement at odds with the wider multilateral trading system they sought.

The second context was Bevin's more general wish to improve relations with France. In this framework, closer economic relations could serve two purposes. For the outside world, a Western bloc devoted to economic co-operation might appear less threatening than a defence pact.[83] Second, as Harvey told a meeting with the Board of Trade in October 1947, 'The Secretary of State was thinking of economic association for political reasons, such as the combatting of Communism.'[84]

Reinforcement of non-Communist forces in Western Europe was a powerful motive behind Marshall Aid, the third context for Anglo-French economic co-operation. France was absolutely central to the European Recovery Programme, by virtue of her size and geographical position and because of the strength of Communism (which in Autumn 1947 prompted the Truman Administration to supply France, along with Italy and Austria, with 'interim aid' for the winter even before funds from the larger programme became available).[85] In the longer term France required aid to have any chance of fulfilling the first (Monnet) Plan.[86] At Bevin's and Bidault's initiative, the European conference to discuss Marshall's Harvard proposals opened on 27 June 1947, barely three weeks after the speech itself. Determined that the Soviets 'must be given no opportunity to cause delay and obstruction',[87] the Western powers readily proceed on their own after Molotov left the table. But Marshall Aid was offered on conditions, the chief of which was the presentation of a co-ordinated recovery plan with provisions for European economic integration. This proved elusive: by early September, the West European delegates to the Paris conference had failed to reach an agreement to satisfy the Americans.

In this context, proposals for a customs union could be interpreted in two very different ways: either as a means to demonstrate to the Americans that Western Europe was serious about economic integration, or as a means, especially if the two empires were included, to achieve a greater degree of economic autonomy, allowing both countries to limit their need to purchase imports with scarce dollars.[88] This latter motivation – which might, if carried much further, have provoked American hostility – appeared most clearly in the discussions on colonial co-operation during the Bevin–Ramadier talks in September 1947, in the subsequent exchanges with Chauvel and Bidault, and in Alphand's proposals for West African co-operation made in December.[89]

Neither plans for colonial co-operation nor those for a customs union involving Britain met with success. Both were essentially Foreign Office projects that fell victim, on the British side, to the other ministries involved. The Colonial Office, mindful of the aspirations of Britain's colonised peoples, were suspicious of anything resembling a league of imperial powers, especially when the inclusion of Belgians, Dutch and Italians was discussed; in any case, as one official observed, the authors of the new proposals 'had no conception of the problems involved and . . . were activated wholly by political motives'.[90] On the customs union, the Board of Trade had blocked Bevin's request for serious discussions in 1946. A year later, Duff Cooper was lamenting that 'officials of the Treasury and the Board of Trade – pig-headed as ever – won't hear of it', adding that 'We need only accept the principle – the thing itself would not come about for years.' Chauvel recalled similar obstructiveness to Bevin's proposals for economic co-operation in negotiations for the Brussels Treaty in 1948.[91] Some of their reasons would reappear in Britain's Common Market debates of the 1960s and 1970s: a European customs union would be at odds with the wider free trade order being created under American auspices, or with Britain's existing relations with the Commonwealth, or with Labour's aspirations to build state socialism in Britain.[92]

The most important difficulty, however, lay in the two countries' balance-of-payments difficulties arising from the post-war disruption of Europe's trade. Before 1939 Britain had run regular trade deficits with continental Europe, largely thanks to big food imports; with France, trade had also included an exchange of French luxury goods, and invisible earnings from tourism, against British raw materials, especially coal. But the war, combined with long-term underinvestment in the mining industry, had turned Britain into a net importer of coal (for which dollars had had to be paid),[93] at the same time as the British temporarily captured former German markets on the continent for industrial goods, especially machine tools. The difficulty lay in finding goods to buy from the Europeans, and especially the French, in the absence of a functioning multilateral world trading system. Europe's food surpluses had disappeared; demand for French luxury goods had plummeted in the context of post-war austerity. Less than 25 per cent of Britain's foreign trade in the years after 1945 was with Europe.[94] In 1946, the value of franc area exports to the sterling area was barely a quarter of trade in the opposite direction.[95] British officials were unsympathetic, arguing that 'The French people are to a large extent responsible for their own difficulties', that 'The nation generally seems more interested in rebuilding its constitution than its economy', and that 'The French must cease to count on charity and get on with reconstruction.'[96] More materially, the British demanded and got payment; under an agreement of 29 April 1946, the French undertook to requisition £20 million in foreign currency and shares held by the French in Britain in order to reimburse debts over three years to 1949 and to reduce imports from the UK.[97] This last readjustment, at the price of severe import restrictions in France,[98] was very successful. In the first half of 1947 France's trade balance with Britain improved dramatically – prompting new British complaints that 'We had been buying all we could from France, but the French acted restrictively.' More specifically, Board of Trade officials complained that France's 'economy was designed to fit a luxury world, whereas everyone now wanted essential goods only'; that Britain needed fewer 'luxury' goods (these included fruit and nuts) and more essentials (especially steel, iron ore, pig iron, scrap iron, bauxite, timber, leather, tanning materials, plus wood products such as pitprops, hardwood, plywood, and sleepers), which were presently unavailable or too expensive. In Autumn 1947, the broad economic view of the Board of Trade remained dismissive: 'with regard to the pooling of resources between ourselves and France, we should be the losers. We should be in the position of holding up France.'[99] Their minister till September 1947, Sir Stafford Cripps, had opposed closer economic integration with France before Blum's visit in January; his successor Harold Wilson showed no inclination to take a broader view.[100]

To overcome such objections would have required a continuous exercise of political will. That of Bevin and the Labour Government was episodic. In the spring of 1946, amid fears of a Communist victory in the elections of 2 June and well-publicised Soviet deliveries of grain to France, they persuaded the Americans to raise deliveries of coal.[101] In January 1947, the Cabinet declared its willingness to discuss 'France's economic difficulties' with Blum – discussions that led to the Dunkirk Treaty.[102] But fear of other European demands, and of weakening Britain's own case for help from the United States, ruled out any charitable treatment of France. On the free trade issue, one of Bevin's last letters to Duff Cooper rallied to the Board of Trade viewpoint – that Britain could not afford to export essential goods in return for French 'luxuries', and that political concessions meant that the French already 'do much better than is warranted on strictly economic grounds'.[103]

The major success of Anglo-French economic co-operation in the immediate post-war period, therefore, lay not in freer trade or closer colonial links, but in the speed with which Bevin and Bidault acted to set up a structure for receiving Marshall Aid at the July 1947 Paris conference. Decisive though this was, in terms both of furthering European recovery and of committing both countries to a Western alignment, it was a response to an American initiative, and one that failed to reach the level of economic co-operation the Americans sought, let alone foster a special Anglo-French relationship.

France, Britain, and the German question

Anglo-French differences over the unfolding Cold War and economic issues came together in opposed policies over Germany. Officially, the two countries agreed in the Dunkirk Treaty to resist any resurgent German threat jointly; even in December 1947, with Cold War battle lines already drawn after the failure of the London conference, Bevin could observe to Bidault that 'he doubted whether Russia was as great a danger as a resurgent Germany might become'.[104] In practice, however, for most of 1944–47 the British took the Russian threat more seriously, and the German one less so, than the French did. Implicit in concerns about the Soviet Union in the Foreign Office and the General Staff was the corollary that the West needed a friendly and restored Germany: as early as July 1944 Sir Alan Brooke, Chief of the Imperial General Staff, believed that Britain should 'foster Germany, gradually build her up, and bring her into a federation of Western Europe' to face a greater Russian threat.[105] Post-war practicalities reinforced that view. Economic revival would cut the costs of the British occupation zone in Germany. Keeping the Americans engaged with Europe required co-operation with them over Germany, including, for example, the suspension of all reparations payments out of the American and British zones from May 1946 and the merger of the two zones, as the basis for what would become the Federal Republic, effective from January 1947. Nothing in the Soviets' behaviour – whether it was the Sovietisation of the eastern zone or their calls for a revival of central government institutions based in Berlin, for reparations from all zones, or for a role in the management of the Ruhr – encouraged the British to believe for long that four-power co-operation in Germany would work.

The French, by contrast, came at the question from the perspective of a nation that had suffered three German invasions in one lifetime. As Cogan argues, France's policy was based on three distinct but related concerns: ending the German military threat, securing France's eastern frontier, and keeping Germany's economic revival behind that of France, both to prevent the re-emergence of a war industries and for reasons of simple justice.[106] Five priorities ensued, outlined by de Gaulle from August 1944 and more or less faithfully adhered to by Bidault for most of the next three years. First, the left bank of the Rhine – the border region through which invading German troops passed – should be occupied indefinitely by British, French, Belgian and Dutch garrisons. Second, the Saar, the small coal-producing region south-east of Luxembourg and bordering France, should be incorporated into France's customs and currency system, with French ownership of the mines. Third, Germany's industrial heartland, the Ruhr, should be permanently detached from the German state and placed under international control, with a share of its coal production earmarked to fuel the recovery of France and the Benelux countries, steel production tightly limited, and certain types of war-related industrial production, such as ball-bearings, banned there altogether.[107] Fourth, France wanted both the 'restitution' of French assets pillaged by Germany during the Occupation and the payment of reparations, of which Ruhr coal could form a portion.[108] Finally, in the long term no strong central government should be permitted in what remained of Germany; and in the short term, no German institutions at all should be created until the boundaries of the future state, especially with the Rhineland and the Ruhr, had been settled.[109]

The French pursued these goals, more specific and detailed than Britain's, with determination. Within their own occupation zone, they requisitioned food, coal, timber, and electricity and imposed high taxes, strict rations, and a wage freeze, achieving (unlike the British and Americans) an $8 million operating surplus in 1947. They declared a customs union with the Saar (which fell within their zone) from 22 December 1946. They used the Council of Foreign Ministers, from September 1945, to veto the creation of central German government agencies (agreed in principle, in the absence of the French, by the Big Three at Potsdam) even for practical issues such as transport.[110] And they sought Soviet support to secure their aims. Auriol claimed that it was precisely to win Soviet backing over the Rhineland that de Gaulle had refused the British alliance in 1944; at two meetings of the Council of Foreign Ministers, at New York in November–December 1946 and at Moscow in March–April 1947, the French again hoped for Soviet backing, especially over the Saar, in return for support for Soviet proposals on reparations.[111]

Some French positions were uncontentious for the British and Americans, who were unworried about the Rhineland occupation as long as they maintained troops in Germany, and who not only conceded French control of the Saar, but proved more receptive than the Soviets on this issue at Moscow in 1947. The Ruhr, by contrast, lay within the British zone – and at the heart of Anglo-French disagreements over Germany. Initially there had been some British support for French positions. Bevin, Duff Cooper, Harvey and Sargent were all concerned that 'the mighty arsenal of the Ruhr should never fall into German hands'; Bevin talked of 'an internationalised Ruhr as the economic powerhouse of a Western Union' and even a 'Rhenanian Republic'.[112] By April 1946, however, the British Cabinet had decided that the Ruhr should stay within Germany, albeit with some international control, the 'socialisation' of its industries, and the Europe-wide distribution of their profits.[113] There were three reasons for this change. First, in February 1946, the Economic and Industrial Planning Staff of the Foreign Office argued that the separation of the Ruhr would bring about economic collapse and long-term poverty throughout Germany, entailing new Allied expenditures. Second, economic dislocation would give the Soviets opportunities, via German Communists, to extend their influence westwards.[114] Third, any internationalisation of the Ruhr would provoke Soviet demands for a role in its administration, which the British increasingly opposed.[115]

Added to differences over the longer-term future of the Ruhr was a clear conflict of interests over the current output of a region that produced over 80 per cent of Germany's coal. The French sought both a guaranteed share of Ruhr coal output and undertakings that Ruhr steel production would stay low. Ruhr coking coal, and coke, had fuelled two-thirds of France's pre-war steel production; they were needed even more now that Britain had practically ceased to export coal.[116] In the medium term, moreover, France sought, through the first Plan, to modernise basic industries so as to match or even to supplant those of Germany, and would need guaranteed imports of Ruhr coal, in larger than pre-war quantities, to achieve this.[117]

The British proved both unable and unwilling to meet French demands. Ruhr coal production had slumped. Throughout 1946, the British zone was producing half or less the quantities of ten years previously. Pits were damaged, British managers inept, and German miners malnourished, obliging the British to spend 'precious dollars to import wheat to feed a population whose calorie intake had dropped to 1,000 per day'.[118] The obvious solution was to make the zone economically self-sustaining, by promoting its highest-value export, steel.[119]

In early 1946, some 3.8 million tons of Ruhr coal were being used each month in the three Western Zones, against exports from the Ruhr of 800,000–900,000 tons, of which just 120,000 were allocated to France by the European Coal Organisation, the Allies' control body; the French wanted monthly exports to rise to 2.2 million tons and to be allocated a quarter of that figure, 550,000 tons, roughly the pre-war level of French imports.[120] The British occupation authorities took a precisely opposite view, pressing for a total moratorium on Ruhr coal exports to hasten reconstruction of the zone.[121] While they were unsuccessful in this, the French goal was never even approached; at Moscow in March 1947, Marshall suggested that France's best route to more Ruhr coal lay via entry into the Anglo-American bizone.

But joining the bizone would entail a radical revision of French conceptions about Germany's long-term future. General Lucius Clay, who governed the American zone, saw his goal, in line with Roosevelt's disengagement plan, as a speedy withdrawal of American troops from a denazified, self-governing, economically viable Germany.[122] Although unification proved increasingly elusive with the Sovietisation of the eastern zone, and although Secretary of State Byrnes committed the United States, in September 1946, to maintaining American troops in Germany indefinitely, the goals of a democratic and economically viable German state – in the West only if necessary – remained, and were increasingly shared by the British. This was no far-sighted or idealistic reconciliation with the old enemy; Bevin, after all, is famously on record as confessing his hatred for the Germans.[123] But as Cold War perspectives spread in the Foreign Office, especially after the events of early 1946 in Iran, the British came to view a divided Germany both as a solution to the German problem and as a bulwark against the Soviet Union. Byrnes's offer of June–September 1946 to merge zones with any willing partner was then seen both as a route to a permanent American commitment in Europe and as a way to slash the operating costs of the British zone while stabilising the economy of the West.[124]

For France, the turning-points over Germany, as over much else, came with the Moscow Conference of March–April 1947, when the Soviets proved disappointingly unsupportive of French needs, and with the Marshall Plan. No European Recovery Programme could incorporate a permanently weakened Germany – even though the French had to swallow very hard before accepting British and American plans to raise the level of German industry in the summer of 1947.[125] By that October, Chauvel was talking to Sargent and Harvey about merging the French with the Anglo-American zones; six months later, Couve de Murville would accept Clay's outline of the process that would lead to the founding of a West German state. At the same time the French were quick to grasp the security implications of 'a new frontier against Russia in Germany which would have to be policed'; in the spring of 1948, Bidault's pleas to Marshall for a permanent American presence in Europe would become increasingly insistent.[126]

It is understandable, then, that no Anglo-French alliance was concluded as long as de Gaulle and Bidault made agreement on Germany a precondition. Even their own officials viewed their demands as excessive and unrealistic.[127] And the British, despite initial sympathy, proved wholly unreceptive, whether to plans for the country's long-term future or to demands for coal. When the French position finally changed, in mid-1947, it was as part of a larger Cold War package which pushed the British into a subordinate role. Even then, the French dilemma of allowing a German economic recovery without a military resurgence remained. That was only addressed by Robert Schuman's direct approach to the Federal Republic in May 1950.

Conclusion

In May 1945, no major international event of the next five years – not the disintegration of the Grand Alliance, nor the extension of America's military presence in Europe, nor the Franco-German *rapprochement* of 1950, nor the Communist victory in China – could be foreseen with certainty. The development of a privileged Anglo-French partnership at the centre of a strategic and economic Western bloc would have looked no more astonishing than any of these – and would have changed the course of European history.

Massigli, Duff Cooper, and many others worked consistently for such an alliance. But in two countries groping for a credible role in a transformed world, political commitment from the top was less consistent. With Churchill and de Gaulle in power, officials and ministers alike were periodically paralysed by the clashes of two great egos. Bidault and Bevin built a good working relationship, but no more. And it would have required unusual vision and political will on either side to transcend the very real obstacles in the way of a special relationship.

That Britain did not forge such a relationship has been viewed as a failure of leadership. For Howorth, 'The United Kingdom could not bring itself to play the European role that history and geography had carved out for it'; for Lipgens, Bevin 'had refused to make Britain the spokesman for Europe and to give a lead to the Continental peoples in fulfilling their vision of Europe's future'.[128] To do so, though, would have meant overcoming not only a four-centuries-old reluctance to take on long-term strategic commitments in Europe, but also the refusal by the Treasury and the Board of Trade to 'hold up France' in a comparable economic commitment, in a context in which Britain faced unprecedented penury and France's spectacular post-war recovery was unimaginable to the most sanguine observer. The strength of the PCF, and endemic governmental instability, inspired little confidence towards France; Germany was viewed as a current problem not a future partner. There was little evidence that the French, at least, were seeking British leadership on the continent; and the misgivings of both superpowers towards a Western bloc were expressed even after the signature of such a mild document as the Dunkirk Treaty. For Britain, the Western bloc idea fell between global ambitions (to continue playing a world role in conjunction with the Americans), and short-term difficulties (the balance of payments).

Nor were the French exempt from responsibility. The PCF acted as a relay for Soviet misgivings. Their global ambition, to act as a 'bridge' between the two superpowers, also sat uneasily with a possible special relationship with the British. The desire for a more or less punitive peace with Germany, coupled with the right to control and benefit from Germany's industrial strength, commanded a wide consensus within France, and diverged increasingly from British and American policy. It took the decisive events of 1947 for the French to be prised from these goals and persuaded to accept a Western alignment and a divided but revived Germany. That policy change was not, of course, completed by the end of 1947. By 1950 the desire to control Germany's recovery, but by new and creative methods, found expression in the Schuman Plan, the Coal and Steel Community, and in due course the privileged partnership with Germany – a partnership from which the British chose to exclude themselves.

Notes

1. A. Bullock, *Ernest Bevin: Foreign Secretary* (London: Heinemann, 1983), p. 144.
2. H. Simonian, *The Privileged Partnership: Franco-German Relations in the European Community, 1969–1984* (Oxford: Oxford University Press, 1985).

3. Cf. Chapter 11. For Duff Cooper, Britain's post-war ambassador to Paris, 'Both are men whose instinct is to say "no" whenever ordinary people would say "yes"': cf. A. Duff Cooper, *Old Men Forget* (London: Rupert Hart-Davis, 1953), p. 335.

4. C. de Gaulle, *War Memoirs*, Vol. III, tr. Richard Howard (London: Weidenfeld and Nicolson, 1960), p. 57.

5. Churchill to Duff Cooper, 20 April 1945, National Archives, Kew (hereafter NA), CAB 120/524/T.555/5.

6. J. Chauvel, *Commentaire, vol. II: d'Alger à Berne, 1944–1952* (Paris: Fayard, 1972), pp. 162–4.

7. NA/FO/141/1093.

8. A. Duff Cooper, *The Duff Cooper Diaries*, ed. John Julius Norwich (London: Weidenfeld and Nicolson, 2005), pp. 370–2; F. Kersaudy, *Churchill and de Gaulle* (London: Collins, 1981), pp. 407, 409.

9. Young, *France, the Cold War and the Western Alliance*, pp. 56, 151; A. Roshwald, 'The Spears Mission in the Levant: 1941–1944', *The Historical Journal* 29.4 (1986), pp. 897–919.

10. H. Macmillan, *The Blast of War, 1939–1945* (London: Macmillan, 1967), pp. 449–50; Duff Cooper, *Old Men Forget*, p. 314.

11. He did the latter in a lengthy memo as early as May 1944. Cf. Ll. Woodward, *British Foreign Policy in the Second World War*, Vol. V (London: HMSO, 1976), p. 190.

12. Woodward, *British Foreign Policy, in the Second World War*, Vol. III (London: HMSO, 1971), pp. 24, 29–33, 39, 64–5, 102–3.

13. A. Eden (Lord Avon), *The Reckoning* (London: Cassell, 1965), pp. 398–9, 447.

14. R. Ovendale, 'Britain, the USA and the European Cold War, 1945–8', *History* 67.220 (1982), pp. 217–36: p. 228; S. Greenwood, 'Ernest Bevin, France, and "Western Union", August 1945–February 1946', *European History Quarterly* 14.3 (1984), pp. 319–37; pp. 320–3.

15. M. Minion, 'The Fabian Society and Europe during the 1940s: the search for a "Socialist Foreign Policy"', *European History Quarterly* 30.2 (2000), pp. 237–70; Bullock, *Bevin*, pp. 145–6.

16. Cf. R. Ulrich-Pier, *René Massigli: une vie de diplomate, 1888–1988*, 2 Vols. (Brussels: Peter Lang, 2006).

17. In a minute of 9 January 1945, quoted in R. Massigli, *Une Comédie des erreurs, 1943–1956: Souvenirs et réflexions sur une étape de l'intégration européenne* (Paris: Plon, 1978), p. 71.

18. Ibid., p. 70.

19. W. Lipgens, *A History of European Integration*, Vol. I (Oxford: Clarendon Press, 1982), p. 170.

20. V. Auriol, *Journal du Septennat*, Vol. II (1948) (Paris: Armand Colin, 1974), pp. 93, 187.

21. A. Shennan, *Rethinking France: Plans for Renewal 1940–1946* (Oxford: Clarendon Press, 1989), pp. 211–12.

22. G. Bidault, *Resistance: the Political Autobiography of Georges Bidault* (London: Weidenfeld and Nicolson, 1967), p. 142.

23. A. Horne, *Macmillan 1894–1956* (London: Macmillan, 1988), p. 189; Macmillan, *The Blast of War*, p. 415.

24. Woodward, *British Foreign Policy*, Vol. III, pp. 19–25.

25. Cf. Roosevelt to Churchill, 28 September 1944, NA/CAB120/524/T1834/4.

26. WM44 (115th) conclusions, Monday 4 September, NA/CAB65/43, p. 127.

27. 'Report of State of Civilian Population in France', SHAEF, 13 June 1944, NA/FO371/41862; 'Opinion in Liberated France', memorandum by the Secretary of

State for Foreign Affairs, 26 June 1944, NA/CAB66/42 (W.P.(44), 346); 'Political situation in Paris', Report by Major K. Younger, 5 September 1944, NA/FO371/41863; 'Conditions in France and Belgium', Report by Major D. Morton, 3 October 1944, NA/CAB65/66, pp. 5–8.

28. 'Conditions in France and Belgium', NA/CAB65/66, pp. 5–8.
29. J. Young, *France, the Cold War and the Western Alliance 1944–49* (Leicester: Leicester University Press, 1990), pp. 22, 39.
30. For the confused recognition endgame, cf. Duff Cooper, *Diaries*, pp. 327–8.
31. C. de Gaulle, *Discours et messages*, Vol. I, 1940–1946 (Paris: Plon, 1970), p. 463.
32. Roosevelt's advisor Harry Hopkins, quoted in J. Young, *Britain, France, and the Unity of Europe, 1945–51* (Leicester: Leicester University Press, 1984), p. 8.
33. A. Deighton, *The Impossible Peace: Britain, the Division of Germany, and the Origins of the Cold War* (Oxford: Clarendon Press, 1990), p. 40.
34. Woodward, *British Foreign Policy*, Vol. III, p. 95.
35. de Gaulle, *Discours et messages*, Vol. I, p. 518.
36. Deighton, *The Impossible Peace*, pp. 22–3.
37. Bullock, *Bevin*, p. 145.
38. Lipgens, *European Integration*, p. 188; NA/CAB122/778, p. 118.
39. NA/BT11/3454, p. 48; J. Kent, 'Bevin's imperialism and Euro-Africa, 1945–49', in Michael Dockrill and John Young (eds), *British Foreign Policy, 1945–56* (London: Macmillan, 1989), pp. 47–76; p. 51.
40. Duff Cooper, letter to Ernest Bevin, 16 October 1947, NA/FO371/67674/Z10270.
41. V. Auriol, *Journal du Septennat*, Vol. I, 1947 (Paris: Armand Colin, 1974), p. 253
42. T.H. Anderson, *The United States, Great Britain and the Cold War, 1944–47* (Columbia: University of Missouri Press, 1981), p. 115.
43. Deighton, *The Impossible Peace*, pp. 25, 62; R. Smith and J. Zametica, 'The Cold Warrior: Clement Attlee reconsidered, 1945–7', *International Affairs* 61.2 (1985), pp. 237–52.
44. S. Greenwood, 'Bevin, the Ruhr and the division of Germany: August 1945–December 1946', *Historical Journal* 29.1 (1986), pp. 203–12; p. 210.
45. Kent, 'Bevin's imperialism and Euro-Africa, 1945–49', p. 56.
46. 'Anglo-French Conversations', minutes of Bevin–Bidault meeting, 17 December 1947, FO371/67674/Z11010.
47. Ovendale, 'Britain, the USA and the European Cold War', p. 217.
48. Bullock, *Bevin*, p. 202.
49. Ovendale, 'Britain, the USA and the European Cold War', p. 227.
50. Young, *France, the Cold War and the Western Alliance*, p. 29.
51. G. Elgey, *La République des illusions, 1945–1951* (Paris: Fayard, 1965), p. 282.
52. 'Anglo-French Conversations', 17 December 1947, NA/FO371/67674/Z11010.
53. J. Baylis, 'British wartime thinking about a post-war European security group', *Review of International Studies* 9 (1983), pp. 265–81; pp. 274–6; Victor Rothwell, *Britain and the Cold War, 1941–47* (London: Cape, 1982), pp. 406–13; Massigli, *Une Comédie des Erreurs*, p. 69.
54. Duff Cooper, *Old Men Forget*, p. 346.
55. Young, *Britain, France, and the Unity of Europe*, p. 5; Greenwood, 'Ernest Bevin, France, and "Western Union"', p. 324.
56. Eden, *Full Circle*, pp. 494–5; Woodward, *British Foreign Policy*, Vol. V, pp. 191–5; Young, *Britain, France, and the Unity of Europe*, p. 27; Young, *France, the Cold War and the Western Alliance*, pp. 76–7.
57. CoS (Secretary, Waterfield) to FO (Harvey), 10 February 1947, NA/CAB122/778.

58. Bevin memo to Cabinet, 26 February 1947, NA/CAB121/400, pp. 135–6.
59. Moscow Embassy to Foreign Office, 4 February 1947, NA/CAB121/400, p. 121.
60. Auriol, *Journal du Septennat*, Vol. I, pp. 123, 673–6.
61. In talks with Duff Cooper and Oliver Harvey, 4 April 1946 (NA/FO800/464, pp. 35–6).
62. B. Zeeman, 'Britain and the Cold War: an alternative approach. The Treaty of Dunkirk example', *European History Quarterly* 16.3 (1986), pp. 343–67, pp. 350, 356; Woodward, *British Foreign Policy*, Vol. v, p. 293.
63. Cf. Deighton, *The Impossible Peace*, p. 38; 'Visit to London of Secretary-General of French Ministry for Foreign Affairs, 19th–22nd October, 1947: Conversation with Secretary of State', NA/FO371/67674/Z9992.
64. Ovendale 'Britain, the USA and the European Cold War', p. 236; Deighton, *The Impossible Peace*, p. 42.
65. Quoted in Lipgens, *European Integration*, p. 192.
66. NA/FO371/67674/Z9992; NA/FO371/67674/Z11010.
67. 'Anglo-American conversations', December 1947, NA/FO371/67674/Z11009.
68. Stapleton to Orme Sargent, 24 December 1947, NA/FO371/67674/Z11126-8.
69. Young, *France, the Cold War and the Western Alliance*, pp. 174, 179–80; C. Cogan, *Forced to Choose: France, the Atlantic Alliance, and NATO – Then and Now* (London: Praeger, 1997), pp. 28–30; M. Vaïsse, 'L'échec d'une Europe franco-britannique', in R. Poidevin (ed.), *Histoire des débuts de la Construction européenne* (Brussels: Bruylant, 1986), pp. 369–89; p. 384.
70. J. Howorth, 'The Marshall Plan, Britain, and European security: defense integration or coat-tail diplomacy?', in M. Schain (ed.), *The Marshall Plan: Fifty Years After* (New York: Palgrave – now Palgrave Macmillan, 2001), pp. 39–59.
71. Holman's report of 4 January 1945 to Sir Anthony Eden on 'Communism in France' (NA/FO371/59975/Z336/14/17) claimed that 'the Communist bogy was magnified out of all proportion, particularly amongst the privileged classes', during the Liberation period; 'it seems evident', it correctly added, 'that the Communist party have received a directive from Moscow not to embarrass seriously the régime of General de Gaulle. It must be just as much in the interests of the Soviet Government as in those of France that conditions here should remain stable during the war period.' Cf. also Duff Cooper to Eden, 20 January 1945, NA/FO371/49071/Z1424/14/17.
72. Quoted in Greenwood, 'Ernest Bevin, France, and "Western Union"', p. 332.
73. Duff Cooper, *Old Men Forget*, p. 366.
74. Cf. Orme Sargent to Bevin, NA/FO371/59953/Z3744/20/17, and Foreign Office meeting, 8 October 1947, in NA/T11/3454, pp. 50–4.
75. Zeeman, 'Britain and the Cold War', pp. 357–8.
76. Bevin to Churchill, 11 April 1946, in NA/FO800/464, p. 47; Anglo-French conversations, 28 November 1947, in NA/FO800/465, pp. 50–1.
77. Deighton, *The Impossible Peace*, p. 163.
78. Duff Cooper to Bevin, 13 November 1947, in FO371/67674; 'Visit to London of Secretary-General of French Foreign Ministry', FO371/67674/Z9992; Bevin to Duff Cooper, 24 November 1947, in NA/FO371/67674/Z10271/25/G.
79. 'Anglo-French Conversations', 17 December 1947, NA/FO371/67674/Z11010.
80. Despite misgivings about the quality of French troops, Montgomery was convinced that 'France is the key-stone of the Western Union' and that Britain must commit to a continental European strategy including West Germany. His views were not shared by the British Chiefs of Staff. Cf. N. Hamilton, *Monty: the Field*

Marshal, 1944–1976 (London: Hamish Hamilton, 1986), pp. 699–700; V. Auriol, *Journal du Septennat*, Vol. II (1948) (Paris: Armand Colin, 1974), p. 64.

81. Young, *Britain, France, and the Unity of Europe*, p. 39; A. Milward, 'The Committee of European Economic Co-Operation (CEEC) and the Advent of the Customs Union', in W. Lipgens, *A History of European Integration*, Vol. I (Oxford: Clarendon Press, 1982), pp. 507–69: p. 550; Duff Cooper, *Diaries*, p. 440; F.M.B. Lynch, *France and the International Economy: From Vichy to the Treaty of Rome* (London: Routledge, 1997), pp. 104–5.

82. Quoted in Bullock, *Ernest Bevin*, p. 104.

83. Greenwood, 'Ernest Bevin, France, and "Western Union" ', p. 324; Cogan, *Forced to Choose*, p. 39.

84. Foreign Office/Board of Trade meeting, 8 October 1947, NA/BT11/3454, pp. 50–4.

85. Milward, 'The Committee of European Economic Co-Operation', p. 544; A. Milward, *The Reconstruction of Western Europe, 1945–51* (London: Routledge, 1992 (original edition 1984)), p. 142; W.I. Hitchcock, *France Restored: Cold War Diplomacy and the Quest for Leadership in Europe, 1944–1954* (Chapel Hill and London: University of North Carolina Press, 1998), pp. 83–6.

86. G. Bossuat, *La France, l'aide américaine et la construction européenne, 1944–1954*, Vol. I (Paris: Ministère des Finances (Comité pour l'histoire économique et financière de la France), 1992), pp. 138, 151.

87. Duff Cooper, *Diaries*, p. 439.

88. Bossuat, *La France*, p. 167.

89. Kent, 'Bevin's Imperialism and Euro-Africa, 1945–49', pp. 58–9.

90. Ibid., p. 63.

91. Milward, 'The Committee of European Economic Co-Operation', p. 554; Duff Cooper, *Diaries*, p. 446; Chauvel, *Commentaire*, II, p. 197.

92. Young, *Britain, France, and the Unity of Europe*, pp. 38–9; Lipgens, *European Integration*, pp. 196–8; 'Anglo-French economic co-operation', Foreign Office meeting, NA/BT11/3454, pp. 50–4.

93. J. Gillingham, *Coal, Steel, and the Rebirth of Europe, 1945–1955* (Cambridge: Cambridge University Press, 1991), p. 84.

94. Milward, 'The Committee of European Economic Co-Operation', p. 510.

95. Lynch, *France and the International Economy*, p. 121; 'Negotiations with France': note by Board of Trade, 18 October 1947, annexe II, NA/BT11/3454, p. 49.

96. Memo on Anglo-French Commercial relations, 25 February 1946, NA/BT11/2631, pp. 13–14.

97. Bossuat, *La France, l'aide américaine et la construction européenne*, pp. 43–5, 59.

98. F. Lynch, 'Resolving the paradox of the Monnet Plan: national and international planning in French reconstruction', *Economic History Review* 37.2 (1984), pp. 229–43; p. 241.

99. Anglo-French Economic Relations: Foreign Office meeting, 8 October 1947, NA/BT11/3454, pp. 53–4; 'Negotiations with France': Board of Trade note, 18 October 1947, NA/BT11/3454, pp. 43–7; Anglo-French Commercial Sub-Committee meeting, 4 November 1947, NA/BT 11/3625.

100. Bullock, *Bevin*, p. 357.

101. Duff Cooper to Sir Oliver Harvey, 15 April 1946, NA/FO371/59975/Z4055/65/171; Orme Sargent to Averell Harriman, 30 May 1946, NA/FO371/58402/UR5058.

102. Cabinet, 4 January 1947: NA/CAB128/9.

103. E. Bevin, letter to Alfred Duff Cooper, 27 November 1947, FO371/67674.
104. 'Anglo-French Conversations', 17 December 1947, FO371/67674/Z11010.
105. Smith and Zametica, 'The Cold Warrior', p. 240; Deighton, *The Impossible Peace*, pp. 6, 25; Field Marshal Lord Alanbrooke, *War Diaries, 1939–1945* (London: Weidenfeld and Nicolson, 2001), p. 575.
106. Cogan, *Forced to Choose*, p. 19.
107. Thus, for example, on 20 March 1946 Bidault stressed that France sought 'a complete political separation of the Rhineland and the Ruhr in relation to the rest of Germany'. Cf. Chauvel, *Commentaire*, Vol. II, p. 165.
108. Ibid., pp. 58, 70, 112; Milward, *The Reconstruction of Western Europe*, p. 128.
109. de Gaulle, *War Memoirs*, Vol. III, pp. 50–1.
110. Young, *France, the Cold War and the Western Alliance*, pp. 60, 82–3, 128–9.
111. Ibid., pp. 128–9, 143–4; Auriol, *Journal du Septennat*, Vol. I, p. 57.
112. Deighton, *The Impossible Peace*, p. 64; Greenwood, 'Bevin, the Ruhr and the division of Germany', p. 203.
113. Milward, *The Reconstruction of Western Europe*, p. 138.
114. Ibid., pp. 205–6; Deighton, *The Impossible Peace*, p. 55.
115. Quoted in Greenwood, 'Bevin, the Ruhr and the division of Germany', p. 210.
116. British coal exports to France fell from 6,156,000 tons in 1938 to 545,000 in 1945. They diminished both in quantity and quality, through 1946, and effectively ceased that December. Cf. NA/BT11/3206; NA/Cab 139/10; Lynch, *France and the International Economy*, pp. 52–4, 59.
117. W. Duchêne, *Jean Monnet, First Statesman of Interdependence* (New York: Norton, 1994), pp. 163–5; Milward, 'The Committee of European Economic Co-Operation', p. 518; Lipgens, *European Integration*, p. 498.
118. Milward, *The Reconstruction of Western Europe*, p. 134; Gillingham, *Coal, Steel, and the Rebirth of Europe*, pp. 85, 180–4; Deighton, *The Impossible Peace*, p. 58.
119. Greenwood, 'Bevin, the Ruhr and the division of Germany', p. 206.
120. Allied Control Authority, Economic Directorate, meeting of 29 May 1946: NA/FO371/58403/UR5273.
121. Treasury meeting, 28 May 1946, NA/FO371/58402/UR5058.
122. Young, *France, the Cold War and the Western Alliance*, p. 83.
123. Bullock, *Bevin*, p. 90.
124. Deighton, *The Impossible Peace*, pp. 91, 102, 105–7, 109.
125. Lynch, 'Resolving the paradox of the Monnet Plan', p. 241; Hitchcock, *France Restored*, pp. 78–9.
126. 'Military aspects of M. Chauvel's final conversation with Sir Orme Sargent and Sir Oliver Harvey', 21 October 1947, FO 371/67674; Young, *France, the Cold War and the Western Alliance*, pp. 180–1, 191.
127. Massigli, *Une Comédie des erreurs*, pp. 68–71; Chauvel, *Commentaire*, Vol. II, p. 151.
128. Howorth, 'The Marshall Plan', p. 40; Lipgens, *European Integration*, p. 189.

Bibliography

Alanbrooke, Field Marshal Lord, *War Diaries, 1939–1945* (London: Weidenfeld and Nicolson, 2001).

Anderson, T., *The United States, Great Britain and the Cold War, 1944–47* (Columbia: University of Missouri Press, 1981).

Auriol, V., *Journal du Septennat*, Vols. I (1947) and II (1948) (Paris: Armand Colin, 1974).

Baylis, J., 'British wartime thinking about a post-war European security group', *Review of International Studies* 9 (1983), pp. 265–81.

Bidault, G., *Resistance: the Political Autobiography of Georges Bidault* (London: Weidenfeld and Nicolson, 1967).

Bossuat, G., *La France, l'aide américaine et la construction européenne, 1944–1954*, Vol. I (Paris: Ministère des Finances, 1992).

Bullock, A., *Ernest Bevin: Foreign Secretary* (London: Heinemann, 1983).

Chauvel, J., *Commentaire*, Vol. II (Paris: Fayard, 1972).

Cogan, C., *Forced to Choose: France, the Atlantic Alliance, and NATO – Then and Now* (London: Praeger, 1997).

de Gaulle, C., *Discours et messages*, Vol. I (1940–1946) (Paris: Plon, 1970).

de Gaulle, C., *War Memoirs*, Vol. III, tr. Richard Howard (London: Weidenfeld and Nicolson, 1960).

Deighton, A., *The Impossible Peace: Britain, the Division of Germany, and the Origins of the Cold War* (Oxford: Clarendon Press, 1990).

Duchêne, W., *Jean Monnet, First Statesman of Interdependence* (New York: Norton, 1994).

Duff Cooper, A., *Old Men Forget* (London: Rupert Hart-Davis, 1953).

Duff Cooper, A., *The Duff Cooper Diaries*, ed. John Julius Norwich (London: Weidenfeld and Nicolson, 2005).

Eden, Sir A., (Lord Avon) *The Reckoning* (London: Cassell, 1965).

Elgey, G., *La République des illusions, 1945–1951* (Paris: Fayard, 1965).

Gillingham, J., *Coal, Steel, and the Rebirth of Europe, 1945–1955* (Cambridge: Cambridge University Press, 1991).

Greenwood, S., 'Bevin, the Ruhr and the division of Germany: August 1945–December 1946', *Historical Journal* 29.1 (1986), pp. 203–12.

Greenwood, S., 'Ernest Bevin, France, and "Western Union", August 1945–February 1946', *European History Quarterly* 14.3 (1984), pp. 319–37.

Hamilton, N., *Monty: the Field Marshal, 1944–1976* (London: Hamish Hamilton, 1986).

Hitchcock, W., *France Restored: Cold War Diplomacy and the Quest for Leadership in Europe, 1944–1954* (Chapel Hill and London: University of North Carolina Press, 1998).

Horne, A., *Macmillan 1894–1956* (London: Macmillan, 1988).

Howorth, J., 'The Marshall Plan, Britain, and European security: defense integration or coat-tail diplomacy?', in Martin Schain (ed.), *The Marshall Plan: Fifty Years After* (New York: Palgrave – now Palgrave Macmillan, 2001), pp. 39–59.

Kent, J., 'Bevin's imperialism and Euro-Africa, 1945–49', in Michael Dockrill and John Young (eds), *British Foreign Policy, 1945–56* (London: Macmillan, 1989), pp. 47–76.

Kersaudy, F., *Churchill and de Gaulle* (London: Collins, 1981).

Lipgens, W., *A History of European Integration*, Vol. I (Oxford: Clarendon Press, 1982).

Lynch, F., 'Resolving the paradox of the Monnet Plan: national and International planning in French reconstruction', *The Economic History Review* 37.2 (1984), pp. 229–43.

Lynch, F., *France and the International Economy: From Vichy to the Treaty of Rome* (London: Routledge, 1997).

Macmillan, H., *The Blast of War, 1939–1945* (London: Macmillan, 1967).

Massigli, R., *Une Comédie des erreurs, 1943–1956: Souvenirs et réflexions sur une étape de l'intégration européenne* (Paris: Plon, 1978).

Milward, A., 'The Committee of European Economic Co-Operation (CEEC) and the advent of the Customs Union', in W. Lipgens, *A History of European Integration*, Vol. I (Oxford: Clarendon Press, 1982, pp. 507–69).

Milward, A., *The Reconstruction of Western Europe, 1945–51* (London: Routledge, 1992 (original edition 1984)).

Minion, M., 'The Fabian Society and Europe during the 1940s: the search for a "Socialist Foreign Policy" ', *European History Quarterly* 30.2 (2000), pp. 237–70.

Ovendale, R., 'Britain, the USA and the European Cold War, 1945–8', *History* 67.220 (1982), pp. 217–36.

Roshwald, A., 'The Spears Mission in the Levant: 1941–1944', *The Historical Journal* 29.4 (1986), pp. 897–919.

Rothwell, V., *Britain and the Cold War, 1941–47* (London: Cape, 1982).

Shennan, A., *Rethinking France: Plans for Renewal 1940–1946* (Oxford: Clarendon Press, 1989).

Simonian, H., *The Privileged Partnership: Franco-German Relations in the European Community, 1969–1984* (Oxford: Oxford University Press, 1985).

Smith, R., and Zametica, J., 'The Cold Warrior: Clement Attlee reconsidered, 1945–7', *International Affairs*, 61.2 (1985), pp. 237–52.

Ulrich-Pier, R., *René Massigli: une vie de diplomate, 1888–1988*, 2 Vols (Brussels: Peter Lang, 2006).

Vaïsse, M., 'L'échec d'une Europe franco-britannique', in Raymond Poidevin (ed.), *Histoire des débuts de la Construction européenne* (Brussels: Complexe, 1986), pp. 369–89.

Woodward, Sir Ll., *British Foreign Policy in the Second World War*, Vols. III (London: HMSO, 1971) and V (London: HMSO, 1976).

Young, J., *Britain, France, and the Unity of Europe, 1945–51* (Leicester: Leicester University Press, 1984).

Young, J., *France, the Cold War and the Western Alliance, 1944–49* (Leicester: Leicester University Press, 1990).

Zeeman, B., 'Britain and the Cold War: an alternative approach. The Treaty of Dunkirk example', *European History Quarterly*, 16.3 (1986), pp. 343–67.

13
Occupation, Liberation, Purges: the Changing Landscape of French Memory

Philippe Buton

The Second World War marked a double crisis for France. The defeat of 1940 provoked a crisis of national identity; the (temporary) death of democracy and the establishment of a regime of the far Right caused a crisis of political identity. The questions raised by the Liberation, and by the purges that went with it, lie at the heart of the efforts of the French people to cope with this twin crisis of identity.

The term Liberation, in the French context, entails an obvious question – *Liberation by whom?* – which in practice breaks down into two. In national terms, did France liberate herself alone, or was France liberated by the Allies? In political terms, insofar as France did liberate herself alone, which political force(s) deserve the credit?

Similarly, the term purge (*épuration*) invites a question – *Who was purged, in the name of what values?* – which also suggests a double answer. On the national level, the 'victims' of the purge can be viewed as a handful of traitors who sold out to the occupier, a group of no internal significance, comparable to the spies shot during the First World War. Treated politically, however, they may be seen as a real political tendency, deserving of censure, certainly, but also of serious analysis as to their motives and coherence.

How the memories of the French managed this double identity crisis is the subject of this chapter.[1] Of course, the diversity of memory is infinite.[2] We will note in the first place *synchronic* variations: each social group has its particular memory. That of prisoners of war is not the same as those of victims of deportation to the Reich for political or racial motives. Memory will also vary with political sympathies. And within each group, each individual will give his or her own memories a unique personal colouring. But *diachronic* variations in memory are equally important. As time passes, some memories fade while others become, if anything, more clear-cut and powerful. Sometimes wholesale revisions of memory take place, on an individual or even a collective level. Finally, *generational* variations, cutting across the synchronic and diachronic dimensions, complicate matters further. Thus those who had experienced the First World War had a more welcoming ear for the discourse of Pétain than those who had not, and a different way of organising their memories.

The sum of these elements amounts to a veritable kaleidoscope of memory. In order to make some sense of the period, this extreme diversity must be transcended – but with the caveat that the broad tendencies that we do discern depend to a considerable degree on the variable chosen.[3] We shall start with the memories of France's different (and conflicting) political sensibilities, before considering the outcomes of their battles – what amount, in other words, to the main features of the three 'landscapes of memory' which have followed one another from the Liberation to the present day.

Liberation and the politics of memory

One line of memory, marked by Gaullism, held a dominant position at the start and retains an eminent one today.[4] In this tradition, the Liberation appears as an incomplete happy end. Over and above the ordeal of the Occupation, France, for Gaullists, faced two mortal dangers, those of subjection from the outside to the 'Anglo-Saxon' powers and from the inside to the PCF. It was de Gaulle's political genius that enabled France to avoid these twin menaces. Alas, however, the General fell victim to the vengeful hostility of the political parties, marginalised under his rule, and to the ingratitude of the French. If he had, despite this, begun the transformation of France – restoring its independence and launching the great economic and social reforms of the period (the Social Security system, the Plan, the nationalisations, and the *comités d'entreprise*) he was unable to conclude his task by achieving the institutional and moral reform that would have permanently foreclosed any option of a return to the wayward Third Republic. After 1958 and de Gaulle's return to power, the Gaullist tradition could salute this new awakening of the French people which had finally allowed their country to close the cycle with the completion of the labours that the Liberation had begun. These historical lessons were drawn, in a particularly exalted form, on 18 and 19 December 1964, during a moving ceremony marking the transfer of the remains of Jean Moulin to join the tombs of the 'great men' of France in the Pantheon.

The purges naturally have no place anywhere in this Gaullist view of history, for their victims were not political opponents, but traitors. And their first punishment remains silence, the *damnatio memoriae*, dear to the Roman Empire or to the Republic of Venice, which confiscates their own punishment from the ranks of collaborators.

For a long while, the rest of the French Right shared broadly the same memory of the Liberation as the Gaullists. The major difference concerned its density and significance. For the Gaullist tradition, the Second World War was a founding event; for the other right-wing forces it was merely traumatic. Bathed in light for the Gaullists, the period includes patches of shade for the traditional Right. It is here that a different view of the purges can be seen, with the appearance, albeit in a muted form, of the idea that the collaborators were guilty, not of treason, but of error. For the liberal Right (which participated closely in the Vichy regime), everything invited a speedy turn of the page. As Georges Pompidou, who did more than anyone else to wreck the hegemony of the Gaullist memory, to the benefit of the traditional Right, observed in 1972, it was time to 'forget those times when the French did not love one another, but were torn apart and even killed each other'.

Continuing the passage from luminous to sombre views of the Liberation, for the far Right all, or nearly, is darkness, aside from a rhetorical concession to the joy of liberation. If the Germans had left, the Americans, more dangerous because more insidious, had taken their place. If the Communists had been contained, it was only on a temporary basis, and by people who were hardly better. France had missed her chance, and returned to the paths of decadence. In this account, the central event is not this 'pseudo'-Liberation, but the purges. It is to the purges, and not to the Second World War itself, that the extreme Right ascribes its own criminalisation, its victim status being enhanced by the legend of latter-day 'September Massacres' (after those of the Revolution) and of a 'permanent purge' and crowned by the iconic figure of Robert Brasillach, the most brilliant – and one of the most viciously anti-semitic – of the collaborationist writers, executed for treason on 6 February 1945.

The memory of the Liberation is equally variegated on the Left. For the Communists, the period goes down as an exceptionally happy one. Of course, not everything was achieved. The purges are viewed as a failure, owing to sabotage. But this setback did not result from the deliberate action of individuals, but from the nature of the economic system. This view reveals a third conception of the collaboration/purges duo – national for the Gaullists, political for the extreme Right, but socio-economic for the Communists. Since it was the bourgeoisie who had collaborated, it was they who should have been punished – a model that echoes the 'government of national desertion' of Marx's *Civil War in France* of 1871. However, continue the Communists, the bourgeoisie was clever enough not to put all its eggs into one basket, and de Gaulle allowed it to save its essential interests. Those interests, though, were not really threatened in the last analysis, because 'the' revolution was not on the agenda. What was, in the Communist view, was to liberate France, and then to begin its economic and social regeneration. A start was certainly made thanks to the work of Communist *résistants*, and then Communist ministers, to whom their party's official history assigns the credit for the structural reforms of the Liberation. Unfortunately, democratic progress was held back, initially by the hostility of de Gaulle and the pusillanimity (if not treason) of the Socialists, and later by the Americans who 'obtained' the removal of Communist ministers the better to subjugate France.

The image of the Liberation in Socialist memory is less idyllic than in that of the Communists; indeed, it could be summed up as a missed opportunity. When Léon Blum declared, in 1945, that socialism was the master of the hour, he meant that the Resistance had drawn heavily on traditional Socialist thinking, all the more readily as the Socialists had won fame and glory in every Resistance movement. It is certainly true that fundamentally at least, the programmatic texts of the Resistance bore the stamp of democratic socialism, the CNR programme representing the archetype of a more general phenomenon in this respect. However, this ideological victory of socialism was not crowned by the political victory of the Socialists. For that reason the balance-sheet of the Liberation is a bitter one in the Socialist account. Far from dominating the electoral landscape or holding the most influential posts in government, the party seemed to hold a permanent supporting role. Used by de Gaulle, neutralised by the constraints first of *tripartisme* and then of the Third Force, the SFIO had lacked any real control over events.

Historical research has shown these regrets to be ill-founded. The SFIO was the spinal column of the Liberation as it was of the Fourth Republic (to which it gave its first president and first prime minister, after having supplied two of the three post-de Gaulle heads of the Provisional Government). In fact, the dissatisfaction engrained in Socialist memories of the Liberation arises in great part from the gulf between, on the one hand, the limited objectives that the party's leadership agreed on between themselves and, on the other hand, the political fantasy of the socialist revolution that has always lain at the heart of Socialist political culture in France and has always been spurred on by Communist outbidding.

The last tradition of political memory, reactivated after 1968 but present from the start, is that of the extreme Left. At the core of this is the cult of the broken dream, of the Liberation betrayed by the leaders of the 'workers' parties – a theme that finds some echoes in Socialist and Communist memories. The evidence of betrayal offered by the far Left is twofold: the absence of any socialist revolution (and indeed, the deterioration of workers' living conditions) during the period, and the sabotage of the purges, especially those of a social and economic order – for in this area the far Left's account resembles a harder version of the Communists'.

The rhetoric of the far Left suggests a vision in white (the revolutionary working class working for a liberation that would be indissociably national *and* social) and black (the betrayal of revolutionary ideals by a PCF that had sold out to a degenerate USSR in some views, to French imperialism in others). The other originality of this line, contrasting with the Socialists and even more with the Communists, is that of giving maximum weight to the events of 1944. This is the subject of the last verse of the Maoist hymn *Les nouveaux partisans*, with its references to 'the arms the traitors thieved in "45" from the people, who are now ready to rise up again and wage war on the bourgeoisie'.

Competition and assimilation: chronology of memorial frameworks

It should be stressed that these different, competing, frameworks of memory were (and are) far from equal in strength. This inequality allows us to discern dominant tendencies, and to distinguish three periods between 1944 and the present. The first of these, running from the Liberation to May 1968, offers a reassuring, but rose-tinted, memory of the Second World War. From 1968, the myths of the earlier period collapsed. There followed a period of considerable uncertainty, marked notably by the extreme fragmentation of frameworks of memory. The confusion lasted a whole generation – right through the Pompidou, Giscard and Mitterrand presidencies (1969–1995). Since the very end of the Mitterrand years, a real revolution in memory has taken place. At the end of at times muted investigations, this now appears to have produced a relative balance, characterised in particular by the convergence of formerly fragmented memories.

The 'resistentialist' myth: 1944–1968

The first period saw a dominant framework of memory forged as soon as the war ended. It is no coincidence that this collective memory was used, right from the start, to promote the resurrection of the French state, to affirm the independence of France, and to legitimate the new government. Its most remarkable trait was to have erased, as if by magic, recollections of defeat or collaboration. This rose-tinted but dominant view of the war was carefully cultivated by the two major political forces of the era, Gaullists and Communists. According to this account, France was at the same time a victim, especially through the initial act of betrayal of 1940, and a victor, having maintained a heroic stance throughout.

France was viewed as a victim because the French saw the Second World War chiefly through a Franco-German prism. For de Gaulle it had been the closing cycle of a thirty years' war, a single struggle from 1914 to 1945 between France and an aggressive Germany. For the PCF, the war arose from the nature of Nazism, and from its drive to destroy both France and the USSR, along with their respective revolutionary legacies of 1789 and 1917. To a dispassionate eye this 'victimisation' of France is far from obvious, and it certainly seems much less clear-cut today. On the contrary, over the 1980s and 1990s, the war came to be seen within a larger framework, that of Europe rather than of nation states. The defining axis that shapes the modern vision of the war for the French is that of Nazism and Jews. Of course, the view of France as victim also completely ignores the question that has received more attention than any other in recent years: was France *to blame*, at least in part? In the 'resistentialist' vision of the Second World War (to borrow Henry Rousso's expression) the answer is clearly No: France – the whole of France – may have bent under the storm, but never ceased to resist in the shadows. Once again, the two dominant frameworks of memory, Gaullist and Communist, converge on a series of key points.

In the first place, both present the Liberation as the culmination of the French people's constant resistance against the occupant. Thus de Gaulle told the people of Bayeux on 14 June 1944, in his first speech on the liberated soil of mainland France, that 'what the country expects of you, behind the front line, is that you continue the fight today, as you have never ceased to do since the start of this war and since June 1940'.[5] This 'resistentialist' myth certainly made it considerably easier for the French to rally around him personally: how could one refuse the seal of a Resistance record, and thus of honour, so cheaply offered? On the Communist side, the same vision dominates. Even today, the Communist literature presents the Liberation as a mass uprising of the French people; the events of Summer 1944 are qualified as a 'national insurrection'. Two films of René Clément, *La Bataille du rail* of 1945 and *Le Père tranquille* of the following year, offer perfect illustrations of this view. In the former film, presented as a documentary, the railwaymen's struggle against the occupant is praised and implicitly made to stand for the struggle of all French workers. In *Le Père tranquille*, plot is more important: a young *résistant* is disappointed by the apparent cowardice of his own father, until he discovers him to be the clandestine chief of the local Resistance network. The moral is clear: even apparent cowards among the French were really cunning *résistants*.

Another element shared by Communists and Gaullists is the view of the Liberation as the achievement of the French people alone, with the role of American and British forces carefully pushed into the background. The accounts of the liberation of Paris given by de Gaulle on 25 August 1944 in front of the Town Hall, and by the Communist leader Jacques Duclos six days later, display a disturbing similarity: neither makes any mention of the US 4th Infantry Division. With Paris a metaphor for the whole of France, the legend of a France liberated entirely through her own efforts could be created; the real defeat of 1940 could be expunged from memory by the mythical victory of 1944; the resistentialist framework of memory could cover over the French identity crisis generated by the war; and the French could see their country as one of the major world powers, after the war as it had been before it.

The third common element of this rose-tinted view of the Second World War, stressed by Gaullists and Communists alike and adopted by most of the French, is the perception of France as a nation betrayed. Vichy is portrayed as nothing more than a handful of traitors who had sold out to the Germans. Indeed, it was the characterisation of their acts as treason that allowed (under Article 75 of the French penal code) purges to be undertaken and collaborators to be shot. In other words, Vichy had no endogenous status; it was a pure product of the German occupant, and not an ounce of blame attaches to France or to the French for what occurred under its rule.

This institutionalisation of a quasi-official memory came at a cost: other, partial memories were blurred out, confined to the historical subconscious, or simply denied. This applied to the memories of specific social groups – Jews, prisoners of war, or labour conscripts, for example – and of political groups, notably the extremes of Right and Left.

In purely quantitative terms, the prime case of such marginalisation is that of prisoners of war.[6] For a long time, this group was practically ostracised from French society; it is revealing that the municipal elections of April–May 1945 were held without waiting for their return. These prisoners had made the 'mistake' of representing a living and permanent reminder of the defeat of 1940. At the Liberation, repressing that embarrassing memory entailed forgetting the signs that recalled it; France sought conquerors, not defeated armies, to buttress the official memory.

Gradually, though still slowly, the cloud of disgrace lifted from above France's former PoWs; they did, after all, represent nearly two million voters. But if they no longer faced open reproaches, they remained unable to attain the positive image of pure suffering. The films on the subject confirm this, by consistently presenting a twin vision of PoWs: on the one hand that of prisoners suffering from their confinement, their lives punctuated by escape attempts, successful and not; on the other hand, that of cunning fellows exercising their resourcefulness on German farms – and German women.

Worse off than the PoWs were another group of ill-loved exiles, those who had worked in Germany under the Service du Travail Obligatoire (STO), instituted in February 1943. The efforts of these former labour conscripts, via their associations, to win rehabilitation, have been constant, controversial, and ultimately not very successful. As early as the summer of 1945 they sought to achieve a form of linguistic rebranding, inventing the term 'deported workers' – the reference to 'deportation' entailing an implicit comparison with racial or political deportees – and then, in January 1946, creating the 'Federation of labour deportees'. Their initiatives led to a series of lawsuits, of which the last, in 1992, produced a ruling banning the use of this term.

France's major 'memory lapse' in these early years of freedom, however, concerned racial deportees, Jews in particular. This was not for lack of information. As Annette Wieviorka has demonstrated, a plethora of survivors' accounts, and plenty of serious, well-documented historical studies, were available from the very start of the post-war period. But neither witnesses nor historians received a hearing.[7] A good indicator of collective memory is to be found in schools, and here the record is shabby: not a word about the Holocaust appears in school textbooks of the period. Before 1960, the only (and rare) references to concentration camps speak of political prisoners – of the Germans and Italians who had been active against the dictatorships of Hitler and Mussolini between the wars, or of the French who protested against the Occupation. The only representation of deportation concerned *résistants* in Buchenwald and Dachau, not Jews sent to Auschwitz. The *only* reference I have found to gas chambers in the textbooks of the period made no mention of Jews. It was only with the fall-out of the Eichmann trial in 1961 that the phenomenon of Jewish deportation was acknowledged, and even then almost all authors showed no understanding of the Holocaust, placing it on the same level as other categories of repression and deportation.[8] Here again, then, we remain in a period when the trauma of defeat led newly-liberated France to seek heroes, not victims.

The memory of three other groups, finally, was completely hidden from view. The first was that of gypsies, victims of Nazi Germany's second genocide, whose fate was recognised within France's collective memory (including that of academic specialists) even later than that of the Holocaust. The deportation of homosexuals, which certainly occurred at least from the French territories of Alsace and Moselle annexed by the Reich, was also totally eclipsed. It was, after all, in blatant contradiction with the stereotype of modern virility that the defeat and the Occupation had so badly damaged in France and that the Liberation sought to maximise by way of compensation.[9] If the memory of homosexuals has been steadily uncovered in recent decades, this is not the case of the final 'hidden memory' of deportees, that of common criminals, who for obvious reasons sought, after their release, to 'upgrade' their category to one more likely to win sympathy.

As with these groups, certain political memories were also blurred or even rubbed out. Of these the most important was, of course, that of the far Right – a structure of memory that, at the Liberation, was simply disqualified as amounting to treason. This result was that the memory of the far Right simply disappeared outside private conversations between friends and family; if victims were unwanted in the France of the Liberation, traitors were doubly so.

After 1947, the memory of the far Right made a slow and confidential reappearance on paper. A common tendency in these rare writings was the attempt to politicise their version of history. Collaborators, according to these accounts, were soldiers not mercenaries, patriots not men who had sold themselves out. Within this current, however, two very different strands coexist. Firstly, Vichyite collaborators presented themselves as patriots who had tried to serve France by protecting her from Germany through negotiation rather than confrontation. Paradoxically, such authors share in the 'Resistentialist' framework of memory: just as, in *Le Père tranquille*, a seeming coward could turn out to be a cunning *résistant*, in Vichyite accounts even a collaborator could emerge as *really* a covert *résistant*. The second strand is represented by collaborationists – those who worked with (and for) the Germans not out of a conservative form of patriotism but from a wish to take an active part in a fascist revolution. This group cultivated a nostalgia for the past brotherhood of arms and gave assistance, albeit weakly, to the phenomenon of Holocaust denial (negationism) that emerged at this time. Their discourse remained, of course, totally marginal.

Roughly the same is true at the other extreme of the political spectrum. For the extreme Left (as for its much larger Communist rival) the Second World War caused acute difficulties of memory. Its first handicap was directly linked to its own fairly inglorious attitude during the war. The Anarchists undertook nothing on a collective level. As for the Trotskyists, their dogmatism led them to treat the Second World War as if it was the First World War, and thus to adopt a Leninist position of 'revolutionary defeatism' that was at odds with practically the whole French population. In short, the extremes of Right and Left, handicapped by the record of their main groups during the war years, were incapable of denting the resistentialist myth of patriotic unity.

The crumbling edifice: 1968–1995

The resistentialist view of the Second World War could not resist the impact of 1968 and after. What followed was a profound break that produced a deeply unsettled pattern of memory, reflected in many of the channels through which memory is transmitted – schools and universities, the media, and political discourse.

In the area of academic history, the main historiographical hiatus is usually dated at 1973, with the publication in France of Robert Paxton's *Vichy France: Old Guard and New Order*.[10] This is broadly correct: even if some iconoclastic books on the subject had appeared previously, it was with Paxton that a new view of Vichy was widely circulated, a view that identified it as both national and guilty. Vichy would henceforth be seen as having originated the policy of Franco-German collaboration; and above all, it would be analysed, not as a German creation, but as a political entity with its own coherence, derived from very well-defined *French* traditions of antisemitism and right-wing antirepublicanism.

At the same time Marcel Ophüls's documentary *Le chagrin et la pitié*, made for television in 1971, banned from the small screen for a decade, but shown in cinemas in the 1970s, shook two pillars of the resistentialist myth. By interviewing former collaborators at length, it both demolished the notion of a France united in resistance, and showed collaboration as a political rather than a merely material choice. In the following years, a cultural wave sometimes known as the 'mode rétro' blurred many moral stances, and memories, relating to the Occupation. Some concluded, too hastily, that because not all of the French had been *résistants*, they must all have been collaborators. Louis Malle's 1974 film *Lacombe Lucien* appeared to suggest that the choice between joining the Resistance and entering Vichy's Milice could be determined by pure chance.

The world of politics was not far behind, and contributed to the questioning of long-accepted certainties, as well as to a huge operation seeking to delegitimise the established authorities. However true the academic studies were, their effect was to open a breach into which the far Right stepped briskly. Henceforth it could present itself as the heir to a real political tradition, not as the representative of a few spies working for the Germans. Collaborationists started to recount their experiences, and historical articles by extreme right-wing authors were published openly. But these activist historians remained true to their doctrine: the GRECE (Groupement d'Études et de Recherches sur la Civilisation Européenne), founded in 1969, attempted to rehabilitate themes and theorists of fascism and of Nazi racism, and the various far-right groups contributed to the spread of negationist theses.

Paradoxically, denials of the existence of gas chambers and the genocide of Jews were spread not only by the far Right but also by activists from the fringes of the far Left as well. We have seen earlier how great were the problems posed by the Second World War for the various extreme left-wing groups. But the Holocaust also represented them with a major doctrinal challenge. It contradicted their vulgar economism, which viewed levels of profit as the motor of all political decisions, and it undermined the moral basis of the far Left's basic creed: its refusal to support one form of imperialism against another or to choose between a 'humanist and democratic' form of capitalism and a 'fascist and racist' type. In an attempt to resolve these two contradictions, part of the far Left began to tread two dangerously slippery slopes.

The first resulted from their economist approach to history, discernible in texts of the far Left on the subject from the early days of the Liberation up to the present. The finest example of the genre is an article from the review *Le Programme communiste*, published almost confidentially at the start of the 1960s but regularly reprinted as a pamphlet over the following decade.[11] The central argument of this text, 'Auschwitz or the Great Alibi', produced by the Bordiguists of the Parti Communiste International, was that since the Jews belonged chiefly to the petty bourgeoisie, their elimination served to promote capitalist concentration and the polarisation of classes; in itself, the elimination of these intermediate classes was typical of capitalism; only the chosen means – genocide – differed in this case; but Nazism was not essentially different from classical capitalism. Inane as it is, the publication of this text speaks volumes about the unease with which the far Left of the time confronted memories of the Second World War.

To preserve the second article of faith of the far Left, the refusal to distinguish between different varieties of the capitalist evil, two strategies were followed. One was to recall the barbaric character of democratic capitalist powers, for example by dwelling on the genocides perpetrated against native Americans or Algerians. Another, however, was to stifle any debate that might disturb far left-wing analyses by denying the existence of the troublesome fact of the genocide itself. Hence the acceptance by a fringe of the French extreme Left of negationist theses from 1970 on. In purely quantitative terms, this phenomenon was tiny, involving fewer than a hundred activists in total. In political terms, on the other hand, it was highly important. As long as negationism was confined to the extreme Right it was totally marginalised, as in Germany, Italy, or Britain – and in France until 1968. Thereafter, however, France became an unusual case as the negationism of the far Right was reinforced by that of the extreme Left – and of a certain number of academics such as Robert Faurisson, Henri Roques, Bernard Notin, and a few others, posing as 'apolitical' researchers. From then on, negationism was no longer a political phenomenon, exclusive to the far Right, and rumours of the 'no smoke without fire' variety could spread rapidly. It took nearly two decades for France's historians to demolish the negationists' arguments and above all to shed light on their real motives. This task now complete, France's negationists have become what they never ceased to be in most other countries, political sects without influence.

It remains true that negationism was wholly marginal within the French far Left. A far more mainstream variety of memory at this end of the spectrum was represented by the Maoists, who tried to appropriate the memory of the Communist Resistance for themselves and against not only the governments of the day, but also the PCF itself. At the start of the 1970s, the most active of the Maoist groups, the Gauche Prolétarienne, stated that France was in a similar position to that of the Occupation. In line with the slogan of May 1968, 'CRS-SS', the police represented the armed forces of the new occupiers of France, the authoritarianism of the Gaullists and the Pompidolians who followed them reproduced that of Vichy, and the 'revisionists' of the PCF were the new collaborators. This carefully-maintained framework of analysis is pregnant with dangers.[12] It aimed, in fact, to allow activists to cross the threshold into 'armed struggle', to give lustre and legitimacy to the present struggle by assimilating it to the glorious days of yore, and in brief to obscure the difference between fascism and democracy, and between occupation and independence.

Rhetorical excesses aside, the far Left did substantial damage to the Resistentialist myth, both by accepting the endogenous character of Vichyism and by sapping the legitimacy of the two leading forces of the Resistance. The myth was also, it is true, attacked at the same time by other political groups. The outcome was that France in this period underwent an unsettled period in relation to the war and the Liberation, during which the various arenas in which memory is situated – academic, political, popular, official, educational – were dissociated from one another.

Among academics, rapid progress was made. Thanks in particular to researchers centred on the Institut d'Histoire du Temps Présent, France's universities developed a scientifically-grounded history of the period. In 1971, the Second World War was included in the syllabus for the first stage of secondary schooling, and from the 1980s the period was well covered in school textbooks.

Paradoxically, it was at this moment that a number of voices were raised in criticism of what was claimed to be the silence of historians, and even an official censorship, on the question. Revealing a continuing sense of unease as to national identity, France entered a period of what Henry Rousso has called 'obsessional memory'.[13] During the 1980s and early 1990s, there was hardly a history book or a television documentary that did not deal with Vichy or the Holocaust. And it became common to present France's role in the harshest possible light: some works, having discovered the antisemitism of Vichy, presented it as equivalent to that of the Germans, or confused Vichy's complicity in crimes against humanity with the active planning and execution of such crimes. A final sign of the 'dissociation' of memory was at the level of the state itself: even while a series of trials of former Vichy civil servants or members of the *milice* got under way, the state authorities continued to recall the resistentialist 'official' history of the war.

This fragmentation of memory allowed the Front National and Jean-Marie Le Pen to intensify the struggle over the historical memory of the war that they had started with the FN's creation in 1972. This campaign, which ran parallel to the far Right's political breakthrough from 1983, took five forms. First, in order to break the logical chain that served to delegitimise the far

Right and its racism, the FN deployed the far Right's historical view of Vichy as a choice that was both tactical and patriotic. The second technique was to blur the wartime divisions of the French by stressing the far Right's role in the Resistance. Thirdly, they sought, in conclusion to the first two points, to suggest that in any case, the Occupation belonged to a past that was of little or no interest. Fourthly, they tried to deny the scope of the atrocities committed in the war: in this light negationism, discreetly supported by the FN leaders, had a clearly political import. Finally, the FN did not shrink from adopting some of the official positions used by the Vichyite far Right during the war, even during its darkest hours. This last attitude was designed chiefly for the FN's own activists. It served both to remind them that the FN remained faithful to the most revolutionary of the far Right's traditions, and to lend specificity and coherence to the far right-wing camp so that if, as it periodically tried to do, the FN reached an alliance with the moderate Right, it would remain immune from the risk of dissolution into the democratic mainstream.

To summarise: the period running from May 1968 to the end of the Mitterrand presidency saw the Resistentialism of the post-war years increasingly confined to the status of official discourse. Within the rest of French society, cacophony reigned: historians undertook a steady and balanced revision of France's wartime past, the media covered the questions of collaboration and the Holocaust with an intensity that was the mirror image of their pre-1968 silence, former Vichyites who had lived unpunished for decades were brought before the courts, and the far Right – aided and abetted by a fraction of the far Left – sought to make Vichy respectable and the Holocaust irrelevant.

Convergence, 1995–

The past decade, by contrast, presents a very different tableau, in which practically the whole range of historical discourses (in universities, schools, politics, and society generally) have clearly converged. This 'revolution in memory' was caused by a single and shocking event, and by the courageous revision of official history that followed. The event, in 1994, was the revelation of the President's Vichyite past, given vivid representation by the photograph of the young François Mitterrand shaking hands with Marshal Pétain.[14] The subsequent official revision was undertaken at the very top, first by Mitterrand's successor Jacques Chirac on 16 July 1995 (the fifty-third anniversary of the notorious round-up of Jews at the Vélodrome d'Hiver), and then by Prime Minister Lionel Jospin in 1997. Its effect was to end the fiction, carefully maintained by all presidents and all governments since the Liberation, of France's role as the innocent victim. Through the voices of Chirac and Jospin, both Right and Left admitted that France had not emerged morally untainted from the Occupation. Thus Chirac stated that 'the criminal folly of the occupiers was backed up by Frenchmen, by the French state . . . France, on that day, committed an irreparable act.' In effect, the President was presenting a diptych: France did have its share of responsibility for the Vichy regime, but France also represented something else, precisely the republican and human values that had fuelled the regime's opponents.

At times, the debate was muddied by the confusion between the concepts of the state, the Republic, and the nation. France is indisputably guilty of having permitted Pétain's crimes; but this historical event would not have taken place without the Occupation. Within this perspective, it is important to analyse the nature of the initial massive support for Pétain. Thus historians separate *maréchalisme* (an attachment to Pétain as an individual, and especially as the victor of Verdun in 1916), *pétainisme* (embodied in Pétain's political speeches and proposals) and *vichysme* (referring to the discourse of, and the measures taken by, governments under Pétain).[15] Similarly, while it is true that, especially at first, the French allowed the Vichy regime to persecute *résistants* and Jews, it is also important to gauge how much they knew. Up to 1942, information on deportations was extremely rare, at least for ordinary citizens. By contrast, studies have shown that public opinion rejected Vichy quite early on, and that from 1942 growing numbers of French assisted its victims by increasingly widespread acts of disobedience. Today, therefore, there is no justification for the claim that the French behaved more shamefully than other peoples placed in an equivalent position. This convergence of historical memory indicates that the major findings of historical research have become part of the common knowledge of politicians and of the general public.

Conclusion

At the Liberation the dominant choice of the resistentialist myth had clear advantages, both for France's status in the world and for the restoration of republican legality. In the medium term, however, it was a choice that left France as a community fragile. By forgetting the Holocaust, the Republic damaged its own power to assimilate new populations which had been one of its strengths since the Revolution. By covering up the defeat of 1940, France's weakness was wiped out, as if by magic. In the real world, however, France remained weak, and this gap between memory and reality took a dramatic turn as France fought out its colonial struggles, first in Indochina and then in Algeria. By concealing Vichy and the daily compromises made with the occupiers, the Resistentialist myth prevented any investigation of the grey areas of French behaviour – a blindness that again had serious consequences during the Algerian war, notably in relation to torture. When the myth itself was exploded, finally, the awakening was cruel. When this occurred, in the aftermath of May 1968, French society was torn apart and political debate radicalised, in a form of punishment for the past ill-treatment of history.

Today, a decade after the 'revolution' of French memory of the mid-1990s, alternative discourses on the period, whether traditional or extreme, have been marginalised. The memory of the Liberation was always a double one, with areas of darkness (the constitutional setbacks for the Gaullists, the failure of the purges for the Communists, the failure of the revolution for the far Left) coexisting with happier memories of independence and freedom regained and the foundation of France's Welfare State. For the great majority of the French, the light is now stronger than the shades. Slowly and progressively assimilated, the memory of the Second World War has been pacified; this identity crisis has been calmed, and one of the areas with potential for the development of extremism has been neutralised. Today, if there is one event that nags at the historical and civic consciousness of the French, it is not the Occupation or the Liberation, but the Algerian war.

Notes

1. The initial steps of my work on this topic appeared in the last chapter of my book *La Joie douloureuse. La Libération de la France* (Brussels: Complexe, 2004), and in 'La memoria collettiva francese della seconda guerra mondiale, crisi d'identità e consolidamento democratico', *Ventunesimo Secolo* 7 (2005), pp. 61–81.

2. Cf. notably the pioneering work edited by P. Nora, *Les lieux de mémoire* (Paris: Gallimard, 1984–1992); R. Gildea, *The Past in French History* (New Haven/London, Yale University Press, 1994); and M.-C. Lavabre, *Le fil rouge. Sociologie de la mémoire communiste* (Paris: Presses de la Fondation Nationale des Sciences Politiques, 1994).

3. Thus, for example, the remarkable work of Henry Rousso uses a different chronology from ours, especially as he analyses the memory of Vichy, not of the Liberation or the purges (H. Rousso, *Le Syndrome de Vichy de 1944 à nos jours* (Paris: Le Seuil, 1987)). The same comment is valid for R. Frank, 'La mémoire empoisonnée', in J.-P. Azéma and F. Bédarida (eds), *La France des années noires*, Vol. II (Paris: Le Seuil, 1993), pp. 483–514; and for the epilogue ('Remembering the Occupation') in J. Jackson, *France: the Dark Years, 1940–1944* (Oxford: Oxford University Press, 2001), pp. 601–32.

4. Cf. P. Nora, 'Gaullistes et communistes', in P. Nora (ed.), *Les lieux de mémoire*; Vol. II, 1997), pp. 2489–532; and contributions by N. Racine-Furlaud ('18 juin 1940 ou 10 juillet 1940. Bataille de mémoires'), M.-C. Lavabre (Mémoire, souvenirs et images de De Gaulle chez les militants communistes'), and L. Gervereau ('Gaullistes et Communistes: les affiches du face à face'), all in S. Courtois and M. Lazar (eds), *50 ans d'une passion française. De Gaulle et les communistes* (Paris: Balland, 1991).

5. C. de Gaulle, *Lettres, notes et carnets. Juin 1943–May 1945* (Paris: Plon, 1983), p. 245.

6. Cf. F. Cochet, *Les exclus de la victoire. Histoire des prisonniers de guerre, déportés et STO (1945–1985)* (Paris: SPM, 1992).

7. A. Wieviorka, *Déportation et génocide. Entre la mémoire et l'oubli* (Paris: Plon, 1992).

8. This is developed further in P. Buton, 'Les camps de déportation dans les manuels scolaires', in F. Bédarida and L. Gervereau (eds), *La Déportation* (Paris–Nanterre, BDIC, 1995), pp. 234–8.

9. Cf. P. Buton, 'La Résistance, la tonte des femmes, et la crise de la masculinité en France', in F. Marcot and D. Musiedlak (eds), *Les Résistances, miroir des régimes d'oppression. Allemagne, France, Italie* (Besançon: Presses Universitaires de Franche-Comté, 2006), pp. 143–55.

10. New York: Knopf, 1972. The French version, *La France de Vichy 1940–1944* was published by Le Seuil in 1973. Cf. H. Rousso, 'L'historien, lieu de mémoire.

Hommage à Robert Paxton' (2000), reprinted in H. Rousso, *Vichy. L'événement, la mémoire, l'histoire* (Paris: Gallimard (collection Folio-histoire), 2001), pp. 453–80.
11. *Auschwitz ou le grand alibi* (Paris: Editions du Parti communiste international, n.d.).
12. Cf. in particular I. Sommier, *La violence politique et son deuil. L'après 68 en France et en Italie* (Rennes: Presses Universitaires de Rennes, 1998); I. Sommier, 'La Résistance comme référence légitimatrice de la violence', *Politix* 17 (1992), pp. 86–103; and P. Buton, 'La gauche et la prise du pouvoir', in J.-J. Becker and G. Candar (eds), *Histoire des gauches en France*, Vol. II (Paris: La Découverte, 2004).
13. E. Conan and H. Rousso, *Vichy, un passé qui ne passe pas* (Paris: Fayard, 1994).
14. P. Péan, *Une jeunesse française. François Mitterrand 1934–1947* (Paris: Fayard, 1994).
15. The following list gives the main lines of this debate, in chronological order. C. Lévy, 'L'opinion française devant le régime de Vichy en 1944', in Comité d'histoire de la Deuxième Guerre mondiale, *La libération de la France* (Paris: Éditions du CNRS, 1976), pp. 343–59; P. Laborie, *Résistants, vichyssois et autres. L'évolution de l'opinion et des comportements dans le Lot de 1939 à 1945* (Paris: Éditions du CNRS, 1980); D. Peschanski, 'Le régime de Vichy a existé', in D. Peschanski (ed.), *Vichy 1940–1944. Archives de guerre d'Angelo Tasca* (Paris and Milan: Éditions du CNRS–Fondazione Feltrinelli, 1986), pp. 3–49; F. Marcot, 'La Résistance et la population, Jura 1944: relations d'une avant-garde et des masses', *Guerres mondiales et Conflits contemporains*, no. 146 (Paris: Presses Universitaires de France, 1987); J.-M. Guillon, *La Résistance dans le Var*, Thèse d'État, Université de Provence, 1989; P. Laborie, *L'opinion française sous Vichy* (Paris: Le Seuil, 1990); P. Laborie, 'L'évolution de l'opinion publique', in L. Gervereau and D. Peschanski (eds), *La propagande sous Vichy, 1940–1944* (Paris–Nanterre, BDIC, 1990), pp. 224–38; J.-M. Flonneau, 'L'évolution de l'opinion publique de 1940 à 1944' in J.-P. Azéma and F. Bédarida (eds), *Vichy et les Français* (Paris: Fayard, 1992), pp. 506–22; A. Lefébure, *Les conversations secrètes des Français sous l'Occupation* (Paris: Plon, 1993); P. Laborie, 'Solidarités et ambivalences de la France moyenne', in J.-P. Azéma and F. Bédarida (eds), *La France des années noires*, Vol. II (Paris: Le Seuil, 1993) pp. 295–333.

Bibliography

Azéma, J.-P., and Bédarida, F. (eds), *La France des années noires*, 2 Vols (Paris: Le Seuil, 1993).

Buton, P., *La France et les Français de la Libération. Vers une France nouvelle?* (Paris–Nanterre: BDIC, 1984).

Buton, P., 'Les camps de déportation dans la manuels scolaires', in F. Bédarida and L. Gervereau (eds), *La Déportation* (Paris–Nanterre: BDIC, 1995), pp. 234–8.

Buton, P., *La Joie douloureuse. La Libération de la France* (Brussels: Complexe, 2004).

Buton, P., 'La gauche et la prise du pouvoir', in J.-J. Becker and G. Candar (eds), *Histoire des gauches en France*, Vol. II (Paris: La Découverte, 2004), pp. 563–83.

Buton, P., 'La Résistance, la tonte des femmes, et la crise de la masculinité en France', in F. Marcot and D. Musiedlak (eds), *Les Résistances, miroir des régimes d'oppression. Allemagne, France, Italie* (Besançon: Presses Universitaires de Franche-Comté, 2006), pp. 143–55.

Cochet, F., *Les exclus de la victoire. Histoire des prisonniers de guerre, déportés et STO (1945–1985)* (Paris: SPM, 1992).

Conan, E., and Rousso, H., *Vichy, un passé qui ne passe pas* (Paris: Fayard, 1994).

Courtois, S., and Lazar, M. (eds), *50 ans d'une passion française. De Gaulle et les communistes* (Paris: Balland, 1991).

Flonneau, J.-M., 'L'évolution de l'opinion publique de 1940 à 1944' in J.-P. Azéma and F. Bédarida (eds), *Vichy et les Français* (Paris: Fayard, 1992), pp. 506–22.

Frank, R., 'Le mémoire empoisonnée', in J.-P. Azéma and F. Bédarida (eds), *La France des années noires*, Vol. II (Paris: Le Seuil, 1993), pp. 483–514.

Gildea, R., *The Past in French History* (New Haven/London: Yale University Press, 1994).

Guillon, J.-M., *La Résistance dans le Var*, Thèse d'État, Université de Provence, 1989.

Jackson, J., *France: the Dark Years, 1940–1944* (Oxford: Oxford University Press, 2001).

Laborie, P., *Résistants, vichyssois et autres. L'évolution de l'opinion et des comportements dans le Lot de 1939 à 1945* (Paris: Éditions du CNRS, 1980).

Laborie, P., *L'opinion française sous Vichy* (Paris: Le Seuil, 1990).

Laborie, P., 'L'évolution de l'opinion publique', in L. Gervereau and D. Peschanski (eds), *La propagande sous Vichy, 1940–1944* (Paris–Nanterre: BDIC, 1990), pp. 224–38.

Laborie, P., 'Solidarités et ambivalences de la France moyenne', in J.-P. Azéma and F. Bédarida (eds), *La France des années noires*, Vol. II (Paris: Le Seuil, 1993), pp. 295–333.

Lavabre, M.-C., *Le fil rouge. Sociologie de la mémoire communiste* (Paris: Presses de la Fondation Nationale des Sciences Politiques, 1994).

Lévy, C., 'L'opinion française devant le régime de Vichy en 1944', in Comité d'histoire de la Deuxième Guerre mondiale, *La libération de la France* (Paris: Éditions du CNRS, 1976), pp. 343–59.

Marcot, F., 'La Résistance et la population, Jura 1944: relations d'une avant-gardeet des masses', *Guerres mondiales et Conflits contemporains*, no. 146 (Paris: Presses Universitaires de France, 1987).

Nora, P., *Les lieux de mémoire*, 3 volumes (Paris: Gallimard (collection Quarto), 1997; original edition in 7 volumes, Gallimard, 1984–1992).

Nora, P., 'Gaullistes et communistes', in P. Nora (ed.), *Les lieux de mémoire*, Vol. II (Paris: Gallimard, 1997), pp. 2489–532.

Peschanski, D., 'Le régime de Vichy a existé', in D. Peschanski (ed.), *Vichy 1940–1944. Archives de guerre d'Angelo Tasca* (Paris and Milan: Éditions du CNRS–Fondazione Feltrinelli, 1986), pp. 3–49.

Rousso, H., *Le Syndrome de Vichy de 1944 à nos jours* (Paris: Le Seuil, 1987) (collection Points Histoire), 1990).

Rousso, H., 'L'historien, lieu de mémoire. Hommage à Robert Paxton' (2000), reprinted in H. Rousso, *Vichy. L'événement, la mémoire, l'histoire* (Paris: Gallimard (collection Folio-histoire), 2001), pp. 453–80.

Sommier, I., 'La Résistance comme référence légitimatrice de la violence', (*Politix* 17, 1992), pp. 86–103.

Sommier, I., *La violence politique et son deuil. L'après 68 en France et en Italie* (Rennes: Presses Universitaires de Rennes, 1998).

Wieviorka, A., *Déportation et génocide. Entre la mémoire et l'oubli* (Paris: Plon, 1992).

Index